Ephesians 2:10

THINGS TO COME

A Brief History of The Bible

THINGS TO COME

TOM NEWMAN

TATE PUBLISHING
AND ENTERPRISES, LLC

Things to Come
Copyright © 2015 by Tom Newman. All rights reserved.

No part of this publication may be reproduced, stored in a retrieval system or transmitted in any way by any means, electronic, mechanical, photocopy, recording or otherwise without the prior permission of the author except as provided by USA copyright law.

Scripture quotations marked "NASB" are taken from the *New American Standard Bible* ®, Copyright © 1960, 1962, 1963, 1968, 1971, 1972, 1973, 1975, 1977, 1995 by The Lockman Foundation. Used by permission. All rights reserved.

The opinions expressed by the author are not necessarily those of Tate Publishing, LLC.

Published by Tate Publishing & Enterprises, LLC
127 E. Trade Center Terrace | Mustang, Oklahoma 73064 USA
1.888.361.9473 | www.tatepublishing.com

Tate Publishing is committed to excellence in the publishing industry. The company reflects the philosophy established by the founders, based on Psalm 68:11,
"The Lord gave the word and great was the company of those who published it."

Book design copyright © 2015 by Tate Publishing, LLC. All rights reserved.
Cover design by Joana Quilantang
Cover photo by Nicole Jenabzadeh
Interior design by Stephanie Woloszyn

Published in the United States of America
ISBN: 978-1-68142-349-4
1. Religion / General
2. Religion / Biblical Meditations / General
15.08.03

To my two children, A. Elizabeth and D. Thomas, who have known the Lord from a very young age and have been a blessing every day of their lives.

ACKNOWLEDGMENTS

My acknowledgments are to God, Jesus Christ, the Holy Spirit, and Scripture. God is completely sovereign, he has created each of us, and we are an integral part of his eternal plan. He is involved in our lives every day. To Christ, his only begotten Son, who came to earth in the flesh to offer us eternal salvation through his sacrificial death. Acknowledgment is also accorded to the Holy Spirit, who shows us God's truths through illumination and enlightenment and is our daily Helper in all things. Last, is God's word, which is God's open communication to us to be heard as frequently as we choose to listen.

I would also like to thank John Woodcock and Gary Baldwin, whose help was invaluable in the production of this work.

CONTENTS

PREFACE	13
INTRODUCTION	17
THE COVENANTS OF GOD	**23**
And the Rest Is History	26
Jerusalem	30
Islam and Christianity: Two Sides to Every Story	31
The Law and Moses	35
The Power of Prayer	38
The Ten Commandments	43
Mankind in the Context of God's Divine Plan	46
The Covenants of God	49
The Covenants of God's Rule	51
THE HOLY SPIRIT	**55**
The Helper	55
The Ministries of the Holy Spirit	57
Being Filled with the Spirit	61
The Elect	63
Born Again: A New Start	66
The Spiritual Gifts of the Holy Spirit	67
Sinless Perfection Is Impossible	72
The Soul and the Spirit	75
The Way of the Spirit and the Way of the Flesh	78
The Conscience of Man	80
Becoming Spiritual	84

Beyond Our Wildest Dreams 86

The New Walk 88

THE PRINCE OF DARKNESS 93

That Serpent of Old Called the Devil 93

Satan's Rebellion 95

The Christian Conflict 97

The Deceiver and the Restrainer 99

The Spiritual Battleground 101

Angels of Light 106

Provisional Reality 108

The Warfare 113

The Works of Satan 118

The Divine Permission of Sin 124

What Does Turning Your Life Over to Christ Mean? 125

The Problem with Sin Is That There Is No Problem with Sin 130

I Will Tell You a Mystery 137

The Book of Life 140

PROVIDENCE AND THE SOVEREIGNTY OF GOD 143

The Sovereignty of God 143

Providence and the Invisible Hand of God 149

The Most Important Thing We Do 152

The Thousand Natural Shocks That Flesh Is Heir To 154

Free Will and the Permissive Will of God 160

Freedom of Choice 164

The Refiner's Fire: Trials, Discipline, Chastisement, ... 168
and Pruning

Some Assembly Required 173

Discipline of Love 177
Chastisement from the Lord 178
Pruning: So That We May Bear More Fruit 183
The Most Extreme Cases 185

THE GREAT TRIBULATION AND THE RAPTURE OF THE SAINTS — 189

The Apostasy of the Church 198
The Sequence of Events 222
The Four Horsemen of the Apocalypse 233
The Judgments of the Seven Trumpets 250
The Rapture of the Saints 257
The Seven Bowls of Wrath 282
The Prostitute Religion 290
The Evolution of Mankind 299
The Final Judgment and the Book of Life 308

THE ALPHA AND THE OMEGA — 317

The New Covenant 317
Jesus Christ 319
The Conundrum of Free Will 323
The Mystery of Faith 327
The First Myth: If I Am Only Good Enough 328
Is It Ever Too Late? 331
The Second Myth: Once Saved, Always Saved 334
Balancing the Books 337
"My Lord and My God" 338
A Personal Relationship with Christ 341
And I Myself Will Raise Him Up 342
That You May Have Joy 343

One Shepherd, One Flock 345

The Unpardonable Sin 348

The Return of the Alpha and the Omega 350

At the Appointed Time 354

Walk Worthy of Your Calling...356

The Temptation of Christ..357

Rejoice and Be Glad for Great Is Your Reward in Heaven 361

Perfection in Faith, Not Perfect..366

The Measure of a Christian 367

What Is Justification?...371

What Is Imputed Righteousness?......................................372

Faith Is an Attitude 375

The Meaning of Life 376

The Absolute Truth..379

EPILOGUE   385

BIBLIOGRAPHY   387

NOTES   389

ADDENDUM   423

America's Heritage: A Christian Nation, ...425
Light for the Whole World

PREFACE

When I set out to write my third book, I found that much of the information in the original *A Brief History of the Bible* was still very good information. I did not want the third book to eclipse the information already published. As a result, I decided to do a re-release of *A Brief History of the Bible* and change the title to *A Brief History of the Bible: Things to Come*. The new information in the re-release is the result of my continual study of Scripture since *A Brief History of the Bible* was published in 2010.

When I first set out to write this manuscript, I was keenly aware that there are two separate realities. I spent a year in Vietnam with the 101st Airborne Division. I was assigned to B Company of the 502$^{nd.}$ In the year I spent with the Five-O-Deuce, we sustained 97 percent casualties and fatalities. It is hard to understand death on such a grand scale, and the experiences caused me to reexamine everything I understood and knew to be true.

In April of 1968, as we advanced on a village in the northeast portion of 1 Corp, the trooper next to me struck a wasp's nest with the butt of his rifle. The wasps swarmed on me and stung me eleven times in the head. I was evacuated by helicopter to the MASH unit at LZ Sally. By the time we arrived, my facial features had completely disappeared because of the swelling from the stings. As they carried me into the emergency room, the doctor looked at me and said, "What in the hell happened to him?" I realized I had bitten one of the wasps that had stung me in the mouth; I removed the wasp from my mouth and offered it up for anyone to see. I then went into anaphylactic shock and suffered cardiac arrest and complete respiratory failure. As soon as I flatlined, my spirit and soul left my body. There were no bright lights, no tunnels leading anywhere, and there was no one waiting to meet me. I just went above the operating table and watched the efforts to revive me. There was no fear, no anxiety, and no concern, just watching and waiting. I was, however, aware of my existence; I was fully conscious, and I knew it was still me. The surgical team withdrew blood from one arm and put new blood into my other arm while they administered shots of adrenaline. As soon as they resuscitated me, I returned into my body.

The next day in the recovery room, I was thinking about the supernatural phenomena I had just experienced and was wondering how I could empirically verify my experience. The ER orderly came by and said, "Oh, I see you're coming around."

I asked him, "Why were you putting blood into one arm and taking it out of the other?"

With a very surprised look, he replied, "How the hell did you know we did that? You were gone."

My experience in the MASH unit in Vietnam had a profound impact on my interpretation of Scripture and the truths that were illuminated to me by the Holy Spirit. Understanding and knowledge can come from either formal education or experience.

There are two separate interrelated realities. The first is provisional reality. It is our touch-and-feel reality that we experience every day on earth. The second is a spiritual or foundational reality, which is populated by God and his celestial beings. It is very difficult to relate information about foundational reality from Scripture to our everyday life. We do not understand the interconnectedness of the two realities. When we read Scripture, we tend

to pass much of it off as metaphorical. However, real significance and meaning for this life is contingent upon understanding the connection between these two realities.

I do not have to wonder about whether there is life after death or not—I know.

Things to Come can form a bridge to understand the connection between foundational and provisional realities. Only by understanding the connection can we understand true reality, which is a blending of the two distinctly unique realities.

The first chapter of *A Brief History of the Bible: Things to Come* is a summary of the Old Testament and the covenants; it sets the stage for the rest of the chapters. Chapters 2 through 6 focus on the New Testament and the interplay between foundational and provisional reality. *Things to Come* does not have to be read like a novel; the information in each chapter can stand by itself.

INTRODUCTION

There are two distinct realities, and they are as different as night and day. And just like night and day, they are inextricably interwoven.

Provisional reality is the touch-and-feel, three-dimensional, material, and corporal reality of earth. It is predictable and governed by the physical laws of God. We experience provisional reality and gain information about our environment through our five senses. We are cognizant of our reality because of the information we receive from our sensory receptors of hearing, sight, touch, smell, and taste. Our minds are able to process the information we receive from our senses and put it into some type of a context that makes sense of physical reality. Our sense of reality comes from our sensory information and our ability to interpret this data and our interaction with things and events that exist within our reality.

However, when we leave the empirical, we have a little more difficulty wrapping our minds around just what something is. What actually is time? Moreover, what is infinity in space? These are more of a cognitive construct than physical realities. Time is simply when. Time is the measurement of the passing of or the duration of events, which only has significance to someone that has an end state and can be aware of that end state.

Foundation reality is a completely different reality as it exists beyond the sensitivity of our sensory receptors. It is a spiritual reality; it is the realm of God and all his celestial beings. It is reality comprised of the immaterial and the incorporeal. For the most part, we are unable to detect very much information about its attributes. Our provisional reality, our empirical style of thinking, and our lack of sensory information limit our ability to perceive and understand a coexisting simultaneous realm in another dimension unless we have been there.

The spectrum of light rays stretches from x-rays to infrared rays. The sensory receptors in our eyes are only able to perceive about ten percent of the entire spectrum. Our sense of sight does not have the ability to penetrate beyond the thin veil, which separates our physical world from the spiritual realm. Because of this disconnect between the two realities and our inability to perceive it, we have difficulty understanding foundational reality or true complete reality, which is a blending of both foundational and provisional realities.

The Bible is the major source of information not only about world history, but about foundational reality as well. Scripture has a plethora of instances that manifest the different nature of physical laws as they apply, and do not apply, to foundational reality. In one instance after Christ's crucifixion, the disciples were afraid of being arrested. They had locked and bolted themselves in a room, and Christ suddenly appeared in their midst.[1] On another occurrence when Christ was about to be captured, the Scripture reads, "He passed through their midst,"[2] or "hid" in their midst.[3] Additionally, when Christ quelled a storm, his disciples wondered in amazement, "What kind of a man is this that even the winds and seas obey Him?"[4] They were equally amazed when he came to their boat walking on the water. Moreover, Christ healed the sick, the lame; he gave sight to the blind[5] and raised Lazarus and others from the dead.[6] My favorite is when Christ time travels: "So they were willing to receive Him into the boat, and immediately the boat was at the land to which they were going."[7] During the transfiguration of Christ, recorded in the books of Matthew, Mark, and Luke, Christ is transformed into an incorporeal state and converses with Elijah and Moses,[8] both of whom had long since passed away. Moreover, Scripture records that Jesus knows what others are thinking.[9] The most amazing, however, is when God suspends time for a day.

> Then Joshua spoke to the Lord in the day when the Lord delivered up the Amorites before the sons of Israel, and he said in sight of Israel. O sun, stand still at Gibeon, and O moon in the valley of Aijalon. So the sun stood still and the moon stopped, until the nation avenged themselves of their enemies. (Joshua 10:12–13)

Whenever Christ encountered demons, their response was always the same. "What business do we have with each other, Jesus of Nazareth? Have You come to destroy us? I know who You are—the Holy One of God!"[10]

Because this is a completely different reality, we do not have any store of information that is relative to the characteristics of foundational reality. We can, however, understand foundational reality as we have God's inspired Word and the enlightenment of the Holy Spirit, who is our helper, and he will guide us into all truth.[11]

The two realities are inextricably interwoven because there is an overlap between the two. There is a meaning and significance in life's circumstances and events as they occur simultaneously in both realities. Situations that are played out in provisional reality have a meaning, and consequences for both realties, as well as the events within foundational reality, have implications for provisional reality. "The angel answered and said to her, 'The Holy Spirit will come upon you, and the power of the Most High will overshadow you; and for that reason the holy Child shall be called the Son of God.'"[12] This event changed the course of human history, and the impact has lasted for over two thousand years.

If we restrict our understanding to only that which we can see and feel, we preclude our ability to understand supernatural events. This means we do not understand true reality.[13] This not only limits our ability to understand life and supernatural intersections; it also limits our ability to find answers to the questions we have about the meaning and significance of life, faith, and eternity. However, just because we cannot perceive foundational reality does not mean it does not exist. We cannot see gravity; however, we know by reason and by evidence that it exists. Just as Scripture tells us, "Faith is belief in the things not seen."[14] There is as much validity in looking for answers in foundational reality as there is in looking for answers in provisional reality. Although we do not perceive the spiritual, we are influenced by it. If we accept all that is physical and rule out all that is in existence in another dimension, then we will never be able to understand our existence or the reasons for events, circumstances, and situations. Without this understanding, we will not understand all that is encompassed in our complete reality, nor will we understand the real extent of God's love for us or the truly hideous nature of sin and Satan.

We are eternal beings. We cannot seek answers only from within this existence. Life on earth is such a small part of the entire span of our eternal existence. Just as you cannot completely understand or make judgments about what a book has to say by reading only one chapter, neither can we understand complete reality from a myopic view of provisional reality alone. Empirical evidence is of the phenomena of provisional reality and our five senses. Faith is of the conviction of foundational reality—the things not seen.[15] If an event or a situation cannot be explained by our empirical process, it may simply be that the occurrence is not of an empiri-

cal nature and, therefore, may only be explained by a supernatural interpretation from within the context of the overlap of realities.

The whole point is that the span of our life, some seventy-odd years,[16] is really insignificant compared to how long we will exist in eternity. Yet, in the short timeframe of this existence, we will decide our destiny and help others decide their destiny for eternity. This is the single most important thing we do in this life.

To "seek first His kingdom and His righteousness"[17] means that I have a perception of provisional reality that is tempered by the understanding that provisional reality exists within foundational reality. The meanings for events in my life come from foundational reality, not provisional reality. Regardless of the events that transpire in provisional reality, I know that "all things work for the good of those who love the Lord."[18] I also understand that there will be things or events in this life that I will not understand because of the differing characteristics of the two realities[19] and my inability to completely comprehend God or foundational reality. However, because of my faith, I trust God[20] that all things are for the best and that I can blindly put my faith in his providence for my life[21] and trust the things not seen. I also understand that although I do not completely understand foundational reality, ultimately it has more bearing on my life and plays a more significant role in my life's experiences than events within provisional reality.[22]

The single most important thing that determines our ultimate destination is our faith. When our faith is the most important thing in our life, faith defines the meaning of events in our life, which in turn dictates our behavior. "But like the Holy One who called you, be holy yourselves also in all your behavior; because it is written, YOU SHALL BE HOLY, FOR I AM HOLY."[23]

What is fascinating about the two different realities, provisional and foundational, is that we actually exist being both physical and spiritual beings right now in both of them. Life in provisional reality is an antecedent.

THE COVENANTS OF GOD

From the beginning of time with the edenic covenant God has defined the parameters for humanity as to what is required to have a significant, worshipful relationship with the Creator. God has outlined the parameters in his covenants, and man has been unable to uphold his end of the agreements ever since. God's covenants are his blueprint for the unfolding of his divine plan as it is unveiled through the exercise of his determined will both within the context of human history and man individually. The covenants of God culminate with his new covenant, in Jesus Christ who establishes all of the requirements necessary for man's salvation and an eternal relationship with God.

In the beginning was the Word, and the Word was with God, and the Word was God. He was in the beginning with God. All things came into being by Him...In Him was life, and the life was the light of men. (John 1:1–5)

When God creates, he creates out of nothing.[24] By his command, that which did not exist is now brought into existence. That is the essence of creating—something only God can do.[25] God is spirit,[26] and the Spirit of God gives life. Christ was begotten, not created.[27] God thought, *I will bring into being a Son from out of my very essence; he will be begotten from me. "You are My Son. Today I have begotten You."*[28] *We will create all that we will choose to create.*

The common threads running through the Bible are the covenants, or agreements, that God has forged with humankind. The Abrahamic covenant was the first of God's theocratic covenants. Theocratic covenants are the covenants of God's rule for humanity. There are three universal covenants and five theocratic covenants.

God established his first covenant with Abraham.[29] The covenant was ratified when Abraham accepted the conditions set out by God. The Scripture foresaw that God would also justify the Gentiles[30] by faith and foretold Abraham, saying, "All the nations will be blessed in you."[31] Those of the Christian faith, from every nation, are blessed through Abraham. Abraham is the father of the Christian faith, and everyone who chooses to believe in the gospel of Jesus Christ is blessed.[32] Believers are blessed in that they have the opportunity to have an eternal reward in heaven and an eternal relationship with God the Father, His Son Jesus Christ, and the Holy Spirit. Hence, those who are Christians from "any tongue, tribe, and nation"[33] are blessed in Abraham through the birth, crucifixion, death, and resurrection of Jesus Christ. Jesus Christ is from the lineage of Abraham,[34] born in the promised land, born to a virgin, from the line of David. He is the fulfillment of scriptural prophecy as the Messiah.[35]

The reason God establishes a covenant with Abraham is to establish Abraham and the Hebrews as his holy people, a people set aside that can have a unique relationship with him.[36] There will also be a future need for establishing the lineage of Jesus Christ.

All that God has decreed in his covenants has already occurred in human history. They have already established the presidencies that will drive future events until the end of human history.[37] The covenants also demonstrate God's direct involvement in the affairs and history of humanity.[38] The people of the earth will know that he is the one and only true God and that all that he has created is under his dominion. God's covenants represent the manifestation of God's will in the course of the human experience.[39] God's covenants are promises, and they are the blueprints for his intersection in both realities. God knows our actions and reactions ahead of time. He shapes the events of history and leads humanity down the preordained path that he has established. He does this to ensure the perfect execution of events such that his divine plan will come to pass[40] "on earth as it is in heaven."

The essence of the Abrahamic covenant is that God asks, Abraham complies,[41] so God blesses him. The significance of this exchange, however, is that it sets the stage for events that are occurring to this very day within the providence of God and his creation. Men are able to make a free will choice for God and choose to obey or disobey him. Worship to be true worship must, by its very nature, be a free will choice. "If you love Me, obey My commandments."[42] Worship is a free will choice, just as is God's grace; neither are, nor can be, a mandate. Within the concept of God's will is also God's permissive will, which allows for the liberty of the free will choices of humanity.

God's divine plan for humanity is not some unfathomable mystery. He communicates his intentions in Scripture so that everyone can understand. "Blessed is he who reads and those who hear the words of the prophecy, and heeds the things, which are written, for the time is near."[43] All of the essential elements of his plans are contained in his covenants. In God's divine plan, he establishes his holy people; at the same time, he makes provisions for the rest of humanity, so that, "whoever believes will in Him have eternal life,"[44] and "God our Savior, who desires all men to be saved and to come to the knowledge of the truth."[45]

TOM NEWMAN

AND THE REST IS HISTORY

Civilization began in the Ur Valley, within the Fertile Crescent, about 4000 BC in the ancient land of Mesopotamia. The Ur Valley is located in Iraq, on the Euphrates River, approximately midway between modern-day Baghdad and the Persian Gulf. It is also considered the most likely location of the garden of eden.

By 4000 BC, we have already had the fall of man. By about 3000 BC, the great flood of Noah had subsided, and the population is again multiplying on the face of the earth. It was not long after the creation of earth and humanity that "Jehovah repented that He had made man on the earth, and He was angered in His heart."[46]

> And Jehovah saw the evil of man was great on the earth, and that every imagination of his thought of his heart was only evil all the day long. And Jehovah said, "I will wipe off man whom I have created from the face of the earth..." (Gen. 6:5,7 Interlinear Hebrew Old Testament)

God then destroyed the inhabitants of the earth with a great, worldwide flood.[47] After the flood, Noah and his family were the only occupants of provisional reality. Even after God had already destroyed all of the inhabitants of the earth once, he found that with the memory of the flood still fresh in their minds, humankind was again evolving as a pagan, godless people.

God wanted to separate from the rest of the inhabitants of the world a people for himself—a holy people. A people that would put him above all else so that he could put them above all others. They would also serve as an example to the rest of the world as a righteous and just people that would honor and worship God as their creator and live in harmony with one another.[48] God would richly bless his people because of their devotion and dedication to him.

One of Noah's sons, Shem, fathered the lineage that produced Abraham. Shem's descendent Abraham was born several genera-

tions after the flood and lived in the Ur Valley. The peoples of Ur were evolving as pagans and worshiped the moon god of nanna. God called out to Abraham and asked him to leave his family and the pagan peoples of Ur and to journey to a land that he would show him.[49]

If Abraham complies, God in turn will do some things for him—six things to be exact. God will make a great nation out of Abraham's descendants. God will bless Abraham, and God will make him famous.[50] In addition, Abraham will be a blessing such that all that bless Abraham will be blessed, and all that curse Abraham will be cursed.[51] This is God's decree, and it applies to God's chosen people[52] then as it does today.

Finally, through Abraham, all of the families of the earth will be blessed.[53] This request by God for Abraham to leave and Abraham's compliance constitutes the Abrahamic covenant.

In compliance with God's request, Abraham leaves the Ur Valley and journeys to where God directs him, which is modern-day Israel.[54] This is done so that Abraham may start the lineage of a new chosen people. They will be God's holy people. Abraham complies with all that God has required, hence God blesses him. In these blessings to Abraham and his people, we see a foreshadowing of future events.

God will bless Abraham, and God will make him famous. As his nation grew and prospered, Abraham did indeed become famous.[55] His fame was not only in his time, but it is recorded in history and throughout the Scriptures. Abraham will be known as the father of the Jewish and the Arabian people.

The nation of Israel and the Jewish people have suffered greatly throughout history because of their stubbornness and rebellious behavior. The Assyrians first subjugated the Hebrews, and then Nebuchadnezzar destroyed their cities and temples and took them captive to serve as slaves in Babylon. After AD 70, many Jews migrated to other parts of the world; it is referred to as the diaspora or the dispersion.[56] Syria also conquered Judah and converted their temple into one that honored Zeus.

Judea became a Roman state under the Roman emperor Nero following Syria's domination of Judea. The Romans utterly destroyed Jerusalem in AD 70 and rebuilt the city in honor of the Greek pagan god Jupiter. The promised land was renamed Syria Palestina, and any Jew entering the city was to be killed.

The fall of Judea created a division between Jews and Christians. The Jews saw their condition as disastrous and the fault of the Christians. The Christians, however, viewed the condition of the Jewish state as God's fulfillment of the curse of his "blessings and the curses"[57] and punishment for their rejection of the Messiah.

The persecution of Jews continued throughout all of Europe from before the time of the Crusades to the Black Death. The Jews were falsely accused of causing the Black Death by poisoning the wells of Christians. Many Jews were killed during this time, and many others were forced to live in specific areas called ghettos. England, France, Germany, and Switzerland expelled their Jewish populations, and most of them fled to Russia and Poland, where they again experienced persecution and systemic massacres called pogroms. Hitler and Nazi Germany attempted to eliminate the Jewish race with the "final solution."[58]

Finally, through Abraham, all of the families of the earth will be blessed, and we truly have been blessed. The people of Israel have provided us with our many prophets. They are the source of the Bible. Most importantly, God's chosen people are the lineage of Jesus Christ. Christ has blessed all people that believe that he is the Son of God[59] with salvation from their sins and the opportunity for eternal life. In this manner, all of the peoples of the world have been blessed.

When Abraham arrived at his destination, God said to him, "Lift up your eyes and look from the place where you are, northward and southward and eastward and westward;[60] for all the land which you see, I will give it to you and to your descendants forever."[61]

The description of the promised land in the Bible[62] would include modern-day Israel, Syria, Lebanon, and Jordan. It is imperative that God defines a place for all of his future events to take place—his stage, as it were, so that everyone can understand his sovereignty, that all things are under his control, and that the events of history are preordained and do not just occur by happenstance.

God again sought a relationship with the people of his creation and wanted them to know him. Israel would be the home for his holy people and the birthplace of Jesus Christ. This would also be the place of the death and resurrection of Christ, the Savior of humanity. Christ will also rule from Jerusalem over the new heaven and the new earth during the millennium. All of these events orchestrated by God had to be connected to a specific people on a land given to them by God. The home of the Messiah, a holy land, and a holy people were all foretold. Otherwise, the connections would be missed. Without all of this deliberate planning by God, the sequence of events would have been perceived as random events, and random events are not perceived to have an author or be attributable to intelligent design.

God's plan is a chosen land, a chosen people, a chosen Savior, and a book, the holy Bible, to explain it all.[63] I will send my Son to earth[64] and let him die[65] as a sacrifice for the sins of humanity. Then I will bring him back to life[66] so that all can see that there is life after death.[67] In addition, they will know that they too may have this eternal life,[68] a holy peaceful existence that lasts forever in foundational reality.[69] That will be my part in this covenant; now what shall I require of them?

> What does the Lord your God require from you, but to fear the Lord your God, to walk in all His ways and love Him, and to serve the Lord your God with all your heart and with all your soul, and to keep the Lord's commandments and His statutes which I am commanding you today for your good. (Deut. 10:12–13)

God also desires that we live in righteousness and with justice.[70] This is all done so that we may know that God is I AM,[71] that he has created everything, and that in return he desires our thankful worship. Then they will know that I have sent my Son to be their salvation because they will have something in their touch-and-feel reality to believe. I want to establish an eternal relationship with them.[72] Moreover, they should love me with all of their heart, mind, and soul,[73] and one other thing, they should love their neighbor as themselves.[74] Then they will know, by faith, what I have planned for them is a future and a hope, not calamity and pain.[75]

JERUSALEM

Jerusalem—located in the heart of the promised land, given to Abraham, Isaac, and Jacob forever[76]—is the key to the endtime events. "When you see Jerusalem surrounded by armies, you know the end is near."[77]

Jerusalem is also the city Jesus Christ will occupy on his return,[78] and it is the site of the final confrontation between good and evil.[79] Currently both Israel and the Muslims claim Jerusalem as the seat of their religions.

Jews and Christians maintain that Jerusalem is where Abraham offered to sacrifice his son, Isaac, to God. Jerusalem is also the site of the ancient Jewish temples. Christ will return to this location at his second coming when he returns as "King of kings and Lord of lords."[80] The New Jerusalem will descend from heaven signifying the new beginning, the "new heaven and the new earth." It is from here in the New Jerusalem that Christ will rule from for the millennium.[81]

The nation of Israel, after their punishment of dispersion for their nonbelief and rebellion,[82] reappeared after a 1,900-year absence. Israel was reestablished[83] as a nation once again in 1948 as a part of the land repositioning after WWII.[84] Since that time,

Israel has had to fight seven wars to maintain its independence.[85] No other nation has disappeared from the face of the earth for 1,900 years and then resurfaced with its religion and culture intact. This is certainly of God's design.[86]

The Muslims also consider Jerusalem holy as they believe Abraham gave this land to them through Ishmael. The Muslims also believe Jerusalem is the site from which their prophet Muhammad ascended to heaven.

On the side of provisional reality, human and national interests predominate. In foundational reality, God's divine plan is unfolding. God says that the promised land that he showed to Abraham will belong to the Jews forever,[87] and he warns everyone against dividing up the land.[88]

Nations and people that are in conflict with the Jewish nation of Israel are not taking issue with Israel; they are taking issue with God. This issue is clearly addressed by God in his many warnings of the blessing and the curse. "Those who bless Israel I will bless; those who curse Israel I will curse."[89]

ISLAM AND CHRISTIANITY: TWO SIDES TO EVERY STORY

Let us put this into historical context. Abraham was called by God to go to Canaan, modern-day Israel, and begin a society of his progeny that would become God's holy people and a great nation. Why was Abraham chosen? Even while living among the pagans of the Ur Valley, Abraham kept God's charge and obeyed his commandments, his statues, and all of God's laws,[90] so God considered him righteous.[91] God asked Abraham, Abraham complied, and the first theocratic covenant was inaugurated.

Abraham had two sons; his first, Ishmael, was conceived by Hagar, a family concubine. Later, according to God's promise, Isaac[92] was born to Abraham's wife, Sarah. God told Abraham that his seed would be perpetuated through Isaac and that Ishmael would also father a great nation.[93] Most of the world's cultures, especially in biblical times, deemed that the firstborn son had the family birthright.[94] In accordance with this belief, the eldest would inherit all of the family's holdings, businesses, family wealth, and position in the community.

The Hebrews believe that Isaac was the true heir of Abraham and Sarah and had claim to the covenant between God and Abraham. Scripture reads, "And Abraham said to God, Oh that Ishmael might live before Thee!" However, God said, "No, but Sarah your wife shall bear you a son, and you shall call his name Isaac, and I will establish My covenant with him for an everlasting covenant for his descendants after him."[95]

The Muslims see Ishmael as the firstborn son of Abraham by his concubine, Hagar,[96] not Isaac his firstborn from his legitimate wife, Sarah.

The Bible records that Abraham was asked to sacrifice his son Isaac to God.[97] The Qur'ān maintains that Abraham offered his son Ishmael as a sacrifice. (We will serve thy God and the God of thy fathers, Abraham, Ishmael, and Isaac.)[98] The Qur'ān further asserts that although God had called out the Hebrews as a great nation, that blessing had been rescinded. It was rescinded because of their evil deeds,[99] for not following the religion of Islam,[100] and for breaking the covenants.[101] ("Some of those who are Jews alter words from their places…, distorting with their tongues and slandering religion…, but Allah has cursed them on account of their disbelief.")[102]

"Certainly they disbelieve who say: Allah is the third of three And there is no God but one God."[103] The third of three is a reference to the Holy Trinity of Christianity. Islam is the only religion acknowledged by Muslims. "And whoever seeks a religion other than Islam, it will not be accepted from him, and in the hereafter he will be one of the losers."[104] "Surely the true religion with Allah is Islam."[105]

God's divine plan conceived in foundational reality is being played out in provisional reality; God told Abraham that he would father many nations.[106] Abraham's son, Isaac, and his wife, Rebekah, had two sons, twins, Esau and Jacob. Ishmael had twelve sons and one daughter. They lived in the land just east of Israel, in a country called Edom, and its people became known as Edomites.[107]

In this first theocratic covenant, we have the beginnings of two nations and two peoples: the Jewish state of Israel and the peoples of Arabia. When Rebekah, Isaac's wife, was pregnant, her unborn children, Esau and Jacob, were struggling within her.[108] Rebekah inquired of God why this was so, and God told her that she had two nations within her. When they were born, it was proclaimed that "one people shall be stronger than the other and that the older will serve the younger."[109] Esau was born first.[110] As it turns out, when Isaac was very old and his health was failing, he sent for Esau to pass on his birthright; however, Jacob deceived Isaac and received the birthright.[111]

Interestingly enough, if there is any condemnation in the whole affair, the Bible gives fault to Esau for giving up his birthright for immediate gratification.[112] Esau was supposed to receive his blessing; however, he was hungry, and before he went to see his father to receive his blessing, he wanted to eat. While he was eating, Jacob disguised himself as Esau, fooling the nearly blind Isaac, and was successful in stealing Esau's birthright blessing.[113]

We too are to learn that immediate gratification or other worldly temptations within provisional reality can also put our birthright or our inheritance—eternal life—at risk. The theft of Esau's birthright by Jacob in actuality is a provisional perception of the event. From a foundational perspective, it was God's will that the birthright should go to Jacob. Abraham knew that he would father a great nation. However, he was not willing to wait for God's timetable. Before Sarah was able to conceive, Abraham had a child by his concubine, Hagar. Sarah was not able to conceive yet because, in God's timetable, "the time was not right"[114] and God had "sealed up her womb."[115]

In God's perfect wisdom, he knew how Abraham would respond, and the two children, one by Hagar and the other by Sarah, would begin two separate nations. These two nations have undeniable ramifications in today's unfolding of historical events. Because of the theft of Esau's birthright by Jacob, Esau harbored a grudge against his brother.[116] Jacob fled from his brother as Esau had vowed to kill him. One night, Jacob had a dream and wrestled with God; God changed Jacob's name to Israel[117] and gave him the same land he had promised to Abraham.[118]

However, these situations only cloud the true distinction. If you are Jewish or Christian, the land belongs to Israel. If you are Muslim, the land belongs to Islam. Wars are never fought over a right and a wrong; they are always fought between two rights. Both the Jews and the Muslims think they are right about being the chosen ones of God. At issue, here are the basic underpinnings of the religions of two peoples. Neither side will disavow their religion, ignore what God or Allah has told them to be true, and be subjugated by their enemy. Neither the Arabs nor the Jews are willing to forgo their beliefs. If one acquiesces to the other, it means they have been living a lie; their culture, their heritage, and their religion will have to be abandoned. Abandoning your religion means that the fate all of those that have died before you are in question, as well as your own destiny. Is your eternity now to be in heaven or hell? Both sides seek to occupy the promised land of Israel and possess the holy city of Jerusalem.

The final resolution and the only permanent solution will come after the great tribulation. Man will never resolve this issue; it will only be resolved by God. The promised land will be the location of the final battle between good and evil.[119] It is not only a promise from God; it is a part of his prophecy.

Although all of this took place in provisional reality, it was orchestrated by God in foundational reality as part of his divine plan for humanity. What is interesting to note is that God knows us so well, he fashions us in the womb[120] and knows how long we will live.[121] He knows how we will respond to events in life, even when we are trying our best to honor him.[122] To God, our sinfulness and all of our behavior, for that matter, is predictable. When Paul refers to the birth of Esau and Jacob in the book of Romans, he quotes God as saying, "Jacob I loved, Esau I hated."[123] Scripture further reveals that this was done to show the sovereignty of God, not because of anything Jacob or Esau had done.[124]

> For it is written Abraham had two sons, one out of the slave woman, Hagar, and one out of the free woman, his wife Sarah. But, indeed, he of the slave woman has been born according to flesh; and he out of the free woman through the promise; which things are being allegorized; for these are two covenants, one, indeed, from Mount Sinai bringing forth slavery, which is Hagar, for Hagar is Mount Sinai in Arabia, and corresponds to the present Jerusalem, and she slaves with her children, But the Jerusalem from above is free, who is the mother of us all; for it has been written, 'Be glad barren one, for more are the children of the desolate rather than she having the husband.' But brothers we are children of promise according to Isaac. But then even as he who was born according to flesh persecuted the one born according to the Spirit, so it is now also, even unto this day. But what say the Scripture? Cast out the slave women and her son, for in no way shall the son of the slave woman inherit with the son of the free woman. (Gal. 4:22–30)

THE LAW AND MOSES

The nation of Israel struggled with their role as God's holy people. They vacillated between righteousness and paganism. This resulted in their living both the blessing and the curse.[125] As God had told his people, "I have laid before you all of the provisions and expectations of a holy people. I have laid before you life and death, chose life." Be obedient to my covenant and things will go well for you; disobey, and suffer the consequences.[126]

Abraham and Sarah gave birth to Isaac, who married Rebekah, who gave birth to Esau and Jacob. Jacob married Rachel, and they gave birth to Joseph. Joseph's brothers were excessively jealous of him and the relationship he had with Jacob, their father. In betrayal, they sold him into slavery to a caravan of Ishmaelites traveling to Egypt. Joseph was sold to Potiphar, one of Pharaoh's officers. The Lord was with Joseph, so he became successful, and he was in the house of his master, the Egyptian. "Now his master saw that the Lord was with him and how the Lord caused all that he did to prosper in his hand. So Joseph found favor in the sight of Potiphar, and became his personal servant."[127]

At this time, there was a worldwide famine. Joseph's family heard there was grain in Egypt, and eventually all of Joseph's family came to Egypt.[128] They stayed in Egypt, married, and grew as a population. The sons of Israel were fruitful, multiplied, and became exceedingly mighty so that in the four hundred and thirty years that they were there, the Hebrews developed into a formidable people.

> Now a new king arose over Egypt, who did not know Joseph and he said, 'Behold, the people of the sons of Israel are more and mightier than we. Come let us deal wisely with them, lest they multiply and in the event of war, they also join themselves to those who hate us, and fight against us, and depart from the land.' So they appointed task masters over them and afflicted them with hard labor. (Exod. 1:7–11)

Some two hundred years before the nation of Israel began to develop as a nation in Egypt, God told Abraham about their future.

> And God said to Abraham, know for certain that your descendants will be strangers in a land that is not theirs, where they will be enslaved and oppressed four hundred years. Then in the fourth generation they will return here. (Gen. 15:13, 16)

THINGS TO COME

Pharaoh commanded the Hebrew midwives that if a Hebrew woman gave birth to a male child, he was to be put to death.[129] Moses was born during this time of persecution, and his mother put him in a wicker basket and set him afloat in the Nile.[130] Pharaoh's daughter found Moses and claimed him to be her own child. As a result, Moses was raised in Pharaoh's household. The new king inflicted hard labor on the Hebrews. One day Moses saw an Egyptian beating a Hebrew, and he killed the Egyptian and went into exile. While Moses was in exile from Egypt, God called to him through a burning bush.[131] God asked him to free the sons of Israel[132] from captivity in Egypt. Moses' birth, subsequent litany of events as the adopted son of Pharaoh, and interactions with the nation of Israel while they were slaves was all precipitated by God to position Moses as the best candidate to free his chosen people.

God, through Moses, brought a series of plagues against Egypt until Pharaoh relented and granted the nation of Israel their leave.[133] However, Pharaoh recanted and pursued the sons of Israel. The hand of God defeated Pharaoh's army. They were held back by the pillar of cloud[134] that blocked their way and allowed time for the sons of Israel to flee. "Lift up your staff and stretch your hand over the sea and divide it, and the sons of Israel shall go through the midst of the sea on dry land."[135]

When the Egyptians pursued, "the Lord overthrew them in the midst of the sea by returning the waters and covered the chariots and the horsemen, even Pharaoh's entire army had gone into the sea after them; not even one of them remained."[136] "And when Israel saw the great power which the Lord had used against the Egyptians, the people feared the Lord, and they believed in the Lord and in his servant Moses."[137]

While the sons of Israel began their journey to the "land flowing with milk and honey,"[138] God called Moses to the summit of Mt. Sinai. Moses ascended Mt. Sinai to receive God's dictates, commandments,[139] and the Mosaic covenant.[140] In actuality, Moses went up on Mt. Sinai several times to receive the Ten Commandments, he received instructions from God,[141] and he sought forgiveness for his people.

The entire history of the Hebrews as it played out in Egypt in provisional reality was orchestrated by God from foundational reality. In Psalms we read that God "called for a famine upon the land," "He sent Joseph, who was sold as a slave," "He caused His people to be very fruitful," and "He turned their heart to hate His people."[142] In the book of Romans, we read that God also had plans for Pharaoh. "For this very purpose I raised you up, to demonstrate my power in you, and that my name might be proclaimed throughout the whole earth."[143]

THE POWER OF PRAYER

In the wilderness, away from Egypt, and in the absence of their leader Moses, the sons of Israel forgot all of the miraculous works that God had orchestrated in freeing them from Pharaoh. When Moses remained on Mt. Sinai for forty days, the faith of the sons of Israel faltered, and they had Aaron make a calf of gold so they could commit idolatry.[144] When Moses confronted Aaron about why he would defile God and make an idol for the people, Aaron's response is a perfect example of our psychological defense mechanism of denial.

> Then Moses said to Aaron "What did this people do to you, that you have brought such great sin upon them?" "And I said to them, whoever has any gold, let them tear it off, so they gave it to me, and I threw it into the fires, and out came this calf."[145]
> (Exod. 32:21, 24)

"Out came this calf," as if Aaron had nothing to do with it, even though Aaron made the calf. "It was the woman, whom you gave me."¹⁴⁶ "It was the serpent."¹⁴⁷ This of course angered God. The Lord said to Moses,

> I have seen this people, and behold, they are an obstinate people [stiff-necked]. And now leave Me alone, that My anger may glow against them, and that I may consume them and I will make of you a great nation. And Moses prayed, "Why, Jehovah does Your anger glow against Your people whom You caused to go up from the land of Egypt with great power, and with a mighty hand? Why should the Egyptians say, 'For evil He has caused them to go up, to kill them in the mountains, and to consume them on the face of the earth?'" (Exod. 32:9–12 IHOT)

Then some very interesting things happened. Moses prayed to God for the sake of his people. Scripture says that God changed his purpose about the harm, which he said he would do to his people.¹⁴⁸ This intercession by Moses for the Jews is exactly the role that Christ fulfills today for all Christians. As far as God is concerned, repentance and prayer will always change things.¹⁴⁹ When Scripture addresses the evil that God intended, or the harm he was going to inflict, these sentiments must be put into context. God cannot do evil, so when Scripture refers to God doing evil, it is that the justice that is meted out by God is perceived by people in provisional reality as evil.

Christ is the mediator between God and Christians.¹⁵⁰ Our sinful behavior cannot be reconciled against God's complete holiness without the intercession of a mediator. Christ qualifies as the only worthy mediator as he took the sins of the world unto himself¹⁵¹ and professes our innocence to God.¹⁵² It is also very interesting to note that because of the prayer of Moses, God changed his purpose in answering Moses' prayer. The original translation reads, "And Jehovah changed His purpose." Another very interesting development is the fate of the idolaters, which exemplifies that

God's holiness cannot be compromised. After the nation of Israel committed idolatry, Moses asked the people,

> Who is for Jehovah? Come to me? All of the sons of Levi assembled to him. And he said to them, So says Jehovah, God of Israel, each one put his sword on his thigh; pass over to and fro and each one kill his brother, each one kill his neighbor, and each one kill his kindred. And about three thousand men of the people fell on that day. (Exod. 32:26–28 IHOT)

Moses then again ascended Mt. Sinai to see if he could make atonement for their sins. Jehovah responded to Moses' prayer by saying, "Whoever has sinned against Me, I will blot him from My book. Now go lead My people to that place which I have spoken to you. Behold, My angel shall go before you. And Jehovah plagued the people because they had made the calf."[153] Although God spared the sons of Israel from complete annihilation, as he did not consume them, their sins of idolatry did not go unpunished. The nation of Israel was struck with a plague, and the three thousand participants in the idol worship were put to death by the sword. Even more disturbing than the loss of life, their names were blotted out of the book of life, which means eternal damnation.[154] Had God overlooked the sins of the nation of Israel, he would have compromised his complete holiness.

Prayer and repentance caused God to change his purpose; however, prayer cannot change who God is. We see sin in a completely different light than God does. God defines what sin is regardless of how we can rationalize our sinful behavior. Jehovah later told Moses what would happen in the immediate future and that he would not personally accompany him and the nation of Israel on their journey to the promised land. God chose not to accompany them because of their propensity for disobedience and their lack of faith.

And I will send an angel before your face, and I will drive out the Canaanites, the Amorites, and the Hittites, and the Perizzites, the Hivites and the Jebusites; to a land flowing with milk and honey. For I will not go up among you, for you are a stiff-necked people, least I consume you on the way. (Exod. 33:2–3 IHOT)

There appears to be a continuum at work in prayer. On the one end, we know that God does not hear the prayers of sinners.[155] Sinners are people who continue in sin without seeking repentance and with no inclination to stop sinning. On the other end of the spectrum are people as righteous as Abraham and Moses who were able to prevail upon God through prayer and repentance, which caused him to change His purpose.[156]

There are two expressed sets of circumstances in life: those that are in theory and those that are a practical application—our real life experiences. Theories and conjectures are either validated or invalidated by real life events. This, at times, can make life an exercise in trial and error as we try to establish life's truths. However, God as the Creator is the author of absolute truth and absolute reality. "The counsel of the Lord stands forever, the plans of his heart from generation to generation."[157] Absolute truth begins with God because whatever God thinks and wills becomes reality.

In the Sinai wilderness, God gave his laws to Moses[158] so he could impart the law to the nation of Israel. Moses prayed, "Now therefore, I pray Thee, if I have found favor in Thy sight, let me know Thy ways, that I may know Thee, so that I may find favor in Thy sight, consider too, that this nation is Thy people."[159] Moses told all of the remaining newly freed slaves from Pharaoh's Egypt what God required of them. The nation of Israel agreed to do all that God had said.[160] This is also known as the Mosaic covenant or the second theocratic covenant.

The Mosaic covenant was never given so that by keeping the law people could be saved. The law made people realize that they were at the mercy of their fallen nature in spite of their best intentions and would not do what God wants them to do.[161] The law was given so that man might realize that he is helpless and hopeless when left to himself, that humanity would realize that the only hope for salvation is to receive the righteousness of God by faith in Jesus.[162] Essentially, because of man's sinful nature, he cannot keep God's commandments, even when they are written in stone.

> Why the Law then? It was added because of transgressions, having been ordained through angels by the agency of a mediator, until the seed should come to whom the promise had been made. For if a Law had been given which was able to impart life, then righteousness would indeed have been based on Law. But the Scripture has shut up all men under sin, that the promise by faith in Jesus Christ might be given to those who believe. (Gal. 3:19, 21–22)

Christians understand that as the law has defined sin and that we are helpless in overcoming our proclivity for sinning by ourselves. We need a Savior, Christ, to intercede for us with God.[163] The law was meant to be a trainer so that God's people would have a guide to differentiate between righteous behavior and behavior that was displeasing to God.[164] The covenant with Moses and the nation of Israel exists in tandem with the covenant God made with Abraham.

Before the law, people did whatever they wanted, whatever was right in their own eyes.[165] God found that man's thoughts were continuously evil. You can drive one hundred miles per hour if you want to if there is no speed limit. There would be no consequences aside from the inherent danger at traveling at that speed. When the sixty-five-miles-per-hour speed limit sign is posted, now you know you are breaking the law. Now there is a right from wrong.

The Mosaic covenant was given to the now-freed sons of Israel, to those who believed and remained steadfast in their dedication to God's promise in the first theocratic covenant. The intent was so that the nation of Israel would develop a relationship with God. They would come to know and understand him and understand his providence regarding the blessing and the curse.[166] It was God's intent that the other nations of the world would also understand this relationship of a nation that was blessed because of its faith and worship of the God of Abraham, and that they too would seek a relationship with God.[167]

However, the nation of Israel became legalistic in the sense that obedience to the letter of the law became more important than the spirit of the law. The Jews honored the law more than they honored God.[168] They became enmeshed in their own rules and traditions and interpreted God's laws in ways other than how God had intended. Religion became a matter of who was the most legal, not who was the most obedient to God.[169]

THE TEN COMMANDMENTS

There are three parts to the Mosaic covenant. The Ten Commandments[170] offer specific commands for our personal life and defines the relationship between man and God. Incidentally, in the original Hebrew translation, the sixth commandment does not read "thou shall not kill" but rather "thou shall not murder."[171] The difference is significant. As for the rest of the Commandments:[172]

- I AM Jehovah your God, who brought you out of Egypt, from the house of bondage. You shall not have any other gods besides Me.

- You shall not make a graven image for yourself, of any likeness which is in the heavens above or which is in the earth beneath, or which is in the waters under the earth; you shall not bow to them, and you shall not serve them; for I am Jehovah your God, a jealous God.

- You shall not take the name of Jehovah your God in vain; for Jehovah will not leave unpunished the one who takes His name in vain.

- Remember the Sabbath day, to keep it holy, six days you shall labor and do all your work; and the seventh day is a Sabbath to Jehovah your God; you shall not do any work, you, and your son, and your daughter, your male slave and your slave girl, and your livestock, and your stranger which is in your gates. For in six days Jehovah made the heavens and the earth, and the sea, and all, which is in them, and He rested on the seventh day; on account of this, Jehovah blessed the Sabbath day and sanctified it.

- Honor your father and your mother, so that your days may be long on the land which Jehovah your God is giving to you.

- You shall not murder.

- You shall not commit adultery.

- You shall not steal.

- You shall not testify a witness of falsehood against your neighbor.

- You shall not covet your neighbor's house; you shall not covet your neighbor's wife, or his male slave, or his slave girl, or his ox, or his ass, or anything which belongs to your neighbor. (Exod. 20:2–17 IHOT)

The second part to the Mosaic covenant is in Exodus chapters 21 through 23. In these chapters, social and civil laws are defined for the Hebrews to guide them in their behavior in a communal setting. The precedent for capital punishment among other laws are also established here: "He that strikes a man so that he dies, surely he shall be put to death.[173] If one strives with a man and he is injured, the other party is responsible for his lost income and his medical bills.[174] If a pregnant woman is struck and there is no injury, the husband may levy a fine. If there is injury, it shall be life for life, eye for eye, and tooth for tooth[175] Or if a man lures a virgin and lies with her, he shall surely pay her dowry for a wife to himself.[176] You shall not take a bribe, for the bribe blinds the seeing one and it perverts the words of the righteous."[177] Moses recorded these statues, some six hundred, and called them the Book of the Covenant. He read them to the people, and they said they would uphold all that God had said. Moses consecrated the covenant with the blood from a sacrifice.[178]

In the third part, also in the book of Exodus, we find the ordinances that describe the religious parameters for the nation of Israel so that they would know God and know how to approach him. "Raise a contribution for Me; from every man whose heart moves him."[179] Also, written here are instructions on how to build a tabernacle so that God may dwell among his people.[180] The book of Exodus also gives instructions for building the ark of the covenant, which is to hold the testimony of God himself.[181]

The remaining chapters go into great detail about the tabernacle: its curtains, inner veils, outer veil, a bronze altar, oil, lampstands, and priests' garments. This may all seem like an excessive amount of focus and attention on God and his tabernacle; however, that was just the point. God wanted to make sure that he became an important part of their everyday lives.

Those who are under the law and reject faith are cursed. No one becomes justified through obedience to the law, no matter how good his or her behavior is. The law is not of faith as explained in the gospel of Jesus Christ; it is the precursor of faith.[182] Christ redeemed all believers from the curse of the law by becoming cursed himself and dying on the cross so that we are justified.[183] The blessing of Abraham came to everyone from every nation that believes that Jesus Christ was and is the Son of God. That he was sent by God[184] as a sacrifice and as the propitiation for the sins of all believers.[185] The Holy Spirit brings enlightenment and illumination[186] to all believers. He is responsible for a believer's faith and guides us through our process of sanctification. Sanctification is the journey all believers take in their process of becoming holy.

All laws that govern man are to have their origins in natural law or God's law, as is revealed in Scripture. Natural law has precedence over man-made laws—one nation under God, as our founding fathers intended that we would continue to fashion our national laws and model our government after the precepts of God. Only by modeling our laws and relationships from Scripture are we able to prepare for future events as they unfold according to God's plan in both realities. Otherwise, we precede down a path of secular solutions in provisional reality, which is secondary to foundational reality—the absolute truth. Secular solutions, although initiated with the greatest sincerity, have very little relevance in God's providence and the unfolding of his divine plan for humanity.

MANKIND IN THE CONTEXT OF GOD'S DIVINE PLAN

The Old Testament is the history of the Jewish people, God's chosen people,[187] and his covenants with them, including the promised land that they are to occupy forever.[188] Moses wrote the first five books of the Bible[189]—Genesis, Exodus, Leviticus, Numbers, and Deuteronomy. They are known to the Jews as the Torah, which are the books of the law. The Torah profiles the Jewish race, its origin, culture, religion, and the requirements for God's holy people. The Torah also explains God's statutes, commandments, and covenants that reveal his divine plan for all of humankind. The most significant event in the history of the Hebrew nation, from their perspective, was the exodus from Egypt to the promised land.

The most significant event in the lives of humanity was the advent of Christ. The next most significant event will be the tribulation period. The exodus is rather like a miniversion of God's divine plan. It is an illustrative example of the interaction between God and man.[190] An analysis of the book of Exodus is especially significant in our provisional knowledge of God and his providence as it is here that we get an unmistakable depiction of the parameters that should characterize our relationship with God.

The Torah lays out God's foundational theology in which he reveals to his people who he is, his attributes, his redemption, his law, and how he is to be worshiped. The Torah specifies that which is acceptable and that which is not acceptable behavior.

Most significantly, God describes the circumstances and events that will determine the progression of humanity. He sets the criteria that will determine all that is to happen based on humankind's free will choices of obedience or disobedience within the framework of God's permissive will. Moreover, through the ministry of a chosen mediator, Moses, and ultimately Jesus, God's purpose in history is accomplished.

God's chosen people, the Hebrews, are enslaved in Egypt, just as we are enslaved in sin. God tells Abraham that his people will be enslaved for 400 years,[191] and 430 years later, Moses leads them out of slavery.[192]

All that is foretold in the Bible by God will happen just as God decrees.[193] Moses left the house of Pharaoh to save his people, just as Christ left his Father's house to save us. Moses served as the mediator between God and the Hebrews to forestall their punishment for their disobedience and idol worship[194] just as Christ mediates for us.[195] On the night of the Passover, the Jews swabbed blood from a lamb over their doorway so that the coming plague would "pass over" them. This exemplifies the role of Christ. He shed his blood so that we too may be delivered from captivity and passed over from the wrath of God. Moses led the Hebrews out of their captivity, just as Christ leads us out of our sinful captivity.[196]

In spite of all that the Hebrews witnessed, the plagues of Egypt,[197] the pillar of cloud,[198] the parting of the Red Sea,[199] and all of the provisions that were made for them—water,[200] manna,[201] and their safety[202]—some still did not believe and honor God.[203]

When God brought the Hebrews to the promised land, the land of Canaan, they sent out spies to reconnoiter the enemy. The twelve spies returned after forty days of spying. All but two, Joshua and Caleb, were fearful and said, in spite of God's promise for victory, they should retreat.[204] The people rebelled; they wanted to stone Moses and return to Egypt.[205] For their unbelief, God made them to wander in the wilderness, one year for every day they had been spying.[206] Because of their continual disobedience, rebellion, and idol worship,[207] the Hebrews were made to wander in the wilderness until all of the unbelievers perished.[208] The remnant of believers—which is only Joshua, Caleb, their children, and those steadfast in their faith,[209] of the original 600,000, plus women and children, that left Egypt[210]—are led into the promised land. This represents a parallel for us today; only a remnant of humanity past, present, and future will spend an eternity in heaven, and others will not.[211]

It is God's desire that we live as righteous people, conducting ourselves in a manner worthy of our relationship with God.[212] We do our best to resist sin[213] and repent of those sins when we are unable to resist[214] temptation. We accept and believe that Christ has paid the debt for our sins.[215] Then out of gratitude for our rescue and the promise of our eternal reward, we willingly obey God's desire that we conduct ourselves righteously and obey his commandments and statues.[216] To be righteous simply means that you are right with God. The promised land of provisional reality is, of course, analogous to heaven—foundational reality.

We all have our own personal wilderness with faith we must pass through. The whole point is to pass through it; if you remain in the wilderness, you too will perish.

THE COVENANTS OF GOD

Although the covenants are established in the Old Testament, their authority and consequences run all the way through to the book of Revelation. In all, God made eight covenants with man. They are important because through these covenants we see God's involvement in the events of man and in the events of history. We not only understand God's sovereignty over his creation; we have the blueprint for human history. We know exactly where history is heading.

The first three covenants are called the universal covenants because they apply to all of humanity and have a universal application. They are the edenic (garden of eden),[217] the Adamic (Adam and Eve after the fall),[218] and the Noahic (Noah after the flood).[219]

The other five covenants are the theocratic covenants because they involve God's governing of humanity. They involve the creation of a holy people and God's eternal plan for our salvation through faith, Christ, and grace. The covenants demonstrate that God has not just created us to progress by happenstance. They show his direct involvement in the lives of people individually, in the development of nations, and in world history.

The first covenant was between God and Adam, the edenic covenant (Eden). Adam was to populate and subdue the earth, exercise dominion over the animals of creation, care for the garden and enjoy its fruits. In other words, man was given stewardship over the earth.[220] However, Adam was told, "Do not eat from the tree of knowledge of good and evil, if you do, surely you will die."[221] On his part, Adam was to refrain from eating the fruit from the tree of knowledge of good and evil under penalty of death. In other words, he was to obey God's one simple commandment.[222] Obey God, and things will go well for you; disobey, and you will experience God's divine judgment.[223] However, free will, the inability to resist temptation and the forces of evil all coalesced and caused Adam and Eve to disobey—the fall. The fall is to fall from the grace of God. All of us have committed the same act of disobedience, our will over God's. However, our role is still to populate, subdue, and exercise dominion over the earth.[224]

The second universal covenant was between God and Adam and was called the Adamic covenant (Adam). This covenant reflects the consequences of disobedience. Adam and Eve were in paradise, however, they chose to do their will instead of God's will. Man had fallen through disobedience, and this new covenant between God and humankind will be in place until the curse of sin is removed. Sin is any departure from what God, as our creator, has decreed.

The second universal covenant also judges Satan and grants him limited success in his endeavors.[225] The snake was commanded to live on its belly and eat dust.[226] The very sight of a snake henceforth would remind people of how repulsive sin is to God. Moreover, it does, especially if you come upon a snake unexpectedly, just as when God sees one of his children sin. Satan's endeavors will be held in check by the restraining powers of the Holy Spirit.[227] Ultimately, Satan's success in this cosmic battle of good and evil will be analogous to a bruise on the heel of Christ, and he will receive a bruise on his head[228] that will prove to be fatal. Satan will be able to lead some astray; however, the coming Messiah will destroy him.[229] Further stipulations of this covenant are the population of the earth will be greatly multiplied, sorrow will be a part of childbirth, and the female will desire her husband.[230] Some may wonder how a female to desire her husband is part of a curse. Noah Webster in1828 defines desire as "an emotion or excitement of the mind, directed to the attainment or possession of an object from which pleasure, sensual, intellectual, or spiritual is expected." When these expectations are not realized to the degree, anticipated conflicts can arise. When our expectations are not realized, we attempt to assume more control over the situation. Man will have to work in order to eat, his gains will be by the sweat of his brow, and physical life is exchanged for death.[231] In short, paradise is gone because of our sinful nature. Life in provisional reality will

be filled with trials and suffering, although we will still be able to find peace and joy.

The third and final universal covenant is made between God and Noah (the Noahic covenant). God by this time destroyed the earth's population with the flood, except Noah and his family. Humanity's destruction came about because of man's disobedience to God's revealed law—man's "violence and wickedness," which amounted to "sin that was so great"[232] that God was sad he had made man.[233] The third covenant essentially reaffirms that all of the conditions set forth in the second covenant between God and Adam are still in place.[234] God established justice within civilization from a provisional perspective as a check against sin and the conditions that necessitated the destruction of humankind, as man was unable to adhere to strictly foundational precepts. This is the beginning of the legal system, which is designed to help man know right from wrong and will serve as guidelines for man's behavior. Additionally, God promises never to destroy the earth by water again. The sign of this promise and a remembrance is that he places a rainbow in the sky after it rains.[235] The rainbow stands as a reminder, for both God and man of his covenant. However, in the New Testament, we learn the next time the world will be destroyed, it will be by fire.[236]

THE COVENANTS OF GOD'S RULE

The next five covenants are the theocratic covenants. God's covenants are our certainty that the events prophesied in the Bible will occur just as God has foretold they would.[237]

The first theocratic covenant is between God and Abraham, the Abrahamic covenant. It is God bestowing upon Abraham the promised land.[238] This covenant is passed on to his son, Isaac,[239] who in turn passes the covenant on to his son Jacob.[240]

The second theocratic covenant is the Mosaic covenant, and it is between God and Moses. In it, God prescribes more behavioral guidelines[241] and reaffirms the promised land for the Hebrews.[242]

The third, the Palestine covenant, is between God and his people. Essentially, it says, "If you will diligently obey the Lord your God, the Lord your God will set you high above all the nations of the earth."[243] Humanity would not live morally according to God's wishes, so God prescribed a myriad of laws that would define appropriate and inappropriate or sinful behavior so people could have guidelines for social, civil, and religious behavior. God did not make laws so that he could condemn or judge people; they were made for our benefit so that we could exercise our free will in choosing to behave righteously rather than sinfully, obedience over rebellion.[244] The system of laws and rules relayed by God were legalistic; they were immediate and conditional.

Deuteronomy contains three sermons by Moses. The first is a historical look back.[245] It recounts the lesson of God's moral judgment on the Hebrews for their unbelief and deliverance during times of obedience. The simple lesson is that obedience brings blessings, and disobedience brings punishment. The second sermon is a current view that if they obey God, the promised land will be theirs. Here also is found all of the testimonies for moral behavior,[246] the statutes for ceremonial duties,[247] and the ordinances for social and civil duties.[248]

The third sermon is forward-looking and tells of the dispersion and the return of the Jewish people to the promised land, a continuation of the blessing and the curse.[249]

The fourth is the Davidic covenant, where God continues the promises for his people that the land of Israel is theirs forever,[250]—an unending dynasty[251] and an everlasting kingdom.[252] "The genealogy of Jesus Christ, the son of David, the son of Abraham" makes the unending dynasty and the everlasting kingdom possible.[253]

The final theocratic covenant is called the new covenant.[254] God will put his law in our hearts so that we will innately understand

God and innately understand good and evil.[255] This understanding will be by the indwelling presence of the Holy Spirit.[256] Lastly, the new covenant is a covenant that will occur in days that are coming[257] and will provide for the forgiveness of sin.[258] The last covenant, the forgiveness of sin enabled by Jesus Christ, is that which was alluded to in the second universal covenant, whereby Jesus Christ would remove the curse of sin. The new covenant augments the legal system with God's system of grace. This is only made possible through the sacrificial death of Christ and the blood he shed for the atonement of our sins.[259] The Messiah will provide for the salvation of all of humanity that believes he is the Son of God.[260]

Man has never been able to live up to the expectations of God, to live in a manner worthy of a child of God. We have always failed to follow the statutes and commandments of God; even his holy people failed.[261] "There is none righteous, not even one; There is none who understands, There is none who seeks for God, All have turned aside…There is none who does good, There is not even one."[262] Therefore, God provided a Savior, and through his sacrifice and the blood he shed on the cross, God forgave and will continue to forgive our iniquity, and he will not remember the sins of believers.[263] When God's holy people rejected the Messiah and had him crucified, the offer of the new covenant was extended to Gentiles—all who believe that Jesus Christ is the Son of God.[264] Christ came to earth to bridge the gap between our sinfulness and God's complete holiness.[265]

Through all of this, we understand that no matter what provisions God makes for man, man is unable to honor God and comply with his will. We will need someone to save us from ourselves—a Savior.[266] God has never broken a covenant.[267] That distinction has always fallen to man. This is proof that humanity is unable to live according to God's expectations. If we are to walk in a manner worthy of our calling, we will need help in accomplishing this task.

The essences of the covenants are that God continually tries to give guidance to humanity. Within the framework of his permissive will, humans continue to do what they think is right in their own eyes. Adam and Eve could not resist temptation. Neither could those that eventually had to be destroyed in the flood and the inhabitants of Sodom and Gomorra. The followers of Moses could not put their faith in a man doing God's bidding, even after witnessing all of the miracles of God.[268] "There is none without sin, no, not even one."[269]

The first four theocratic covenants were unable to quell the spirit of human rebellion and the challenges of man's free will choices. It was left to God to provide a solution, as man was unable to save himself from his sins. Humankind needed a Savior. Jesus Christ is the perfect solution, God in the flesh to take the punishment for the sins of humanity. Man is incapable of performing God's will and conducting themselves in such a way as God would consider them—us—righteous. The new covenant inaugurates God's system of grace through the death and shed blood of Christ. That is why at the Last Supper, Christ took the cup, gave thanks, and gave the cup to his disciples, saying, "Drink from it, all of you; for this is My blood of the covenant, which is poured out for many for forgiveness of sins."[270]

THE HOLY SPIRIT

The Holy Spirit is described by Christ as the Helper, and he is to be the source of truth and illumination for every believer. The Holy Spirit, among other things, also imparts within us the fruits of the Spirit and his spiritual gifts. Being filled with the Spirit is the manifestation of the Spirit functioning within the idiosyncratic personality of the believer. It is not so much how filled we are with the Spirit, but how much we are willing to yield to the Spirit to allow the filling.

THE HELPER

We must understand three things about the Bible. The Bible is the inspired Word of God.[271] It is communication from God himself to his people, from foundational reality to provisional reality.

Second, the Bible is like a code, which means it is intended for some people and not for others.[272] It is the language of two realities.

Third, like every code, there has to be a key, a key that allows the intended

recipient to be able to decipher the message.[273] The key for understanding the Bible is the Holy Spirit. When Christ was about to be crucified, he told his disciples that he would ask the Father to send a Helper, and that the Helper would be the Spirit of truth.[274]

However, not everyone would be able to benefit from the Helper, only the followers of Jesus Christ. The Helper, the Holy Spirit, will teach us all things.[275] He teaches us by enlightenment, revelation, and he conveys information from God to his people.

The Holy Spirit of the Trinity interacts with us[276] and intervenes on our behalf in two ways. He restrains Satan, and he conveys messages from God to us and from us to God.[277] His restraining powers[278] limit the effects that Satan can have in provisional reality. The Holy Spirit is in constant engagement with the prince of darkness, limiting his ability to wage war. The Holy Spirit is a Helper because he contends with our fallen, sin nature and is the only existing power by which a believer's human nature is ever controlled. The Holy Spirit is constantly in our midst working beyond the veil that shields this reality from foundational reality. The Holy Spirit is active and engaged in both foundational and provisional reality.

The divine method of overcoming evil is the power we are given by the indwelling Holy Spirit. He also gives us the ability to know good from evil and to recognize the influences that Satan can cast over unbelievers and the cosmos world institutions. The Holy Spirit not only limits the power of Satan; he also provides us with truth through enlightenment. The truth that the Holy Spirit leads all believers to comprehend is that we are inherently sinful and deserving of the wrath of God. To be saved, we must believe that Christ is the Savior. It is not our words that profess this truth, but the words of Christ himself. "Jesus said to them, I am the way and the truth and the life, no one comes to the Father except through Me."[279]

Man must believe that he has sinned, and, because he has sinned, he needs a Savior. That Savior is Jesus Christ, the Son of the

living God,[280] and salvation is only possible through Jesus Christ and in him alone. Moreover, this saving work was accomplished through his sacrificial death. He suffered the punishment for all of our sins so that we may have eternal life. If this truth is hidden, it is hidden to the lost, "in whom the god of this world has blinded the minds of them that do not believe."[281]

We exist in provisional reality and do not readily perceive the further dimensions of reality that simultaneously exists in the realm of foundational reality. Our empirical-thinking process is oriented to provisional reality because that is the reality we see. We do not readily understand foundational reality because we cannot see it, and because we cannot see it or interact with it, we do not know what or how to think about it. Every time an angel appears to someone in the New Testament, the angels begin their conversation with "Do not be afraid."[282] This should tell us something about our inability to comprehend the supernatural. Additionally, when Jesus changed the physical laws of nature by walking on water[283] or raising people from the dead,[284] he cautioned people not to be afraid. This understanding can only come by revelation and enlightenment from the Holy Spirit, and that is contingent on the maturity of a Christian's spirituality.

THE MINISTRIES OF THE HOLY SPIRIT

In the present age, there are twelve ministries of the Holy Spirit: enlightenment,[285] revelation,[286] prophecy,[287] filling or indwelling,[288] administering gifts to believers,[289] and restraining evil by restraining Satan.[290] Additionally, the Holy Spirit is responsible for care and growth of the church,[291] making available to us the fruits of the Spirit,[292] and bearing witness to us.[293] The Holy Spirit also prays for us.[294] He gives power to believers to witness[295] and to overcome evil. The Holy Spirit is the conduit by which we receive

God's love.[296] A brief explanation of the ministries of the Holy Spirit will help us understand the bridge he provides between foundational and provisional reality.

Enlightenment or illumination is the process whereby the Holy Spirit opens the understanding of God to believers as they read Scripture. Scriptural interpretation is very idiosyncratic as the Holy Spirit delivers specific messages relevant to a believer's growth, walk, or needed counsel. This is why the Bible is referred to as the living Word or the living Bible.

Closely related to enlightenment is the ministry of revelation and prophecy. This ministry is to ensure God's Word, statues, and thoughts are made known to us. The truths revealed to us from the Holy Spirit are not from him, they are from the depths of God.[297] The ministry of revelation is directed toward the individual believer. It is the only hope that man will turn intelligently and completely by faith to Jesus Christ as one's Savior. Revelation is the Spirit's power to give understanding to the believer as they experience the Word of God. Without the Holy Spirit's revelations, God's Word is often difficult to understand, which makes it difficult to apply biblical truths to one's life. Revelation also involves the Holy Spirit's ability to impart to some believers the gift of prophecy. The origins of prophecy begin with the Spirit's ability to relay that which he hears of God's thoughts and reveal those thoughts to those selected for that gift. Prophecy is not limited to predicting future events; it is also meant to include the ability to interpret scriptural truths to impart to others.

The believer is required to have a heightened sense of awareness as to how the Holy Spirit communicates his message. The message is from foundational reality; as such, there will be a tendency for us not to recognize the message as one originating from the Holy Spirit. Messages from the Holy Spirit are often subtle and may be easy to miss. They can, however, be conveyed while we read Scripture or through a messenger sent by God. Messages can also come from a friend, or they can be impressions formed in our mind by the Holy Spirit. We must be attentive, focused, and understand that we can receive messages from supernatural entities. The challenge can be not only discerning the message, but its source as well. The more we are aware of the overlap of the two realities, the more attuned and receptive we tend to be to the supernatural. Any involvement of the Holy Spirit in our life is a supernatural experience. A message from the Holy Spirit will honor God, reveal God's work in our life, and portray what is required of us. "I have many more things to say to you, but you cannot bear them now. But when He, the Spirit of truth comes, He will guide you into all truth."[298]

The third ministry is that of filling or indwelling. If we are believers, the Holy Spirit indwells us, and that means he is living within us and we are his temples.[299] With the Spirit indwelling us, we are able to be influenced by his presence and we can receive supernatural power from his presence. How much influence and power is dependent upon how much we yield ourselves to his presence.

The fourth ministry is related to the third. When we are open to the Holy Spirit, he makes a variety of supernatural gifts available to us. Spiritual gifts are recorded in Scripture, and they include gifts of wisdom, helping, discernment, knowledge, faith, healing, miracles, prophecy, teaching, giving, mercy, exhortation, apostleship, ministering, hospitality, and pastoring.[300]

The fifth ministry is that of restraining, and it is directed toward Satan and his minions. The Holy Spirit restrains the amount of evil Satan can do in provisional reality. It is a ministry by which the manifestation of evil is restricted to certain divinely predetermined thresholds. God and Satan discuss some of these limitations in the book of Job.[301] However, our best indication of what these restraints are limiting is found in the book of Revelation. The book of Revelation reveals the events in provisional reality during the tribulation period when the Restrainer has been removed. The definition of the restraint lies in the disparity between evil in today's provisional reality and evil as it is portrayed in the book of Revelation—tomorrow's reality.

> For the mystery of lawlessness is already at work [Satan]; only He who now restrains [the Holy Spirit] will do so until He is taken out of the way. Then that lawless one will be revealed whom the Lord will slay with the breath of His mouth and bring to an end by the appearance of His coming. (2 Thess. 2:7–8)

The arrival of the Holy Spirit into provisional reality is called Pentecost. He came to earth to fill the void that was left by Christ's departure at his resurrection.[302]

The sixth ministry of the Holy Spirit was to guide the church through its development,[303] ensure its development, and provide for the enlightenment of clergy and parishioners.

The seventh ministry is the fruits of the Holy Spirit. The fruits are love, joy, peace, patience, kindness, goodness, faithfulness, gentleness, and self-control.[304] The fruits of the Spirit will characterize his message, and they are the traits the Holy Spirit imparts to us for the conduct of our everyday affairs.

The eighth ministry of the Holy Spirit, witnessing, involves communication between realities. The ninth also is a direct commission from God, that the Holy Spirit will bear witness[305] to the believer. The communications ministry also entails the Holy Spirit convicting the world of its sin.[306] He also gives the believer the ability to discern[307] between good and evil. We understand from Scripture that the Holy Spirit receives his information directly from God, and he is to relay that information to believers. The information is not for nonbelievers because to them, it is all foolishness.[308] The information the Holy Spirit will reveal to the yielded believer is all truth, even from the depths of God.[309] God has said that he will impart his laws and knowledge of Himself within us, and He does this through the Holy Spirit.[310]

The tenth ministry is that the Holy Spirit prays for us. The significance of this ministry is that the Holy Spirit searches the depths of God and knows a man's innermost thoughts.[311] With this information, he can intercede for us in praying to God. The Holy Spirit uses groaning[312] in his prayers, which is a far superior mode of communication to our verbal communication in significance and meaning. Through the culmination of these blessings bestowed on the believer by the Holy Spirit, we receive the power to witness boldly, we have a power for living courageously and seeking justice, and we have the power to overcome evil.[313] The Holy Spirit will always pray for us; if we do not know how to pray for or about something, we can ask him to pray to God directly for us.[314] Prayer is the conduit for love between God and his people. We ask, and as long as our prayers are in conformity to God's will, he answers us.[315]

BEING FILLED WITH THE SPIRIT

The Bible speaks of the filling or the indwelling of the Spirit or that one is to be filled with the Spirit.[316] This is the very center of the concept of a spiritual life. When a believer is filled with the Spirit, he is accountable to the Holy Spirit and is the benefactor of all of the ministries of the Holy Spirit. Because we are filled and availed to the ministries of the Holy Spirit, we are in possession of all of the power required for resisting evil and for service to our Lord. The Holy Spirit gives us the supernatural ability in provisional reality to counter Satan's influences from foundational reality. The more we accommodate ourselves to the fruits and gifts of the Spirit, the more effective we will become in our preordained good works.[317] We exert less control over our life and let the Holy Spirit exert more.

The degree to which one is influenced by the Holy Spirit or filled with the Spirit is contingent upon the degree to which one accommodates themselves to the Holy Spirit. The more one adjusts themselves to the influences, promptings, and sensing of the Spirit, the more one is guided by the truth, which is Jesus Christ, and the more supernatural one's life becomes. "No man can come to Me except the Father which has sent Me draws him; and I will raise him up at the last day."[318]

The believer that is indwelt has three ministries. First, the spiritual life calls for a deliverance from the power of the three great enemies of God and man, which is provisional reality: the secular world, the flesh, and Satan and all of his minions, collectively referred to as the cosmos.

Second, the spiritual life calls for the manifestation of divine grace, which is all of the virtues of one called out of darkness into the Light.[319] We are without question responsible to our Creator for our behavior and our morality,[320] just as children are responsible to their parents.

Third, the new Spirit-led Christian has a new authority. The new authority brings new responsibilities for us and our brothers and sisters. We are brothers and sisters in Christ because we all have the same Father. Our new responsibilities encompass overcoming evil and being holy because God is holy.[321] We have the responsibility to others as well, ensuring their salvation; the harvest is plentiful, but the workers are few.[322] We are also to follow the examples demonstrated by Christ during his tenure on earth.

The whole point of the indwelling Holy Spirit is to enable the Christian to have the supernatural power to "run the race that is set before us,"[323] "fight the good fight,"[324] "walk in the light,"[325] and "walk in the newness of life."[326] The Holy Spirit is the countermeasure to the dual reality we live in; it is how God levels the playing field. Through the power of the Holy Spirit, we are able to live by Christ's example. We are able to go where God wants us to go, to be what God wants us to be, and to do what God wants us to do.

The confession of every known sin and maintaining the principle of reliance upon the Spirit in our everyday endeavors depends on the individual's free will choice to be yielded, to give up control to the Holy Spirit. We are to be submitted to God and adhere to his guidelines for our behavior, which we know full well, because they are in Scripture. "All Scripture is inspired by God and is profitable for teaching for training in righteousness, that the man of God may be adequately equipped for every good work."[327] Moreover, we possess the information innately.[328] We are also ever guided by our conscience and the Holy Spirit. We are not alone in this; we are supernaturally aided by the indwelling Holy Spirit.

Here is the whole point. The manner of life required of the child of God is not a plea for something the believer must do to be saved or continue to do to be saved. It is rather a pattern of behavior that exemplifies the gratitude we have for all that has been done by God, Christ, and the Holy Spirit in securing our salvation.

THE ELECT

There is a select group of people called the elect.[329] The elect are predetermined and preordained to be saved and to spend an eternity in heaven. They will spend eternity in foundational reality with fellow elects, God the Father, Jesus Christ, the Holy Spirit, and the entire host of celestial beings. The elect are the certain number of people that are called[330] by God. They will understand and believe in the Lord Jesus Christ as the Savior and the only source of salvation for humanity. The originally chosen people of God were the children of Israel. When they rejected Christ, that rejection opened the way for Gentiles to be among those destined to an eternal existence in heaven.[331] "I have other sheep, which are not of this fold; I must bring them also, and they will hear My voice; and they will become one flock with one Shepherd."[332]

However, it is God's wish that not one of these should perish.[333] If one of his elect is about to be lost, God will intervene in their life to assure their salvation.[334] People come to a faith in God and Jesus Christ by the enlightening ministry of the Holy Spirit. With that enlightenment comes the understanding that Christ is the answer to every need we will have in provisional reality. The individual called by God is thereby able to receive Christ as their personal Savior. Only those drawn by God come to Christ in faith.[335] We are called by God and drawn to faith by the Holy Spirit.[336] Unbelievers who resist their innate knowledge of God and the influences of the Holy Spirit have their minds veiled to the truth. Only those who turn to God will have their veil removed.[337] For life's important issues, we should seek counsel from yielded fellow believers.

> For this is the will of My Father, that everyone who beholds the Son believes in Him, may have eternal life; and I Myself will raise him up on the last day. (John 6:40)

> No man can come to Me, except the Father which hath sent Me draw him; and I will raise him up on the last day. (John 6:44)

Christ came to earth for many reasons: to overcome death, to destroy the works of the devil,[338] to take away our sins,[339] and to bring salvation to all men.[340] He was also God among us,[341] so that we could know him personally. He also came to earth so that we would have a new ideal for daily living, an example of an exalted character, and a new pattern for daily life.[342] God appeals to Christians for conduct in our daily life that is in accordance with our high calling: "Be ye perfect for I Am perfect,"[343] and "Be ye holy for I Am holy."[344] We are to emulate Christ because, as Christians, we have been asked to.[345] We do not change our behavior to conform to Christ's model so that we may be saved; we change our behavior because we are saved. It must never be thought that we earn our salvation by righteous living.[346] Two very pervasive lies that are perpetuated by Satan are that men can forgive the sins of another man[347] and that by being a good person, we will be saved.[348] Many good people will spend eternity in hell. We can never earn our way into heaven by our good behavior. The path to an eternity with God has been paved for us by the death of Christ on the cross.

The magnitude of Christ's death is not easy for us to comprehend, nor is his capacity for love, mercy, and his ability to forgive. A perfect, immortal God becomes flesh so that he may come into provisional reality and offer himself as a sacrifice for all sinners so that they may be saved and have eternal life in paradise. The very sinners that he has come to save murder him, and as they are in the process of murdering him, he asks his Father to forgive them. When Christ said, "Father, forgive them for they know not what they do," he was asking forgiveness from a perspective of foundational reality. Because they were responding to situations in provisional reality, with no acknowledgment of foundational reality. That is why Christ said, "They know not what they do." It should be impossible for an immortal being to die, but Christ did. The two concepts are wholly supernatural: immortality and the death of someone that is immortal. The ability to have eternal life creates the true motive for holy living, a God-honoring lifestyle. Without exception, all that receive the gift of eternal life do so on the sole human requirement of believing in Jesus Christ as their Savior. "And in none other is there salvation; for neither is there any other name under heaven that is given among men, wherein we must be saved."[349] Life itself is difficult to define, and the concept of eternal life as a transformed being is hard for our empirical understanding to conceive.

> So also is the resurrection of the dead. It is sown a perishable body, it is raised an imperishable body. It is sown a natural body, it is raised a spiritual body. If there is a natural body, there is also a spiritual body. (1 Cor 15:42, 44)

If there is a provisional reality, then there is a foundational reality.

BORN AGAIN: A NEW START

The transformation we undergo after death is not our first transformation. Christians experience regeneration. Regeneration results in a fundamental change in the individual. We become a new being with new capabilities. The new life given to the Christians is manifested in new ways of thinking, new behaviors, new motivations in life, and new spiritual powers. The new nature has a longing for God and a desire to do his will. This produces a drastic change in our manner of life, our outlook, and our priorities. This is what is meant by faith without works is dead.[350] If you have truly been regenerated, born again, it will be apparent in your everyday behavior. However, even after we accept Christ as our Savior and choose to dedicate our life to Christianity, we still experience remnants of the old self; old thoughts and temptations linger. We are still subject to demonic influences.

The power for victory over sin lies in the indwelling Holy Spirit, which is the presence of God within us. The new nature provides the will for us to do the will of God. Our new power from God provides the means by which this end is accomplished in spite of our human condition. This new being has a new capacity for love, joy, peace, sorrow, compassion, and guidance. We turn from our self-interests to God's interest. We now have the ability, if we pursue it, to be able to comprehend the existence and the interconnectedness of the two realities. We can also now understand the relevance of Satan and the influence he is able to exert as the prince of darkness in provisional reality.

Old thoughts and habits die hard, but their influences will become less and less with time as we grow in faith. Naiveté in Christians can often produce disappointment by the lack of an overnight transformation. We need to remember there is a completely different reality that exists beyond that which we are able to perceive—a reality populated with spiritual beings, both good and evil, that can reach beyond the chasm that separates provisional reality from foundational reality and exert their influences. However, they can never interfere with our free will. Even God holds free will sacred. A regenerated person is still capable of sinning. Primarily because of our basic sinful nature and our ability to exercise our free will in the choices we make. A state of sinless perfection can never be reached. James tells us, "But each one is tempted when he is carried away and enticed by his own lusts."[351]

In the last analysis, the experiences of this life are only antecedent to the larger experiences the regenerated person will have after deliverance from the presence and temptation of sin.

THE SPIRITUAL GIFTS OF THE HOLY SPIRIT

The spiritual life is the result of a voluntary choice to do God's will, and consequently it can be said that whosoever will may come.[352] It then follows that whosoever will may attain victory over evil. This is how we ultimately bear the responsibility for our own behavior. We are accountable to God, our Creator, for our morality. The unsaved cannot make a choice for Christ until moved to do so by the actions of the Holy Spirit. In the same manner, Christians do not make a choice for spirituality until moved to do so by the Spirit working in their minds. Living a spiritual life on the basis of faith is gaining the ability to overcome evil and to perform every good work.[353]

The Spirit expresses himself in nine distinct characteristics that are reflected through the Christian's new behavioral repertoire. These fruits of the Spirit are love, joy, peace, patience, kindness, goodness, faithfulness, gentleness, and self-control.[354] Doing the will of God is not accomplished by virtue of the fact that one is saved. It is accomplished in those who are saved and do not walk according to the flesh, but according to the Spirit.[355] These nine characteristics constitute the essential elements of Christian character or the new man. The contrast is between Christians who depend on their own resources and do not trust God and those Christians who depend on the power of the indwelling Spirit. Love, joy, and peace are experienced as an inner tranquility in spite of foreboding circumstances or conditions. "Do not let your heart be troubled, nor let it be fearful."[356] Gentleness is not being less than one really is; it is rather not pretending to be more. "The servant of the Lord must not strive, but be gentle unto all men."[357] Self-control is responsibility for your behavior and walking worthy of your calling. Patience is waiting for everything to happen according to God's timetable while we are being anxious for nothing.[358] We cast our anxiety upon the Lord because we know that he cares for us.[359] Kindness and goodness are behaviors that result from motivations that are based on not thinking more highly of ourselves than we ought to and helping others to surpass themselves.[360] Faithfulness is having as a guiding principle for interpreting events in provisional reality of "we know that all things happen for the good to those who love the Lord."[361]

The afflictions and desires of the flesh will demonstrate themselves through the works of the flesh not held in check by the power of the Holy Spirit. The indwelt and responding Christian will love what God loves and hate what God hates. Love is the key to his redemptive program. Received, it becomes our salvation; released to others, it becomes our service. This is the state of a believer in provisional reality who trusts God and leans not on his own understanding[362] but knows that all things work to the good for those who love the Lord.

> Love not the world, neither the things that are in the world. If any man loves the world, the love of the Father is not in him. For all that is in the world, the lust of the flesh, and the lust of the eyes, and the pride of life is not of the Father, but is of the world. (1 John 2:15–16)

Christians must love the lost people of the cosmos and strive for their salvation. At the same time, we hate the satanic system in which we are placed and know we are not to become spotted or stained by it.[363] The presence of compassion in a believer is nothing other than the expression of divine love from God himself being expressed through the believer. Divine love is the dynamic, motivating force in the spiritual life that attracts us to other believers to ensure that the salvation of their souls is secure. Satan's influences within the cosmos tend to subvert this divine love and turn it into a physical attraction and tempt the believers into committing sexual sin. In this manner, instead of a believer assuring the salvation of a fellow Christian, they both have entered into one of Satan's snares.[364]

In God's divine plan, a man and a woman are attracted to each other. They fall in love, become wed, leave their parents, cleave to each other, and become one flesh.[365] The result of marriage is a commitment to each another based on a vow to God, to love one another until death do we part.[366] The blessing of an intimate relationship,[367] with all of its pleasures,[368] is based on this solid foundation. This kind of a commitment, ensured by a promise to God during the wedding ceremony that "until death do we part," gives the relationship the commitment to weather any storm.

The flaming arrows of Satan and his deception turn this blessing into a curse. People meet, become attracted to one another, and become involved in a sexual relationship. They both know that God considers this sinful behavior, and they experience feelings of guilt. They rationalize away their guilt by convincing themselves that they are in love; this is another demonic deception. A relationship based on deception cannot be truthful. The eventual breakup not only causes a broken heart, but this pain is compounded by the knowledge that God was right, and the behavior has been sinful. Guilt reappears, and the lost love is replaced with feelings of worthlessness. A sense of worthlessness distances us from a perfectly Holy God and pushes us closer to Satan. We seek to be consoled from others rather than seek forgiveness from God. God not only repeatedly warns us about sexual immorality, it is his will that we abstain from it.[369] His warning is so strong that he tells us to flee from it.[370] Not avoid it or cautiously refrain, he says flee. Those that will not find their way to heaven include the cowardly, unbelieving, abominable, murderers, immoral persons, sorcerers, idolaters, liars, fornicators, adulterers, homosexuals, drunkards, swindlers, revilers, and those that are sexual immoral.[371]

Spiritual gifts are not to be confused with natural talents or abilities. A spiritual gift is the Holy Spirit working through the personality of the Christian to accomplish a particular service. Spiritual gifts are latent and are only expressed after a Christian has achieved salvation; they are a function of the new nature.

Spirituality in itself does not bring spiritual gifts. They are only manifested when there is an accommodation made to the Holy Spirit and the believer has a right relationship with God. What is the right relationship? The right adjustment is a complete dependence on the Holy Spirit and complete submission to God. Submission is an abandonment of self-will and complete obedience to do only that which is pleasing to God.[372] "Submit therefore to God, Resist the devil and he will flee from you. Draw near to God and He will draw near to you."[373] Without the right relationship to God, there cannot be a manifestation of one's spiritual gifts. To be unyielding to the Holy Spirit will also hinder our ability to receive guidance and counsel from the Holy Spirit. Spiritual gifts are divinely given to Christians when these two criteria are met, and they are given strictly as a result of God's sovereignty.

No two Christians are alike, nor have they had the same experiences. Our gifts may be the same, the gift of wisdom or service, but the manifestation of gifts will be idiosyncratic to our personality and our life's experiences. So many people go through life wondering what life is all about. They feel as if they have missed something, or they are not satisfied in spite of wealth or success. If they are not living out the expression of their spiritual gift or gifts, they are missing something—their calling. "The gifts and the calling of God are irrevocable."[374] The gifts of the Holy Spirit are:

> Now there are varieties of gifts, but the same Spirit. And there are varieties of ministries, and the same Lord. And there are varieties of effects, but the same God who works all things in all persons. But to each one is given the manifestation of the Spirit for the common good. For to one is given the word of wisdom through the Spirit, and to another the word of knowledge according to the same Spirit; to another faith by the same Spirit, and to another gifts of healing by the one Spirit, and to another the effecting of miracles, and to another prophecy, and to another the distinguishing of spirits, to another various kinds of tongues, and to another the interpretation of tongues. But one and the same Spirit works all these things, distributing to each one individually just as He wills. (1 Cor 12:7–10, 28–30)

> Since we have gifts that differ according to the grace given to us, each of us is to exercise them accordingly; if prophecy, according to the portion of his faith; if service, in his service; or he who teaches, in his teaching; or he who exhorts, in his exhortation; he who gives, with liberality; he who leads, with diligence; he who shows mercy; with cheerfulness. (Romans 12:6–8)

> And He gave some as apostles, and some as prophets, and some as evangelists, and some as pastors and teachers, for the equipping of the saints for the work of service, to the building up of the body of Christ; until we all attain to the unity of the faith, and of the knowledge of the Son of God, to a mature man, to the measure of the stature which belongs to the fullness of Christ. (Eph 4:11–13)

Spiritual gifts are used by the Christian through the fruits of the Spirit to reap the harvest. The harvest is the salvation of the souls of humanity, to and for the glory of God.

It is incredibly rewarding to have an experience that involves both realities. From provisional reality, we can be involved in the activities of the supernatural and doing the work of God. God leads us and gives us guidance and counsel through the Holy Spirit. The leading is not necessarily some outward sign or signal. More often, it is a conviction about the rightness, or wrongness of something as the Holy Spirit forms impressions on our minds.

> I have many more things to say to you, but you cannot bear now, but when He, the Spirit of truth comes, He will guide you into all truth, for He will not speak on His own initiative, but whatever He hears, He will speak, and He will disclose to you what is to come. (John 16:12–13)

SINLESS PERFECTION IS IMPOSSIBLE

Even with the power of the Holy Spirit indwelling us, we must be cautious. Satan has the ability to form impressions on our minds as he did with Judas,[375] Peter,[376] and others.[377] Moreover, he and his minions masquerade as angels of light.[378] Any message from God will be in keeping with his holy character. The results of the message will be to his glory and honor. It will accomplish salvation for you or for others. There must always be a balance of mind—a rational, objective perspective. People that are involved in cults, mysticism, or astrology do not have the right relationship with God and are easily subject to false doctrines.[379] It is far more likely that any information they are receiving is from Satan or his minions.

> Do not turn to mediums or spiritists; do not seek them out to be defiled by them. I am the Lord your God. (Lev 19:31)

He made his sons pass through the fire in the valley of Ben-hinnom; and he practiced witchcraft, used divination, practiced sorcery and dealt with mediums and spiritists. He did much evil in the sight of Lord, provoking Him to anger. (2 Cor 33:6)

There are also considerations that should be made for undue fatigue, depression, or other cognitive anomalies that may interfere with the rational thought process of a normal individual. If you are not walking in the truth,[380] there is a possibility the message will be misunderstood. The message will be delayed. Instead, you will be moved closer to a right relationship with God through his direct intervention in your life. God's direct intervention involves his management of people, circumstances, and events in provisional reality. God is persistent in the salvation of his elect. We are predestinated[381] for salvation,[382] and it is his will that not one of us will be lost to eternal life. A right relationship with God implies a constant striving toward moral and holy perfection. To walk in the light, one must submit to God's will. Only then will the blood of Christ continuously cleanse us, and our relationship with God is maintained. Our relationship is not contingent on sinless perfection that is impossible. As long as we are present in our mortal bodies in provisional reality, we will sin. It is required of us that we constantly adjust ourselves to God's standards for our behavior by repenting of our sins and conforming our behavior to that which is good and acceptable to God.[383]

This whole matter of "judging ourselves so that we may not be judged"[384] is to understand our behavior as sinful (judge ourselves). Then we ask for forgiveness, which is granted because of the sacrificial blood of Christ. Then we are not to recommit the same sin. In this manner, we will not have to be judged by God as sinful. We can slip from righteousness into judgment and deserving of discipline.

"If we confess our sins, He is faithful and righteous to forgive us our sins and to cleanse us from all unrighteousness."[385]

The Christian must agree with God about what is and what is not acceptable behavior from God's perspective if the right relationship is to be maintained. "Can two walk together, unless they agree?"[386] We must conform to God's expectations and standards and not fashion God to meet our desires.

As Christians, we are not punished for our sins. The price for our sins has been paid by Christ. His payment was sufficient for all sins—past, present, and future. Salvation is for all who believe in the gospel of Jesus Christ.[387] The trials and tribulations imposed on us in provisional reality are for our spiritual maturation.[388] God will not allow his children to live in such a manner that will deny them the priceless blessing, which he longs to endow on all of his elect. God uses discipline to keep us on track, to get us back on track.

Although God does not punish believers, suffering is a part of our existence in provisional reality. Suffering brings us to a new level of character development. This new level is achieved because our endurance in suffering brings about our perfection.[389] The amount by which we are changed by our life's experiences is a measurement of our growth. All too often, we do not work hard enough at our own growth, and God must intervene. He intervenes for two reasons: to ensure our salvation and to ensure that we are able to accomplish all that he wants us to accomplish. We should not take this charge lightly.

The full utilization of our God-given talents, gifts, and abilities is illustrated in the parable of the talents.[390] In this parable, three servants are given talents; one is given five talents, one is given two, and the last is given one. The man (Jesus) who gave them the talents departs on a journey, and when he returns, he inquires as to what each has done with his talents. The one who had five doubled his to ten. Likewise, the one who received two had doubled his to four, to which the master replies, "Well done, good and faithful servants, you were faithful in a few things; I will put you in charge of many things."[391] The last servant, having received one, was afraid

of losing his talent and being punished, so he hid his talent. He only had the one talent to account for when the master returned. The master lost his cool; he took the one talent away from the servant and called him wicked, lazy, and worthless.[392] Then he cast the slave into the eternal fire.[393] The talents are a form of money; there were many forms of money in use at the time. It is interesting that the word *talent* is used, as talent has a completely different meaning for us today. We can substitute talents meaning money as talents meaning God-given abilities. The parable illustrates the gifts that have been imparted to us by the Holy Spirit and the price for not utilizing them. God has a plan for the ages, and part of that plan includes the life of each and every one of his elect. That plan is carried out in our life when we are reborn, indwelt, and adjusted to the Holy Spirit. Then we will do God's will in our lives and not our own will. Our will for our life is not a part of God's eternal divine plan.

THE SOUL AND THE SPIRIT

The spirit of man and life are from God; they are gifts freely given. God's breath imparts life in us and the very image of God, which is in essence life itself.[394] Man is spiritual as far as he lives and acts according to his divine origin and in accordance with the promptings of the Holy Spirit and one's conscience. Man's cognitive ability and our personality—the who we are—is our soul. The nature of God that we possess is from the indwelling Holy Spirit. In the original account of the creation, there is a marked distinction made between the body and the spirit. The body is from the earth; the spirit is from God. The body and spirit are not only represented as different substances but also as having different origins. The body shall return to dust,[395] and the spirit shall return to God. God breathes into man the breath of life,[396] and this demonstrates that the spirit is not earthly or material. The spirit has its origin immediately from God. Our bodies are derived from our earthly parents. The Holy Spirit works in and through the human spirit,[397] but this is not said of the human soul, which is the source of our free will. The flesh wars against the spirit because they have different motives. The flesh is of provisional reality, and the spirit is of foundational reality.[398]

The soul is that idiosyncratic element of a person that makes that person unique. The soul of man is the bridge between the body and the spirit. The destiny of one's soul is contingent on ones faith. The soul may go either to heaven or to hell. The spirits indwells a person at the moment of genuine faith. God is a Trinity, consisting of God the Father, the Son, and the Holy Spirit. In like manner, we are created in God's image, a trinity—body, soul, and spirit. At death, our body returns to dust, our spirit and soul depart from the body to heaven, and we are like angels[399] waiting Christ's return when we will be given our resurrected bodies.[400] The indwelling spirit returns to God and our soul and spirit to the destiny secured by our free-will choices.[401] For purposes of clarity, the soul is our individual uniqueness; it is who we are as a person. The body is our vehicle for the time that we have on earth,[402] and it returns to the ground,[403] ashes to ashes, dust to dust. The indwelling spirit, which occurs after our regeneration, is the very part of us that is the essence of God within us and gives us supernatural abilities.

Two verses that distinguish between soul and spirit are:

And the very God of peace sanctify you wholly; and I pray God your whole spirit and soul and body be preserved blameless unto the coming of the Lord Jesus Christ. (1 Thess 5:23)

For the word of God is quick, and powerful, and sharper than any two-edged sword, piercing even to the dividing asunder of soul and spirit, and is a discerner of the thoughts and intents of the heart. (Heb. 4:12)

Man's soul is an individual possession. The spirit, however, is the life principle of man derived from God. In death, the spirit is yielded to the Lord:

> Father, into Thy hands I commend My spirit: and having said this, He gave up the ghost. (Luke 23:46, Interlinear Greek New Testament)

> And they stoned Stephen, calling upon the Lord, and saying, Lord Jesus, receive my spirit. (Acts 7:59)

> To deliver such a one unto Satan for the destruction of the flesh, that the spirit may be saved in the day of the Lord Jesus. (1 Cor. 5:5)

In essence, there are two spirits. The spirit that indwells us is from God. The other, within biblical context, refers to our life principle, which maintains life for our soul. Both spirits have their origin and continuance in foundational reality. The more our spirit is in alignment with the indwelling spirit, the more spiritual we are, the more supernatural. The more we exhibit the fruits of the Spirit, the more in alignment we are with the Holy Spirit. This is a very conscience effort on our part because the flesh wars against the spirit. Hence, we are called upon to rule over our own spirit.[404] "Like a city that is broken into and without walls is a man who has no control over his spirit."[405] To rule over our spirit is to ensure that the will of our spirit is always in accordance with God's intentions. Christ himself warns us in Matthew, "Watch and pray that you enter not into temptation: the spirit indeed is willing, but the flesh is weak."[406] Additionally, we are warned against being overmastered by a wrong spirit.

When man submits to the power of sin, a new direction is given to his mind. He comes under a spirit of whoredom.[407] "For the spirit of whoredom hath caused them to err, and they have played the harlot, departing from under their God." One becomes "proud in spirit"[408] instead of having a "quiet spirit which is precious in the sight of God."[409] We act foolishly when we are rebellious in spirit[410] because this gives way to anger and sin.[411]

The faithful in spirit are the people who resist the temptations of evil in provisional reality. "Be subject therefore unto God; resist the devil, and he will flee from you."[412] The divine Spirit is the source of all life, and its power is exercised within our reality.[413] Man is spirit because he is created in God's image and as such is dependent upon God. Man also has a body unlike the angels. Body, soul, and spirit are nothing other than the real basis of the three elements of our being. We experience world consciousness (physical life, through our senses), self-consciousness (personal life, soul), and God consciousness (spirituality), a trinity.

THE WAY OF THE SPIRIT AND THE WAY OF THE FLESH

There are essentially two kinds of people: nonbelievers and Christians. Christians believe that Jesus Christ is the Son of God who became flesh and came into provisional reality to die on the cross as a sacrifice for the sins we commit. This provision made by Christ allows God to accept us without compromising his holiness.

A nonbeliever is in all appearances no different then a Christian. However, nonbelievers are primarily influenced by provisional reality. They lack the supernatural essence of a Christian. The Christian is a transformed person that has an assurance of eternal life. Christians are also indwelt by the Holy Spirit. The nonbeliever does not physically have the indwelling spirit. Both have two very different life motives, and both will have completely different destinies.

The Christian is to be sanctified wholly in his three-fold life—the physical life of the body, the individual life of the soul, and the inner life of the spirit. The function of the soul is on a more rudimentary sphere of provisional reality. The spirit is from foundational reality. "Abstain from fleshly lusts, which war against the soul."[414] Scripture acknowledges this dichotomy, which exists within our complete reality. "It is sown a natural body; it is raised a spiritual body. If there is a natural body, there is also a spiritual body."[415] The fundamental question is whether the flesh or the Spirit of God shall dominate the believer's life. To live according to the flesh is to be in the way of death,[416] and to live according to the Spirit is to be in the way of life[417] with its victory over the flesh and over death. The evil character of the flesh is in opposition to the Spirit of God.[418] Since no unregenerate person acknowledges the presence of the Holy Spirit, this conflict is between what the Christian is in himself—flesh—and the Spirit of God who indwells him. This warfare belongs only to the child of God. The only conflict within the nonbeliever is with their conscience. Once the nonbeliever has quenched the Spirit and quieted the conscience, the remaining influences are those of Satan and his minions.

> For the law of the Spirit of life in Christ Jesus hath made me free from the law of sin and death. For what the law could not do, in that it was weak through the flesh, God sending His own Son in the likeness of sinful flesh, and for sin, condemned sin in the flesh; that the righteousness of the law might be fulfilled in us, who walk not after the flesh, but after the Spirit. (Rom. 8:2–4 IGNT)

The human mind may be related to that which is good or to that which is evil. The carnal mind is enmity against God.[419] A man's intellect is the general term for the mind in reference to its capacity for understanding and thought. For the believer that understanding that we possess is augmented by the power of the Holy Spirit and his ability to show us things to come and to teach us all truths. The Holy Spirit also illuminates our understanding and inspires thoughts and ideas in our minds. This information is made known to the believer by enlightenment and discernment. Paul even said that he was compelled to do things by the Holy Spirit.[420] We are told, "the mind controlled by the Spirit is life and peace."[421]

The nonbeliever is more completely under the influences of Satan. Nonbelievers do not possess the counter balance provided by the indwelling Spirit. "Wherein you once walked according to the course of this world, according to the prince of the powers of the air, of the spirit that now works in the sons of disobedience."[422] It is our choice how much influence we yield to the indwelling Holy Spirit. Whether we like it or not, we will always be tempted by the influences of Satan.

Our intellect, our emotions, and our will all experience the drawing spoken of in John 6:44. The drawing is a divine influence referred to as being called by God. Faith, or confidence in God, is a divinely wrought state. To those who are subject to the will of God, there is ever-increasing knowledge of the truth. Acquiring the truth is a progressive acclamation of understanding more. The more a Christian commits himself to Christ in thought, in Scripture, and in his behavior, the more understanding is revealed to the Christian. This commitment is not any different from any other desire to succeed in sports, job, marriage, or as parents. The expanding depth of knowledge made available by the ever-increasing intimate relationship with God through the Son and the enlightenment of the Holy Spirit.[423]

THE CONSCIENCE OF MAN

The implications of our behavior play a significant role in determining our destiny. God will not allow his predetermined elect to stray very far from their chosen path. God's plan will culminate in their salvation and eternal life.[424] God's chosen are disciplined,

whereas the natural man or the unregenerate are punished for practicing evil.[425] When our behavior is not in keeping with God's morality, we have a sense of wrong before we exhibit certain behaviors, which is a prompting from the Holy Spirit through our conscience.

The supernatural entity that communicates the convictions of the Holy Spirit to us is our conscience.[426]

There are few mysteries as complicated as the human conscience. It is the most pronounced and the most direct link between foundational and provisional reality, I hasten to add, in addition to the Scripture. There is nothing else that so directly influences us and is so reflective of who God wants us to be and what he wants us to do than our conscience.[427]

The cognitive impressions, which are imparted by our conscience regarding our behavior, our morality, our thoughts, and our feelings, serve as guides for our daily living and the appropriateness or inappropriateness of our behavior. Our conscience is the entity that fulfills God's promise that he has imprinted within us his laws and the very knowledge of his being.[428] In spite of the fact that there is a lot about man and our fallen nature that is contrary to God's nature, a believer's conscience always reflects God's divine ideal.[429]

Our conscience functions independently of our will and in effect sits in judgment over our thoughts, feelings, and behavior. The human conscience not only informs us with impressions about today, but it also impresses us about the future and the way things should be. The conscience through the power of its ability to inform us through impressions makes known to us that which is sinful. Our conscience serves as an internal guide as to what is right and wrong.[430] The information the conscience holds comes from the Holy Spirit, and the Holy Spirit must depend upon our will to enforce its dictates.

The Bible does not teach that Christians will not sin. It does teach us, however, that because of our fallen nature, we will sin until we are removed from our physical bodies.[431] Moreover, our conscience informs us what sin is, and we have the indwelling Holy Spirit that enables us to resist sin. In our resistance, we not only defy sin, we defeat Satan.[432] The more we are attuned to our conscience, the more we are made aware of God's morality and his desires for our life. A believer cannot sin without suffering feelings of guilt and a sense doing wrong. The guilt and remorse is due to the presence of the Holy Spirit within the believer and his convicting ministry, which will move us to repentance.

Unregenerate men who do not have the Spirit indwelling them could never experience this reaction of the divine nature against sin.[433] The unregenerate that is void of the Holy Spirit has a conscience that is weak and defiled.[434] The indwelling Spirit constitutes a ground for distinction between those who are the children of God and those who are not. The Christian is first made aware of the morality of an issue by the correct and true answer being immediately impressed upon one's conscious. A Christian with the support of the Holy Spirit is able to resist the temptations of sin and honor the moral judgment received from God and imposed on them by their conscience. We all have a conscience; the strength of its influence is dependent upon the degree to which we are yielded to the Holy Spirit.

To say something is a human trait means that the trait is in common with most people, and as such, it makes these human processes somewhat predictable. The human thinking procedure of processing ideas follows a predictable pattern. When we contemplate doing something we know is wrong, we listen to our conscience and make a decision to proceed or not. If we choose to proceed, we go through a process of rationalizing our behavior until we convince ourselves it is okay. When one fails to resist sin, they will need to silence their conscience before committing the sinful behavior. This is accomplished by employing one of the many defense mechanisms we humans use when we need to change the truth about something. We will use denial ("It's really not a sin"), rationalization (Well, everyone was doing it"), or projecting where fate or bad luck is to blame, and then we commit the act and submit to sin. When the act has been committed, the strength of our conviction changes when we see the consequences of our aberrant behavior, and we realize we allowed ourselves to yield to temptation. The response then of the conscience is to impose feelings of guilt, that supernatural agency that is intended to drive us to seek forgiveness. We acknowledge the sin, confess it, and ask for forgiveness, which also implies an abstinence from repeating the act.[435]

This process keeps us in conformity to God's morality. Or else we again, employ defense mechanisms to change our perception of the reality of our behavior. Although we have sinned, asked for and been forgiven, sin changes us and sin that has not been forgiven destroys us. This process of rationalization is augmented by satanic influences. "The spirit is willing but the flesh is weak."[436] This is why we are advised in Scripture to take every thought captive.[437] We are even given a model:

> Finally, brethren, whatever is true, whatever is honorable, whatever is right, whatever is pure, whatever is lovely, whatever is of good repute, if there is any excellence and if anything worthy of praise, let your mind dwell on these things. (Phil. 4:8)

The feelings of guilt that we experience are the result of our disobedience to God. We know when we are disobedient because of our conscience, which reflects the innate knowledge we have of God, and this knowledge makes us aware of his requirements for our behavior.[438] We can lie to ourselves, but we cannot lie to God or the Holy Spirit, so we choose to ignore them.

The Biblical testimony concerning our conscience is that it exists supernaturally in the regenerate and that it also exists in the unregenerate. However, without the Spirit, one's conscience is ineffective. The conscience of the unregenerate is defiled,[439] evil,[440] convicting,[441] and seared.[442] The supernatural conscience in the Christian is far more complex. A real question is raised as to whether the Christian lives by his conscience at all. The Apostle Paul significantly states that his conscience bore him witness in the Holy Ghost.[443]

The Spirit employs the conscience as his means of expression, impression, and communication. Our conscience is the medium by which the Holy Spirit communicates with us, from foundational reality to provisional reality. This relationship between the Holy Spirit and our conscience is the very definition of the nature of the human conscience.

BECOMING SPIRITUAL

If we rely on our defense mechanism and ignore the promptings from the Holy Spirit, we become hardened or desensitized to our feelings of guilt.[444] When we become desensitized to the Holy Spirit, we are no longer sensitive to his promptings, enlightenment, or guidance. This quenching[445] of the Spirit opens the way to more disobedience, and that is why we are warned not to quench the Spirit.

When we make a decision to yield ourselves to the Holy Spirit, the more we become attuned to his enlightenment, the more spiritual we become. When we become spiritual, that means we undergo a transition from our human nature to one that is supernatural. We need to realize the seriousness of sin. This realization comes from understanding the ramifications our sinful behavior has on our destiny. To realize the horrendous nature of sin, all we really need to do is fully comprehend the price paid for our recompense and our salvation, the death of God on the cross.[446]

If we are one of God's elect and choose to ignore the warnings of either our conscience or the Holy Spirit, God will intervene directly in our lives. Godly intervention is designed to cause us to consider our situation and to appeal directly to him in prayer. We can be assured of this intervention because our fate has been predestinated.[447] Inherent in the concept of predestination is a known outcome. God's intervention ensures that outcome. The appeal will always be answered by the Holy Spirit. The answer will come in different ways for different people. The most important criteria is that we are watchful for the intervention. It may come to us from the Holy Spirit while reading Scripture, or it may come to us while we are in prayer. God also uses other agents: friends, an event we observe; it may even be delivered by a supernatural entity. "We may entertain angels, unaware."[448] We of course rarely recognize the entity as supernatural. We have an inherent inability as residents of provisional reality to recognize anything from foundational reality or to discern the supernatural. The message rarely comes from people we seek out, but rather from the people God sends to us with his message. The people we seek out tend to have the message we want to hear, and it may have very little to do with the truth. The Holy Spirit not only provides illumination; he is also the source of all communication between God and man.[449] Christ's request to God concerning the Holy Spirit was that he would send a Helper for humankind, and that Helper would abide within man—the indwelling Holy Spirit, who reveals all truth.

> I will ask the Father, and He will give you another Helper, that He may be with you forever; that is the Spirit of truth, whom the world cannot receive, because it does not see Him or know Him, but you know Him because He abides with you and will be in you. (John 14:16–17)

The unregenerate person lives completely in provisional reality—a single-dimension existence. Christians live in both realities because we have a supernatural spirit within us, and the spirit being part of us makes us supernatural.

BEYOND OUR WILDEST DREAMS

A spiritual life is strived for not out of fear of eternal damnation or fear of chastisement; although it may have started there, it is done out of gratitude because we are saved. "I am comforted to know that my troubles are producing an eternal glory that will one day supersede the worst misery endured on earth."[450] In the divine plan, human will determines the whole course of the believer's life and ultimate destiny. A free-will choice for God and faith in Jesus Christ assures one of an eternal glory. A free-will choice not to believe is a choice for eternal damnation.

If we are submitted to God, we make the choices that are well pleasing to God; we will delight to do His will.[451] It is simply a matter of every person is either under the power of Satan or under the power of God.[452]

Satan and his followers teach a gospel of reformation and salvation won by human efforts. Rather than salvation won by faith alone, in Christ alone, in grace alone, which is unrelated to any human effort or virtue. We cannot make the choice for God unless we are under the influence of the Holy Spirit. The Holy Spirit in turn gives us the supernatural power to resist evil, endure, and even overcome evil. "Because greater is He that is in you [the Holy Spirit], than he that is in the world [Satan]."[453]

Every Christian must learn to be receptive to and magnify the reality of the Spirit's indwelling holy presence. We must become familiar with the Spirit's way of communicating to us. To walk in the Spirit is not a series of renewed commitments, it is a constant casting of one's self upon the Spirit with the confidence and anticipation that all needed support will be realized. Only then can the Holy Spirit energize the Christian to do that, which is well pleasing to God[454] and empower the Christian to overcome the solicitations of Satan.

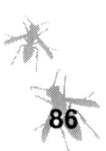

When we are fully yielded to the Holy Spirit, we are able to overcome our sinful nature. After we have our own sinfulness under control, we are then to take a stance against the wiles (strategies) of the devil.[455] We are to wrestle against the rulers of darkness of provisional reality.[456] This is not a passive spectator role; this is an active engagement in the spiritual warfare, a commission much greater than we are able to accomplish on our own. This is precisely why it is so important that we are doing God's will and not our own. To do what we want, to do our will, is to do Satan's will. If we are not doing the will of God, we can never be participants in the spiritual warfare for the sake of righteousness. When the Christian is yielded to the Holy Spirit, s/he is spiritual because s/he is spirit filled. The Spirit is free to fulfill all the purposes and desires of God in the believer's life. Jesus Christ exemplifies God's will, when he says, "He came to do the will of His Father."[457]

Christ came to earth to physically reveal foundational reality to us, the multidimensional nature of our existence. We are exhorted to expose the deeds of darkness,[458] and we are given authority to tread on serpents and scorpions and over all power of Satan.[459] If this was God's will for Christ, it is Christ's will for us because "I and the Father are One."[460] Christ asked of the Father that we not to be taken out of the world, but that we should instead be protected from evil[461] so that we may do his will.

The New Testament teaches victory over all evil in provisional reality, the flesh, or fallen nature, and the devil by the constant enabling power of the Holy Spirit.[462] Scripture and the Holy Spirit give us all of the information we need to have confidence in God's plan for salvation. There is no mystery, no surprise ending; the book of Revelation tells us how the warfare ends. Satan is cast into the lake of fire,[463] Christ brings a new heaven and a new earth,[464] and the Lord Jesus Christ himself is the government over the new creation.[465]

If people go to the lake of fire, it is because they, like Satan and his minions, of their own free will, have adopted a philosophy of independence toward God. This independent philosophy is the very essence of sin.[466]

THE NEW WALK

God's plan for each believer's daily life incorporates the method by which that life should be lived. However, two procedures are possible, dependence upon one's own ability or dependence upon the power of the indwelling Spirit. These two methods are completely incompatible. Any attempt to live by supernatural or spiritual standards while depending on human resources or secular solutions will fall far short of the mark even though we have the best intentions. The attitude of any person toward the Word of God is a certain indication of the innermost character and reality of that person's spiritual state.

Scripture teaches there are two types of Christians: those who "abide in Christ" and pseudo-Christians who "abide not."[467] That is Christians who are walking in the light and those who are walking in darkness.[468] All believers have the Spirit in them; however, some do not allow the Spirit to lead them. This has to do with the quality of one's daily life. It is not a matter of saved and unsaved; it is a finer line than that. It is a matter of life's motivation—God honoring or self-honoring. Our degree of commitment is all-important to our process of sanctification. James warns us about being double-minded, and if we are, we are not to expect anything from the Lord.[469] He also tells us that the onus is on us. "Draw near to God, and He will draw near to you."[470]

The deciding factor is who is in control, the flesh or the spirit. Flesh cannot inherit the kingdom, nor can a person that has not made the transition from flesh to spirit through rebirth. If a person is not conforming their behavior to the expectations of Christ, the question is, Does this person really believe? Which then begs the question, Were they ever really saved? The indwelling of the Holy

Spirit has tremendous significance in the lives of those who recognize his influence and power.

One's new obligation after rebirth is not to make ourselves accepted. That has already transpired; rather, we are now to walk worthy[471] of one who has been accepted.

Christ captures the essence of the believer's relationship to himself when he talks about the vine and the branches. "Every branch in Me that beareth not fruit, shall be cast off and thrown in the fire."[472] The obligation of the branch is to continue in the relationship to the vine—to continue to receive all the sustenance that is necessary for growth and life. The divine life or energy may flow into the branch so that the branch may bear fruit. For the believer to be fruitful, the believer must remain in an obedient relation to Christ, wherein the power of the Spirit may be realized in and through the believer.

The experience of indwelling is unique in that it is a personal relationship with a living spiritual entity rather than conformity to a set of rules. Any relationship to God, which is less than a complete accommodation, must be considered that of the natural man. There is a great transition from the condition of being unsaved to that of the saved. There is also a transition for the Christian from the natural state to that of the spiritual state. The transition for the Christian is brought about by the release of the Holy Spirit's power within the believer when the needed accommodation to the Spirit is made. The spiritual state of existence is not a once and for all accomplishment; it must be nurtured and sustained by the spirit's renewal, sustaining the new walk, prayer, reading God's Word, and following his will. All of this is the process of sanctification, our process of becoming holy.

Filled with the Spirit, means a full and unrestrained demonstration of the nature of the Spirit in the thoughts and behavior of the believer. This means allowing the Spirit to accomplish all that he came into the believer to do. Of all of the ministries of the Holy Spirit, indwelling is the only one that requires human cooperation.

We are told to be filled with the Spirit,[473] which clearly implies that it is in our capacity to accomplish the filling, to make the necessary adjustment to allow it to happen. We cannot be lukewarm about our commitment. When Christ was talking about the church of Laodicea, he said, "Because you are lukewarm, neither hot or cold, I will spit you out."[474]

The Christian's own faithfulness determines the degree of filling. Not all believers are so yielded to God as to be filled. Filling is the source of all right Christian experiences and is the sufficient force behind all Christian service and accommodating the will of God. Filling does not require us to become or to be someone else. The Spirit manifests himself through our own personality. However, now we are able to exercise the gifts we have been blessed with from God for our idiosyncratic service. There is a perfect match, predestinated, foreknown, and a link between a believer's individual personality and the role one is to play in God's divine plan. In the grand scheme of things, our idiosyncratic personality is here for reasons other than our own amusement. In human relationships, if I respond to you as me, my motives are self-serving. If, however, I respond exhibiting the fruits of the Spirit, my behavior is other-serving and God-honoring.

Our personality is designed for some particular service, and it is because of our particular personality makeup we are able to fulfill the role we are destined to fulfill. The concept of being filled with the Spirit is not a matter of getting more of the Spirit, rather the Spirit getting more of the Christian.

When the Spirit has control of all of the believer, he is able to manifest in him the character of Christ. Spirituality, on the other hand, or for one to be spiritual, is to experience the divine purpose and plan in one's daily life through the power of the indwelling Spirit. The believer is able to execute God's plan and overcome evil, all to the glory and service of God. Overcoming evil begins with our realization of our supernatural qualities. Spirituality is what makes our lives and us supernatural. The solution is found in our accommodation to the indwelling Holy Spirit, who can accomplish every aspect of overcoming evil. All that is required of a person is to have a sufficient dependency on the Spirit. We should be ever attuned to our conscience and sensitive to the urgings of the Spirit so that we can follow his direction. Being spiritual, then, is responding to the Spirit and not to the natural inclinations of our human, fallen nature,[475] the influences of Satan,[476] or to become spotted by provisional reality.[477]

Evil is a very real part of our everyday reality because of the active power of Satan, his minions, and our sinful nature. When we have accommodated ourselves to the Spirit and the Spirit is energized in our life, we have all of the supernatural power we need to overcome evil. Once we have overcome evil, we are then able to promote that which is good, that which is in God's will and plan for our lives. The diametrically opposed properties of overcoming evil are that evil cannot be overcome without the energizing power of the Spirit, and this supernatural power of the Spirit cannot be experienced where evil is not being overcome. Overcoming evil is not a passive activity. You have to be actively involved in resisting demonic temptations and influences. This is the very essence of the spiritual warfare that goes on every day between foundational and provisional reality, between them and us.

Spirituality is not just the suppression of evil and restraining ourselves from sinful behavior. It is also an outward expression of our obligation to live a fruitful life modeled after Christ. This is the "you in Me and I in you."[478] We are to conduct ourselves with all of the attributes of Christ. This is possible because of our coexistence with him, because of our new birth, and by the sustaining power of the indwelling Holy Spirit. An unregenerate person cannot overcome evil or the desires of the flesh because they do not have the desire or the aid of the Holy Spirit.

> Now the works of the flesh are manifest, which are these; adultery, fornication, uncleanness, lasciviousness [lewdness], idola-

> try, witchcraft [sorcery], hatred, variance [a difference between what is expected of a child of God and what occurs], emulation [jealous rivalry], wrath, strife, sedition [rebellion against authority], heresies, envying, murders, drunkenness, reveling [uproarious behavior], they which do such things shall not inherit the kingdom of God. (Gal. 5:16–21)

Which is to say, "Putting off the old man."

> But the Spirit is love, joy, peace, longsuffering, gentleness, goodness, faith, meekness, temperance, against such there is no law. (Gal. 5:22–23)

"Putting on the new man."

THE PRINCE OF DARKNESS

"For our battle is not against flesh and blood." Ever since Satan left his domain and tempted Eve to cause the fall of humanity, we have been inextricably interwoven in the cosmic battle between good and evil. We are participants in a warfare where Satan is trying to achieve his five "I wills," a battle for the most part, that is beyond our purview. Satan, sin, and evil all play a role in God's divine plan for humanity. If they did not, God simply would not have allowed them to exist. Our will exists within the purview of God's permissive will. We are responsible for our free will choice, for that which lies beyond our will, and within the permissive will of God, we have his blessings in his system of grace.

THAT SERPENT OF OLD CALLED THE DEVIL

Evil must continue along with good until each shall reach its determined end. That evil will be judged and dismissed forever is the assuring testimony of the Scriptures.[479]

> And the slaves [angels] of the landowner [Christ] came and said to him, "Sir, did you not sow good seed in your field? How then does it have tares?" And He said to them "an enemy [Satan] has done this and the slaves said then do you want us to go and gather them up?" But He said "No, lest while you are gathering up the tares [unsaved], you may up root the wheat [saved] with them, allow both to grow together [provisional reality] until the harvest; and in the time of the harvest I will say to the reapers, [angels] first gather up the tares and bind them in bundles to burn them up [hell]; but gather the wheat into My barn [Heaven]. (Matt. 13:27–30)

Everything written in the Bible is inspired by God. Everything recorded in Scripture has its origins with God, therefore all Scripture is good for teaching, rebuke, and understanding.[480] One of the major themes in the Bible is the truth concerning Satan, who was the originator of sin. He is the promoter of evil in both foundational and provisional reality, and a tenacious opponent of the occupants of the earth.

We are warned in Scripture that we should not be ignorant of Satan's or of his devices.[481] The Bible gives us full warning of whom Satan is and exactly what it is he is trying to accomplish. He is the one "which deceiveth the whole world"[482] and he "roams the earth looking for whom he may devour."[483] Christians are warned not to be taken captive by him.[484] Yet, in spite of these warnings, people choose to believe that Satan and his minions do not really exist. He is considered by many to be a figure of speech, a biblical illustrative example of evil. However, figures of speech are not created angels [485] that sin and rebel against God.[486] They serve in realms of darkness and are doomed to a final and dreadful judgment at the hand of God. "Into the eternal fire which is prepared for the devil and his angels."[487]

SATAN'S REBELLION

One consolation for all Christians is that we know evil not only exists by God's permission, but God also limits its expression by commissioning the Holy Spirit to restrain Satan and his minions.[488] The Holy Spirit limits their influences to divinely established parameters.

Satan is the originator of lying[489] and he convinces people to believe his lies because he has the ability to veil unbelievers' and skeptics' minds from the truth.[490] Scripture also reveals that because of the veiling, many will not believe in the saving blood of Christ.[491] As a result, those that do not believe will not be saved. The natural man, as opposed to the spiritual man, who is indwelt by the Holy Spirit, does not consider the inextricably interdependent existence between foundational and provisional reality.[492]

The concept of a dual reality is not just that we exist in a physical reality and the celestial creations of God exist in a spiritual reality. Foundational reality is not limited by the physical laws that govern provisional reality. There is an overlap between the two. God first created the angels in numbers too high to count.[493] Then God created man a little lower than the angels.[494] However, after life in provisional reality, we will be transformed into a spiritual form, live in foundational reality, and even sit in judgment of the angels.[495] The angels to be judged are those that rebelled against God—Satan and his minions.

In that, rebellion unrighteousness was found in Satan,[496] and he refused to submit to the will of God. The inequity that was in Satan's heart was seen by God as Satan's five "I wills."[497] These five "I wills" constituted his rebellion. Satan's desires were to obtain: (1) the highest possible heavenly position, (2) regal rights both in heaven and on earth, (3) Messianic recognition, (4) to have the glory which belongs only to God, and (5) a likeness to the Most High, the possessor of heaven and earth.

God is the Creator of all that exists. Satan's attempt to create a copy will be a counterfeit system, and like any counterfeit, it looks like the real thing but has no value because it has no worth behind it. In essence, all sin is patterned after Satan's inequity. Man does not want to be told what to do or live by someone else's guidelines. "We will not have this man to rule over us."[498] Therefore, they do their will instead of God's will. As the creator, God, has sovereignty over his creation—man, angels, and the universe. Sin constitutes the created deviating from the Creators intended purpose. "Shall the clay say to the potter, why have you made me thus."[499]

The natural man, or those who are lost, prefer the darkness to the light, which is Christ. The Light exposes the evil in their deeds, and they prefer not to acknowledge their sins because that would require that they change their behavior and the way they think.[500] Essentially, the relationship is from darkness to light, from doing self-will to doing God's will. The five "I wills" of Satan constitute original sin. Sin is disobedience to God and putting self-will before God's will. This is also the premise of Satan's big lie that he has used and always will use to deceive humanity. It is the same lie Satan used in the garden of eden, "you will be as Eleom,"[501] and "surely you will not die." With Adam and Eve's rebellion came the corresponding punishment—death for the species. "Surely they will die."[502]

The real significance of the interaction in the garden of eden between Eve and Satan, aside from it hastening humanity's fall from grace with God, is that an entity from foundational reality interacted with someone in provisional reality to undermine the relationship between God and man.

In this single encounter, humankind would forever be inextricably interwoven in the warfare between good and evil. Inextricably interwoven because events in either reality can and do have consequences for the other reality.

The crucifixion of Christ on the cross in provisional reality has very specific implications for both realities. Humankind was provided a Savior, death was overcome, and Satan was defeated. There are a litany of events in one reality that have consequences for the other reality: the creation of angels, the creation of mankind,[503] Satan's rebellion, the temptation of Eve,[504] the fallen angels, some angels leaving there first estate,[505] the flood,[506] the immaculate conception,[507] the birth of Christ,[508] the teachings of Christ,[509] the crucifixion of Christ,[510] his subsequent ascension,[511] the indwelling Holy Spirit,[512] the entire host of miracles performed by Christ,[513] and the continual intervention of God into our everyday lives.[514]

Adam and Eve were punished for their sins as was Satan because at the time of their offense, there was no provision for salvation. God set the precedence for the significance of sacrifices by performing the first sacrifice when he slew animals to make the clothing for Adam and Eve.[515] The clothing was to cover them because now they knew they were naked, and they were ashamed.[516] They now knew the difference between good and evil because in their disobedience, they committed the first sin. The animals God used in the first sacrifice covered the first sin, Christ, as the last sacrifice, will cover all sins.

Prior to their rebellion, Adam and Eve lived in perfect obedience to God, and God communicated directly with them in paradise.[517] Since the fall, we have been participants in the cosmic battle between angels' light-and-dark warfare of cataclysmic proportions that has been permitted by God.

THE CHRISTIAN CONFLICT

A vast majority of the challenges experienced by Christians in their lives' trials are wholly accounted for within three specific aspects of provisional reality. First, the world as it exists today is under the influence and charge of the prince of darkness.[518] Satan is the god of this world[519]—provisional reality.

Second, we continually battle the desires of the flesh because of our rebellion and our subsequent fallen nature. Our evil nature and our rebellion, which dominates the flesh, were born of Satan and his lie in the garden of Eden.

Third, Satan continues to attack God's plan for salvation and eternity.

These attacks are from foundational reality, supernatural influences in provisional reality. This supernatural spiritual activity constitutes the spiritual warfare.

God is perfect in every way. He is all-knowing,[520] (omniscience), he is present everywhere[521] (omnipresent), and he is all-powerful[522] (omnipotent). He can never err or be deceived.[523] Through the degenerating power of sin, Satan, as did Adam, became an entirely different being from that which God had intended for them as his creations. The philosophy of Satan is a lie in the sense that it contradicts that which is infinitely true, and all that God says is infinitely true. Satan rules provisional reality, influencing all those who inhabit the earth.

The essence of the spiritual warfare, our warning that spiritual warfare is a real life phenomenon, and our call to arms is written in the book of Ephesians.

> Put on the whole armor of God, that we may be able to withstand the wiles of the devil [be unaffected by the enticements of Satan] and that our wrestling is not against flesh and blood but instead, it is against the principalities, against the spiritual hosts of wickedness in the heavenly places. [Satan and his minions within foundational reality exerting their influence within provisional reality.] (Eph. 6:11–12)

Principalities are territories that are ruled by a prince; in this case, the territory is provisional reality, and Satan is the prince of darkness, and he wanders to and fro on the earth,[524] "seeking whom he may devour."[525] The spiritual hosts of wickedness are the fallen angels or Satan's minions that followed Satan in his rebellion against God. They also chose to do their own will instead of God's.

THINGS TO COME

There is some inherent benefit to our own dual existence. Our physical existence separates us from all of God's other celestial creations. This benefit is evidenced by the scriptural reference that, Christ, while human, "was for a little while lower than the angels,"[526] and that we will sit in judgment of the angels.[527] More than anything else, this was a precipitating factor compounded with Satan's pride and arrogance, which comprised the seeds for rebellion. Satan's five "I wills" reveal the true motivation of Satan's desires, and they are an anathema against the Creator, God's plan, and his purpose. In order for Satan to accomplish the goals of his rebellion, he must gain authority over heaven and earth, which he cannot accomplish.

The essential evil character of sin or its basic nature from which all sin originates is the unwillingness on the part of the created, to be that which God, the Creator, has preordained. Not only for our lives individually, but also for our various roles in the eternal providence of God's plan for foundational reality.

God is sovereign over his creation,[528] and we are to do his will, not ours. In obedience we will accomplish that which God has preordained to occur for us in our lives[529] and ultimately within the framework of God's plan for the ages. In order for a play to recreate the story line, the actors must follow their roles, say their lines, and follow the lead of the director.

THE DECEIVER AND THE RESTRAINER

Satan was created perfect in every way. His perfection generated self-sufficiency, pride, and a sense of meism. His pride and arrogance changed his perceptions of reality such that he deemed that he no longer needed God. Because of his delusion, he chose to rebel against God's authority and will. Satan sought to define his own path, assert his own will, and develop his own philosophy.

He desired to replace God. In addition to Satan's rebellion against God, he is also the deceiver of the whole world.[530]

A major part of this deception is for Satan to remain a nonentity. To remain obscure enough that we, the people of provisional reality, do not believe he is real.[531] Satan's wrathful presence on earth during the entire history of humankind is largely responsible for all of the hate, agony, pain, and suffering endured by man.

Scripture reveals to us the true nature of Satan. He is the god of this world,[532] a murderer,[533] and the ruler of all demons.[534] He is the world forces of darkness spoken of in Ephesians.[535] He is the father of all lies.[536] He tempts men to sin,[537] he is deceitful,[538] evil,[539] cowardly,[540] and he terrorizes[541] and afflicts[542] unbelievers. Satan repudiated God; he deceived some of the angels and drew a third of them into his rebellion.[543] He weakens the nations,[544] and he destroys cities and countries[545] and causes war on earth,[546] with all of its horrors and atrocities. Satan tempted Christ;[547] Satan entered Judas and prompted him to betray the Son of God.[548] He blinds the minds of those who are lost.[549] Satan takes the word out of the hearts of the unsaved,[550] lest they should believe and be saved. He sends his minions with wiles and snares, which are described as trickery and cunning to nonbelievers to tempt and distract the saints from accomplishing their preordained good works.

Satan exercises and abuses the power of death.[551] He is opposed to God.[552] He persecutes the saints,[553] and he is the father of all lies.[554] He causes pain, misery, and suffering for all humankind.[555] That which exists today that is contrary to God's very nature is by design from Satan or those he has been able to influence in provisional reality.[556] Just as Scripture tells us we will know a tree by its fruit, we will also know the author of events by the attributes of the event.

As long as people are deceived and do not believe that Satan is a real entity, interacting within this reality,[557] God will continue to be blamed for all of the misery, suffering, and pain on earth.

God is a loving and compassionate God who never changes.[558] We can be angry with Satan, we can hate Satan, but we should never be angry with God.[559]

Your fate in destiny is set by your choice. One day you will either awake to an ecstasy of love and beauty beyond your wildest dreams, in our Father's house, and "what I have planned for you is a future and a hope."[560] Or, you will awaken to an eternity of horrendous suffering, pain, and darkness. A destiny that you will endure forever, cast into outer darkness, and the lake of fire, which is the second death.[561] A soul forever removed from God.

THE SPIRITUAL BATTLEGROUND

Christians are in provisional reality; however, we are not to be a part of it. We are aliens and are to be ever steadfast in our Christianity.[562] "Love not the world, neither the things that are in the world."[563] Our example was Christ. Although he lived among men, he always did that which was well pleasing to his father.[564] The whole cosmos system is not just humanity in provisional reality; it also includes its entire composition and all of the prevailing influences of Satan—its lusts, principles, motives, course, and inevitable end. All that is not of God lies in the power and bondage of Satan. The believer is warned not to love the things of provisional reality, which are wholly evil in God's estimation and are not, therefore, loved by him.[565] The cosmos world system is as much the work of Satan in everyday life as the Holy Spirit, the Restrainer,[566] is a part of everyday life. Both are, for the most part, unacknowledged as dimensions of our provisional reality. If you are of God, God controls your destiny; if you are not, you are of Satan, and Satan controls your destiny.[567]

Provisional reality is not a battleground where God is contending with Satan for supremacy. The spiritual warfare is something which God has permitted so that the lie may have its fullest unveiling and run its full course. God is sovereign. Provisional reality is a spiritual battleground where forces of good and evil are contending for the souls of men. God created Satan. Satan is not on an equal footing with God. Satan is on an equal footing with Michael, another created angel. Satan the created cannot defeat God the creator. That is why we have the book of Revelation, where God reveals to us the ending, so we know how it all comes out. "Thy kingdom come, Thy will be done, on earth as it is in heaven."[568] Satan is not the keeper of the gates of hell; he, like everyone else there is a prisoner. The lie must run its full course that it may be judged not as a mere hypothesis or incipient venture, but in the complete and final exhibition of its antigod character.[569]

This evil in provisional reality is the very thing from which the Christian has been given the authority from Christ[570] and power from the indwelling Holy Spirit to overcome.[571] The commission from Jesus to his disciples—and all Christians are disciples of Jesus—was "open the eyes of the unbelieving and turn them from darkness to light, and from the power of Satan to God, so that they may receive forgiveness from their sins."[572] Christ told his disciples that he was here to do the will of his Father, not to do his own will.[573] The New Testament describes the role of the Christian as that of a soldier both standing his/her ground and using divine weapons to tear down the strongholds of evil. "Stand firm against the schemes of the devil,[574] be on the alert."[575]

Satan has specific schemes to influence our children so they resist our spiritual teachings and guidance. He wants to lead them away from God and into destruction. Scripture tells us that we should not be taken by surprise by Satan's schemes because we know what they are.[576] We know what they are because he has demonstrated them to us, and they are revealed in Scripture.

Satan rebelled against God, and he attacked Adam and Eve, the first couple, by deception and caused them to break their promise and their vow to God. His influences effect couples today to get them to break their vows to God to love, honor, and cherish in sickness and in health until death.

Satan attacks morality and religion with his influences. Constant exposure to sex, violence, and moral decadence desensitizes us to its ungodly nature, and it gradually becomes less offensive. Eventually these sinful venues become accepted. Soon we rationalize that we are not responsible for our own behavior, it is the media, poor influences, or our environment. "It was the woman."[577] "It was the serpent."[578] Satan wants us to believe that we are victims because then we are less likely to have an effective strategy to resist temptation and his influences.

As a parent, we must confront ungodly values, attitudes, and behaviors. We are responsible for instilling Christian values in our children and exemplifying the difference between Christian values and the values of provisional reality.[579] We are to be the commensurate role models. We can say anything we like to our children in terms of values, appropriate behavior, and all of the dos and don'ts we expect. However, it is our behavior over time that will have the biggest impact.

There is a direct correlation between spiritual maturity and spiritual strength. "The harvest is ready, but the workers are few."[580] Every soldier must be prepared for battle, and in every battle we have to expect casualties; casualties are a consequence of any war. Believers are prepared when they are fully indwelt by the Holy Spirit and doing God's will rather than fulfilling their own desires. We also have assurances that angels are sent to assist us.[581] If we are faithful, he will strengthen us and protect us from the prince of darkness.[582] We also have the assurance of Scripture that whatever God promises, he will deliver.[583]

We have been anointed from the Holy Spirit by the power of God.[584] Christ has sent us into the world, and our spiritual authority comes from this anointing. Our authority is to be used to overcome evil, as it exists in provisional reality. We are to walk in the light and to help set others free from the oppression of the prince of darkness.

With this anointing and the aid of the Holy Spirit, we have the power and authority to penetrate the veil that separates the two realities.

We are not to be passive bystanders in this cosmic civil war. We are ambassadors of Christ,[585] and we understand our role. As ambassadors, we are diplomatic officials appointed by God in foundational reality to represent him and his message in provisional reality. To prove the strength of God's truth through our faith and our willing participation in the unfolding of God's plan.

The original Greek version uses the word *combat* and not *fight* in "I have combated a good combat."[586] Combat is a much stronger word with very strong inferences. However, the literal English translation was cumbersome, so *combat* was replaced with *fight*. The interpretation then is that the elect, those that have come to earth as ambassadors to Christ, are not only to model our behavior after Christ's example, but we are to fulfill the will of God in the same manner that Christ did. As such, we are to be children of God without fault in the midst of a crooked and perverse generation, among whom we are to be lights of the world.[587]

In light of all of the disclosures of Scripture, we can know that any religion that suggests a transformed, regenerated world because of human effort is merely a deception. God declares that provisional reality is to continue with increasing deception and to continue to be the embodiment of the lie until it is crushed by the infinite power of the returning King.[588] Indeed, Christians are exhorted to be instant in season and out of season in the saving of individuals.[589] It is not the reason of man, but the revelation of God, which points out that governments, morals, education, art, commercialism, vast enterprises and organizations, and much of religious activity are influenced by Satan in the cosmos system.[590] Satan would have us save the world rather than one another.

According to 1 John, "He that does the will of God; he abides forever."[591] To do the will of God is to do the truth; to act apart from God is to do the lie. The present relation of God to provi-

sional reality, beyond his sovereign permission and restraint of it, is to save out of it an elect people for his heavenly glory.[592] However, our ability to understand the motives and thinking of God, who is omniscient and omnipotent, is completely inadequate. The enmity of Satan is not only toward the person of God from whom he and his minions have everything to fear.[593] "We know You Jesus Son of God; have You come to torment us before the time?"[594] His enmity is also toward every true child of God. There are an abundant number of scriptures to prove that Satan makes unceasing efforts to negatively influence the life and service of the Christian with his schemes,[595] flaming arrows,[596] and prowling around on the earth seeking whom he might devour.[597]

Thus, the believer becomes a medium of connection, an unknown participant in the spiritual warfare, between the God of creation and the rebellion of Satan.

God is just, and to be just, your standards cannot change and must apply equally to all. God must punish evil because he is perfectly holy, and sin compromises that holiness. To ignore or condone sin would compromise God's very nature.

> These things I have spoken unto you, that in Me you might have peace. In the world you shall have tribulation; but be of good cheer; I have overcome the world. (John 16:33)

As God's creations, we are wholly accountable to God, just as our children are accountable to us. We are especially accountable for our morality. God as Creator would not leave his children without the guidelines for what is and what is not acceptable in terms of behavior and his expectations. All of these guidelines were exemplified by Christ in his role as Messiah, his lifestyle, his teachings, and they are recorded in Scripture for our continual reference.

In light of the signs of the times, it is not safe to subscribe blindly to that which promises general good simply because it is good and is garnished with the teachings of the Bible. It is no longer the case that good is all on the one side and evil all on the other. We are encouraged in Scripture to hone our skills in our ability to discern between good and evil. However this capacity does not come to just anyone, it is a skill of a mature Christian.[598]

Any religious offering that does not profess that Christ came to earth in the flesh to offer salvation to men through his sacrificial death, no matter how thoroughly externally religious they are, they are teachings from Satan.[599] The test as to the presence of the spirit of the antichrist is one who denies the Father and Son as they are professed to be in the Bible and Christianity.[600] All false religions will leave their followers in the doom of everlasting banishment from the presence of God. True religion is of God having promise of the life that now is, and of that which is to come.[601]

ANGELS OF LIGHT

Christ is the way and the only way to God.[602] Christ, angels and the Holy Spirit are the only protection from the prince of darkness and his minions who disguise themselves as angels of light.[603] There is no greater mystery than for God to allow Satan to pursue his lie to its full consummation. There is no redemption for Satan or any other fallen angel. This foregone conclusion produces immense hatred on Satan's part toward God and his elect.

Satan continually involves himself in religion as the best means to attack his only real enemy—the true believers in provisional reality, Christians. Satan's dominant purpose is not to be unlike God, but rather to adapt much of what Christianity teaches, except the one and only primary concept—that of salvation through faith in Jesus Christ.

Worship is so essential to Satan that he will demand the worship from the people of provisional reality under a penalty of death.[604] Christ tells us that "just as we know when summer is close by the budding of the trees,[605] we to will know when the end is near by the signs of the times." Chief among the signs is that evil men and evil conditions will progressively worsen.[606] Paul describes the predicted satanic systems of the last days in his second letter to Timothy. Paul talks of difficult times that will come because men will be lovers of self, lovers of money, and they will be boastful, arrogant, revilers, disobedient to parents, ungrateful, and unholy.[607] Paul's focus is on people's behavior; we either take our cues from God and Scripture, or we take our cues from Satan and that which he has created in provisional reality.[608]

It is a challenge to keep an even perspective because we live in a reality that is heavily influenced by Satan. To maintain our balance, we must be indwelt, praying, reading, and meditating on Scripture and practicing the gospel of Jesus Christ. Without this counterbalance, the only influences, or the predominate influences we are exposed to, are Satan's. Satan's influences are in our schools, TV shows, movies, and music; increasingly they are designed to desensitize us to Satan's evil and put us at odds with the gospel and teaching of Jesus Christ. We are also warned against those who teach a false doctrine although they may appear to be based on religious principles. Their offers will be so attractive and externally so religious that many will be drawn away, and some will even depart from the faith.[609]

All religions, except Christianity and even then some ministers, do not necessarily know the real mission they have. Being unregenerate persons of provisional reality and thus blinded to the real gospel, they are sincere, preaching and teaching the gospel of Satan delivered to them by the prince of darkness. Their gospel is one of human reason and human decency, which appeals to human independence and self-sufficiency. If one is not born again, their teachings in spiritual matters will be misleading, an unknown deception. All religions and ministers are to be judged by their perception toward the doctrine of the blood redemption of Christ. Many are easily led to fix their attention upon secondary things, provisional reality, and to neglect wholly this one primary truth the redeeming grace of God made possible only through the death and shed blood of Jesus Christ.

Satan's doctrine is based on provisional reality, secondary things, tangible and seen, while the primary and essential things are spiritual and unseen.[610] Satan has blinded the minds of the unbelievers, and they are lost to these eternal truths. The idea that man will stand on a basis of personal worthiness is the perpetuation of the lie into the twenty-first century. No man can forgive the sins of another, only God can do that.[611] Man can try to be righteous, however, none is without sin,[612] and redemption comes from faith in Jesus Christ, and in him only.[613] It does not come from our good deeds or being a good person. The souls of many good people, who lack faith and a personal relationship with Jesus Christ, will be found in the confines of hell.

God created man; as a result of that origin, man sustains an inherent moral responsibility to be like God in conduct, as man is like God by creation. God has commanded that we are to "Be ye holy; for I am Holy"[614] and "Ye therefore shall be perfect, as your heavenly Father is perfect.[615] On this ground, all moral conduct is based, for there is no other basis on which our behavior could rest. Man's actions are right when conformed to the character of God, and wrong when they do not. No other basis for a distinction between good and evil exists. When men reject God and seek to find their own way through the problems of human life, their futile efforts are of little value. "By faith we understand that the worlds were prepared by the word of God, so that what is seen was not made out of things which are visible."[616]

PROVISIONAL REALITY

Satan's attacks are directed at vulnerable individuals of influence and the institutions in the cosmos system. Through his deceptive influences, he tries to undermine religion and our morality. The Bible tells us that there were angels that "kept not their first estate."[617] Their first estate would be as angels doing the things they were commissioned to do by God, to be messengers, to aid and protect the elect, and to perform their appointed tasks.

Scripture also reveals that these fallen angels found the daughters of man to be extremely beautiful.[618] They came to earth and cohabited with them, creating offspring that were considered giants, called Nephilim.[619] Nephilim has two meanings; one is "giant," and the other is "the fallen." The Nephilim are giants, fallen ones, or both. This could very well have been the kernel of truth that evolved into Greek mythology. In mythology, gods are portrayed as living on mountains and coming down to interact and, in some instances, cohabiting with humans. We cannot be sure how these fallen angels took human form; perhaps they indwelt humans or maybe even possessed humans. There are many instances of demon possession in the Bible. The unions between women of earth and the angels that "kept not their first estate" would have produced offspring with a genetic mixture of the two, contaminating the human gene pool with the seeds of evil. We have evidence of this in Scripture: "you are of your father the devil"[620] or "children of the devil."[621] The flood was the means by which God, after judging that the earth was wholly evil and that "God was sorry that he had made man,"[622] chose to cleanse the human genetic pool of this contamination, to extinguish the physical seeds of evil. God commissioned the flood to destroy all of the human inhabitants of the earth, except for eight—the family and in-laws of Noah, whom God found to be righteous.[623] The angels that left their first estate and cohabited with the daughters of men are forever confined to darkness until the Day of Judgment.[624]

The consequences of not acknowledging the interactions between God and his creation and the insidious influences of Satan in our everyday lives means we do not assign the true causality to the origins of events and circumstances.

As such, we embrace a system heavily influenced by the deceptions of Satan. Provisional reality suffers from its satanic influences and embraces godless governments and continual armed conflicts.

Continual exposure to satanic decadence lessens our sensitivity to its sinful nature. The distinction between right and wrong becomes blurred. Provisional reality is opposed to God as worldliness is opposed to spirituality in the same manner that the desires of the flesh are opposed to the desires of the Spirit.[625] The world is wholly under the delusions of Satan's deception.[626] Demonic and satanic influences and activities are prompted by secular motives; the first is to hinder salvation through Christ, and the other is to extend the authority of Satan himself.

Demonic influences are exercised both to mislead the unsaved and to wage an unceasing battle against the believer. Satan's four primary vehicles to accomplish his plan are to continue the decadence of provisional reality. Satan's flaming arrows tempt us away and weaken our faith. These arrows jeopardize our relationships with fellow Christians, spouses, family, friends, and God. He will continue to veil the truth to the yet to be saved and the lost.[627]

Rebellion is a transformation of the significance of the interests and morality of the Creator to the interests of the created. In order for this aberration of reason to be believed, it must be accompanied by irrational emotions and an excessive self-interest that clouds the voice of reason and ignores the indwelling Holy Spirit. The defiance of rebellion is a change in the perception of reality. We often see this pattern in teenage rebellion. Reality is as reality is perceived, and we should never impose our perception of reality over the perception of God's. In the unsaved, the flaming arrows begin as influences and coupled with the veiling of ones mind; eventually, these two factors lead to a hardening of one's heart.[628] Consequently, one manifests more decadent behavior as one is subject to increasingly more satanic influences. So we are told to take every thought captive,[629] to stop this process before our rationalization process renders us susceptible to Satan's influences and results in our sinning.

Prayer and reading Scripture can serve as a counterbalance to this never-ending onslaught of Satan's deceptions and misinfor-

mation. The more you know about God, and the better you know God, the more your faith matures. As you submit to God and resist Satan, he will flee from you. Draw nearer to God, and He will draw nearer to you.[630]

> And we know that we are of God, and the whole world lies in wickedness. (1 John 5:19)

There is so much of Satan's influence in today's society that we no longer consider many things as evil or sinful even though God has not changed his standards. We have negotiated away our standards, rationalized our morality, and shrugged our shoulders at Satan's continued encroachments into our lives.

To call it all evil, we would have to take responsibility for its proliferation. It is easier to ignore Satan and think that he is not a real entity and that he is not hunting to the death the souls of men. Rather we blame adolescence, society, governments, drugs, movies, and violence, when in fact these are all symptoms of Satan's influences. Those that have been blinded to the truth by Satan are the ones that lead the charge of tolerance. They misuse the intent of freedom of speech. They limit prayer in schools. They seek acceptance for things prohibited in the Bible, call the murder of abortion "pro-choice," and proliferate the very influences of Satan. "Not only do they do it but they encourage others to do it."[631] We blame circumstances and society instead of our own behavioral choices. It is not man's role to condone what God has condemned.

The cosmos is a vast order or system that Satan has promoted, which conforms to Satan's ideals, aims, and methods. It is civilization now, right here in provisional reality, functioning as it does apart from God.

We exist in provisional reality, and very few people expect God to intervene in their daily lives. Yet God is blamed for all of the misfortunes that befall man. Either God involves himself in our life or he does not. A loving compassionate God would not intervene in our lives for the sole purpose of causing pain and suffering. That would be contrary to his very nature.[632] Everything that happens occurs within the permissive will of God and is an expression of his absolute sovereignty.

The pain and suffering that exists today in our lives is the work of Satan. Pain and suffering comes from his cosmos system, our poor choices, and evil deeds of others. Additionally we have our own fallen nature, physical laws, and the consequences of those laws. God's involvement in our life is a blessing, assistance, protection, and promise for eternal hope.[633] We can discern the invisible hand of God and Satan in events, circumstances, and in history. However, all too often, almost always we miss it. We do not recognize God's intervention in our life, and we fail to recognize satanic influences within provisional reality.

The evil character of Satan, ignited by his ambitious pride and perpetuated by his untruths, results in a philosophy that is contrary to God's teachings. Satan, who had the seal of perfection, was created with wisdom that is full and perfect in beauty.[634] He was a victim of his own flattery, and his pride distorted his judgment. Satan's self-interest became more important than the precepts of God. This distortion in the perception of God's love and care for his creations always happens when someone puts their self-interests above everything else. With the obscuring of reason, which self-interest engenders, it is possible to be so misguided as to adopt the very opposite philosophy of life, which God's infinite wisdom has ordained for his creation.

Satan proposes by his conceit and excessive self-interest to advance his cause to heaven and transform himself into the very likeness of God. Satan valued himself above all else, even the will and the very sovereignty of God. "He abode not in the truth, and that he is the father of lies."[635]

It is one thing to come to an understanding that Satan is a real live personality whose influences we encounter on a daily basis. It is a completely separate understanding to know that Satan is not the sole cause of all of the natural shocks that flesh is heir to. We continually make decisions in our lives, decisions that have consequences for good and for misfortune. We make decisions that cause our own pain. Good and bad decisions about school, friends, free-time activities, who we marry, where we live, living together, careers, sex, drugs, drinking, and pornography. Our decisions should be God honoring not self-honoring. We can make a few poor decisions, and suddenly we are thirty years old and wondering how things could have gone so wrong.

True reality is that there are two realities, provisional and foundational, and that we actually exist, right now, in both of them.

Our perceptions of empirical phenomena lead us to form conclusions and assumptions about the nature of provisional reality and customary relationships. When we observe events that are connected in sequence and in time, we make causal assumptions about the nature of provisional reality. However, these assumptions are based on provisional reality, and our tendency is not to consider aspects or facets of intervening foundational reality. Empirical information from our senses defines provisional reality. The aspects of foundational reality are rarely perceived by our senses. This is why some things remain a mystery or why we do not always have all the answers.

THE WARFARE

What is this experience we call life? We are born into physical bodies that are patterned after God's creativity and his genetic code. Our bodies are subject to the vulnerabilities of our genetics. Sometimes chromosomes do not split right, and sometimes they are defective. This creates anomalies and premature deaths, the results of which we do not always understand. Death always seems premature to us, but it is never premature with God, it always occurs at exactly the right time. Before we have lived one day, God records the day of our death.[636] "Precious in the sight of God is the death of His saints."[637] For the most part, our personality is preprogrammed; the design of which has been predetermined by God for our unique role in his plan. God forms us in the womb.[638] The Trinity prepares us for our role through our learning's and the experiences orchestrated in our life. These life experiences give us the abilities and skills we will need to work in conjunction with our spiritual gifts to accomplish his plan for our life. God also gives us wisdom and skills in the crafts we will need.[639]

We function within these personality parameters by using our free will to make choices and decisions that have consequences for good and evil. Does this mean that we are preprogrammed? To the extent that God chooses when we are to be born and when we will die. He weaves us together in the womb[640] and decides where and when we will live[641] and who will be our parents. This process predetermines many of our influences and experiences and makes certain that some paths are available and others are not. Our personal history influences our perception of reality and the person we have become. All of the agencies employed by God to ensure the salvation of the elect originate in the realm of foundational reality.

When we have a brush with death and our life is spared, we do not often attribute it to God unless we are very gifted in discernment. We attribute it to luck or to our own skills and abilities or haphazardly refer to a guardian angel or to God without fully realizing that is exactly what has happened—divine protection. "For He will give His angels charge concerning you, to guard you in all your ways."[642]

Our personality makeup and the experiences we go through are all part of God's divine plan for our salvation. However, because we perceive that we have complete free will, we believe we are in charge of our own destiny. Scripture clearly tells us that God foreknew those that would be conformed to the image of his Son, and these he predestined for glory.[643]

In order for God's plan to come to fruition, there has to be an orchestration by God of the events in our life. A visual image for this is that we exist in provisional reality, and provisional reality is God's hologram. For the most part when God intervenes in our life, it is without our knowledge. Our physical body is vulnerable to diseases, viruses, microscopic pathogens, and destructive effects of free radicals, accidents, and injuries.

We are subject to sin by our own fallen nature and the influences of evil demonic beings that we cannot even see. They are dedicated to our destruction. Our very existence is threatened by the evil actions of others, violent crimes, states of war, famine, the consequences of natural disasters and laws of nature that can work for or against us. Life is a condition of being dependent on uncertainty. Without faith in God, life may seem like an exercise in futility, because it is. It is subject to all of the above without rhyme or reason, with no outcome other than death and darkness.

Christians believe that life is an antecedent. We may not understand all that life is about; however, we have faith and hope in God's compassion and his ultimate justice in all things. God's justice will prevail, if not in provisional reality, then in foundational reality.

Our experiences are bringing us to a point where God wants us to be; without the experiences, we would not accomplish our preordained service or arrive at our preordained destination of eternal life. "And we know that in all things God works for the good of those who love Him, who have been called according to His purpose."[644] Mark Twain said, "The two most important days in your life are the day you are born, and the day you find out why."

The spiritual warfare that goes on all around us is a constant battle. It is an ongoing other-dimension conflict between good and evil initiated by Satan's rebellion and brought into provisional reality with the creation and fall of humankind. It is a battle Satan wages against humanity to achieve his five "I wills." The consequence of this spiritual warfare is the loss of human souls. In everything we do, we are to bring glory to God. We do things to glorify God because he created us and has offered us eternal life. Satan wants us to glorify him so he can take God's place. When we allow Satan to be the god of our life, we denounce God. We trade the eternal existence of our soul in paradise for one of eternal torment. Forever separated from God. We exchange all that is good, pure, righteous, and holy for lies, pain, and suffering. For we know in part (we know this provisional reality) and prophesy in part (the supernatural part that we can only speculate about) until the perfection comes (Christ), and we perceive all of reality as it really is. Then we will remember our past physical existence, and we will know the other state of spiritual existence.[645]

A loving, compassionate God would not create us only to have us suffer, die, and disintegrate into nothingness. The reason God gives us the Holy Spirit is so that we are not defenseless in provisional reality. The Holy Spirit enables us to combat and overcome evil. God's system of grace sounds too easy; believe that our salvation is through Jesus Christ and Christ alone, and we will be saved.[646] It is the compassionate working of a God that knows not all that happens is entirely our fault.

When we do not yield ourselves to the control of the Holy Spirit, we are targets for Satan's minions, who devise and advance schemes[647] and flaming arrows[648] against the inhabitants of provisional reality. Satan and his minions try to convince us that God is not to be trusted and that salvation through Jesus Christ is beyond our grasp because we are not good enough.

If we are yielded to the Spirit, then we are exhibiting the characteristics of the spirit. It is part of our personality and in our behavioral repertoire. Our normal conduct is now walking in the Spirit. People that are not saved are not yielded to the Spirit, and they are exhibiting behaviors that are characteristics of the influences of Satan and his minions. They perpetuate their schemes by influencing us through his institutions and those that are not protected by the Spirit.

THINGS TO COME

> But I say, walk by the Spirit, and you shall not fulfill the lust of the flesh. For the flesh lusts against the Spirit, and the Spirit against the flesh; for these are contrary the one to the other; that you may not do the things that you would. But if you are led by the Spirit, you are not under the law. Now the works of the flesh are manifest, which are these: fornication, uncleanness, lasciviousness, idolatry, sorcery, enmities, strife, jealousies, wrath, factions, divisions, parties, envying, drunkenness, reveling, and such like; of which I forewarn you, even as I did forewarn you, that they who practice such things shall not inherit the kingdom of God. But the fruit of the Spirit is love, joy, peace, longsuffering, kindness, goodness, faithfulness, meekness, self-control; against such there is no law. And they that are of Christ Jesus have crucified the flesh with the passions and the lusts thereof. If we live by the Spirit, by the Spirit let us also walk. Let us not become vainglorious, provoking one another, envying one another. (Gal. 5:16–26)

> For He delivered us from the domain of darkness, and transferred us to the kingdom of His beloved Son. (Col. 1:13)

> In which you formerly walked according to the course of this world, according to the prince of the power of the air, of the spirit that is now working in the sons of disobedience. (Eph. 2:2)

Victory over the cosmos is only gained by the superior power of the indwelling Holy Spirit. "Greater is He that is in you [the Holy Spirit], than he [Satan] that is in the world."[649] The change in a believer's life from self-sufficiency to Holy Spirit dependency is a supernatural experience. The believer is not aware of any physical transformation. The Spirit does not work outside of the normal functioning of human will, nor is it necessarily a conscious experience.

However, if a Christian is attuned to the Spirit, differences can be noted. There is an inner peace, a comfort from knowing "all things work for the good of those who love God." Additionally, one will notice that their motives and priorities have changed. There are continual victories in the internal warfare against Satan's influences. "It is God, which works in you both to will [with your own will] and to do [with your own doing] His good pleasure [God's will]."[650] Yielding to the Spirit is not a believer's withdrawal from an active participation in one's life. The believer continues to remain in the heat of the battle, becoming more effective, which actually increases one's involvement and the significance of the believer's work. The conflict is not a test of strength against an outside foe. It is a warfare within the Christian, who realizes that we have no real power to determine the issues without being strengthened by the Holy Spirit.

THE WORKS OF SATAN

God is sovereign over all of his creation, and we are part of his creation. God is self-existent, self-sufficient, eternal, infinite, holy, righteous, just, and merciful. He is love, hope, peace, joy, omnipresent, omniscieny, and omnipotent. God never changes,[651] and he is wholly incomprehensible.[652] That is why he sent his Son, so we could begin to understand him. We are encouraged to take every thought captive.[653] This is to protect Christians from Satan's eve-present influences in the cosmos world system. God has said whatever is good, whatever is pure, whatever is of good repute, dwell on these things.[654] The Holy Spirit brings, love, joy, peace, patience, kindness, goodness, faithfulness, gentleness, self-control.[655] All of these attributes are of God because they emanate from God. All that is contrary to this is of Satan, and they are the tools that he uses to draw us away from faith in Jesus Christ. The unregenerate are people whose personalities are not yet controlled by the indwelling Holy Spirit.

When we as Christian are born again, we receive the Holy Spirit, and we "put off the old man."[656] We change from a self-centered life to a God centered life. However, even after giving our lives to Christ, we have to deal with old habits, thoughts, and temptations. The more our behavior strayed or was influenced by Satan before we became born again, the more prevalent these old influences will be, and the harder they will be to overcome. This is one of the reasons Scripture places so much emphasis on good and righteous behavior.

Once you commit a sin, it is always easier to recommit the same sin. This is the difficulty people have with turning over a new leaf. A part of spiritual oppression is that demonic influences continue to tempt people with sins from the past. By Satan's design, sin is such that the behavior is never satisfying. Hence, people are tempted to try it again, or more frequently, each time upping the ante. There is always the deception that next time will be enough, and it never is. That is why we continue to sin and why we can still be tempted even after being born again. This vicious cycle constitutes spiritual oppression. However, we are told in Scripture that if we, submit to God, and resist the devil, he will flee from us.[657]

When a person is born again, there is a transformation from the natural man to the spiritual man. This transformation brings us closer to understanding the complete reality of both foundational reality and provisional reality. Our sanctification, which is our process of becoming holy, takes time. Believers are all in a process of maturation, dependent upon God's patience, guidance, instruction, and our willingness. We must be willing to commit ourselves to Christ and to the Holy Spirit. We must be attuned to God's intervention and the Holy Spirit's message to receive this counsel.

Sin originates from our own fallen nature, our desire to put ourselves first, Satan's influences, the work of his minions, and the consequences of living in his cosmos system.[658] This situation is complicated by our ability to make free-will choices. Additionally, there are those we interact with that are lost, operating under demonic influences, and are unknowingly helping Satan achieve his goals. He accomplishes this by furthering the decadence of the cosmos system. By causing the conditions in provisional reality to become progressively worse, people can rationalize away their sinful behavior. As conditions worsen, it appears to the faint of heart that God is less and less in control, and this causes people to lose faith and confidence in God.

We just need to remember, "All things happen for the good to those that love God."[659] We usually do not find joy in our trials and tribulation.[660] They are heartfelt pain and sorrow. However, the message is every event has an eternally good purpose by God. We may not understand the implications within the context of complete reality, but we have God's assurances that everything serves a purpose for good. Until we are able to comprehend the vastness of God's plan, we are sustained by our faith, hope, and love.[661]

We need to acknowledge that we do live in an unseen spiritual world inhabited by intelligent, supernatural beings that promote good and evil.

The unsaved are constantly veiled from understanding the gospel.[662] In addition, when the Spirit would draw them, their minds are often filled with doubt, skepticism, and misinformation. Their inability to believe in Christ is a mystery to themselves, and nothing but the direct illuminating power of the Holy Spirit in conviction can open their eyes and deliver them from their ignorance and fears. The believer is often mystified and frustrated by the inability of a lost person to grasp the concept of salvation, the Holy Trinity, the reality of Satan, and the blood redemption of Christ. It is all foolishness to the unsaved.[663]

Every person is dependent upon God not only for our very existence and sustenance, but also for our righteousness. Sin severs the spirit and soul from God.[664] Apart from God, the spirit and soul are deprived of God's favor and of his strength to uphold righteousness and resist evil. Deprived of God's favor and sustaining power, we become self-directed. This has been the direct apostasy of the fallen angels, the reason for their abandonment of faith. Hatred of God produces a hatred of all good, of all beings that are good, and envy at their happiness. From hatred and envy springs the desire to corrupt whatever is good and disrupt those who have joy and hope.

Satan is called the destroyer because he delights in destroying everything that is good and everything that God has blessed. He goes about as a roaring loin, seeking whom he may devour.[665] The powers of Satan and his minions are limited. They are not omnipotent and can do nothing outside the permissive will of God.[666]

There is a significant effect in commitment or the cumulative effect of commitments. The more you commit to God, the more that is revealed to you, the more able you are to become Christ-like in behavior and in your spirituality. The more you submit to satanic influences, = the more you become like him; the more commitment, the more of him is revealed to you. This is not a one-time decision; it is an ever-evolving process from superficial to supernatural. The minions made a free-will choice to change their nature because they changed their purpose. They willingly stepped outside the preordained plan of God. Consequently, they will be cast into the lake of brimstone and fire; it will be no different for nonbelievers.

Satan and his minions have been around for a long time since their fall. They are probably very knowledgeable about the human race and about our weaknesses and frailties. Satan does not attack the average person; he is a single entity in a world of seven billion people. That is why he tries to influence people that have a great deal of influence—people in governments, schools, media outlets, celebrities, pastors, military, gangs, etc. His minions involve themselves with the unregenerate to increase their decadence and those not yet protected by the Holy Spirit. However, they cannot coerce our will. They cannot compel any other being to comply with their designs.

It is man's ability to exercise free will, to choose his own destiny. The implication is that free will is everything, and that is true to the extent that one chooses not to love and honor God, then life is an open choice. However, if one chooses to honor God, then his or her life is to be that which God has planned for them. When Satan understands that you have committed yourself to Christ and that you are going to trust God no matter what, his influences are greatly diminished. The choice is ours—a life ruled by God or ruled by Satan, an eternity of unimaginable blessing, or an eternity of horrific pain, suffering, and loneliness.

Satan and his minions have power over nature when permitted to use it,[667] but they can create nothing, nor can they employ God's creation in any means other than as he decrees.[668] The knowledge of Satan's limitations should be a source of great reassurance to Christians. It is a reassurance to those who understand the daily interaction and conflict in the spiritual warfare that rages in provisional reality with the powers of darkness. In truth, God can also use Satan as an instrument to chasten and correct his erring saints.[669]

Choosing a life dedicated to God limits one's behavioral options; fewer things are okay. Many people, in their shortsightedness, simply do not want to miss out on anything. They want to keep their options open. Hence, they remain uncommitted to God and do not accept Christ as a personal Savior. However, this choice really means, "I don't want to give up anything." They would not have this man to rule over them.[670] People are willing to sacrifice an eternal existence in heaven for a few pleasures on earth. Who is really missing out? Faith is forsaking the seen for the unseen.[671]

On that final Day of Judgment, everyone will be judged. The elect will be judged according to their faith and their works. In the same manner as those portrayed in the parables of the ten talents[672] and the ten virgins,[673] the unfaithful will be judged for their nonbelief. They will suffer the appropriate fate for their free-will choices and their deeds.[674] The judgment for believers is to grant them their crowns of life and to assign them their rewards for eternity.[675] The judgment for nonbelievers is to assign their punishment. Because of their nonbelief, the sacrificial blood of Christ does not protect them.[676] There is no salvation for those

who knowingly violate God's morality, pray for forgiveness, and yet continue in their sins.[677] God does not hear the prayers of sinners as sin separates us from God.[678]

> Simon, Simon, behold, Satan has demanded permission to sift you as wheat: but I have prayed for you, that your faith may not fail; and you, when once you have turned again, strengthen your brother. (Luke 22:31–32)

> You are to deliver such a one unto Satan for the destruction of the flesh, that the spirit may be saved in the day of the Lord Jesus. (1 Cor. 5:5)

> Of whom is Hymenaeus and Alexander; whom I delivered unto Satan, that they might be taught not to blaspheme. (1 Tim. 1:20)

The Bible often describes events that we are unable to comprehend and are likened to a mystery. As with all mysteries associated with God, they are events we do not understand because we cannot explain them. The reasons we do not comprehend are not always just a lack of information, but also, there are limits to what we have the ability to comprehend. There are no limits with God.[679] Physical evidence is of the phenomena of provisional reality. We have difficulty understanding things that lie beyond provisional reality.

Faith is the evidence of foundational reality. If you do not have faith, there is no foundational reality in your life or in your future.

If an event or a situation cannot be explained by an understanding of provisional reality, it may simply be that it is not of a physical nature. Understanding may only come from a view of foundational reality; it may only be explained by a spiritual interpretation.[680] The cardinal point of faith is that whatever comes to pass, no matter how calamitous it may appear in the moment, there is reason for joy and confidence.[681] True faith transcends the events of provisional reality, and we know that all things work together for the good of those that love God.[682] "If we endure, we shall also reign with Him."[683] This can be a difficult concept for us to understand because "all things working for good" is based on a perception from foundational reality, not from the view we have in provisional reality. It is extremely difficult to see the good in our pain and suffering.[684] Peter tells us that when we believe God and everything he says, our faith and corresponding assurances will give us hope. Our hope will lessen the impact of sorrow and fears as uncertainty is replaced with peace and confidence.[685] The Christian who puts his trust in providence perceives a world in which even the natural laws of the universe yield to the sovereignty of God. "What kind of a man is this, that even the winds and the sea obey Him?"[686] A sovereign God would desire that we would choose good and not evil. He desires that we exercise our free-will choice in honoring his commandments and the statutes of his Son, Jesus Christ. The reason so much significance is placed on the power of choice is that in the simple act of choosing we determine our destiny for eternity. Simply, we choose to fulfill God's will or we do not.

THE DIVINE PERMISSION OF SIN

The presence of sin in the world is because God has chosen to allow its existence. We can only conclude that this is the case, or He would have destroyed Satan at the beginning of his rebellion. If God had crushed Satan as soon as he rebelled, our relationship with God would be based on fear of punishment. A relationship based on fear and punishment is not the kind of a relationship that God seeks. As the God of love and mercy, he seeks those who will make a free will choice to reciprocate his love. As such, sin must fit into God's divinely preordained plan. Sin, pain, and suffering must be an integral part of God's eternal plan, or he would have chosen a different course.

Only an omniscient God can conceive of every possible course of action and the outcome of each alternative. We can only conclude that life as we know it is the best possible course of action deemed by God to accomplish his desired outcome. The divine purpose of sin has not been specifically revealed to us. We will not be able to understand complete reality until we have a spiritual vantage point after our death and subsequent transformation. Although no sin is allowed outside of the permissive will of God, God is absolutely holy and the very definition of holy. Therefore, God is free from the slightest complicity in evil, although he does permit evil to exist.

There is immeasurable evil in provisional reality, and it causes incomprehensible suffering. However, it is a part of faith to believe that somehow evil fulfills a necessary part of God's divine plan. His plan with absolute certainty will achieve his perfectly conceived outcome. God's plan for the ages is the best plan that could have been conceived by infinite wisdom, executed by infinite power and will be the fullest expression of God's infinite love and a complete manifestation of his glory. Our finite minds cannot grasp the conceptualizations of an infinite God. One of the basic tenants of God is his incomprehensible nature.[687] It is our faith in God's love and our complete ability to trust in him that gives us the ability to endure unto the end. It is this confidence that will give us peace through our existence here in provisional reality.

WHAT DOES TURNING YOUR LIFE OVER TO CHRIST MEAN?

Sin in its fundamental character is the unwillingness of people to have "this man rule over us."[688] It is being in charge of our own lives direction as opposed to turning that control over to God.[689] What does it mean to turn your life over to God? When we turn our lives over to God, that means the decisions we make and the things we do are God-honoring. We make decisions and conduct ourselves in a way that we know will please God. Turning our lives over means we stop doing our will; we change the way we think, which will change our behavior. And how do we change the way we think?

First, we adopt the fruits of the Spirit—which are love, joy, peace, long-suffering, kindness, goodness, faith, meekness, self-control—as our motivation for our behavior.

Second, we become so familiar with Scripture that when we encounter various situations in life, we have biblical references that come to mind. It is analogous to learning a foreign language, and you become so proficient at that language that you begin to think in that language. We allow the Holy Spirit to become our internal valuing process. Our valuing process must be based on God's precepts, not on our own.

Third, we behave in accordance with the examples set for us by Christ while he was here in provisional reality. He quoted Scripture from memory. He sought time alone to be with God, and he prayed without ceasing.

Last, we are all called in Scripture to do our best, to work as if we are working for the Lord and not for men.[690] We are to work without grumbling or complaining, and we are to provide for our families.[691] We are to engage our daily endeavors to the best of our ability.[692] Pray to God for wisdom, counsel, and guidance that we make the best decision we can make, and then trust God with the outcome. The outcome will be in your best interest. "Cast all your anxiety on Him because He cares for you."[693] "The Lord is faithful to all His promises and loving toward all He has made."[694]

We can pray about the outcome; however, we are not to be anxious for any reason.[695] If it does not turn out the way we wanted it to, it turned out the way God wanted, which ultimately was in our best interest. Sometimes the outcome is a blessing, and it works out as we had hoped and prayed. Sometimes it turns out just the opposite. Sometimes it seems like we are being ignored. It is not unlike a toddler's request; they may not understand their parents' lack of compliance or seemly inconsistent response. However, we must remember to seek first His kingdom and His righteousness[696] to see life from a godly perspective. This requires us to look at things with an understanding from foundational reality. Our prayers are not answered because we have the wrong motives.[697] Our motives may not be God honoring, or it may simply be that our request does not fit God's plan.[698]

Sometimes we pray for the impossible, even a miracle, and in God's sovereignty, he can intervene. However, he does not always intervene because of your prayer. The intervention may have been because the situation changed, people responded, and the answered prayer will somehow reveal God's glory. The answered prayer will be in response to foundational reality, not provisional reality. Remember the most important thing in your life is determining where you spend eternity. Jesus did not raise Lazarus from the dead because of everyone's prayers (provisional reality). He raised him from the dead because they all knew he was a healer, and now was the time for them to know he was the resurrection and the life (foundational reality).[699] Scripture tells us to ask for anything we want in accordance with God's will, and God will hear our request.[700] It follows then that what is prayed for must in and of itself be God honoring and must conform to God's will. We cannot expect God to answer a prayer that is contrary to his will and purpose or runs contrary to his eternal plan. Events, circumstances, and challenges are situations that provide opportunities for us to grow as we are guided by God's involvement in our life. We should respond with the full knowledge of God's benevolence.

Our unwillingness to turn our life over may be expressed in many ways. The sinful nature of sin is reflected in the penalties, which are righteously imposed on those who choose to sin.[701] The doom of Satan,[702] the sentence of unregenerate men,[703] the outer darkness,[704] the lake of fire, and the great tribulation[705] are all just punishment for the single free-will act of disbelief. All the suffering of this life bears testimony to the presence of sin. God, being perfectly just and perfectly holy, could only have a just response, one that is commensurate with the contemptible nature of sin.

The holy character of God is the standard of that which is good and perfect.[706] Empirically, it is difficult for us to be able to understand the horrific nature of sin. We are seduced by demonic influences and tempted with sin all of the time. However, we can gain an understanding of the true nature of sin, its offense to God by understanding what punishment sin is met with, and the price paid for its atonement.[707] God is the creator of everything that exists.[708] He invented the game, and he wrote the rules.

A constant state of sin exists that can be relieved only by the prevailing power of the indwelling Holy Spirit. Sin is only forgiven when we repent, ask for forgiveness, and understand that this is possible only through belief in Christ and in the sacrificial blood, which Christ shed for us. This allows the sinner to enter into God's benevolent system of grace. God's interpretation of sin is the absolute truth. Absolute truth, as it applies to provisional reality, can only be understood or known from foundational reality. There are truths in provisional reality;[709] however, the absolute truth can only be revealed by the Creator of reality. As God, he has complete knowledge; being the author of both realities is the only source of what is truth, and God's truth is absolute.

The penalty for the unregenerate is the outer darkness where there is a gnashing of teeth.[710] Punishment is confinement to the lake of fire, and it is an eternity in torment. This is not the will of an arbitrary or insensitive God; it is a reflection of the truly horrendous nature of sin. The punishment that is meted out is absolute justice for those that are disobedient.[711] It is because we would rather define these things—good and evil, right and wrong—ourselves that we struggle with turning everything over to God. In absolute truth, it is his definition of right and wrong and not ours. This is a very old and well-quoted Scripture verse, "And people choose the darkness because they were afraid of the

light."[712] We as creations of God must come to understand that it is not a matter of not finding fault with God for his harshness but rather realizing that his justice will be done. God is a God of love and compassion.[713] However, he is also the God of justice and cannot ignore sin.[714] A constant state of sin exists that can only be relieved for the individual through the prevailing power of the indwelling Holy Spirit[715] and our free-will choice for obedience.

Within provisional reality, we have a tendency, like Satan, to be focused on self. Why did this happen to me? This is not in my best interest! If I do it, will the result be what is best for me? However, life is not about what is in it for us; it is about what are God's requirements. If it is our expectation to spend an eternity with God in heaven, we had better accomplish everything on earth that he desires for us to accomplish.[716] "Work out your salvation with fear and trembling."[717]

God could have saved souls without the sacrifice of his Son. However, the death of his Son as a sacrifice is required only because God cannot compromise his holy character by making light of sin. It is the very structure of the gospel that God is infinitely righteous in his attitude toward sinners. This means perfect and eternal condemnation unless the demands of infinite holiness are righteously met. We can never live up to or reach those requirements, so Christ intervened on our behalf.[718] Life is about a big-picture perspective; foundational reality is the big picture. However, we can be so caught up in the details of provisional reality that we lose sight of the real purpose of life.[719] What is most important? What happens to us in our seventy years in provisional reality, or what happens for eternity in foundational reality?

TOM NEWMAN

THE PROBLEM WITH SIN IS THAT THERE IS NO PROBLEM WITH SIN

The very essence of our sinful nature is motivated by our self-will and our self-serving proclivities. These activities are a departure from that, which having been divinely purposed, was and ever must be God's truth. This truth was substituted by the lie of Satan, which included not only the repudiation of God but also the adoption of an antigod philosophy. This antigod philosophy is manifest in almost every aspects of provisional reality.[720] Adam and Eve, although they were enticed, committed the same sin as did Satan. They chose self-will over following the will of God.[721] Today we commit the same sin when we do it our way, not God's way. We assume an independence from God by departing from God's will and purpose.[722] God warned Adam and Eve that if they ate of the tree of knowledge, they would surely die.[723] Their actions had several significant ramifications for humanity. First, they experienced spiritual separation from God by their disobedience. They dramatically changed the nature of their relationship with God; they no longer were bestowed with all of God's blessings. They were thrown out of the garden. Not only would their blessings be significantly reduced, man was no different from the fallen angels in their vulnerabilities. As a result, all were cursed—man, woman, and Satan.

New with the fall is that man would now experience physical death, which is the separation of their spirit and soul from the body. Those who continued in disobedience would now also experience the second death,[724] which is the eternal separation of the soul and the spirit from God in the lake of fire.[725] When Adam sinned against God in his rebellion, he and Eve came under the domination of Satan. They had literally surrendered to Satan. Those that are lost are under demonic influences to the extent that their minds are blinded concerning the gospel of their eternal salvation, and demonic influences energizes their activities.[726]

"And God saw that the wickedness of man was great in the earth, and every imagination of the thoughts of his heart was only evil continually."[727] Since God, being perfect, cannot err, sin could not come into existence until another form of being was created; following upon God's creative act, the highest of angels sinned. Satan's rebellion was conceived by his unholy pride and his willingness to exchange the perfection of God's ideal and destiny, which was designed in infinite love, wisdom, and power by the Creator. However, we, as Satan, often choose the wretched warfare of a self-centered life with its eternal agonizing and inevitable end in the experience of death and everlasting torment.

> And you were dead in your trespasses and sins, in which you formerly walked according to the course of this world, according to the prince of the power of the air, of the spirit that is now working in the sons of disobedience. (Matt. 25:41)

The created, whether angel or human, is by creation not only the property of the Creator by rights of creation,[728] but as created, we are wholly dependent on the Creator.[729] There are only two philosophies of life. One is to be conformed to the will of God, which is the original divine arrangement, and the other is rebellion, to forsake the Creator and renounce his authority and purpose, which is Satan's philosophy.[730] The history of provisional reality is characterized by man's inability to conform to the expectations of God and for man to continually fall short and resist conforming to God's will.[731] The angelic being Satan, Adam and Eve, Noah's generation, and God's chosen people were all unwilling to live by God's will. They chose instead to live in rebellion instead of living in obedience, and that has been, for the most part, the course of humanity ever since.

The first two children were Cain and Abel. One worshipped God; the other, out of jealousy, became the first murderer and killed his brother.[732] In the book of Genesis, we need only get as far as chapter 6 to read, "The Lord saw that the wickedness of man was great and that every intent of man's thoughts were continually evil."[733] Because of the sin in the world, God was sorry that He had made man and He was grieved in His heart.[734] Superimposed on these conditions within provisional reality is foundational reality. Satan and a third of the angels rebelled against God's sovereign authority and embarked on a path of doing their will, not God's.[735]

So how did we get from two people in paradise to the utter destruction of humanity in so short of a period? Just before the Genesis 7, which describes the great flood, we read of Methuselah, who lived to be 969 years old.[736] We can assume at the time of the flood civilization would have been in existence for a little over a thousand years. The population of the earth at that time could have been about a billion people.

The real question is why God allowed sin at all. The holy character of God is the final and only standard by which moral values, motivation, and subsequent behavior may be judged. God looks to our motives.[737] God's standards for behavior are conveyed to us in Scripture, innately, by our conscience, and for Christians by the indwelling Holy Spirit. All of which should lead us to a desire to please God.[738] To the one who disregards God, there are no moral standards other than social custom, peers, self-will, or the dictates of an uncertain and rebellious personality.

The ultimate act of rebellion is against the innate awareness of what God requires of us.[739] When that rebellion is against the very nature of God's goodness and holiness, pardonable sin is transformed to a state of evil. Sin is sinful because it is unlike God. God is the standard of holiness. His character is that which sets the definition of sin. When our behavior is contrary to God's standard or is contrary to his character, then our behavior is sinful. We are responsible to God, the creator.[740] This point is illustrated in Scripture when the question is raised, does the pottery have the right to ask the potter why it was made as it was?[741]

Our most fundamental requirement is to be exactly who God has designed us to be in order that we may accomplish all that he has intended for us to be and to do. By following God's will and obeying his scriptural guidelines, we can become that person. When we rebel and follow our own will, we are not able to accomplish that which God has designed for us. That is called missing the mark and thus constitutes sin.[742] This not only means that we are to be righteous in our behavior and to conduct ourselves in a manner that will ensure we are able to accomplish all that God has predestined for us to accomplish.[743] We are to walk worthy of our calling.[744] It is evidently the purpose of God to secure a company of beings, both human and angelic, for his eternal glory so that in the coming ages, he may show the incomparable riches of his grace.[745] The elect must have the quality of character to resist evil by making a free-will choice of faith over evil. We must have the insight to see the value of an eternity offered by Christ in foundational reality over the immediate gratification offered by Satan in provisional reality.

Man cannot make a choice between good and evil unless evil exists. Sin exists for the sole purpose of free will. If sin did not exist, we would not be able to make a free-will choice to sin or to resist sin. It is in God's plan that his redeemed souls are purified by Christ's sacrificial blood and ransomed by the death of God on the cross. The New Testament tells us that God and Christ are one in the same.[746] In effect, it was God who was crucified on the cross. This expression of divine love and the exercise of such a sacrifice are only possible if sin is present in provisional reality. We learn the true nature of sin from the suffering it causes, the penalties that God has decreed for those who commit sin, and by the extraordinary price that was paid for sin to be counted null and void. Man's desire for the knowledge of good and evil began with Adam and Eve. We as humans continue our proclivity to choose evil over God's guidelines for good. Without sin, for all of its pain and suffering it causes, there would be nothing for us to choose between. There would be no free will, and without free will, there would be no faith—there would be nothing to believe in. There would be no free-will worship of God or free-will expression of love for him. There must be a reason God wants a group of people who will exercise their free-will choices to love and honor him. Of all of God's creation, Christ and man alone will experience life in both realities. We are also told in Scriptures that our experience is something angels are observing.[747]

The essential fact of the principle of evil, which if it is to be judged by God, must be brought out into an open demonstration of its actual character. Such a demonstration could not be secured with sin existing as a hypothetical issue. Satan's schemes and snares include desensitizing us to the truly vile nature of sin by surrounding us with it. His influences make us feel that we are so susceptible to sin and therefore too far from the reach of Christ's sacrificial death to be saved. I understand what darkness is because I have been where there is no light. Without that experience, I can only imagine what darkness must be like. Much like I can only imagine what heaven will be like. However, if I experience the reality of it then, I know there is a difference. Then I can make a free-will choice. To honor, trust, and worship God only means something if I have a choice. Therefore, the problem with sin, aside from the pain it causes, is that there is no problem with sin. The alternative to free-will choices is no choices. Without choices, our behaviors would be predetermined, much as the programmed behavior of animals. Birds migrate south, beavers build dams, and salmon return to the stream where they were spawned; these are all examples of DNA-preprogrammed behavior. They exhibit these behaviors today just as they have since the beginning of time. Where is the evolution of a species in this? Without the ability to choose, we could not decide to have faith in God. We would not be able to choose to worship God or to obey his commandments. The choice between good and evil can only be made if they both exist.[748]

Sin exists, and we are not able to be sinless. An antidote must be provided so that not all are lost because of sin. Christ is the perfect solution. God desires redeemed free-will souls, purified by sacrificial blood and purchased at an infinite cost. Only if these conditions are met will God's holiness not be compromised. The expression of such divine love and the exercise of such an extreme sacrifice are possible only when sin is present in the world. We can only come to understand these truths by experience, revelation, and the enlightening work of the Holy Spirit.

In the third temptation of Christ by Satan, Christ was offered all the kingdoms of the world if he would worship Satan.[749] This is also God's plan for his Son that he will rule all of the kingdoms. Satan's path was without pain and suffering—possession without the crucifixion and disobedience to God. God had offered Christ all the kingdoms as well; however, there would be challenges and suffering along God's path. The lesson here is the lie of Satan, the easy way in exchange for something that was not real. Satan did not have genuine ownership. Temporarily, he could give the kingdoms to Christ. However, Satan will have no possessions when he is cast into the abyss. Just as everything we have is from God. Christ only did that which was well pleasing to the Father,[750] and he only did the will of the Father. He never did his own will. He was obedient, and he never took the easy way. "Narrow is the gate, and constricted is the way and few are those who find it."[751] Christ suffered, but because of his obedience, faith, and motivation to do only the will of his Father, he was able to endure, prevail, and demonstrate absolute perfection. Christ was made perfect by his suffering as his faith never wavered. In this perfect obedience, he became the perfect sacrifice. Moreover, he will rule all of the kingdoms of all the worlds for ages to come.

We have a proclivity to do evil, a proclivity to sin. Man has, in his limited sense, the knowledge of good and evil.[752] With that knowledge, man can elect, by a free-will choice, to walk with God. By faith, we conform to the morality of God, forsaking the seen for the unseen, forsaking provisional reality for foundational reality. Alternatively, man can choose to act independent from God and seek his own course as did Satan, Adam, and a multitude of others. Sin and Satan's rebellion had to become concrete, and evil had to become real and prove its unlikeness to God. Satan's purpose is to construct a cosmos system, such as now exists, and it is being tested to the end that sin may be judged in all its veritable wickedness and utterly destroyed.[753] There will be objects of grace, those that choose of their own free will to honor and worship God the Father, as Christ chose to do.[754] This in turn, demanded the permission of sin in the world. Moreover, those who by their free-will choice believe in God and his Son are to be the recipients of God's grace and eternal salvation,[755] secured by Christ's death on the cross.

The entire duration of humanity's tenure from the garden of eden to the tribulation, including Satan, the conflict between good and evil, the existence of sin, and Jesus Christ, the salvation for humanity, serves a specific purpose, and all is within God's divine plan. The choice for obedience on the part of those who are saved is the grounds of God's commendation and reward. Christians will stand before God eternally identified as those who by their own free-will choice elected to walk with him.[756] The chief end of man is to glorify God. All that God has created—man, angels, metaphysical creatures—all will glorify God and contribute to his eternal glory.[757] Some will receive the manifestation of his grace and love in all of its perfection in paradise, and some will experience only his wrath for an eternity.

The challenge that sin creates is more than a mere conflict between good and evil in our every day existence. It involves the measureless and timeless issues in the conflict between God, angels, Satan, and his minions. The ongoing battle in the celestial sphere of foundational reality brought to provisional reality with the creation and fall of man. Sin is sinful because it is unlike God. Sin is any lack of conformity to God's ideals or commandments, not only a lack of conformity to the letter of the law but to the Spirit of the law, as well.

> In order that in the ages to come He might show the surpassing riches of His grace in kindness toward us in Christ Jesus. (Eph. 2:7)

> What if God, although willing to demonstrate His wrath and to make His power known, endured with much patience vessels of wrath prepared for destruction. (Rom. 9:22)

If there are any doubts, we have the book of Revelation that tells how the history of humanity, the fate of Satan, and his minions concludes. God bats one thousand on all of the predictions of the Bible. Jesus Christ, martyred for our sins, returns in power and glory to rule the new heaven and the new earth.[758] A perfect and holy God could only devise a plan that would be a true reflection of himself, the God of love, mercy, grace, and justice. When we fail to understand events of this life, it is only because we lack understanding of our perfect God and his perfect and holy motives. The issues are greater than the sphere of human observation and understanding. The ultimate triumph, which is yet to be, will glorify God with a glory otherwise unattainable[759] by any other means. His elect will share in that glory. As for Satan and his minions, they will be consigned without hope to the lake of fire[760] forever.

I WILL TELL YOU A MYSTERY

So why is all of this necessary? It is one thing to know the path, and it is a completely different matter to walk on the path. When things are relatively secure, and things are going fairly well, it is easy for us to say that we trust the Lord. The true test is do we still love, trust, and honor God when things do not go well? In times of trial, our thought process and our behavior will reveal the measure of our faith. Our spiritual weaknesses will also be revealed, and should we choose to shore up those weaknesses by obeying God's will, we will be blessed for our endeavors. If we choose to ignore our shortcomings, God will guide us through trials to shore up our weaknesses. Is our faith the same when we are in trials as when everything is going well? Are we anxious for nothing?[761] We need to take everything out of the provisional perspective and view everything from a foundational perspective. The solutions are found in our relationship with God, not with a provisional solution to our trial. When our relationship is right with God, or we have made the necessary adjustment, God will provide the way out. Ultimately, it is more important that we trust God rather than man.[762] It is equally important that our life is orientated toward foundational reality rather than provisional reality.[763]

We tend to place too much emphasis on life, on the here and now. The death of any Christian is a cause for rejoicing.[764] We have a Savior that has overcome death, and he was resurrected to prove this reality to us. In his resurrection, Christ proved there is life after death. There were over five hundred witnesses to Christ in his risen state.[765] The deaths of loved ones are not really tragedies if they are Christians. They have gone to paradise to live with the Lord. They have gone home. Seek first a kingdom perception of reality. "So also is the resurrection of the dead. It is sown a perishable body, it is raised an imperishable body."[766] "Behold, I tell you a mystery; we shall not all sleep, but we shall all be changed, in a moment, in the twinkling of an eye."[767] This does not discount the loss we feel in the death of a loved one and the void that is created by that loss. However, we are not created for time; we are created for eternity, and we will rejoin all of our brothers and sisters in paradise. When we do lose a loved one, we have regrets if things have been left unsaid or things were left undone. These will only serve to magnify the loss. I wonder how we will feel if, when we are in paradise, someone we cared about is not there for eternity with us because we did not take the time to make sure they knew the Lord. We did not take the time to make sure they were saved. Was it because talking about the gospel might make them or us feel uncomfortable? I wonder how uncomfortable they will feel in hell.

> For whoever is ashamed of Me and My words in this adulterous and sinful generation, the Son of Man will also be ashamed of him when He comes in the glory of His Father with the holy angels. (Mark 8:38)

Sin in the world is more than just that we have a choice in our behavioral options. Sin is the essence of the historical battle between good and evil that has raged since the rebellion of Satan. Sin is a conflict between the holiness, righteousness, and purity of God and all that is diametrically opposed to all that God is. The standards, which God maintains, are the standards for all of his created beings. He as Creator, and we as created, are subject to all that he decrees for our conduct and morality during our existence. The reward for subscribing to this philosophy is eternal life. The punishment for choosing the alternate philosophy is eternal damnation, consigned without hope to the lake of fire with all of the fallen angels.[768] If God did not fulfill this promise, he would not be just or truthful. A perfectly holy God cannot err; he cannot be untruthful, nor can he be unjust.

All human beings acting independently who are not concerned to fulfill the divine purpose that God has preordained for them are reenacting this same sin of Satan. The destiny is the same as that of the devil and all his minions. Ambition and pride caused Satan to exchange God's paradise designed with infinite love, wisdom, and power for the wretched warfare of a self-centered life with its eternal agonizing in death.

There are only two philosophies of life. One is to be conformed to the will of God, which is the original divine arrangement. The other is to forsake the Creator and renounce his authority and purpose. Herein lies the fundamentals of the before-time spiritual battle between good and evil, continuing into the twenty-first century and encompassing man since his fall. In its fundamental character, sin is inclusive of a restless unwillingness to a passive unwillingness on the part of man to be obedient to his Creator, who in his infinite wisdom, has a plan for all of his creation. The holy character of God is the standard of that which is good. It follows that sin is as evil as it appears to be when viewed from the vantage point of the holiness of God. The sinful character of sin is reflected in the penalties, which are righteously imposed against those who commit sin, from Satan and his minions to humankind. Faith without works is dead. The works are what we do when we are living in obedience. If we try to be obedient without knowing Scripture from reading and mediation, we are doing what we think is right. Just as Satan did, we put ourselves on God's throne.

THE BOOK OF LIFE

The cosmos system exists as it does today because of God's permissive will, the presence of Satan, his minions, and the Holy Spirit's restraint. Evil is manifested by exalting self and is characterized by power, jealously, self-interest, indifference, and neglect. Evil is the antithesis of God's design for provisional reality that he provided in eden because he is a God of love, compassion, peace, care, and benevolence. We are warned of the consequences of sin and told to avoid it at all costs. God knew if he allowed us to have free will, that we would struggle with resisting temptation and that we would choose to sin. However, without free will, we cannot freely choose to worship, love, and honor God. God granted us free will and continuously preaches, teaches, and expounds on the dangers of sin. Free will was absolutely necessary, in spite of the cost, for us to choose to believe, to have faith, and to come to know God through Jesus Christ. There is much about God and his thoughts that we, with our empirical cognitive style, are not able to comprehend.[769] Our finite minds cannot comprehend the thoughts, ideas, and plans conceived by an infinite mind no more than a two-year-old child can comprehend the ideas of his/her parents. God, being perfectly holy, cannot be implicated in sin other than permitting it to exist.

God as creator owns all that he creates.[770] We are indebted to God not only for our existence but for our sustenance as well.[771] We also know that we are to conform ourselves to the image of Christ and follow his example.[772] In the Greek language, sin means that a prescribed mark or ideal has been missed. The mark or ideals that we are looking to achieve are the requirements that God has for those he has created and called. He makes his requirements known to us innately[773] by his commandments,[774] statues, his Son, the Holy Spirit, and his revealed will in Scripture.[775] It appears at times that this little allowance of sin has progressed to the point of challenging the very outcome of this human experience. It is not just a little sin; sin is pervasive and seems to be the norm rather than the exception.

Sin includes not only doing what you know you should not do but also not doing what you know you should do.[776] If you feel, sense, or think you should do something, and the nature of the thing is God-honoring, and you choose not to do it, that is a sin. How do we know whether the influences we experience are from God or if they are satanic? If the message is one of love, compassion, care, or salvation, it is from God. If, on the other hand, the message promotes self and is contrary to the will of God, it is satanic.

Satanic influences are the champion of psychological defense mechanisms, and he makes it easy for us to justify just about any behavior. The decisions we make every day in business, friendships, in the counsel and advice we give are opportunities within the context of the cosmic battle of good and evil. If the conclusion or behavior we come to is God-honoring, we have scored a victory for God in this battle of light and dark. If, however, we acquiesce to Satan's influence, we have scored a victory for Satan. You will be saved and have eternal life if you believe that Jesus Christ is the Son of God and that he came to earth so that he could serve as the payment for the sins of mankind.[777] Within this context, there will be a day of judgment where people are judged for their deeds if their name is not found in the Lamb's Book of Life.

If your name is written in the Book of Life, then your judgment will be based on rewards and not on punishment.[778] In comparison to who God is and who we are as his creations, we have all missed the mark when it comes to his parameters, "Be holy, be perfect." By this line of reasoning we have all failed and are sinful. Whether we want to accept this or not, it is not our interpretations that matters. It is the word of God that we have all come up short.[779] We have all turned aside; together we have become corrupt. There is no one who does good, not even one.[780] It is God's assessment that not one of us is holy and that we all have sinned. We have to acknowledge that we are sinners and, therefore, in need of a Savior. All sin is accomplished within the purview of God's permissive will. We must acknowledge that God is sovereign and has complete say over his creation,[781] being that we are all sinners and in need of salvation, which, according to God's divine plan, has been provided by the sacrifice of his Son, Jesus Christ.[782] It is within God's sovereignty and a part of his plan to allow us to fail, to sin, and then as only God can do, provide for us the means of salvation.[783] Being just and holy, however, there cannot be any reconciliation for sin where the sinner has not sought repentance.[784] Sin that has not been forgiven must be punished; otherwise, God is not just.[785] If we continue in our sins after we have come to faith in Jesus Christ, we must pay the penalty for our own sins because the sacrificial death of Christ can no longer serve as atonement for our sins.[786]

PROVIDENCE AND THE SOVEREIGNTY OF GOD

God is sovereign over all that he has created. God created everything out of nothing, and as the Creator, he alone is the source of absolute reality and absolute truth. He created our provisional reality to exist as a subset of his foundational reality. God did not create us for provisional reality; he created us for foundational reality. He created us to be eternal beings.

THE SOVEREIGNTY OF GOD

We like to think that we are in control of our own destiny and that our empirical style of reasoning does not easily acquiesce to the possibility of supernatural involvement in our lives. We have a hard time with this concept because if it were true, it would lessen our autonomy. Moreover, we are hard-pressed to acknowledge that there are supernatural influences at work that tempt us frequently and regularly. Yet

Scripture is inundated with examples of a supernatural realm and God's intervention in the lives of all that he has created. We are clay in the potter's hand.[787]

Rebekah was pregnant and her children were struggling within her womb, so she inquired of God as to the cause.[788] God told Rebekah that two nations were in her womb and that the two peoples would become separated.[789] When we fail to acknowledge that there is supernatural involvement in history and in our lives, we are unable to see cause and effect relationships between God and what happens in provisional reality.

God told Moses that he had raised up Pharaoh to demonstrate his own power through Moses so that God's name may be proclaimed throughout the earth.[790] The example is that the only reason God brought Pharaoh to such a highly elevated position with so much power is that by defeating Pharaoh, everyone would know who the real, true God is. They would know God's sovereignty. Pharaoh, who thought he was a god, believed that he was in control of his life and all else for that matter. Pharaoh thought that he was responsible for all of his own success and power. He was devastated, and Egypt fell from significance when everything was taken away by the power of God through Moses. Prior to the exodus, Egypt was the supreme military power along the Mediterranean coast; with their demise, the path was clear for the small tribes of Israel to conquer Canaan. The people of Egypt also came to know the sovereignty of God of Israel through the plagues brought through the messenger of God.[791] Each of the plagues God brought against Egypt was in direct defiance to the various gods they worshiped. Through his plagues, God demonstrated his absolute sovereignty over all of provisional reality. When we do not expect God to intervene in our life or in history, we do not look for his intervention; as a result, we do not acknowledge his supernatural presence in our everyday affairs. Consequently, we miss the point of his intervention. We may miss his involvement in our own life, and we may miss what it is that God would have us do. "Man's steps are ordained by the Lord."[792] "Nor is it in a man who walks to direct his steps."[793]

Many people sense emptiness or that something is missing in their lives. They question the significance or meaning of life and their purpose. These are promptings from the Holy Spirit to encourage those that are called by God, to seek God, and discover his purpose for them in their lives.

Not everyone is called, and we do not know how many are called. We are just certain that some are called by God—his elect.[794] The offer of salvation through Jesus Christ is open to everyone.

Cornelius was a Gentile that lived in the time just after the crucifixion of Christ.[795] Cornelius was a devout man who feared God. He was also an officer in the Roman Army. Cornelius prayed to God continually and gave alms to the poor of Israel.[796] One day, Cornelius had a vision where an angel of God appeared to him and told him to send for Simon Peter,[797] one of the disciples. Cornelius sent his servants to invite Peter to his home. Simultaneously, to Cornelius's experience, Simon Peter was up on his rooftop praying. Scripture tells us he fell into a trance.[798] While Simon Peter was in this trance, he had a vision. In the vision, the sky opened up and an object like a great white sheet came down, filled with four-footed animals, crawling creatures, and all sorts of birds. Then a voice told Peter to get up and eat. Peter responded that he would not eat because these things were "unclean, and therefore unholy."[799] The voice responded to Peter and said, "What God has cleansed, no longer consider unholy."[800] When Cornelius's servants invited Simon Peter, he accompanied them to his home. Simon Peter arrived at the home of Cornelius, who had gathered all of his friends and family together to hear what Peter had to say. Simon preached the gospel to this gathering. This is the first time the gospel was preached to Gentiles, and it opened the door for salvation through Jesus Christ to all Gentiles.[801] While Peter was preaching the gospel to the household and family members of Cornelius, "the Holy Spirit descended on all of them that were 'listening' to the message."[802] Those that were not listening did not receive the Holy Spirit.

The ability to answer our call is the result of our being willing to listen and in being yielded to the Holy Spirit.[803] We must also be resisting evil[804] and walking in a manner worthy of our calling.[805] These criteria will establish our relationship with God. Some responsibilities of faith fall to us, and we are responsible for their execution. We cannot do whatever it is we want to do and nonchalantly say, "If I did it, it must have been the will of God," or "It is all in God's hands." We will always be responsible for our own behavior. That is what free will is all about, the ability to choose, and there will always be consequences—good or bad—for those choices. Jesus Christ has done everything for our salvation. However, we must work at yielding ourselves to the Holy Spirit. We must work at restraining our sinful nature. This is accomplished by overcoming evil influences and building our relationship with God.[806] Sin interferes with the progress of our process of sanctification by sabotaging our relationship with God.[807] The call for some can be a false start. If we are still looking to satisfy our own desires and our own will, any attempt will result in a halfhearted pursuit in our commitment to Christ. "No one can serve two masters."[808]

Satan also plays a role with his provisional reality influences; his flaming arrows distract us from our process of sanctification.[809] When we are caught up in these diversions, we want to have what other people have, or we may want to be like someone else, and then we engage in behaviors to gain those things, which will distract us from our preordained path.[810] These arrows do distract us from our course that God has preplanned for us, and that is why envy, pride, ambition, and jealousy are considered sins.[811] These distractions may not just be temporary setbacks; it may take years for us to overcome them and get back on track. These setbacks are our challenges in our process of sanctification. While we are being distracted, we may miss the opportunity with God, and he may pass the opportunity on to someone else. For God, everything

in his eternal plan has to be accomplished in a timely manner. For others, they may not recognize their call until later in life. In addition to the distraction, some of us do not take the supernatural things very seriously and tend to think we have been put here in provisional reality for our own amusement.

A God that has infinite power,[812] infinite knowledge,[813] and is ever present,[814] monitors, is aware, and intervenes in any aspect or any event in the lives of all of his children. God has the capacity to be involved with all of us simultaneously. Scripture does not say some things are possible with God, but all things. All things are possible, and nothing is impossible for God.

Another remarkable feature of God's plan is that, as we are told in Scripture, we will know God from the world around us.[815] We can come to know the characteristics of God by the world he has created. God has created all that we are, all that we see—the entire universe and even dimensions of existence that we cannot see. The ability to create means to make something out of nothing. Therefore, God, along with Jesus Christ[816] and within the presence of the Holy Spirit,[817] created[818] the earth and the universe. Created from God's spoken word, and the word was Jesus Christ, and in Christ, all things were created.[819] It is easier to understand that God can do all of this than it is to understand that planets, stars, and galaxies are infinite and go on in space forever and that everything has just occurred by happenstance. Intelligent design is self-evident by the predictability of all of the physical laws of nature.

Scientists speculate about a big bang theory, a sudden explosion that created the universe. A single event caused everything to spring into existence. The single event is God, and his creation was the big bang. It was the conclusion of atheist-turned-believer Albert Einstein that there has to be a higher power to maintain the delicate balance in the universe that prevents planets and stars from colliding with each other or spinning off into space. After Einstein's religious conversion, he maintained that he was then able to leave behind his empirical thinking style and was able to conjecture theories that are still being proven today. Einstein in 1933 conjectured the existence of black holes that he referred to as the brakes of the universe. He also proposed that the speed of light is the ultimate speed limit, which he referred to as God's universal quarantine. (The speed of light is the ultimate speed limit because as matter accelerates, it expands, and when it has reached the speed of light, it has expanded to the point that there is nothing left to push against to gain more acceleration.)

We are able to know God, the Son, and the Holy Spirit. "For since the creation of the world His invisible attributes, His eternal power and divine nature, have been clearly seen, being understood through what has been made, so that they are without excuse."[820] In the same manner, we come to know an artist or an author by their works. The majesty of the mountains, the power of the water in the oceans, the breathtaking beauty of autumn in the Rocky Mountains, the wonder of the Aurora Borealis, the wrath of a volcano, the quiet beauty of a sunset or the miracle of birth—all are glorious works of God. We are children of God, and God is looking for us to have the same innocence and obedience that children possess.[821] God tells us that a part of pure and undefiled religion is for us to remain unstained by the world.[822] He also says that friendship with the world is hostility to God and that whoever is friend of the world is an enemy of God.[823]

We can discern God's intervention in our lives, in events, in circumstances, and in history. However, unless we truly believe that God involves himself in our everyday activities, we are not prepared for his involvement. Consequently, we miss the significance of his intervention, and that can lead us to miss what God has called us to do. Generally, we do not perceive foundational reality as a part of our everyday life, nor do we understand a godly perspective on our everyday existence.[824]

We were not made for provisional reality or ourselves; we were made by God and for God and for foundational reality. Our time here is just a stepping-off point.[825] The real significance of our existence is that we were made as eternal beings in God's image.

There are some things, however, that are mysteries of God.[826] We may never truly know the answers while we are in provisional reality. To what extent do Satan and his minions influence history and us? There are some calamities we just cannot understand! For the most part, they are all mysteries. The answers of which will not be revealed to us until we enter eternity.[827] We are told that the Holy Spirit can reveal all things;[828] the Bible just does not say when. A part of faith, however, is to trust God and know that all things as they transpire are a part of God's eternal plan. Life in provisional reality is the unfolding of God's plan day by day.

PROVIDENCE AND THE INVISIBLE HAND OF GOD

God's holy character and universal morality must be upheld in provisional reality.[829] Christians recognize this axiom and take it as a personal responsibility for their life. "YOU SHALL BE HOLY, FOR I AM HOLY."[830] Christ was sent as a living example, a role model for our behavior.[831] This is not a holier-than-thou attitude. It is a striving to do all that God desires of his elect, which is, "If you love Me, keep My commandments."[832] We are also to encourage others to find faith in Jesus Christ so that they too may be saved. This is referred to as the great commission.[833] "The harvest is plentiful, but the workers are few."[834]

God's providence is our assurance that all God has preordained and predestined to happen will in fact happen. This is as certain as the unchangeable nature of God.[835] Whatever God chooses to impose will be just and right and will be a perfect fulfillment of his holy will. All that God had predicted in the Old Testament to happen has already happened. All of the predicted events up to the book of Revelation are a part of human history. Revelation is the last chapter of human history, and all of the events depicted in Revelation will happen just as they are recorded.

Because of the abstract nature of the writing style in the book of Revelation, many think the book is not to be taken literally. However, John is taken up into heaven to be shown a preview of what is to come.[836] His translation is a perfect example of how difficult it is for the empirical mind to put into words, events, and scenes from foundational reality.[837] Empirical explanations will always fall short with similes and analogies from provisional reality attempting to describe foundational reality.

The end state of those that are lost is both conscious[838] and, just as the afterlife in paradise, it is also eternal. The nature of the plan of salvation is such that it does not incorporate partial compliance, nor can it be executed on the grounds of good intentions. Faith in Jesus Christ, as Savior and the grace of God[839] are solely responsible for our salvation.[840]

In the Old Testament, God's chosen people had a straightforward proposition with God.[841] When the people of Israel were obedient to God, they were blessed.[842] When they were disobedient, God used trials and tribulations to correct his erring people.[843] As uncomplicated as this proposition was, Israel was never able to maintain an obedient state with God.[844] They were not able to live by the letter of the law.[845] They continually lost faith in the sovereignty of God[846] and tried to define their own destiny.

The arrival of the Messiah brought a new arrangement, a new covenant, whereby all of our sins were transferred onto Jesus so that we, as long as we had faith in all that Christ was able to do, would appear acceptable or justified in the eyes of God. As long as we could not meet God's high and holy standards, a substitute was sent to compensate for our shortcomings. Under this new arraignment, the focus was taken off a chosen people, and the relationship evolved into a personal relationship. The new covenant brought a one on one relationship between the believer and the Savior. God, being sovereign, is able to do whatever he chooses to do.[847] The clarifying truth is that God has an elect company from all nations.[848] Not one of the elect will fail to hear and respond to God's call.[849]

Just as sheep respond to the voice of their shepherd,[850] we respond to the call of God. In the days of Christ where people herded sheep, all of the village's sheep would be penned up at night for safety's sake. The sheep are easier to guard when they are penned, and they can be guarded with fewer people. In the morning when the shepherd opens the gate and calls his sheep, only his sheep will respond to his voice by coming out of the fenced area. The others will not respond until they hear their shepherd's voice.[851] The created, whether angel or human, is not only the property of the Creator, but also wholly dependent on the Creator[852] for its sustenance and its very existence. The created will also be held accountable by the Creator for obedience and their behavior.

When Christians encounter events and situations that we do not understand, we have faith that what God tells us in the Bible is true.[853] These truths are designed to give us information to help us with our challenges, as well as our blessings. Aside from Scripture, the Holy Spirit is also a medium for God to communicate his message to us. We by faith understand that all things happen for good to those who love the Lord[854] and that we are to be steadfast in our faith.[855] In spite of our lack of understanding of God's purpose in events, he always has our sanctification in mind. We also know by faith that nothing is impossible with God.[856] We also know that God has planned a future and a hope[857] for us. That all good gifts come down from heaven and that they are from God.[858] A further truth from Scripture is that Christ has gone to prepare a place for us in his Father's house.[859] An absolute truth is that Jesus Christ is the one and only way to God.[860]

Christians know that the conditions for their salvation have been established by Christ. However, there are requirements for salvation. We must realize that as sinners we need saving from the wrath of God's justice. We must also believe that salvation comes through Jesus Christ alone. A person that believes this to be true subscribes to a belief system that is centered on God's holiness and the triune state of God's existence.[861] Some people struggle with this concept of a triune God. The Trinity means that God is God and the Holy Trinity is comprised of God, Jesus Christ, and the Holy Spirit. We are to devote ourselves to God.[862] "And He said to him, You shall love the Lord your God with all your heart, and with all your soul, and with all your mind."

THE MOST IMPORTANT THING WE DO

This is not an empirical evaluation of providence; it is an attempt to put reason from our empirical nature into the mysteries of God. Our current existence in provisional reality only gives us a partial glimpse of the whole truth; for the rest we must have faith.[863] God does, however, tell us how much significance we are to place on our existence here in provisional reality. We are to view our lives here as tenuously as "a blade of grass"[864] or "a vapor."[865] These analogies seem severe; however, our God is a God of love, mercy, and grace. We misinterpret what God means because it is hard for us to understand his message.[866] We tend to view everything from what is important to us in provisional reality, not from a godly perspective, not from a view of foundational reality.[867] These analogies are not meant to trivialize our earthly existence. They are supposed to give us a means of putting our seventy years of physical life[868] into a perspective that is relevant to our eternal existence. We are not mortal beings; we have a short stay[869] on earth in human form,[870] and then we will exist for an eternity.[871] The people that you know today that are in Christ, you will know forever.[872] The message that God is trying to convey to us is that compared to what awaits us in eternity, our experience here in provisional reality is as insignificant as a candle in the wind.[873]

The whole point is that the span of our life, some seventy-odd years, is really insignificant compared to how long we will exist in eternity. Yet, in the short timeframe of this existence, we will decide our destiny and help others decide their destiny for eternity. This is the single most important thing we do in this life.

That is precisely why the Bible puts so much emphasis on witnessing to other people, on fellowship, and on stewardship. That feeling people have that something is missing in their life is exactly this, the Holy Spirit urging them not to miss out on eternity. The people that Christians are and the way they live their lives, "as beacons to the world,"[874] "as lamps on the hill,"[875] are designed so that people will seek us out because there is something in our life that is missing in theirs. Moreover, we are to be "ready in season and out,"[876] to be able to respond to others. When we are cautious or doubtful or unsure[877] about what we should say, these doubts are the flaming arrows[878] from Satan. Disregard them and say what is in your heart; the Holy Spirit will guide your conversation.[879] It is not up to us to convert everyone; we are just to plant the seed, let the Holy Spirit conduct his influence, and be there for continued fellowship. A person may finally "get it" the fifteenth time they hear the gospel message. You may be the first, tenth, or the fifteenth person to present that message.

As Americans, and being exceedingly blessed of God as we are, we put too much emphasis on provisional reality when we should in fact look forward to our existence in paradise.[880] Death for a Christian should be a celebration.[881] We know that Christ has overcome death because he was resurrected.[882] Our departed loved one has been resurrected, gone to live with Jesus Christ for an eternity[883] in paradise.[884] "Precious in the sight of the Lord is the death of His saints."[885] "But we do not want you to be uninformed, brethren, about those who are asleep, so that you will not grieve as do the rest who have no hope."[886] However, in provisional reality, we do grieve the loss of loved ones because they are gone, and we will miss them. Their absence creates a void until we rejoin them. The death of a loved one also makes us aware of a new dimension to our reality. We seem to have a different sense about our own mortality and the tenuous nature of life. However, if they were saved, we celebrate because they have entered eternity and are present with the Lord in foundational reality. There are no second chances when it comes to eternity. The true value of our experiences has to be taken in the context of both realities. The emphasis of our motives should be on our dual existence, not focused on the singularity of provisional reality. Our actions, thoughts, and intentions have a meaning for our life. However, they are significantly more enriched and profoundly more meaningful when taken in context of both realities.

God is always on the side of righteousness. Injustice is real; it occurs every day, and it is part of provisional reality. The present reality of injustice will be rectified in the final judgment.[887] God also knew we would struggle with the concept of multidimensional realities; that is why he sent his Son.[888] So that we could have a living, real life example of the two states of existence and know that after death there is life.[889] A lot of this we must take on faith. That is why he has given us so much counsel in Scripture regarding staying the course, keeping faith, fighting the good fight,[890] and trusting in him and his final judgment.[891] Our patience is not too much to ask. God has been patient with us in delaying the culmination of human history.[892] He is patient and desires that "all men to be saved and to come to the knowledge of the truth."[893]

THE THOUSAND NATURAL SHOCKS THAT FLESH IS HEIR TO

The Christian who puts his/her trust in providence perceives a world in which even the physical laws of the universe can be changed or altered by the sovereignty of God.[894] Our sovereign God desires that by our own free will, we will choose good and not evil.[895] That we will choose to obey his commandments. "If you love Me, you will keep My commandments."[896] The reason so much significance is placed on the power of choice is that in the simple free will act of choosing, we determine our destiny for eternity. The whole point of a Christian existence is obedience to God. When God or Jesus repeats something in Scripture, it must be important. "If you love Me, you will keep My commandments" is stated four times in John[897] and three more times in 1 John.[898]

God is sovereign, yet we still have free will to the extent that God has allowed it under his permissive will. The extent of our free will defines what we are responsible to God for, and that which is beyond our free will falls within God's sovereignty and grace. God's system of grace is the gift of eternal life in exchange for the single requirement of faith. A belief in the incarnate God, our Lord Jesus Christ,[899] whose blood was shed as a ransom for our sinful nature.[900] This only makes sense for beings that are unknowingly subject to a daily barrage of influences from unobservable spiritual entities who are relentlessly attempting to undermine the Christian's faith and beliefs. Belief in Christ is our amnesty for all that we are guilty of in thought, word, and deed, for that which we have done, and that which we have left undone. The warfare encompasses all of the demonic influences in provisional reality, and we are justly compensated by the mysterious system of God's grace.

We tend to be apprehensive of a system that offers so much and appears to require so little on our part. Faith, just faith in Jesus Christ alone, and we receive a magnum opus reward of eternal life. However, this is only so because we are not cognizant of all that we are enmeshed in while we are in provisional reality. At our transfiguration,[901] we will be aware of the significance of our battle. Only then will we understand the significance of our efforts and the justice and mercy in this incredible gift of eternal life granted to us by the grace of God. Only by knowing the opposite nature of something can we really understand the true nature of something. Right from wrong, truth from falsehood, seen from the unseen, material from the immaterial, and good from evil. While we are in our physical state, we cannot know the true nature and dimensions of our existence. If everything were inexplicably laid out, we would have knowledge, but we would not have faith. Faith is a belief in the existence of things that do not exist in provisional reality.[902] However, we know that they exist, that we believe in them to the degree that our belief governs our behavior. We shall be known by our works.[903] The experiences of this dimension are not as important as the dimensions of this experience!

Many people will not study the Bible because Scripture details too many activities from which people must abstain. They believe that if they followed biblical dictates, they would miss out on too much fun. Ignorance is not bliss; it can cost you your eternity. Ignorance will never be an excuse; it is not in this life, and it will not be in the next. We are without excuse.[904] We can ignore the Bible, we can ignore God, and we can quench the Spirit. However, it will still not be enough; we will still know the truth. If we are truly honest with ourselves, we cannot ignore our conscience, which will reveal that which we know innately about God.[905]

There is shallowness to life if it remains in the single dimension of provisional reality. Real meaning and depth for life comes from experiencing the supernatural in your existence here on earth.

We know that God causes all things to work together for good to those who love God, to those who are called according to His purpose.[906] Paul does not say here that all things that happen to us are good things. In fact, bad and painful things happen to all of us. Things that squelch our spirit and leave us devastated. Yet all of the bad things that happen to us are working together for our good. The bad that we experience is redeemed in the providence of God. This means that God brings good out of the evil and the suffering that we experience.[907] To say that all things work together for good is not the same thing as saying that all the things that happen to us are, necessarily in themselves, good things. Yet if these things are working together for our good, then in an ultimate sense, it is good that they happen to us. Even though we may not understand their significance because we do not see the application to our life, we know through faith that God cares for us. We struggle with all of the suffering we somehow think Christians should be exempt. Christians, like everyone else, experience the "thousand natural shocks that flesh is heir to." However, if we have saving faith, we will experience less discipline, chastisement, and scourging than those less sanctified. To understand the good in everything, we must understand our experiences from a perspective of foundational reality. That is why we must seek the kingdom first and all His righteousness. In theory, it is easy to understand the premise that all things work together for good to those who love God and are called according to His purpose, but to establish this as a basic tenant of our belief system is another matter.

To believe in God is not the same thing as believing God. Believing God means we believe everything he says. Believing in God means we trust him to be right, true, and faithful no matter what happens in our life. We cannot believe in God unless we first believe God.

We should trust God explicitly with our life, and that trust replaces any doubt we would have. The result is that we will not be anxious for anything.[908] Because we know we can cast all of our anxiety on him because He cares for us.[909] We may think that nothing bad will ever happen to us if we belong to Christ. Then when something challenging does happen, we know the strength of our faith by our actions and reaction.

Provisional reality is not meant to be paradise; that is what foundational reality is with a corresponding different set of conditions. However, as Christians, we endure provisional reality because we know that all of our experiences have a purpose and a meaning.[910] We know that everything happens in accordance with God's divine plans, both for us individually and for humanity. If we do not look for God in all of the experience of our life, we miss most of his involvement. We can be proactive in our own growth by looking for significance in those supernatural experiences that occur in our life. "But seek first His kingdom and His righteousness, and all these things will be given to you as well."[911] We should also pay close attention to events that appear to be a coincidence or luck. God can change the physical laws of nature,[912] and he intervenes directly in our lives.[913] His involvement in our life makes much more sense than a coincidence would. It takes more faith to believe that everything is random and that the universe and life transpires by happenstance. It requires less faith to believe there is a God who is orchestrating millions of events every day. Some may ask how simultaneous intervention in every Christian's life can be accomplished every day. When we come to understand the magnitude of God and how he is able to accomplish everything, we too will continually worship God as all of the angels in heaven are currently doing. "Nothing is impossible with God." "Holy, Holy, Holy, is the Lord God Almighty, who was, and is, and is to come."[914]

If we overlook an opportunity for growth through blessings, we may be setting our own stage for our continued growth through trials. We are closest to God when we are in trouble or when we are suffering. However, we can make a free-will choice to be close to God[915] all of the time. During our trials, we get a good understanding of how well we believe in God. God does not put us through trials so that he can see how strong our faith is; being omniscient, he already knows. God puts us through trials so that we become aware of where our faith is lacking so that we understand our need for change or growth. Endurance through these trials sustains our growth; if we endure, we will grow,[916] run the race,[917] fight the fight.[918] If we quit, give up, or stop having faith in God, we have failed the test, missed our opportunity, and aborted the progress God was fashioning in our process of sanctification. If we endure, our endurance[919] sees us through the test so that we will grow; that growth enables character development and allows us to grow more next time. As we emerge from the other side of each growth experience, we will find that we have a deeper faith, more trust in God, and a better understanding of the whole process. We have grown closer to God, and we have improved our personal relationship with him. Trials always develop our character. If God wants us to learn how to love others, he puts us with some pretty unlovable people. "For momentarily, light affliction is producing for us an eternal weight of glory far beyond all comprehension."[920] That is why James tells us to count it all joy when we experience trials.[921] We will always think the growth and our newfound faith and perceptions were worth whatever it was we had to endure. The degree of testing is not the same for everyone; to whom much has been given, much will be required.[922]

Everything that we have is a gift from God, and we are to use God's blessings for his purposes. Christ used his gifts for the glorification of God and the redemption of the souls of all believers. Christ never used his gifts to further or better his cause; in fact, he did not use them when he could have because that would have been in direct violation of God's eternal plan. "Do you think I cannot call on My Father, and He will at once put at My disposal twelve legions of angels? But how then would the Scripture be fulfilled that says that it must happen in this way."[923] God will take any of us when we ask Christ into our life, and then the shaping process begins. If you are one of God's elect, the shaping process began before you accepted Christ, just to make sure that you would. Conversely, there are people that avoid using their talents and disregard their calling from God. The parable of the talents in Matthew and Mark gives an ominous preview of this and of those that choose this path. The master calls the servant that does not use his talents "slothful and lazy" and casts him into the "outer darkness" where there is "gnashing of teeth."[924]

If we do not understand the process of growth and development, we are told to ask for wisdom,[925] and it will be given to us freely so that we may understand.[926] God is sovereign, our key role is obedience, and we are to work out our salvation with fear and trembling.[927] These are the only requirements necessary for most of what happens in our lives. If we do not hold God as sovereign, and if we are not obedient, there is a good chance we may not see an eternity with God. (He who began a perfect work in you.)[928] This steadfast trust upon God allows us to accept situations where justice or right does not prevail. If we suffer unjustly, it may only seem unfair because we are not trusting God through faith, and we are trying to view our situation from a perspective of provisional reality.[929] Something can, in fact, appear to be unfair before we understand all that there is to know about it. We must trust God that although we do not understand, we know enough of God's character to help us accept it until we are able to understand.[930] This process is all a part of the essence of faith. The process of growing through life's trials is that we learn through experience, and what we learn changes us. The amount or degree of change is the measure of how much we grew.

FREE WILL AND THE PERMISSIVE WILL OF GOD

God has a specific plan for his elect, "called for the very purpose that you might inherit a blessing [eternity]."[931] The blueprint for God's plan is divine foreknowledge, divine predestination, divine calling, divine justification, and divine glorification. Christians are designated as "the called according to His purpose."[932] All of "those thus called" includes all of those who are saved; it also includes those who are yet to be saved. The yet-to-be-saved are those whose understanding is presently blinded by Satan.[933] They are rejecting or ignoring the gospel and will continue to do so until they too are enlightened by the Holy Spirit.

> And whom He foreknew, He also predestinated to become conformed to the image of His Son...and whom He predes-

THINGS TO COME

tinated, these He also called; and whom He called, these He also justified; and whom He justified, these He also glorified." All that are predestinated are called, and all who are called are justified.⁹³⁴ (Rom. 8:28–30)

The object lesson in provisional reality is for Christians to conform to the image of His Son. The election of believers is within God's absolute sovereignty. We may think that we have free will, our decisions are our own, and we are in charge of our own destiny. This is certainly a valid construct for provisional reality. However, in the larger design of things, complete reality encompasses both provisional and foundational reality. Our perception of our capabilities is in complete accordance with provisional reality. Within the purview of God's infinite domain, our perception of free will is a subset of what infinite free will would entail.

It is the same as when you let your five-year-old exercise his or her free will and play outside but stay in our yard. The five-year-old is exercising his or her free will; however, within the confines of the safety of our yard, the parent's will is also being exercised. Will they rebel and go outside the yard, and what will you do, out of love, if they do?

Christians are to evangelize to the yet to be saved. It is how they get started on their process of sanctification. Little more needs to be accomplished than to make them receptive to the Holy Spirit, who will pick up where we leave off. The Holy Spirit will enlighten the mind of an unsaved individual about the reality of Christ as the Savior. The Holy Spirit creates within the person a yearning for salvation, a desire to know Christ, and a longing to please and honor God. When a person responds in this manner, they are exercising their own free will in developing their own relationship with Christ. There are incidences of foundational reality that influence us every day in ways that are beyond our ability to comprehend. This supernatural involvement is how the predestination of what is foreknown is accomplished. There is an election of the Father that "not one of these will ever be lost."[935] That is why God intervenes in our lives. It is equally true that not every person sees the Son;[936] not everyone will be saved. Some are fated to an eternity of damnation.[937] If God did not spare the angels that did not honor their first estate and confined them in chains in hell to wait for the Day of Judgment,[938] why do some think their sins will be overlooked and they will be spared? "And if it is with difficulty that the righteous is saved, what will become of the godless man and the sinner?"[939] He is a God of love and mercy; however, he is also a God of justice. If God does not exercise his justice and does not punish unrepentant sinners, then he is not just. If he is not just, then he is not the God of love and mercy. God must be true to his nature and be all that he says he is and do all that he has said he will do. When we try to evangelize to the lost, they think the gospel of Jesus Christ is all foolishness,[940] and our words are lost on them. However, we do not know the difference between the lost and the to-be-saved, so we cannot differentiate; we must evangelize to everyone. We especially try to reach people we care about because it matters to us where they will spend eternity.

By the vision, which the Holy Spirit engenders, we immediately see Christ as the answer to every need that we will have in time or eternity. The challenge in our daily walk is to put all of our trust in Christ. To do that, we must abandon all confidence in ourselves and abandon secular solutions[941] to our everyday challenges. However, the ability to submit oneself to God is extremely difficult. It is foreign to our human nature. We are fiercely independent and like to think that we are in charge of our own destiny. It is only when we try to maintain control of everything that we have difficulty sorting through the events of life.

The ultimate reality is that if you are one of God's elect, and if you are walking in truth, everything that happens in your life is either ordained, permitted, or orchestrated by God, and more specifically, by the Holy Spirit. "All things work together for good to those that love the Lord."[942]

There is not an entity of will itself. Will is not a thing or something that has an identity of its own; it is a theoretical construct. The fact of the will is a psychological truth, while the freedom of the will is theological. The will usually acts as we are moved or influenced by our intellect and our emotions. One's will is a deliberate cognitive act, and the strength of one's ability to maintain those thoughts or ideas is identified as one's will or will power. There are strong-willed people, those that have the tenacity to maintain their convictions in spite of much opposition, hardship, peer pressure, or even demonic influences. There are also weak-willed people that are unable to maintain their convictions and are easily influenced by others, by Satan and false doctrines. There are also a host of those that fall somewhere in between.

One's will then is contingent upon one's ability to steadfastly enforce that which has been cognitively created. Because the will has a degree of variability to it, we can postulate that it is part of our individual makeup and therefore part of our personality. In essence, our intellect is our ability to choose between good and evil. Our will gives us the ability to carry out and enforce our desires, motives, and ideals and to direct our activities to obtain specific outcomes or desired goals. The will does not function alone; it works in conjunction with our intellect and our emotions, which are the foundations of our personality. A strong will is founded in conviction, and that conviction comes from a belief in absolute truth.

The core of our personality is expressed as our personality states, and from our individual states spring our personality traits. Our traits include attitudes, integrity, honesty, dedication, ethics, sense of humor, all of which drive our motives. Personality states tend to be rather enduring, our hardwiring. Conversely, traits are like software and can be modified. Our personality states are the filters by which we see and interpret the world and subsequently are the cornerstones for the development of our internal valuing process. In essence, the strength of our will determines how strongly we act on or enforce our convictions. Influences that we receive can

be from the indwelling Holy Spirit, Satan, or his minions, peers, institutions, family, friends, parents, angels, books, movies, TV, the Web, and life's experiences. It is left to the Holy Spirit and the individual to discern the origins of influences. Because Satan and his minions masquerade as spirits of light,[943] we are told to hold every thought captive.[944] To guard against these influences and to not be deceived by false doctrines that go against what we have been taught.[945] By consistently following the influences of goodness, what is right, and what is truthful, we develop character, integrity, and our moral fiber. All of these working in concert form our internal value system and our beliefs. Our free-will choices determine our direction, our service, and our destiny. By free-will choices, we become bondservants of sin or servants of righteousness.[946] To put a finer point on it, we are responsible for all of our own beliefs and our actions. All of our decisions have consequences for good or evil; they affect our direction in life and our ultimate destiny in eternity.

FREEDOM OF CHOICE

Free will is man's ability to make choices, choices that not only affect one's life: where should I live? What occupation should I hold? How much school do I need? Whom should I marry? A free-will choice ultimately will determine where we spend eternity. We can choose to believe in the salvation brought by Jesus Christ, experience a spiritual rebirth, and receive the indwelling Holy Spirit, which imparts within us the very nature of Christ. Alternatively, we can choose spiritual death as when someone chooses not to believe and becomes susceptible to satanic philosophies and influences. The nature of one's life and the fate of one's future destiny are inexplicably interwoven in our free will decisions.

If man is to be deemed responsible for his actions, he must have some degree of freedom or control over his actions. Our freedom to

act does not have to be completely free and absolute. To whatever degree God allows us to have freedom to act, we are responsible for our actions within the scope of that latitude. We will also be held accountable to God for those free-will decisions and our subsequent behaviors.[947] We are free only to the degree that God allows us our freedom. This is the permissive will of God.[948]

The decision one makes dictates the manner of life which one embraces, godly or satanic. God's will is always exercised by his infinite wisdom and benevolence. Satan chose to do his will rather than God's will. This was a rebellious rejection of God's will, and Satan's decision was within the parameters of the permissive will of God. This is the precedence of man's free-will choice for rebellion and sin.

There are, after all, two choices in life: to be a Christian or to not be a Christian.[949] They are, in fact, two very different philosophies of life. Satan's lie and all rebellion against God are not only a misrepresentation of the person and character of God, but also a distortion of God's will, purpose, and plan. The fact remains that the created, angel or man, is designed to be guided by God alone, not by the evil influences of Satan, and certainly not by conceited self-will. Who is better able to lead you to the realization of your full potential and purpose? You from the confines of a single reality perception, or God from infinite knowledge of both realities and his omniscient, preordained view into the future? You can, with the resources you have, be all that you can be. On the other hand, you can follow God's direction for your life and be all that God wants you to be and complete whatever supernatural role God has preordained for you.[950]

When we attempt an independent, self-directed life, that is the same free-will choice Satan made. God himself, with all that enters into his perfect plan and purpose, is truth in its absolute and unlimited sense. God has created all things; resultantly, he is the originator of how things should be and the sole author of what is true. Any deviation from what God has ordained as true is untrue.

To continue with God in the course he has designed is the highest destiny possible for any person or angel. To depart from that course is to experience the present and future penalties of evil. There is little wonder that misery, pain, and suffering abound in the world when it is recognized that a majority of people live without any conscious reliance upon God, his plan, his purpose and will not acknowledge the reality of Satan. Without the influences of God in your life, the influences you experience will be those of Satan. The conundrum is that people think they are guiding themselves without realizing it is demonic influences from a different reality that are forming impressions in their minds or inflicting sparks in their emotions. The character of sin is defined as missing the mark.[951] In effect, it is missing God's perfect purpose, which is doing your will for your life and not doing God's will. This is missing the mark.

The evil nature of sin is not limited to rebellion against God and turning from his will and plan. It also encompasses all of the behaviors and consequences that result from this separation. Sin continues to elevate self and professes a different and completely God-dishonoring manner of life. Satan's sin was not simply sinful in its rejection of God. It also entailed a contrary philosophy of life, accompanied with behavior that is contrary to the will and plan of God. The lie is a substitution of self for God and the assumption of a self-designed plan of life other than that purposed by the Creator. This is the lie Paul writes about in 2 Timothy where he tells us that we are to serve God's purposes not ours.[952] This is what Christ was referring to when he said of Satan, "He abode not in the truth." "Satan is a liar, and the father of it [lies]."[953] A partial or compromising departure from God is impossible. God is either everything in your life, or He is nothing.[954] This is not a gray area; you are either in God's court, or you are in Satan's.[955] Either you are under the influences of the indwelling Holy Spirit, or you are under the influences of Satan. Moreover, it is a part of Satan's deception and his veiling of the truth that has people believe that he, Satan, does not really exist. He wants people to believe that he is just a symbol of evil and not a real personality. If he does not exist, we cannot expect him to exert any influence over our lives, and we will not have any defensive strategies. Given that this is the case, a person sees all of these influences as self-originating; they assume that they are evil and not worthy of forgiveness from a perfectly Holy God. Once someone convinces himself or herself that they are not worthy of salvation, they prefer the darkness to the light. It is easier to have fun if we do not have to conform to God's morality. All too often, the only reason for rebellion is that the rebellion allows us to push the envelope on free will. Often it is not in fact rebellion; it is a mindset and a self-justification that allows one to violate God's morality by exceeding the permissive will of God.

Everyone knows when he or she has exceeded God's permissive will that is why we have a conscience, that communication medium from the indwelling Holy Spirit. The Holy Spirit issues the first warning. If the warning is ignored in this initial process of distancing oneself from God, that person, just like Satan, will be allowed some degree of latitude before there is divine intervention. When we begin to distance ourself from God, Satan's influence becomes greater, and the Spirit's influence becomes less. Christ always did only those things that were well pleasing to his Father. Christ is our role model,[956] and Christ was obedient unto his death. "Oh but if this could pass from Me, but not My will be done but Yours."[957]

In the most drastic testing that Satan could impose upon Christ, he did not sin by departing from the precise purpose that his Father had for him. Christ said, "I am the truth."[958] He was not only God; he was the truth manifested in the flesh. Our choice is simply the truth or the lie. Few things in life are this cut-and-dried. However, if we are able to make this distinction, a lot of gray area goes away, and things do get simpler. The lie is not merely an untruth, as no one could ever be as God, but rather the lie consists of rejecting God. In our rejection, we discard his purpose for man during our existence in provisional reality and ultimately in our eternal spiritual destiny. Satan wants all worship directed toward him.[959] With the encounter in the garden of eden, which resulted in the fall of man, humanity became an unwilling participant in this cosmic battle between good and evil, angels light and dark. Humanity, unable to battle a spiritual warfare from the confines of provisional reality, needed help, which was granted through the Holy Spirit. Man needed the saving grace from this spiritual warfare that only a Savior sent by God could accomplish. Christ was sent to destroy the work of Satan.[960]

All will be judged by God solely because they believed the lie and did not believe the truth and found pleasure in iniquity, immorality, injustice, or wickedness. Or that we believed in the sacrificial death of his Son and God's benevolent system of grace,[961] and these will be saved.

THE REFINER'S FIRE: TRIALS, DISCIPLINE, CHASTISEMENT, AND PRUNING

James tells us that when we experience suffering, we are to count it all joy, and Peter tells us to rejoice in our suffering.[962] These perceptions are from an awareness that when we are suffering in our trials,[963] we are experiencing God's direct involvement in our lives. God is intimately involved in every aspect of the believer's life.[964] God's involvement makes our experience supernatural.[965] To count suffering all joy is a tough message because no one likes to endure suffering. However, James and Peter are telling us that in the process of spiritual maturation, suffering is part of the process of growth. The reason we count suffering as joy is that it is a symptom of the ongoing process of our sanctification. Our growth and the degree or length of our suffering is contingent upon our ability to be receptive to the process. Because we are developing, changing, and God is participating specifically in this process, we count it joy now to ease the pain, knowing the outcome will be our crown of life.[966] God will provide for us beyond our wildest expectations.[967] The knowledge of God's direct involvement in our lives and especially in our trials sustains us and gives us the ability to endure the experience.[968] We are closest to God when we are in trouble, in pain, or suffering. When we are at our worst, God is at his best; when we are at our weakest, he is our strength.[969] True faith transcends the empirical constrictions of reason and dispels the bewilderment caused by a lack of understanding.[970] The concepts of life's trials and God's sovereign discipline can at times be difficult to differentiate.

The beginning of understanding is fearing the Lord[971] and realizing five very important concepts. First, if you are one of God's children, everything that happens in your life is ordained, permitted, or orchestrated by the Holy Spirit. He is directly involved in your life, and that is all part of his sovereignty.

Second, all things work for the good of those who love the Lord. God always has our best interest at heart, even though we may not always think that is the case.

Thirdly, Scripture cautions us that obtaining our salvation may not be as easy as we might think, especially if we think our salvation is contingent upon being a good person. Pay close attention. "It is through many tribulations that we will be able to enter the kingdom of God,"[972] "conduct yourselves in fear during the time of your stay upon the earth,"[973] "work out your salvation with fear and trembling,"[974] and "if it is with difficulty that the righteous are saved, what will become of the godless man and the sinner?"[975]

The fourth very important point is, we know that whatever challenges life presents, we will never be required to withstand more than we can endure.[976] In addition, we can have complete confidence that God will never abandon us.[977]

Last, whatever we endure will pale in comparison to the rewards that await us in heaven.[978]

In the evolution of God's classroom, we have discipline, chastisement, pruning, scourging, and punishment. God has said, "Blessed is a man who perseveres under trial; for once he has been approved, he will receive the crown of life, which the Lord has promised to those who love Him."[979]

God never punishes his elect. There is no need for punishment, although we may misinterpret our suffering as punishment. Christ's crucifixion has already paid the price for all of the repentant sins of all of the Christian's past, present, and future.

God is merciful and chooses for trials an area where we have the greatest amount of sensitivity. On the surface that may appear unsympathetic. However, if we consider that any area of special significance for us will naturally be one that we will be most sensitive to, thereby making us immediately responsive and focused. Our heightened response will of course reduce the time we are under duress. During these times of discipline, chastisement, and pruning, we must be especially attuned to God's supernatural involvement in our life. If we do not acknowledge these supernatural interventions, we will misinterpret the purpose of the discipline or the chastisement. Instead of learning the lesson or fine-tuning our character, the demonic influences distance us from God. The reason the influences are so effective is that most people do not think Satan is a real personality, so they disregard anything as coming from him. When we fall prey to these influences during these times, our attitude becomes, "Why me?" and we become angry with God. Alternately, if we acknowledge God's involvement in our life, we seek to understand our current suffering through prayer, Scripture, and the Holy Spirit.

Nothing is more important to God than ensuring that we will spend our eternity with him.[980] He has already manifested his love for us by sending his Son to die for us.[981] If our focus is not on seeking first His kingdom of heaven and His righteousness, we will suffer many trials and tribulations before we figure it out. God does not ambush us. He gives fair and frequent warnings before he

gently begins the process. Thus being aware, we may still choose to ignore or deny the Holy Spirit as to why we are being afflicted. God is just, compassionate, and filled with love for his creations. His will is never capricious.[982] In keeping with God's holy character, he does not chastise without making his reasons known to those he is about to correct. It is made known to us by a conscious awareness from the Holy Spirit. The believer may choose to acknowledge or choose to ignore their conscious awareness of the message. However, many just do not acknowledge the message. They have not gotten out of the box of empirical thinking. The whole idea of the supernatural involvement just escapes them. Some hear the Spirit, but they discount it because they will have to give up something. On the other hand, they may have to do something they do not want to do. The empirical challenge here is that you sense the message from the Holy Spirit, you know it's right, and you know you should respond. However, the weight of your empirical thinking and our touch-and-feel reality cause you to discount the message. It may be that you are embarrassed to do what you are asked, or it is out of your comfort zone. You may be asked to talk to a wayward family member or a friend about their salvation. Remember, if you do not do as you are asked, you are being disobedient. Remember also, Christ warns us that if we do not acknowledge him before men, he will not acknowledge us before his Father. God is very persistent. He may also choose to employ a variety of agents to convey his message: scripture, angels, a friend, a parent, a teacher, even strangers. At times God uses events or circumstances to guide us toward his message; either way the truth will be made known to you, and the truth will set you free.[983] God is omnipresent, omnipotent, and omniscient; there is nothing that is impossible for God.

If you are yielded to the Holy Spirit and submitted to God, you must count it all joy.[984] We know that God cares for us.[985] His promise for us is a future of prosperity and hope and not calamity.[986] We have to view all of our challenges with this acknowledgment. Then we will have the right perspective. Everyone must be cautious of intentionally or unintentionally missing the message. We do employ many subconscious defense mechanisms that are designed by Satan to blur or confuse the message. It is also possible that we dismiss the still, small voice of the Holy Spirit because we are not convinced that supernatural entities, light, or dark, from an overlapping reality can indirectly interact or influence us.

As our process of sanctification proceeds, we come to a place where, because of our faith, our inheritance for eternity has been secured.[987] The process of growth will continue. Pruning, discipline, and chastisements are all strategies that God uses to ensure the fulfillment of our role in his divine plan. Just what is God's divine plan? God's plan is to ensure that all of those that he has predestined, his elect, will come to faith in Jesus Christ, offering them salvation, and thereby ensuring their place in eternity.[988] Not everyone gets to heaven on his or her own initiative; some people need help. The whole purpose of this is that God will have a company of his children that have made a free-will choice to join him in eternity.[989] The purpose of which, as far as we can ascertain from our limited perspective from provisional reality, is that God's divine plan will be a complete manifestation of his system of grace. Exhibiting his love, compassion, mercy, and care for us. Ultimately, it will be the glorification of his holiness and the creation of a standard by which all may be saved, in ages and worlds to come.[990]

We do not really know God. God is inconceivable to our empirical cognitive style.[991] His thoughts are not our thoughts; his ways are not our ways. His thoughts are higher than our thoughts.[992] God's predestination that the elect will be saved does not necessarily preclude those that are currently lost from being saved; in fact it is God's desire that all would repent, believe, and be saved.[993]

God knows everything; the past and the future are his present. God, being omniscient, knows everyone that will accept his message and come to faith. If God knew that before we were born, then in that sense, our acceptance of faith was foreknown. Reality is as it is perceived; to God, all the saved are foreknown, therefore predestinated. To us we do not know, so to us it is a free-will choice. From a perspective in foundational reality God has chosen, before time began, who would accept his offer of salvation, he knows all that will be saved. From a view in provisional reality, we do not know if we are one of the elect or not. Without this knowledge, it appears to us to be a free-will choice to believe in salvation through the Jesus Christ. Foundationally, it is God's election; provisionally for us, it appears to be a free-will choice. One proviso in this whole process is that we do not know who are the elect and who are not and at what point in their life they come to saving grace.

It is fairly obvious to see that the plan God has evolved is really the one we would prefer, in spite of its pain and challenges. God's system of grace is perpetual grace. It can apply to any that choose to exercise a free-will choice to be saved. The reason James and Peter tell us that when we go through trials and the ensuing suffering, we are "to count it all joy,"[994] is because the trials will produce in us the ability to endure and that endurance will produce in us perfection.[995] The final result of this process is our receiving the crown of life—eternity in the presence of the triune God.[996]

SOME ASSEMBLY REQUIRED

Trials are the experiences we encounter in life that are a part of God's eternal plan and they serve to correct his erring saints. They provide opportunities for growth, instruction, ensure our salvation, develop our character, and ready us for the tasks that God has called us to do. These trials can be reminders to keep us on the straight and narrow. "For narrow is the gate, and constricted is the way and few are those who find it."[997] Trials also serve to cause us to mature as Christians and to develop Christlikeness and character traits that are Christ-centered. Only God can change a personality! We are never more aware of our need for God than when we are suffering and in need of his strength, mercy, and grace. The work that

God has begun in us will not cease until we have achieved the position God has planned for us,[998] and we achieve the character traits that are required by God.

Once our salvation has been accomplished, we are to rescue as many others as we can for the salvation of their souls. A rescue implies some overt activity; rescues do not just happen. This process involves overcoming evil not just for us, but for others as well, actively involving ourselves in the cosmic battle of good and evil. It may not be apparent now how significant this cosmic warfare is; however, the significance will be ever so apparent when we have gone through the transition from provisional reality into foundational reality. We measure the significance of things by their results. Each converted sinner causes rejoicing in heaven.[999] What other work can we possibly do that will have the significance of causing rejoicing in heaven? This is meaningful work, efforts that have real value, because the results are eternal.

Trials are testing that produce endurance. By our ability to endure our trials, we are able to stick with our challenge until the trial has produced God's intended result. The result is reflected in a change in us—a change in who we are, in how we think, and in how we behave.[1000] This process of change is our process of growth in our continuing process of sanctification or becoming holy. The changes that occur are in the strengthening of our faith and the development of our character. These changes will cause changes in our personality, which will result in our changed behavior. Our growth is measured by the change that occurred in us as we went through our trial and the Holy Spirit revealed new truths to us.

If we have the right attitude about our trials, an obedient and submissive spirit can limit their duration. The time we spend in rebellion, denial, self-pity, or being angry with God only delays the growth or development that the trial is supposed to accomplish. Realizing that God is sovereign, we should look for what our experiences mean. How God is trying to guide our sanctification. We are his because he has created us.[1001] "Man's steps are ordained by the Lord. How then can man understand his way?"[1002] A trial will run its course until it has produced the desired result that God has intended. That may be to grow our faith and character to a sufficient level that will guarantee our place in heaven. It may be to affect the lives of others, to bring them to the Father and to salvation. It may also just be a stage of development with more to come. The Holy Spirit will also use events and situations in our life to equip us for our assigned good works. The growth pattern is similar for everyone; however, the severity or the frequency is more of an idiosyncratic nature. "To whom much has been given, much will be required." The suffering that is caused by trials is also a very effective means to restrain us from our sinful ways.[1003] "I will never leave you or forsake you." Always ask for God's help when you are going through trials.

It is through these trials that our salvation is secured.[1004] Keep in mind that the part we are to play can be here in provisional reality, or it may not be until we are in foundational reality that everything will be fully actualized. Trials always bring us closer to God, and in that closeness, we are better able to communicate with God. In our suffering, we are more attuned to the messages from the Holy Spirit. The crux of the matter is that we have choices; we can choose to pay attention to God, or we can ignore God's message. Hearing the message and responding to the small inner voice of truth does not always mean the suffering will stop; we just may be priming ourselves for more growth.[1005] If we choose to ignore the message, that will not stop the refiner's fire;[1006] it will just prolong the process. However, God is compassionate, and we will never be given more than we are able to bear.[1007]

Everyone that is called has a role to fulfill in God's divine plan. "For we are His workmanship, created in Christ Jesus for good works, which God prepared beforehand so that we would walk in them."[1008] God began the process of our salvation both globally and individually before we were born into provisional reality.[1009] Globally, this was accomplished by Christ's death on the cross. Individually, this happens when we apply the sacrifice of Jesus Christ to our life through faith and accept that Christ is our personal Savior.[1010] We are enveloped in this process because our calling from God is irrevocable.[1011] The primary responsibility of any Christian is obedience,[1012] getting through all of life's challenges so that God can mold us into the person he wants us to be.[1013] "The horse is prepared for the day of battle, but victory belongs to the Lord."[1014] We are created by God, he knew us before we were born,[1015] and he created us in the womb.[1016] God has even determined the number of days we will be alive.[1017] He has a specific role for us to perform. We must be in possession of the right character traits, not only for performing our role but also to be successful in completing our good works. It took Moses forty years in the wilderness to be readied for the work God was preparing for him. Half of a normal person's life was the time needed to develop and evolve Moses's faith, character, and attitude.

Jonah had a crash course. He needed to be molded for his responsibility and endured a very severe experience for a short period to instill his obedience. God told Jonah to go to the people of Nineveh and preach repentance because their wickedness was great.[1018] Jonah did not like the people of Nineveh; he did not want them to be saved. He instead wished for God's wrath to be upon them. He calculated that if he went and preached, God would spare them. If he did not give them the message and they did not repent, God would destroy them. Therefore, instead of going to Nineveh, he went the other way.[1019] God needed to teach Jonah obedience. Three days in the stomach of a great fish,[1020] I think, would mold anyone into perfect obedience. Jonah's challenge was obedience to God. The intensity of the experience can remedy that in a short period of time. Personality changes are a lot more complicated and generally require a process of evolution over time, with many starts and stops, depending on our cooperation. It took Moses forty years to bring the changes in him for a life of work. Jonah took three days' training for a very brief mission. God interacts with us in

THINGS TO COME

a variety of ways: through correction, through blessings, through guidance from the Holy Spirit and by protecting us from danger. Jonah's story is simple and straightforward, and our lives can be a lot more complicated. However, simple instructions are the easiest to follow. "Some assembly required" applies to all of us.

DISCIPLINE OF LOVE

Another means of God's intervention for correction aside from life's trials is through discipline. Simply put, discipline is God's means of correcting our erring ways,[1021] in much the same manner as a father disciplines his child.[1022] Godly discipline in one form or another is an experience that all of God's children will endure.[1023] Discipline from God, for most of us, is accomplished by God's direct intervention in our lives.

However, if we are attuned to our calling and sensitive to the prompting of the Holy Spirit, we can see God at work in our lives every day.[1024]

For the most part, discipline is necessary because of the influences of Satan, his minions, and our propensity for wanting to live life by our standards and not God's. God disciplines us because of his love for us[1025] so that we will be motivated to learn and obey his statutes and commandments. It is God's desire that we should inherit his kingdom, to be with him for all eternity.[1026]

Parents discipline their children when they perceive that they have gone astray or when they are not putting forth their best effort. We all want the best for our children and want to see them heading down "the narrow path" and making the best of their opportunities. God has similar motives when he disciplines us, his children. However, when God disciplines, it is with a view to the realization of the high and holy purposes that God has determined for those that he has called.[1027] Godly discipline is first and foremost for our good in our process of sanctification. If we are deviating from our intended mark, we need to be brought back on track, or we will not reach our destination. Knowing about the human parent-child relationship gives us insights, intuitively, and from observing the world around us[1028] so that it is apparent, by example, that God is working in our lives. When children are deviating from our expectations, whether it's academic performance or unacceptable behavior, they can expect that we will bring some pressure to bear to modify their behavior. We as children of God are in the same type of a relationship. Confession is self-judgment. Repentance and obedience serves to rend unnecessary any continued painful discipline from God, just as the apologies from our children soften our resolve. However, all confession requires repentance, which is a promise to turn from that specific sin and not to repeat it.[1029] Suffering keeps us from sinning.[1030] Discipline serves to check our wayward ways and ensure our continued sanctification. However, discipline is not the only intervention God will use to correct his own or to ensure our continued development. Confession and a realization of the changes that we need to make are the intended outcome of discipline.[1031] God resorts to discipline for his chosen ones[1032] that are still sinful and rebellious[1033] so that they will not be condemned along with the rest of the cosmos world[1034] and its population of unregenerate people. Discipline will get us back on track; its intensity and duration will be exactly that which was required for God to accomplish his objective, not one tear, or one day, or one sigh more. Discipline is the route for those that are seeking their own path.[1035]

CHASTISEMENT FROM THE LORD

Chastisement is for those that have committed themselves to Christ, and although committed, there are still character development issues that need to be addressed. Chastisement has more of a parallel to Christ's suffering than to discipline. Through our suffering, we are to become more Christlike[1036] and to continue in our development of our obedience to God.[1037]

Here is the whole point about repeated godly discipline and chastisement. Life would be much easier if, when God changes us, we would stay changed;[1038] there was a reason God wanted us to change to begin with.

God is forcing a change in us; we are in need of some type of an adjustment, in obedience, in faith, in our character, or in our relationships. However, all too often, once we have come through our trials, we go right back to where or who we were before the trial. Once God has changed us—whether it is in obedience, humbleness, patience, faithfulness, or our spirituality or self-control[1039]—whatever change he has made, we should maintain that changed nature. If we do not, we are setting ourselves up to repeat a period of chastisement. God may also assign the task that was ours to perform to someone else, and we will lose our opportunity to store up rewards for ourselves in heaven. Discipline is used for correction or to change our sinful behavior. Chastisement, although more severe than discipline, is used for education and character development within the child of God. Both discipline and chastisement are a demonstration of the divine love God has for us. Everyone that is chastised is aware through the Holy Spirit why he or she is being chastised. We even understand the love that is involved in this process. In order for us to be aware that the messages are from the Holy Spirit, we have to first understand that trails have little to do with provisional reality. Provisional reality is only the setting for the godly supernatural experience. Life is God's classroom.

The solution comes in our responding to God's lesson, in our obedience to his will. What is the lesson? That is the information that comes from the Holy Spirit. We can benefit if we are only receptive enough to receive it. Where am I falling short? What is amiss in my life? What is it about me that is not complete that God would like to see? What is preventing me from accomplishing my mission? This process can be very frustrating if you do not have a good understanding of what God requires of you. However, all of the answers are available in the Bible and through the aid of the Holy Spirit. A good way to avoid all of the testing is to have a thorough understanding of God's requirements. Scripture is very explicit about what we should and should not do. Read the Scriptures, and If you love Me, obey My commandments, and you will be richly blessed. An integral part of this process is prayer and introspection. Usually the first answer to come to us is from the Holy Spirit, and that is the one we try to rationalize away. We may not know during the process what is being accomplished; however, if we submit to the experience, we will know after we have come through it. All of us need to be tested and sometimes seemingly to our limit.[1040] "He who has begun a perfect work in you will continue until the day of Jesus Christ."[1041] The intuitive sense we have about our specific trial is the imparting of the truth to us by the Holy Spirit. The process is to render us receptive to obedience so that God may accomplish his will for our life. That does not always mean people will immediately respond to the correction. Some may act with defiance and stray further; some may become angry with God,[1042] and that is because they do not have a submissive spirit to God's sovereignty, and consequently, they are acting in rebellion toward God. Additionally, because of our empirical cognitive style, some people just do not get it. They do not understand that God is sovereign and that he is exercising his right over his children.

Supernatural things do happen in our lives in provisional reality. They are like the seeds planted in the parable in the book of Matthew.[1043] Some seeds fell on rocky places where the roots could not develop, so the believer had no firm root in himself, no firm foundation in his religion, and no trust in God, and at the first sign of affliction, he immediately fell away from the faith.[1044] Other seeds fell among the thorns, which is likened to receiving the faith; however, the concerns of this life and wanting to have more material things chokes out the person's faith, and they are unfruitful.[1045] Other seeds fell by the side of the road, which is an inappropriate place for seeding, because the roots cannot develop. A faith that has no roots or commitment is vulnerable, and the evil one can easily come by and steal the word because this person's faith is so immature that they do not understand their own spirituality, nor do they understand the relationship they are to have with God.[1046] They trust men, not God.[1047] Life is not a rehearsal; it is the real thing, and only Christians are getting out alive.

We are cautioned in the book of Job, Proverbs, and Isaiah 45:9 about being angry with God.[1048] Instead, we are to have the right attitude and consider trials good experiences and a needed adjustment to who we are. Defiance in these circumstances is not the outright rebellion of Satan. It is rather a frustration caused by a lack of understanding of God's sovereignty. It is a failure to trust God in that he is a God of his word and that all things do work for the best to those that love the Lord. The challenge with being submissive to God is that in the cosmos world system we have been deceived by Satan that we have our rights. Only from a kingdom perspective are we able to see these trying circumstances as course changes, warnings, and lessons from God. It may take a while to figure it all out, but if we are humble, submissive, obedient, responsive to the prompting of the Holy Spirit, praying for answers, and reading Scripture, then the answers, wisdom, and insight will come.

There are many paths from which we may choose. However, there is only one path to righteousness. There are many paths we all have for our particular idiosyncratic walk with the Lord.[1049] "The path is wide that leads to destruction and narrow is the gate and constricted is the way that leads to salvation and few are those that find it."[1050] The particular path we are to walk to accomplish the things that God requires of us in our process of sanctification is referred to as our calling.[1051] The process of sanctification will result in an eternal existence in God's presence.

There are two key elements here for understanding life's trials. First, our calling is irrevocable.[1052] That means if we are one of those that were predestined by God, or called, He will guide us until we meet the requirements of that calling. Just as he did Moses, Noah, David, Mary, Jonah, Joseph, et al. The calling, being irrevocable, necessitates the corrective measures of discipline, chastisement, and pruning; they are all a part of our process of sanctification.

Second, God is sovereign; everything will conform to his eternal plan.[1053] The more resisting we do, the longer and more frequent or severe the trials will be. The Christian may avoid repeated chastisement and discipline if they respond. By correcting their erring ways, they will further develop their faith and their relationship with God.

All of these processes, discipline, chastisement, and pruning are godly interventions into our lives to ensure God's perfect will is achieved for our lives and for God's eternal plan. The Christian's err may not only be sin; it may also be that the Christian is not heading in the direction that God has intended for them. In addition, it can be that their current path will not bring them to their ultimate destiny of salvation. It could be that one's current path will not lead them to the work that they have been preordained to accomplish.[1054]

Rebellion is the path of pain, sorrow, hurt, suffering, and death. However, our free-will choices can eliminate most of this and soften the rest. The process for God's plan: his elect, were predetermined before the world was created, and they are called by God. The elect are wired to be able to respond to the Holy Spirit and come to faith in Jesus Christ. Because we love him, we obey his commandments.[1055] This obedience results in the right character reflecting the characteristics, or fruits, of the Holy Spirit. True Christians will be those who will choose good over evil[1056] and are able to overcome sin. Their behavior will manifest faith, obedience, and submission to God's will. We are to put aside all bitterness, anger, wrath, and slander, as well as all malice.[1057] We are instructed

to be kind to one another, tenderhearted, forgiving, and walking in love just as Christ did.[1058] We are also to know with certainty that no immoral or impure person has an inheritance with Christ and God in eternity.[1059]

PRUNING: SO THAT WE MAY BEAR MORE FRUIT

Pruning is the process whereby our challenges cause us to grow in faith. During pruning, our challenges are specifically directed at our spiritual growth. Pruning is unique to Christian's that are on the right path. It is God's [1060] manner of growing us in our process of sanctification. We are pruned so that we may bear more fruit, that is to say, that we will be encouraged to develop to our full potential. "Every branch in Me that bears no fruit, He takes it away: and every branch that bears fruit, He prunes it, that it may bear more fruit."[1061]

There is a concept within psychology called self-actualization. If one is self-actualized, it means they have reached their full potential, whatever that potential is. They have been able to maximize all of their genetic proclivities and have been able to maximize themselves within the context of their environment. Pruning is God's way of ensuring that we are self-actualized from a spiritual perspective. Bearing more fruit parallels maximizing our potential. "To those have been given much, much will be required."[1062] The much we have been given can certainly qualify as blessings. Blessings bestowed on us from God can have a multiplicity of manifestations. They can be our gifts from the Holy Spirit or the talents and abilities that God has blessed us with. He also blesses us with circumstances in provisional reality to use for the benefit of his kingdom. If we misuse these blessings or they are left underutilized, God will intervene to ensure our full potential is realized, and that his blessings are not ill-spent. Pruning is all rather on the positive side; it is instructional, and its purpose is to fine-tune us. How we use our blessings is summarized in the parables of Matthew: "Well done, good and faithful slave"[1063] or "Wicked and lazy slave."[1064] We know that God uses pruning so that we might grow and bear more fruit.[1065] The pruning processes are the challenges that God will put us through, the refiner's fire,[1066] so that we might achieve perfection in our faith.[1067]

When Jesus Christ is talking to his disciples and explaining their relationship, he uses the analogy that he is the vine, they are the branches, and God is the vinedresser.[1068] Christ explains that the only way his disciples can accomplish their tasks, to bear fruit, is through their relationship with Christ.[1069] Just as the only way the branches live is by the nourishment made available to them by their connectedness to the vine.[1070] The process by which the disciples will be able to accomplish their tasks is by maintaining their connectedness to Christ. This connectedness applies to us as well. Christ gives the disciples a blatant warning when he tells them that the branches that bear not fruit are cut off and thrown in the fire, and those that do bear fruit will be pruned so that they may bear more fruit.[1071]

The pruning process for us, is often painful, and is akin to the refiner's fire. It is how new growth is established by God in our lives. We can envision growth as change. After a pruning, we have reduced the size of the branch by cutting it back. However, by cutting back the branch, the nourishment from the vine can be channeled into producing more fruit because not as many nutrients will be required for the growth of wood. The development of our fruits of the spirit grow us spiritually. The wood is our growth and development under the influences of provisional reality.[1072] Pruning is a deliberate act done at exactly the right time of the year to stimulate fruit production. Proper care and sustenance allows the cut ends to heal, and the branch produces more fruit than they would have without being pruned. If the pruned branch does not receive proper sustenance, the branch can develop decay and disease, as when our trials drive us away from God, breaking our connectedness and weakening our faith.

There are other references in Scripture with analogies to this process of purification or the refiner's fire.[1073] The refiner's fire is the process of purifying metals with heat. In the process of purification of silver, the application of heat causes the ore to separate from the silver.[1074] The ore and other impurities rise to the surface and may be skimmed off; what remains is pure silver. This process continues throughout the life of the Christian. The process of sanctification is a continual process of purification until we are transfigured and present with the Lord.

THE MOST EXTREME CASES

The whole process that God uses for our sanctification begins with our call and the work of the Holy Spirit. Our response to his call and yielding to the indwelling of the Holy Spirit is all part of our predestined mission. All through this process, God continues to interact with us to guide, teach, and mold our development to ensure our salvation and to develop us as citizens of an eternal kingdom.[1075] Through this process, if we have remained rebellious and continued to live in our sinful nature, which means we have been unwilling to yield to God's sovereignty and unwilling to be obedient, there is a final strategy.[1076]

Scourging is that major life-changing event that shocks us into awareness. Scourging is best characterized as a severe trial that is designed to break the will of one of God's elect that continues in rebellion and a self-directed lifestyle. It is reserved for those that have deviated so far from their intended path that their very soul is in jeopardy. They are following their own dictates, living in darkness by choice, and living a lifestyle characterized as sinful by God's standard. They are ignoring their conscience and have ignored the Holy Spirit for so long that they are no longer aware of the Holy Spirit's influence. Scourging is unlike discipline or chastisement because of its severity. Scourging is a last chance at retrieving someone from the dominion of darkness, and it is designed to conquer the will. It will result in a surrendered life, which is characterized by someone that has completely "turned around" or "turned over a new leaf."

We are all familiar with these types of situations; they are the materials of Christian testimonies. They are car accidents, abuse, cancer, attempted suicide, drug use, illnesses, job loss, alcoholism, participation in wars, to mention a few. They are events so shocking that when we experience and survive them, we understand that we are not in charge. We understand that we survived by the intervention and the grace of God. Our survival puts us in a reciprocating frame of mind, and we either want to pay God back, or we want to be a person worthy of being saved. This strictly provisional, yet supernatural, experience is mirrored by the person that discovers Christ as their Savior. However, it is not only their physical life that has been preserved; it is their eternal life as well. This type of an epiphany causes the changes in people that make believers out of those that were nonbelievers. It also impacts those that think they were doing enough to be safe but still enough removed to be in charge of their own life. Scourging is mentioned in Psalm 39:10 as something that overcomes someone, an overwhelming discipline that breaks the spirit or that can even consume a person's wealth. The implications here are that anything can be accomplished by God to ensure the salvation of one of his own. Nothing in this reality takes precedence over any element of foundational reality.

God's morality will be upheld in the universe and all of the inhabitants of heaven will be holy and perfect according to God's good and perfect will.

While it is true that all that is necessary to be saved is to believe in Jesus Christ as our savior, all of the other requirements—obeying the commandments, fighting the good fight, remaining steadfast, not being spotted by the world—all come naturally after we are saved. It is all done out of gratitude[1077] for our eternal salvation provided by the grace of God through the sacrifice of Christ and not through anything we have done. If the change in our behavior is not willfully forthcoming, we have to question whether we were really saved at all. Christ gave his life for us; we are to give our life to him.

THE GREAT TRIBULATION AND THE RAPTURE OF THE SAINTS

And the word of the LORD came to me, saying, "Son of man, speak to the sons of your people and say to them, 'If I bring a sword upon a land, and the people of the land take one man from among them and make him their watchman, and he sees the sword coming upon the land and blows on the trumpet and warns the people, then he who hears the sound of the trumpet and does not take warning, and a sword comes and takes him away, his blood will be on his *own* head. He heard the sound of the trumpet but did not take warning; his blood will be on himself. But had he taken warning, he would have delivered his life. But if the watchman sees the sword coming and does not blow the trumpet and the people are not warned, and a sword comes and takes a person from them, he is taken away in his iniquity; but his blood I will require from the watchman's hand.' Now as for you, son of man, I have appointed you a watchman for the house of Israel; so you will hear a message from My mouth and give them warning from Me. When I say to the wicked, 'O wicked man, you will surely die,' and you do not speak to warn the wicked from his way, that wicked man shall die in his iniquity, but his blood I will require from your hand. But if you on your part warn a wicked man to turn from his way and he does not turn from his way, he will die in his iniquity, but you have delivered your life." (Ezek. 33:1–9)

Scriptural prophecy states that in the end-times, there will be a time of tremendous distress on the earth and on its inhabitants. This time of distress is referred to as the tribulation or as "the hour of trial that is coming upon the whole habitable world."[1078] Trial in this application, according to the Greek text, is "a putting to proof by experiment of good or evil, discipline, or provocation." The tribulation ends when Christ returns to the earth on a white horse, wearing his robe dripping with blood, accompanied by his army, dressed in white linen, also riding on white horses.[1079] This event is referred to as Christ's second coming.

The word *rapture* does not appear in the Bible. However, in the original Greek translation of the New Testament the word *harpazō* is used in 1 Thessalonians 4:17, "Then we who are alive and remain will be caught up [*harpazō*] together with them in the clouds to meet the Lord in the air, and so we shall always be with the Lord." According to *Strong's Complete Dictionary of Bible Words*[1080], *harpazō* means, "to seize, catch [away, up], pluck, pull, take [by force]." This verse is most often cited as the Biblical truth of the impending rapture or the removal of the saints from the earth during the end-times.

The significance of the rapture and the tribulation period is that these are the events in the final days—the time of the end, or the last days of human history.[1081] The events will occur at the appointed time.[1082] Except for the remnant, everyone else will enter into eternity,[1083] either to the joy and peace of everlasting life in paradise, or to eternal suffering in the confines and damnation of hell forever.[1084]

There are three very distinctive and separate schools of thought on when the rapture will occur. Adherents to the three theories of thought are those who presume the rapture will occur before, during, or at the end of the tribulation. There are also those who believe that there will not be a rapture, so we must look to Scripture and not the precepts of men.

Those holding the belief that the rapture will happen before the tribulation begins are pre-tribulationists. They base their thinking on scriptural references that assert the brethren, or the elect, are "not in darkness," and "that day will not overtake us [the elect]."[1085] Additionally, Scripture reveals that God has not destined us for wrath.[1086] The assumption here is that the wrath of God is the tribulation period and that his children will not have to endure the great distress that is about to befall mankind.

Mid-tribulationists base their view on Scripture such as:

> For then there will be a great tribulation, such as has not occurred since the beginning of the world until now, nor ever shall. And unless those days had been cut short, no life would have been saved; but for the sake of the elect those days shall be cut short. (Matt. 24:21–22)

The understanding here is that if the elect are spared because the tribulation is cut short, they must be in the tribulation.

Finally, the post-tribulationists are those that believe that the rapture will not happen until after the great tribulation has run its course. "But the one who endures to the end, he shall be saved."[1087]

> But immediately after the tribulation of those days the sun will be darkened, and the moon will not give it's light, and the stars will fall from the sky, and the powers of the heavens will be shaken, and then *the sign* of the Son of Man will appear in the sky, and then all the tribes of the earth will mourn, and they will see the Son of Man coming on the cloud of the sky with power and great glory. (Matt. 24:29–30)

Christ said that when he returns on the clouds, that would be the sign of the end, and this verse states that immediately after the tribulation, the Son of Man will appear.

We cannot ignore the fact that, every Scripture is God-breathed and profitable for teaching, for reproof, for correction, for instruction, in righteousness[1088] It is not our role to interpret Scripture such that it supports a preconceived position or conjectures. We must let Scripture and the Holy Spirit guide us in our understanding.[1089] Additionally, we must be careful of trying to define events and situations or reading too much into what the word actually says. Twenty percent of Scripture is devoted to prophecy, hence prophecy is too important to ignore.

There are four instances recorded in Scripture where Daniel and John, who are receiving visions of future events, are told not to write or reveal the nature of an event that relates to the last days. John is instructed by his revealing angel not to declare what the seven peals of thunder spoke.[1090]

Gabriel instructs Daniel not to write down his last dream but to keep it secret.[1091]

> The ram which you saw with the two horns represents the kings of Media and Persia. The shaggy goat represents the kingdom of Greece…The broken horn and the four horns that arose in its place represent four kingdoms which will arise from his nation in the latter period, a king will arise, insolent and skilled in intrigue. His power will be mighty, but not by his own power… and will destroy mighty men and the holy people. He will cause deceit to succeed by his influence and he will destroy many while they are at ease, but keep the vision secret. (Dan. 8:20–23, 24, 25, 26)

Alexander the Great from Greece followed the Medes and the Persians as the next Middle East kingdom. The four kingdoms that arose in its place were the Seleucids, then the Romans, followed by the Mongols, then the last Middle Eastern empire, that of the Ottoman Turks. The next to emerge will be the rule of the Antichrist, whose power comes from Satan.

The second time Daniel is told not to reveal what he knows is commanded by the angel Michael.

> And at that time Michael shall stand up, the great ruler who stands for the sons of your people, (the angel Michael, guards the people of Israel). And there shall be a time of distress, such as has not been from the existence of a nation until that time, [tribulation]. And at that time your people shall be delivered, everyone that shall be found written in the Book [remnant]. And those who are wise shall shine as the brightness of the firmament, and those who turn many to righteousness as the stars forever and ever [overcomers]. But you, O Daniel, *shut up the words and seal the book* to the end time. Many shall run to and fro, and knowledge shall be increase. (Dan. 12:1–4, IHOT)

The above reference to knowledge increasing refers to the appointed time of the end; as we get closer, more information that was previously concealed by John and Daniel will become available from the Holy Spirit. It does not mean that one of the signs of the end-times is that secular knowledge will increase. The world's store of knowledge continues to increase with every generation and will continue to do so until the end. Christ tells us the Holy Spirit will lead us into all truth; and he will disclose what is to come, the increased knowledge will be his revelations.[1092] The placement of the words in parentheses will become apparent as we proceed.

The next warning for silence from Michael takes on a very ominous tone.

> And I heard the man dressed in linen who swore by Him who lives forever that it would be for a time, times, and half a time, and as soon as they finish breaking the power of the holy people, all these events will be complete. As for me, I heard but could not understand; so I said, "My lord, what will be the outcome of

these events?" And he said, "Go your way Daniel, for *these words are concealed and sealed up until the end time.*" (Dan. 12:7–10)

When Christ had spoken his last to his disciples after his crucifixion, he was lifted up and while "they were looking a cloud received him out of their sight."[1093] Immediately, two angels appeared and told the disciples, just as Jesus had been taken up, so would He return.[1094] This is very different from the second coming of Christ as recorded in Revelation where it says, "And I saw heaven opened, and behold a white horse and He who sat upon it is called Faithful, and True; and in righteousness He judges and wages war."[1095]

When Christ returns in the clouds to gather His elect, this event will constitute the rapture.[1096] We are told in Scripture that the Holy Spirit will be with us forever.[1097] We are also told that "the mystery of lawlessness already is working; only he holding back now, until it comes out of the midst."[1098] It is generally believed that if the Holy Spirit cannot be taken from us, and if Christ is going to call the Holy Spirit to heaven, we must accompany the Holy Spirit to heaven, initiating the rapture. Scripture says he will be taken out of the midst; it does not specifically say he is taken to heaven. Additionally, the Holy Spirit can be taken out of the midst; even if that does mean taken to heaven, the point is that his restraint is removed. The Holy Spirit is omnipresent and indwells every believer so he can remain indwelling every believer even if he is taken out of the midst.

There are several references to Christ returning on a cloud for His elect, and one reference as to when He actually does return on a cloud. One of the references is in Matthew, and we will get to that in a moment. The other references are noted below, and we have already looked at the reference in the book of Acts.

> For the Lord Himself will descend from heaven with a shout… Then we who remain alive will be caught up [*harpazō*, raptured] together with them in *the clouds* to a meeting with the Lord

THINGS TO COME

in the air, and so we will always be with the Lord. (1 Thess. 4:16–17, IGNT)

Behold, He is coming *with the clouds* and every eye will see Him. (Rev. 1:7)

I was looking in the night visions. And behold, one like the Son of man came with *the clouds* of the heavens. (Dan. 7:13, IHOT)

Jesus said to him, "You said it. I tell you more. From this time you shall see the Son of man sitting off the right hand of power, and coming *on the clouds of the heavens.*" (Matt. 26:64, IGNT)

And then they will see the Son of man coming *in the clouds* with great power and glory. (Mark 13:26)

There is also a very interesting reference to Christ returning on a cloud to Egypt in Isaiah, which will incite Egyptians against Egyptians, and they will fight against each other. Ultimately, the Egyptians will return to worshipping the Lord.[1099] The majority of Egyptians were Christian from AD 400 to 800, even after the Muslim invasion and conquest. The Coptic Christians, as Christians are called in Egypt, remain the largest Christian community in the Middle East.

The prelude to the tribulation, according to Paul in 2 Thessalonians 2:3, is that the apostasy must come first, and the man of lawlessness is revealed. The apostasy is defined in *Strong's Dictionary* as "a defection from the truth, falling away, forsaking." Apostasy, in this context, is any theory or teaching that takes us away from Scriptural truths and attempts to lead us astray. Christ said to Pilate, "For this I have been born, and for this I have come into the world, to testify to the truth."[1100] The role of the church, according to Paul is "the church of the living God, the pillar and support of the truth."[1101] "For this is good and acceptable before

God our deliverer, who desires all men to be delivered and come to a full knowledge of the truth."[1102] The apostasy of the church, the defection from the truth, has begun today in the current teachings in many churches. When the church fails in its primary objective, Christ will intervene. The apostasy of today's church, fueled by satanic influences in provisional reality, will culminate in the progressive birth pangs of the teachings of the antichrist.

In Matthew, Christ explains to his disciples that there will be signs of the end-times, and as we get closer to the end, the signs will increase in intensity and frequency, like birth pangs.[1103] As the defection from the truth of the church continues through its birth pangs, its increasing apostasy, false doctrines will increase in frequency and intensity. The apostasy will ultimately culminate as recorded in Revelation.

> And it deceives those dwelling on the earth, because of the signs which were given to it to do before the beast, saying to those dwelling on the earth to make an image to the beast who has the wound of the sword and lived. And was given to it to give a spirit to the image of the beast, so that the image of the beast might even speak, and might cause as many as would not worship the image of the beast to be killed. And the small and the great, and the rich and the poor, and the freeman and the slaves, it causes that they give to them all a mark on their right hand, or on their forehead, even that not any could buy or sell, except the one having the mark, or the name of the beast or the number of his name. (Rev. 13:14–17, IGNT)

> As if the Day of the Lord has come. Do not let anyone deceive you in any way, because, that Day will not come unless first comes the falling away (apostasy), and the man of sin is revealed, the son of perdition. The one opposing and exalting himself over everything being called God, or object of worship, so as for him to sit in the temple of God as God, showing himself that he is a god. (2 Thess. 2:2–4, IGNT)

Many Christians believe that just before the horrendous times of the tribulation begin, believers will be removed from the earth in the rapture, citing verses such as, "to wait for His Son from heaven, whom He raised from the dead, that is Jesus, who rescues us from the wrath to come."[1104] In 1 Thessalonians, Paul is addressing chapter 5 to the brethren. "For God has not destined us for wrath, but for obtaining salvation through our Lord Jesus Christ."[1105] The concept here of salvation is the qualifier for wrath in these verses. In the context of salvation, the wrath of God is the wrath that resides on all unrepentant sinners, all who have not put their faith in Christ. Christ's death on the cross was the propitiation, the appeasement of God's wrath, for all believers. This means that because believers are trusting in Christ sacrificial death to remove their sins, they will not experience the wrath of God at judgment.[1106] This is not the wrath of the tribulation referred to in Revelation. "For the great day of His wrath has come; and who is able to stand?"[1107]

The same can be said of "and eagerly to await His Son from Heaven, whom He raised from the dead, Jesus, the One delivering us from the wrath to come."[1108] Again in this verse, we understand that wrath is taken in context with the rest of the verse. True believers are delivered from the wrath to come by Jesus being raised from the dead—everlasting life instead of "he who does not obey the Son shall not see life, but the wrath of God abides on him."[1109] The escape from wrath is God's wrath on unrepentant sinners; it is not an escape from the tribulation, "the hour of testing which is about to come upon the whole world."[1110]

We must keep in mind that Christ was the propitiation, which means that He appeased the wrath of God by taking all of our sins onto himself. Thereby, we that have put our trust in Christ will be spared from God's wrath at the time of judgment, as recorded in the Psalms. "Thou dost hate all who do iniquity."[1111] To be a sinner simply means that you sin as we all do; however, sinners that are unrepentant, their sins remain with them, as does the wrath of God remain on them.

TOM NEWMAN

THE APOSTASY OF THE CHURCH

The three synoptic gospels and the book of John give us a biographical look at Christ and his three-year ministry. During Christ's ministry, he preached the gospel message. "Repent for the kingdom of heaven is at hand."[1112] He also taught his disciples and readied them for their world outreach of the gospel message. The activities of the disciples and the Holy Spirit resulted in the formation and spread of the gospel through the realization of the church. The gospels end with the crucifixion and resurrection of Christ. Christ reappears in the book of Revelation, and one of the first things he does is make an assessment of the seven churches—what he finds favorable, and what he has against them.

There are a couple of ways to look at the seven churches in Revelation. One is that the churches represent the evolution of the church through time. Second is to view the seven churches as the types of churches that exist today. Both ways are a means of gaining an understanding and are equally true and give us an understanding of a conceptualization of the church. One thing is obvious: churches have some shortcomings. Christ's criticisms of the church give us an understanding of what apostasy looks like. The seven churches referenced in Revelation 2–3 were all located in Turkey.

The church at Ephesus:

> I know your works and your labors and your patience, and that you cannot bear evil ones… And I know you bore up and on account of My name you have labored and have not wearied. *But I have this against you* that you left your first love. Then remember from where you have fallen, and repent, and do the first works. And if not, I am coming to you quickly, and will remove your lampstand from its place, unless you repent. But you have this that you hate the works of the Nicolaitans, which I also hate. (Rev. 2:1–7)

To the church in Smyrna:

> I know your works, and the affliction, and the poverty; but you are rich. And I know the evil speaking of those saying themselves to be Jews [Christians], and they are not, but are a synagogue [church] of Satan. (Rev. 2:8–11)

To the church at Pergamum:

> I know your works, and where you dwell, where the throne of Satan is. And you hold My name, and did not deny My faith. *But I have a few things against you.* That you have there those holding the teachings of Balaam, who taught Balak to throw a stumbling-block before the sons of Israel to eat idol-sacrifices, and to commit fornication. So you also hold to the teachings of the Nicolaitans, which thing I hate. Repent but if not, I will come to you quickly, and I will make war with them by the sword of My mouth. (Rev. 2:12–17)

To the church in Thyatira:

> I know your works, and the love, and the ministry, and the faith, and your patience, and your works; and the last more than the first. *But I have a few things against you*, that you allow the woman Jezebel to teach, she saying herself to be a prophetess, and to cause My slaves to go astray, and to commit fornication, and to eat idol-sacrifices. And I gave time to her that she might repent of her fornications. And she did not repent... unless they repent of their works... And I will give to each of you according to your works. But I say to you and to the rest in Thyatira, as many as do not have this teaching, and who did not know the deep things of Satan, but what you have, hold until I shall come." (Rev. 2:18–28)

TOM NEWMAN

To the church in Sardis:

> To the church in Sardis. I know your deeds, that you have a name that you are alive, but you are dead. Wake up be watching and establish the things that remain, which are about to die; for I have not found your deeds completed in the sight of My God. So remember what you have received and heard; and keep it, and repent. Therefore if you do not wake up, I will come like a thief, and you will not know at what hour I will come to you. But you have a few people in Sardis who have not soiled their garments; and they will walk with Me in white, for they are worthy. (Rev. 3:1–6)

> And to the angel of the church in Philadelphia write; He who is holy, who is true, who has the key of David… I know your deeds, Behold, I have put before you an open door which no one can shut, because you have a little power, and have kept My word, and have not denied My name. Behold, I will cause those of the synagogue of Satan, who say that they are Jews and are not, but lie – I will make them come and bow down at your feet, and make them know that I have loved you. *Because you have kept the word of My patience, I also will keep you from the hour of trial which is about to come upon the whole world, in order to try those who dwell on the earth.* I am coming quickly; hold fast what you have, so that no one will take your crown. (Rev. 3:7–13)

To the church in Laodicea:

> I know your deeds, that you are neither cold nor hot; I wish that you were cold or hot. So because you are lukewarm, and neither hot nor cold, I will spit you out of My mouth. Because you say, "I am rich, and have become wealthy, and have need of nothing," and you do not know that you are wretched and miserable and poor and blind and naked. Those whom I love, I reprove and discipline; therefore be zealous and repent Behold, I stand at the door and knock; if anyone hears My voice and opens the door,

I will come in to him and will dine with him, and he with Me. (Rev. 3:14–22)

Christ also had some things to say to the Pharisees and the Sadducees, the governance of the church in Jerusalem. The things that Christ had against them were that they put their traditions above the commandments of God,[1113] they were teaching as doctrine the precepts of men,[1114] they valued the offering more than the altar,[1115] and they neglected the weightier provisions of the law.[1116]

> Even so you too outwardly appear righteous to men, but inwardly you are full of hypocrisy and lawlessness. (Matt. 23:28)

The first thing to notice is that the church in Philadelphia is the only church without any condemnation from Christ. This is also the only church where Christ says he will keep them from the hour of testing that is about to come on the whole habitable earth[1117] "because they have kept the word of My patience and not denied My name." *Strong's* defines patience as "to stay under, have fortitude, persevere, and endure constancy," which is a quality of being faithful, dependable, and unchanging. We can consider the members of this church as true committed Christians, overcomers, living a life in obedience to Christ. This does not mean that only a specific church denomination has it right. Rather those individual believers, with constancy and a personal relationship with Christ, live in complete obedience, possessing attributes that Christ considers worthy will qualify as overcomers.[1118] As well as a few mentioned in Sardis and Thyatira who do not hold to false teachings. Those who walk in a manner worthy of the calling with which you have been called.[1119] Christ died for us; we should live for Him.[1120]

It's not really clear from historical accounts what the Nicolaitians believed other than general references to eating things sacrificed to idols and fornication, which may be linked to temple prostitution. The definition is intentionally vague so that the lesson may apply to any church doctrine that is contrary to the teachings of Christ and therefore worthy of condemnation. To remove the lampstand means that Christ will remove His Spirit from that church.

Christ says the church at Ephesus has left its first love, which was preaching the truth of the gospel message of Christ. A church's primary responsibility is preserving the truth in professing and protecting the gospel message to and for the congregation.[1121] "The manifold wisdom of God might now be made known through the church to the rulers and the authorities."[1122] He tells them to remember their origin and to turn back to a church that is consistent with Christ's original design of preserving and presenting the truth. These are an assessment; however, they are also warnings for churches to repent and return to professing the truth of the gospel message of Jesus Christ. "And have kept My word, and have not denied My name."

The church is to profess the whole Gospel message, that salvation comes through Christ alone by faith alone in grace alone, and that the wrath of God abides on every unrepentant sinner. In fact, those seeking to be justified by the law have fallen from grace.[1123]

> For by grace you have been saved through faith; and that not of yourself, it is the gift of God, not as a result of works, that no one should boast. (Eph. 2:8–10)

> Nevertheless, knowing that a man is not justified by the works of the Law but through faith in Christ Jesus, even we have believed in Christ Jesus that we may be justified by faith in Christ, and not by the works of the Law; since by the works of the Law shall no flesh be justified. (Gal. 2:16)

Paul says that he preaches the whole gospel.[1124] This means he teaches the good news as well as the bad news. There can be no good news without the bad news. We are sinners, for there is none that is without sin, and all of us are in need of a Savior. A Savior from what? From the wrath of God against all sinners.[1125] Because of false doctrines and false teachings, the precepts of men, Christians are deceived into complacency and slothfulness of inactivity. When what we need are patriots and zealots. We can teach that God so loved the world that He sent His only begotten Son as a propitiation for our sins. But that is only half of the equation; the other half is that God sends unrepentant sinners to hell. This is the good news and the bad, and there really is no good news unless you understand the bad news. A church that teaches only the good news is a church in apostasy. We can only seek the God of Zion, Christ, after we understand the God of Mount Sinai.[1126] "The fear of Him may remain with you, so that you may not sin."[1127]

Why would a church just teach the good news, to abandon its first love? So that no one in the congregation is offended. Some people are more comfortable not knowing that there will be consequences for their behavior and that the wrath of God abides on them. If people love the darkness rather than the light because the light exposes their sin, then just preach that God is love, and He loves you in spite of your sins. This is completely contrary to what Scripture teaches. People made to feel uncomfortable in a church will look for a new church, hence, the strategy of churches is to soften the gospel message. Many people do not want to commit their life to Christ; they are afraid they will have to give up too much, too much stuff in provisional reality—the temporary stuff. The church responds by leaving their first love. They water down the gospel message and preach easy grace and that God loves a sinner.[1128]

There are some commonalities here, but I will have to define the fine line that separates naiveté from apostates. There are pseudo-Christians because they are deceived by having adopted the false teachings from the church or self-deceived by thinking they have a better understanding of Scripture than what it actually says and then profess what they think is truth. Such as adopting the philosophy of the Hindu Gandhi who used to say, "Hate the sin, love the sinner." This is an untenable proposition; you cannot separate the sin from the sinner. God does not send sins to hell; he sends unrepentant sinners to hell. The watered-down gospel is a deception that causes complacency in Christians and actually quenches the Holy Spirit in His work. We are told not to quench the Spirit. Pseudo-Christians think that because God is love, all is forgiven by a little prayer, an "I'm sorry" prayer, yet they do not show reverence or fear or obedience to Christ because they don't have to; it's really not required from the God of love.

In the Greek, there are ten different uses of the word love. In the instance of "God is love (*agapē*)," the interpretation is benevolence. In the instance of, "love your neighbor as yourself (*agapaō*)," the interpretation is in a moral or social sense.

The book of Acts profiles the foundation of the church. There are thirteen major sermons in the book of Acts. Ten times we are told about fear, reverence, and obedience to the Lord. Never once is there a mention of love for a sinner or of God's love for sinners; in fact, the word *love* is not even mentioned in the book of Acts.

> When I say to the wicked one, surely you shall die and you do not speak to warn the wicked one from his way, the wicked one shall die in his iniquity. But I will require his blood from your hand. But you if you warn the wicked from his way, to turn from it, and he does not turn from it, and he does not turn from his way he shall die in his iniquity, but you have delivered your soul…I do not have pleasure in the death of the wicked, except in the wicked turning from his way, and so to live. Turn, turn from your evil ways! For why will you die. (Ezek. 33:8–9, 11, IHOT)

Let's be perfectly clear about what the Holy Spirit means in Scripture by and how he defines love. Love is not some emotional sentimentality. Love is obedience, obedience to all of the commandments of Scripture. The only activities in provisional reality that are of any consequence are actions that have an implication for foundational reality. "If you love Me, obey My commandments."[1129]

> For this is the love [*agapē*] of God that we should keep His commandments. (1 John 5:3)

> And this is love [*agapē*] that we should walk according to His commandments. (2 John 1:6)

Love here is rendered benevolence—charity.

> He who does not love [*agapaō*] Me does not keep my word. (John 14:24)

This is the social or moral sense application, the teachings of Christ and the law of Moses as it were. Excluding the ceremonial and sacrificial precepts of the Old Testament, as these were replaced by Christ.

If we know someone that does not consider Christ as their personal Savior, we are to give them the gospel message. We are to turn fellow believers from their sins; this is the reciprocation of the love that was expressed to us—obedience.[1130] "Speak to the wicked one." God desires that all men come to a knowledge of the truth.[1131] When we tell a sinner God loves them anyway in spite of their sin, we are lying to that person heading for destruction. If we loved them, we would tell them the truth. "Repent for the kingdom of heaven is at hand." "Anyone who goes too far and does not abide in the teaching of Christ, does not have God, the one who abides in the teaching, he has both the Father and the Son."[1132] "When I say to the wicked one, surely you shall die and you do not speak to warn the wicked one he will die in his inequity. But I will require his blood from your hand."

TOM NEWMAN

We sometimes confuse love with compassion. Love is obedience. Compassion is the expression of Christ's love within us.[1133] Christ enlightens every man[1134] to help, care for and safeguard others, especially in ensuring their eternal salvation. "As God's chosen people, cloth yourselves with compassion."[1135] The compassion we feel towards others is pure; it is from Christ and comes directly to us from the presence of the Holy Spirit within us. Compassion has no ulterior motives. The only problem we as fallen people have with compassion is when we ignore the source and we quench the Spirit. God tells us that he will give us a new heart and put a new Spirit within us; He will remove our heart of stone and give us a heart of flesh.[1136] However, there is a precondition. "I will put My Spirit within you and make you to walk in that which is in My statutes, and My judgments you shall keep and do them."[1137] When we as committed Christians express our compassion to others, it brings glory to God. When nonbelievers and pseudo-Christians express compassion, it brings glory to them. The Holy Spirit works on nonbelievers and from within for Christians. We are also warned not to quench our spirit of compassion.[1138] Our compassion motivates us to protect the oppressed, disadvantaged, "the widow and the orphan."

Love is best understood by Christ in the garden of Gethsemane.[1139] We need to understand Christ's prayers from a perspective of foundational reality. A provisional view would have us see the cup that Christ wanted to pass from Him as the trial—flogging, ridicule, and ultimate death in His crucifixion. Christ knew it would soon be over; it was all in provisional reality. We are even told that for the joy that awaited Him He went through with the preordained plan.[1140] "God so loved (social and moral sense) the world that He gave His only begotten Son, that whosoever shall believe, will have eternal life.[1141]" God loves mankind, his creation; in a general sense, he does not love sinners.

We define Christ's love from this in that He laid down His life for us[1142] for our salvation, which means sparing us from the

wrath of God.[1143] However, what is really at stake here and the true definition of love is how much He was willing to do in obedience. "For this is the love of God, that we keep His commandments."[1144] Christ, being God, being perfectly righteous, perfectly holy, was about to take all of the sins of the world on Himself, to sacrifice His perfect Holiness and become what He and His Father utterly detest—sin, sinfulness. Fear (reverence) of the Lord is the beginning of wisdom.[1145] We cannot understand anything until we understand the purity and holiness of God the Father, Christ the Son, and the Holy Spirit, which we will never fully understand in provisional reality.[1146] Our humility comes from understanding that Christ sacrificed his complete holiness to take our sins on himself. "Woe is me, for I am ruined! Because I am a man of unclean lips, and I live among a people of unclean lips; For my eyes have seen the King, the Lord of Hosts."[1147] When you try to understand the holiness of God, you begin to understand what Christ gave up for us and what love really is. When Christ was covered in our sins, God could not bear the sight and turned His gaze away from His Son. Christ cried out, "Father, why have you forsaken Me,"[1148] I have done what You asked and now You cannot even bear to look at Me! This is love: the expression of complete obedience to God, obedience unto death. And God has said to us, "This is My beloved Son, listen to Him."[1149] Unconditional love exists within the person of the Holy Trinity and with our children from the age of about one or two, until they are spotted by the world. This is the unconditional obedience and trust Christ is talking about when he says we must be as children to enter into the kingdom.[1150]

There is a simple equation defining God's love—His conditional love:

> He who has My commandments and keeps them, he it is who loves Me, and he who loves Me shall be loved by My Father, and I will love him, and will disclose Myself to him. (John 14:21)

If anyone loves Me, he will keep My word; and My Father will love him, and We will come to him, and make Our abode with him. (John 14:23)

All of these references to love are *agapaō*, the social and moral sense.

If you keep the commandments of Christ, you are demonstrating your love for Christ by your obedience. If you are demonstrating your love for Christ by your obedience, then, and only then, the Father loves you. "For who has known the mind of the Lord, or who became his counselor?"[1151] We should take God at his word and understand his definition and not reinterpret what he has said to something more to our liking.

> You have wearied the Lord with your words. Yet you say, "How have we wearied Him?" In that you say, "Everyone who does evil is good in the sight of the Lord, and He delights in them." (Mal. 2:17)

> For Thou art not a God who takes pleasure in wickedness; No evil dwells with Thee…Thou dost hate all who do iniquity. Thou dost destroy those who speak falsehood; The Lord abhors the man of bloodshed and deceit. (Ps. 5:4–6)

> God is a righteous judge, and a God who has indignation every day. If a man does not repent, He will sharpen His sword. (Ps. 7:11–12)

> The Lord tests the righteous and the wicked, And the one who loves violence His souls hates. (Ps. 11:5)

"You shall love [*agapaō*, social and moral] the Lord your God with all your heart, and with all your soul, and with all your mind. This is the great and foremost commandment. The second is like it;

You shall love [*agapaō*] your neighbor as yourself. On these two commandments depend the whole Law and the prophets."[1152] This means that if you love someone, you will do them no harm. Love them as you love yourself. That's pretty easy; no harm, and do things that are beneficial to and for them. Love is a principle of action—the action of obedience. "Bear one another's burdens, and thus fulfill the law of Christ."[1153] This is the spirit of the law, and if you love one another, you do not have to be as concerned about the letter of the law because in a love veneration, you are not doing things that are prohibited under the law. In this, the law is fulfilled in a social and moral sense. Again we have to stretch ourselves to understand God and not bring him down to our level. God has removed all of the illusions. He has no limit; his love is love as we understand it times ten thousand. His mercy is mercy as we understand it times infinity. His grace is grace as we understand it times eternity.

People experience a range of moods and display different aspects of their personality on a daily basis, depending on circumstances, relationships, and events. All of God's attributes are manifested in full force at all times in equal presence. He is a God of love and mercy just as He is a God of wrath and justice.

We lull ourselves into a false sense of security by placing too much emphasis on God being a God of love. Without understanding His complete nature, his judicial nature, and his corresponding ability to demonstrate his wrath. We think we can appease God by our own good intentions. However, we must remember, "For the Lord your God is a consuming fire, a jealous God." [1154] who will tolerate nothing as more important in your life than your devotion to him. Remember Abraham and God's request that he sacrifice his beloved son?[1155] By doing so and demonstrating his faithful obedience to God, he was considered worthy. "It is a terrifying thing to fall into the hands of the living God."[1156] "God is love" is stated twice in the Bible,[1157] and over three hundred times we are told to fear God.[1158] To fear the Lord means a reverential awe of

God, a reverence for His power, holiness, and glory and a proper respect for His wrath and anger.

The church in apostasy has sold out the truth for the offering plate and a bigger congregation. They have sold out the truth and remain silent about the declining morality in our society and political policies that infringe on our religious liberties, all so they can keep their 501 3C status to keep the money coming in. To sell easy grace, God's free love, and prosperity sells out the soul of the church and the souls of the congregation. This church is neither hot nor cold; it condemns no one's behavior. The good news of salvation has very little meaning if a person does not know they may be headed for an eternity of damnation because their current lifestyle is provoking the wrath of God, not his love.

The wealthy church that is really in poverty is a church of Satan because it is worldly; its cares and concerns are of provisional reality and not the welfare of the eternal souls of the congregation. "And to cause My slaves to go astray and to commit fornication." The congregation is comfortable with the watered-down gospel. A church in apostasy preaches whatever its congregation wants to hear, to the point of being a church of Satan. This church preaches tolerance and denies the truth of Scripture, Christ says, "Wake up." This is a church that has gay pastors and performs weddings among same-sex couples, which God considers an abomination.[1159] It is a church of Satan because they choose to disregard the teachings of Scripture and set themselves up as lawgivers and the authority on morality while what they profess is blasphemy. "You shall not lie with a male as one lies with a female; it is an abomination."[1160] Fallen man can never be his own lawgiver and judge. Who is to decide what is right and what is wrong for the individual or for society? Fallen man, who hates the light and suppresses the truth? This is exactly why Christians are under persecution in America; progressives do not want to be accountable to God. This is the "neglecting the weightier provisions of the law."

For the wrath of God is revealed from heaven against all ungodliness and unrighteousness of men who suppress the truth in unrighteousness, because that which is known about God is evident within them; for God made it evident to them. For since the creation of the world His invisible attributes, His eternal power and divine nature, have been clearly seen, being understood through what has been made, so that they are without excuse. For even though they knew God, they did not honor Him as God or give thanks, but they became futile in their speculations, and their foolish heart was darkened. Professing to be wise, they became fools, and exchanged the glory of the incorruptible God for an image in the form of corruptible man. Therefore God gave them over in the lusts of their hearts to impurity, so that their bodies would be dishonored among them. For they exchanged the truth of God for a lie, and worshiped and served the creature rather than the Creator, who is blessed forever. Amen. For this reason God gave them over to degrading passions; for their women exchanged the natural function for that which is unnatural, and in the same way also the men abandoned the natural function of the woman and burned in their desire toward one another, men with men committing indecent acts and receiving in their own persons the due penalty of their error. (Rom. 1:18–27)

The church of Pergamum is the church of Satan located in Islamic west Turkey. The Arab nations before their subjugation into Islam and the teachings of Muhammad ascribed to the teachings of Balaam as well as other pagan deities. I think that no one can deny that Islam continually throws stumbling blocks to Israel, especially the Muslim nations of Lebanon (Hezbollah), Gaza (Hamas), Iran, Iraq, and Syria. This is the only church where Christ warns "repent but if not, I will come to you quickly, and I will make war with them by the sword of My mouth."[1161] This is the same imagery from the second coming of Christ. "From His mouth comes a sharp sword, so that with it He may strike down the nations." [1162]The church of Pergamum is the church of coexistence and strives to bring Muslims into the fold. The purpose of missionaries is to go out into the world to spread the gospel, not bring unbelievers into the congregation.¹¹⁶³ This is obvious from the criticism of Christ to the seven churches. Christ also speaks of church discipline to maintain the integrity of the congregation.¹¹⁶⁴ Christ also refers to this in the parable of the leaven and the loaves of bread.¹¹⁶⁵ Islam is the spirit of the Antichrist as the Qur'ān teaches that Christ did not come in the flesh and denies His deity. John tells us that those that profess this message are the spirit of the Antichrist.¹¹⁶⁶ This understanding applies to any church that tolerates behavior or doctrine that is contrary to the teachings of Christ or distorts the gospel of Christ. If anyone "preaches a gospel contrary to what we know to be the truth, even an angel from heaven, let them be accursed."¹¹⁶⁷

> For many deceivers have gone out into the world, those who do not acknowledge Jesus Christ as coming in the flesh. This is the deceiver and the antichrist. Watch yourself that you do not lose what we have accomplished, but that you may receive a full reward. Anyone who goes too far and does not abide in the teaching of Christ, does not have God; the one who abides in the teaching, he has both the Father and the Son. (2 John 7–9)

Christ said, "No one can come to the Father except through Me."¹¹⁶⁸ We receive salvation, the promise of eternal life, through our faith in Christ, that his sacrificial death was sufficient for the atonement of all sins. Any religion that teaches Christ's death on the cross was not sufficient, or that it didn't happen and that we must do something to insure our own salvation, is a church in apostasy.

At the Council of Trent in 1545, the Catholic Church adopted their canons in response to the challenges of Martin Luther.

Canon 9 records, "If anyone says the sinner is justified by faith alone, let him be damned."

Canon 24 says, "If anyone says that the righteousness received is not preserved and increased before God through good works, let him be damned."

Canon 32 reads, "If anyone says that the good works of the one justified are in such a manner the gifts of God that they are not also the good merits of him justified, let him be damned."

This is a dead church that replaces God's word with the traditions of men. Though it is rich, it is poor, blind, and naked. Its focus is on the accumulation of wealth through indulgencies and works for salvation rather than professing the sufficiency of the work of Christ on the cross.

The Holy Spirit tells us in Ephesians, "For by grace you have been saved through faith; and that not of yourselves, it is the gift of God; not a result of works, so that no one may boast."[1169]

"If you love Me, obey My commandments." We are obedient in our reciprocation of the love shown to us as a means of gratitude for obtaining salvation. When we think that by our good deeds we insure our salvation, we are saying that Christ's sacrificial death was not enough. However, "and there is salvation in no one else, for there is no other name under heaven that has been given among men by which we must be saved."[1170] Motives are extremely important as they reveal intent. In obedient love out of gratitude, the glory goes to God for his grace in what Christ has done for us. Good works to secure salvation gives the glory to man and denies the sacrificial work of Christ on the cross. The purpose of man is to bring glory to God.[1171]

The idea of erosion exemplifies apostasy. Over time, the wind, the sun, and rain eat away at rocks, mountains, riverbanks—everything in nature. In the same fashion, elements of culture eat away at our moral foundation by eroding the scriptural principles that established our morality in the first place. The Bible predicted this state of affairs as an ever-present phenomenon—in ancient history as well as today. For men loved the darkness rather than the light because their deeds were evil, so they suppress the truth. The sons of darkness do not want to be condemned for their behavior so they change the morality of the culture under the guise of civil rights, personal rights, and tolerance. "But evil men and imposters will proceed from bad to worse, deceiving and being deceived."[1172] However, no rational changes the absolutes of God's decrees for mankind. It has never been, nor will it ever be, in man's authority to condone what God has condemned. The progressive agenda wants to remove God from schools, society, and the military and label anyone of the Christian faith as intolerant. Many are deceived. A true Christian is not intolerant if they are following what is revealed in Scripture.

The church, clergy, deacons, elders, and congregation are to be above reproach; they are to be holy and blameless before the eyes of God.[1173] Some think we have evolved to a higher state of being and know better than God. The church is supposed to be the guardian, preserver, and presenter of the truth. Satan attempts to deceive the church by mingling his children with God's.[1174] Satan unites church and state in Islam and sows false doctrine in America to separate the church and state in an attempt to divide and conquer. He weakens the state through immorality and the church by influencing pastors and elders with his influences and false doctrines.

Our founding fathers, weary of the state church, the church of England, where they were taxed to support the church that would then enact the decrees of the state, established the church free from governmental intervention. It was never their intent to have natural law, morality, and the precepts of Christ removed from government, but to protect them from the government. The Mayflower Compact, the primer to the Constitution, signed in 1620 by the settlers in the Plymouth colony, stated the colonies were established "for the glory of God and the advancement of the Christian faith."[1175] Of course this is not taught in our schools. Change our history, and you change who we are.

THINGS TO COME

One of the buds of spring for being misled is political correctness, where the culture persecutes people for saying what they think is true in spite of the constitutional right of freedom of speech. What has happened on our watch? We are seeing unprecedented persecution of Christians and Christian organizations in America where expression of Christian values, ideas, and the mention of God are being suppressed, harassed, and penalized in spite of the constitutional guarantee of freedom of religion. We have taken prayer to the God of Christianity out of schools, nativity scenes out of commercial settings, and the Ten Commandments out of our courthouses, even though Moses and the Ten Commandments adorn the front of the US Supreme Court building. The process for establishing persecution historically has been political correctness to suppress the truth, then intimidation of those found violators of political correctness. These first two steps lead to activism, which results in persecution and physical violence. The government then condemns the violence when they set up the first two steps to begin with. To appease the situation, the government then passes laws to ensure their agenda. Many are deceived.

Political correctness is the strategy that Satan uses to condemn Christianity. Political correctness denies freedom of religion for Christians. One of the very basic tenants this country was founded on—freedom from religious persecution. Political correctness calls the murder of abortion, pro-choice, and the sins of homosexuality[1176] an alternate lifestyle. On our watch, we have rampant pornography, a worldwide sex-slave industry, and genocide in many third-world countries with the spilling of much innocent blood. We have a fifty percent divorce rate, violating our vows to God, fifty million aborted babies in America, declining morality, and a pervasive drug culture. We are told to make more than we need so we have something to give to those in need.[1177] But we have put all of our excess into idols—our toys—disregarding this commandment from God. "Whoever has the most toys when they die wins!" We render token assistance for the poor and starving. Forty thousand children die every day worldwide because of poor nutrition and water that is not fit to drink. What is the solution from the UN? "Let them eat bugs." We do very little other than lip service to stop worldwide terrorism, especially from Islam. Where are the Christian, Jewish, Buddhist, Hindu, Catholic, Mormon suicide bombers? There aren't any; the only suicide bombers that shed innocent blood are from the religion of peace, Islam. We turn our backs to Israel living in constant threats and daily rocket attacks, and somehow Israel is to blame.[1178] "Woe to those who call evil good and good evil." We let our politicians waste our time, effort, and tax dollars on saving Mother Earth with lies about global warming and climate change. Panic to control CO^2 emissions, when they are a naturally occurring trace gas. And as Ronald Reagan pointed out, "Approximately 80% of our air pollution stems from hydrocarbons released by vegetation, so let's not go overboard in setting and enforcing tough emission standards from man-made sources." It is all a scam to control the world's wealth and allocate resources away from where they are needed most—to foster the progressive's hidden agenda. Whoever controls the money, controls the population. According to the World Economic Forum, the nations of the world spent $1 billion per day to tackle global warming in 2012, which is half of the $700 billion they say is needed. Global warming has already been exposed as a hoax. Christ and the Father want us to save souls; Satan and his agents want us to save Mother Earth. "Many are deceived."

We know that in the past God's reasons for causing the flood was man's wickedness, that every intent of the thoughts of man's heart was evil. and because "they say to God, 'Depart from us! We do not even desire the knowledge of Your ways.' Who is the Almighty that we should serve Him, and what would we gain if we entreat Him?"[1179] This is at the opposite end of the spectrum of understanding God's sovereignty and obedience. Sodom and Gomorra were destroyed as an example for us because of the citizen's sexual immorality and homosexuality.

"And if He condemned the cities of Sodom and Gomorra to destruction by reducing them to ashes, having made them an example to those who would live ungodly lives thereafter."[1180] These are additional precursors for the buds of spring. Christ's first warning to his disciples regarding the end-times was, "See to it that no one misleads you." We have been warned to beware of those that call evil good and good evil. Another bud of spring is the gathering of Israel as a nation in 1948, which started the eschatology clock ticking. In the final analysis, the further we get from God's plan for humanity, the further we are from God's holiness, the closer we are to the end, which in actuality is a new beginning.

The buds of spring are based on God's precedent. What we do not know is when God will say enough is enough. We do know what the deciding factors were for the flood and for Sodom and Gomorra. We know from Scripture what God abhors. He abhors when his creations deny his sovereignty, his principles, his commandments, and the statutes of his Son. We have blatant disregard for the council of God. "You shall not take the name of the Lord your God in vain, for the Lord will not leave him unpunished who takes His name in vain."[1181] How many take this commandment against blasphemy seriously? OMG. Thou shall not, murder, steal, commit adultery, bear false witness, covet, take a bribe, honor your father and your mother, and you shall keep the Sabbath. "If because of the Sabbath you turn from doing your own pleasure on My holy day, honor it, desisting from your own ways, from seeking your own pleasure."[1182] This is honoring the Sabbath, not just going to church. He is a just God and does not want us to have any idols. An idol is anything that is more important in your life than God; pride of self, money, fame, ambition, success, and greed are all examples of idols. What the Trinity abhors is spelled out in Scripture, and those practicing these things will not inherit the kingdom of heaven.

Thomas Jefferson once said, "I have quit the newspaper and am a better man for it." Today's deception, satanic influences that we are warned about in Scripture, comes in a large part through TV programming and especially most news outlets. The scripting in TV shows have brought us from *Father Knows Best* to Homer Simpson, motivated by a desire to destabilize the American family, a cornerstone of America's strength. TV's portrayal of decadence makes people think their sinful behavior is commonplace. The information comes so fast there is little time to analyze the worthiness of the information. TV programming is contrived to consume our time and keeps us from the deeper things of life. The TV script will have the protagonist portray a strong argument for the progressive message, and the village idiot presents a contrary, very weak defense. Then the prerecorded laughter or applause reinforces the deception. The news attempts to deceive its viewers by portraying America as a post-Christian society. In a July 2011 report, the Barna Group found "among the religious beliefs that have remained relatively constant over the past twenty years were the percentage of adults who describe themselves as Christians (84%), those who say their religious faith is very important in their life today (56%), and those who have made a 'personal commitment to Jesus Christ that is still important in my life today' (65%)." America is a Christian nation. Christians need to vote, to vote for Christians and to vote for conservatives before this nation is fundamentally transformed from "One nation under God." I have quit TV and am a better man for it.

Satan is a solitary creature—finite and not omnipresent. He cannot possible involve himself with the seven billion plus inhabitants of the earth, although he does have minions he can dispatch to the most susceptible. For the most part, Satan works on the people that run the world's institutions, churches, governments, and organizations. He also influences politicians, celebrities, those in the news and entertainment industry to help spread his deceptions, to deceive the many. If you don't realize these influences are satanic, you won't be on guard, and you won't have a defense for yourself or your family.

THINGS TO COME

In Job 1, God and Satan are having a conversation. Many translations for verse 8 read, "Have you considered My servant Job?" However, the original Hebrew text reads, "Have you set your heart on My servant Job because there is none like him?" Satan is not targeting the average Christian. His deceptions and the corresponding influences are seen everywhere in the secular strongholds of provisional reality, and their symptoms are political correctness, tolerance, racism, decadence in entertainment, sex industry, drugs, pro-choice, alternate lifestyles, evolution, global warming, Islam the religion of peace and God is love as a theology. "Woe to those who call evil good and good evil." Satan's primary vehicles of attack, his flaming arrows, are the demonic influences he is able to orchestrate in provisional reality within people of influence in the world's institutions. We are aware of his evil influences that he has manifested in provisional reality and often are tempted by them. They are all of the other choices we are tempted to make, and do make, that are not found in, "if you love Me, obey My commandments." "That which proceeds out of the man, that is what defiles the man."[1183] We do not sin because we are being attacked by Satan; we sin because we are fallen, "The heart is more deceitful than all else and is desperately sick" and because we choose to.

Foundational and provisional realities are both real, and we live right now in both of them, as we are both physical and spiritual beings. As we look for answers to life's challenges, we cannot ignore foundational reality. To understand the whole truth, we need to look at the whole of reality. The best source of information about foundational reality is the Scripture and the continuing revelations of the Holy Spirit.

There are consequences for limiting our understanding to just provisional reality, which is only half of our reality. When we limit our understanding, we come up with things like the theory of evolution.

When Darwin was hatching this theory, science was just beginning to develop cell theory. They didn't have a clue about

DNA. This was the same year Louis Pasteur said, "Hey, dummies, life just doesn't mysteriously happen, flies lay eggs, and when they hatch, we get maggots." And all the people said, "Oh." When people used to see maggots just appear on meat they thought, *Life just happens.* They didn't know that flies laid eggs.

Evolution states that life just happened from organic matter and that over time, things in provisional reality just evolved and continued to develop.

Evolution attempts to explain the brain but cannot explain the mind or consciousness.

Evolution teaches survival of the fittest, disregarding the reality of man's empathy, compassion, and altruistic motivations.

Evolution attempts to explain the body but cannot explain the spirit or the soul. Evolution cannot explain anything in foundational reality.

There are no—zero—fossils that show a transitional phase of a species changing from one species into another.

So why are the lies taught to our kids in the classroom? Because the progressive agenda is to suppress the truth. "We will not have this man to rule over us!"[1184] "And "men loved the darkness rather than the light because their deeds were evil." We suppress the truth so that God can be discredited. If God can be discredited, he is no longer relevant; we no longer have any accountability to him. There also will no longer be godly origins for our constitution and our inalienable rights.

The only rights we will have are the ones prescribed by man, and any right given by a man can be taken away by a man.

Creation, the truth had to be replaced with evolution, the lie. "See that no one misleads you." "We hold these truths to be self-evident, that all men are created equal, that they are endowed by their Creator with certain unalienable Rights, that among these are Life, Liberty, and the pursuit of Happiness.—That to secure these rights, Governments are instituted among Men, deriving their just powers from the consent of the governed,—That whenever any

Form of Government becomes destructive of these ends, it is the Right of the People to alter or to abolish it, and to institute a new Government…This is why progressives want gun control.

A continuing part of the apostasy of the church is to avoid the subject of God's wrath—justice and fury over the unrepentant sinner. The familiar refrain to any sinner that "God loves you no matter what" is completely contrary to the teachings of Scripture. This pernicious lie is so prevalent from the apostate pulpit today that those good-intending Christians seeking to evangelize repeat the same hypocrisy. "Then watch out that the light in you is not darkness."[1185] All sin is an affront to God's holiness. Only God can determine what justice is demanded for sin. "The wages of sin is death, and there is not one who is without sin." The incarnate Christ came to earth to save us from the wrath of God. God's appeasement for God's wrath, which rests on all of us, is because of our sinful nature. When Christ took all of our sins on Himself, He died; the wages of sin is death. His death paid the price for all of our sins. With the penalty of sin paid, all sins were forgiven, and He was raised from death to life, just as we are when we are forgiven. With the debt of sin paid, there is life—eternal life. The proof that all of this is true is the resurrection of Jesus Christ,[1186] witnessed by over five hundred people.[1187]

When I use the term *progressive*, it is not necessarily referring to liberals or the Democratic Party; it is people and policies designed to subvert America as a world power and the only nation with a creed of "One Nation under God." As an armed citizenry, we cannot be forced in subjugation, so an alternate strategy must be employed. The strategy is to diminish, corrupt, and muzzle the truth. The deception is designed to release as information only that which will further the progressive agenda and to distort or not release the rest. The truth is muzzled by political correctness, broadening and misapplying the term *racist*, accusing people of Islamophobia. It also includes professing tolerance only so that when someone that does not agree can be labeled intolerant; this tool is particularly effective in trying to silence Christians. They are all demonic strategies designed to prevent people from professing the truth. All of these tactics have as their goal to undermine that fact that America is a Christian nation and to negate our God-given inalienable rights. For the most part, this agenda has been left to the news media and in most instances Hollywood. However, as of late we have politicians that have joined the fray with misinformation and spin that borders on outright deception and dishonesty. These are the false doctrines and false teachers. "See that no one mislead you." "Apostasy must come first, and the man of lawlessness is revealed."

THE SEQUENCE OF EVENTS

To help sort all of this out, we need to follow exactly what Scripture says. The tribulation begins when the Holy Spirit's restraint is removed, and immediately the son of perdition, the Antichrist, is revealed as the rider on the white horse of the four horsemen of the apocalypse. During the tribulation the sword, famine, pestilence, and wild beasts will kill many and a fourth of the world given to the horsemen's authority.

The sequence of events for the end-times are detailed in Matthew 24. In verse 3, the disciples ask Christ, "What is the sign of Your coming and of the end of the age?" This question is not answered until verse 30 because a lot of things will happen in the interim. Verse 30 reads:

> And then *the sign* of the Son of Man will appear in the heavens. And then all the tribes of the land will wail. And they will see *the Son of Man coming on the clouds of heaven* with power and much glory. And He will send His angels with a great sound of a trumpet, and they will gather His elect from the four winds; from the ends of heaven to their ends. (Matt. 24:30–31, IGNT)

Christ is saying that the sign of the end of the age is His return on the cloud to gather His elect, which we understand from 1 Thessalonians 4:17 to be the rapture.

It is important to identify the sign the disciples ask for right away so that the sign does not get lost in the rest of the details of chapter 24. The disciples ask when the sign will appear; however, the first thing Christ says is, "See to it that no one misleads you,"[1188] a warning against being deceived from the truth—apostasy. Christ's immediate response is specific to the disciples but applies to all of us as well. They are to remember "obey My commandments" even after he is gone. They are not to deviate from what he has taught and will teach them—the truth. As with all Scripture being God-breathed, it is good for teaching, reproof, correction, and training in righteousness.[1189] Scripture has a historical, future, spiritual, as well as a present-day application, both individually and for mankind. Christ warns his disciples that many will come in his name, and they will cause many to err. He then warns about wars and rumors of wars, yet cautions them about not being disturbed by this because they must take place, but this is not yet the end. These are just the beginning of throes (birth pangs). In verse 9, it says, "Then they will deliver you up to affliction, and will kill you; and you will be hated by all nations for My name's sake." He also cautions them in verse 10 of Christian persecution. "And then many will be offended, [intolerant] and they will deliver up one another, and will hate one another. Lawlessness shall be multiplied; the love of many will grow cold. But the one who endures to the end, that one will be saved."[1190]

In chapters two and three of the book of Revelation, Christ talks to John about enduring to the end. Christ calls those that are able to endure overcomers. It is important to know what awaits those who overcome. Overcome in the Greek is *nikaō*, which means to conquer, prevail, or get the victory. John tells us that believers are able to overcome because "greater is He who is in you [Holy Spirit] than he who is in the world."[1191] God has also promised that "are they not all ministering spirits, sent out to render service for the sake of those who will inherit salvation?" "The angel of the Lord encamps around those who fear Him, and rescues them."[1192] These are also assurances that Satan does not have the ability to attack the average indwelt Christian. "Submit to God, resist the devil, and he will flee from you."

We gain information about overcomers in Revelation 2–3, "To the one overcoming, I will give him to eat of the tree of life" (Rev. 2:7). "Be faithful until death, and I will give you the crown of life" (Rev. 2:10). "The one overcoming will not at all be hurt by the second death" Rev. 3:11). "To the one overcoming, I will give to him a white stone, and on the stone a new name having been written, which no one knows except the one receiving it" (Rev. 3:17). "And the one overcoming and keeping My works until the end, I will give to him authority over the nations, and he will shepherd them with an iron staff" (Rev 2:26). "The one overcoming; this one shall be clothed in white garments, and I will not at all blot his name out of the Book of Life, and I will acknowledge his name before My Father, and before His angels" (Rev. 3:5) "The one overcoming, I will make him a pillar in the temple of My God, and he shall not go out any more. And I will write the name of My God on him, and the name of the city of My God, the New Jerusalem which comes down out of heaven from My God, and My new name" (Rev. 3:12). "The one overcoming, I will give to him to sit with Me in My throne, as I also overcame and sat with My Father in His throne" (Rev. 3:21)

Mattew 24:14 says, "The gospel of the kingdom shall be preached in all the earth for a testimony to all the nations; and then will come the end."

In review, many people are going to be deceived. Lawlessness will increase, and love will grow cold. Christians are hated by nations, persecuted, and killed for their unrelenting faith in Jesus Christ and their alleged intolerance and racist attitudes. Lawlessness is the slaughter of many Christians and Jews. Love or affection growing cold is the unwillingness of many to try and stop the shedding of innocent blood. Christ cautions us not to be misled or frightened when we hear about wars; wars are going to continue as they are inherent with the actions of fallen man under satanic influences. Nation will rise against nation; there will be famines and earthquakes. These things are just the beginning of birth pangs. We can understand from this statement that as we get closer to the end, these events, or birth pangs, will occur with more frequency and greater intensity. But the one who endures until the end will be saved. And the gospel must be preached to the whole world.

We see the beginnings of this persecution today and remember these are the beginning of birth pangs, so all of these events Christ is warning about will increase in frequency and intensity as we get closer to the end. The persecution of Christians is already being escalated with killing of Christians in Muslim nations today in the Middle East, and in Ethiopia, Nigeria, Sudan, Kenya, Pakistan, Bangladesh, Kazakhstan, India, Uzbekistan, Laos, etc.[1193] And it will get worse.[1194]

In the words of Andrew White, an Anglican priest in Iraq, "Then one day, ISIS, the Islamic State, the Islamic caliphate, came to Nineveh and they hounded all of them [Christians] out. Not some, all of them. And they killed huge numbers. They chopped their children in half; they chopped their heads off." Andrew, whose own five-year-old son was beheaded by ISIS. A five-year-old boy, before the age of reason, could never go against his father's wishes, and he is beheaded. People that are able to commit such horrific acts are people that have made a free-will choice to yield to Satan's influences and have come to the point that they are completely dominated by him and his bloodlust. This is the same evil that was on the other side of the flood.

"The Lord abhors the man of bloodshed and deceit.[1195] And the one who loves violence His soul hates.[1196] In order that they all may be judged who did not believe the truth, but took pleasure in wickedness."[1197]

> He said to His disciples, "It is inevitable that stumbling blocks come, but woe to him through whom they come! It would be better for him if a millstone were hung around his neck and he were thrown into the sea, than that he would cause one of these little ones to stumble." (Luke 17:1–2)

Matthew 24:15 continues:

> Then when you see the abomination of desolation which was spoken of by Daniel the prophet, standing in the holy place, then let those in Judea flee on the mountains.

These will constitute the remnant of Israel. When Daniel talks about the abomination of desolation, quoting from the original Hebrew text;

> And from the time the regular sacrifice shall be taken away, and the abomination that makes desolates set up, a thousand two hundred and ninety days shall occur. Blessed is he who waits and comes to the 1,335 days. (Dan. 12:11–12)

Verse 21 issues the warning that "for then there will be a great tribulation, such as has not occurred since the beginning of the world until now, nor ever shall."

The seven-year time frame for the tribulation is based on a theory about the seventy weeks recorded in Daniel. The theory attempts to explain Daniel's reference to the abomination of desolation taking place midway through the tribulation, such that the tribulation will last for seven years, ignoring the 1,335 days.

When the sacrifices are stopped, taken away, and the Antichrist declares himself as god, "the abomination of desolation,"

THINGS TO COME

1,290 days have transpired since the beginning of the tribulation period. And blessed are those who wait until 1,335 days when the ongoing tribulation period is cut short.

> Seventy weeks have been decreed for your people and your holy city, to finish the transgressions, to make an end to sin, to make atonement for iniquity, to bring in everything righteousness, to seal up vision and prophecy and to anoint the most holy place (the new temple) So you are to know and discern that from the issuing of a decree to restore and rebuild Jerusalem until the Messiah the Prince there will be seven weeks and sixty-two weeks; it will be built again, with plaza and moat, even in times of distress. Then after sixty-two weeks the Messiah will be cut off and have nothing and the people of the prince who is to come will destroy the city and the sanctuary…And he will make a firm covenant with the many for one week, but in the middle of the week he will put a stop to sacrifice and grain offerings. (Dan. 9:24–27)

Seventy weeks or seventy years have been decreed for Israel in captivity to get their act together. The Hebrews were given into the hands of Nebuchadnezzar as punishment for their unfaithfulness. The first temple was destroyed August 16, 586 BC by King Nebuchadnezzar.[1198] Cyrus the Great issued a decree in 539 BC to rebuild the temple.[1199] Work on the second temple was halted while King Darius ordered a search of the records to see if Cyrus did in fact issue a decree to rebuild the temple. When it was found, work on the temple was resumed in 521 BC.[1200] Seven years later, the second temple was completed, according to Ezra 6:15, on the third day of the month of Adar; it was the sixth year of the reign of King Darius, which is March 12, 515 BC.[1201] Seventy years after the first temple was destroyed, the second temple was completed. The seventy weeks of Daniel are about rebuilding the second temple.

People that want to make the seventy weeks about a seven-year tribulation period cite Nehemiah 2 as the beginning of the seventy weeks. In 445 BC, Nehemiah was commissioned to rebuild the wall *by the temple*,[1202] which was completed in fifty-two days.[1203] The temple had already been rebuilt.

The reference to the Messiah is unclear; we all know that Christ is the Messiah. However, Cyrus the Great, who issued the decree to rebuild the temple,[1204] was called God's anointed one,[1205] which also means Messiah. Joshua and Zerubbabel of the Davidic line are also perceived as messianic in that their role is to complete the building of the temple, which they did.[1206] Daniel says, "The Messiah will be cut off and have nothing." It is implausible that Christ would ever be in that position, to have nothing, as all things were made by Him, for Him and through Him, visible and invisible.[1207]

Daniel then prophesizes that the temple and the city will be destroyed by "the people of the prince who is to come." This came to pass in AD 70 when Titus, the son of Caesar, utterly destroyed Jerusalem and the second temple.

If we look at the Antichrist being revealed as the rider of the white horse of the four horses of the apocalypse, and 1,290 (3.5 years) days later we see the abomination of desolation the rest, of the verses make sense. Daniel says the abomination of desolation is the midpoint of the tribulation.[1208] The revelation of the Antichrist will bring the Orthodox Jews back to temple worship and ritual sacrifices, otherwise the sacrifices could not be stopped by the Antichrist as recorded in Daniel.[1209]

The Dome of the Rock, the Muslims mosque in Jerusalem, located on the Temple Mount, the sight of both Jewish Temples, is the place where God chose to display His divine presence. If there is to be a Jewish third temple for the sacrifices, it is hard to conceive of it being any place else. The Temple Mount is holy to Islam because it is alleged that this is the spot where Muhammad ascended into heaven. The Dome of the Rock, completed in AD

691, was patterned after the Church of the Holy Sepulchre. Conceivably, there could be a sharing of this site, holy to both religions as part of a peace negotiation. During the crusades of 1099, when the knights recaptured Jerusalem, the mosque was converted back into a church.

When the Antichrist stops the sacrifices, he then declares himself as god and demands to be worshipped. This act would constitute the abomination of desolation and could happen without the Jews having to rebuild their temple to Jehovah. Scripture does not specifically say there will be rebuilding of a third temple.

> And in the middle of the week he shall cause the sacrifice and the offering to cease; and on a corner of the altar, desolating abominations, even until the end." (Dan. 9:27, IHOT)

At 1,290 days, the rapture has occurred, and all these events will be completed. What follows are the seven bowl judgments, and if they occur in forty-five days, we have the 1,335 days spoken of by Daniel.[1210] This last forty-five days is cutting the time short of the tribulation. "And except those days were shortened, not any flesh would be saved—but on account of the elect, [the Jewish remnant], those days will be shortened."[1211] The remnant of Israel on Mount Zion is the only flesh to survive the hour of testing that is coming on the whole habitable world.[1212] Christ says in verse 15 that that when the people in Judea see the abomination of desolation, they should flee into the mountains. Everyone else has either been raptured or killed by the end of the 1,335 days, the end of the time of the Gentiles. The Jewish remnant, in flesh, will go into the New Jerusalem. As the only physical survivors of the great tribulation, they will have the responsibility of procreating the new earth. All of those predestined to be saved have been saved; an additional 1,290 days is not necessary to destroy the remaining heathens that would not repent of their murders. That can be accomplished in forty-five days.

> I do not want you to be ignorant of this mystery, brothers and sisters, so that you may not be conceited: Israel has experienced a hardening in part until the full number of the Gentiles has come in, and in this way all Israel will be saved. As it is written: "The deliverer will come from Zion; He will turn godlessness away from Jacob. And this is My covenant with them when I take away their sins." As far as the gospel is concerned, they are enemies for your sake; but as far as election is concerned, they are loved on account of the patriarchs, for God's gifts and His call are irrevocable. (Rom. 11:25–29)

Israel's rejection of Christ was not entirely their fault as God had hardened their heart so the blessings of eternal life could be made to the gentiles as well. As such God, for His name's sake, has delivered the remnant into the mountains, Mount Zion, for protection from the Antichrist and his army.[1213] The Jewish remnant, those written in the book, are by reason the Messianic Jews alive at the time of the tribulation.[1214]

> In that day the remnant of Israel, the survivors of Jacob…will truly rely on the LORD, the Holy One of Israel. A remnant will return, a remnant of Jacob will return to the Mighty God. Though your people be like the sand by the sea, Israel, only a remnant will return. Destruction has been decreed, overwhelming and righteous. The Lord, the LORD Almighty, will carry out the destruction decreed upon the whole land. Therefore this is what the Lord, the LORD Almighty, says: "My people who live in Zion, do not be afraid of the Assyrians, who beat you with a rod and lift up a club against you, as Egypt did. Very soon My anger against you will end and My wrath will be directed to their destruction." (Isa. 10:20–25)

Christ has delivered His chosen people to Mount Zion as a safe haven. Initially, the Assyrians were from Turkey, Syria, Iraq, and Iran.

THINGS TO COME

Because Israel was fulfilling the role God had decreed for them and in that their hardened heart was not entirely of their choosing and because God will always honor His covenants. The elect Jews will experience God's just mercy. "I bring near my righteousness, it is not far off; And my salvation will not delay. And I will grant salvation in Zion, And My glory for Israel."[1215]

> Who is a God like you, who pardons sin and forgives the transgression of the remnant of His inheritance? You do not stay angry forever but delight to show mercy. You will again have compassion on us; You will tread our sins underfoot and hurl all our iniquities into the depths of the sea. You will be faithful to Jacob, and show love to Abraham, as You pledged on oath to our ancestors in days long ago. (Mic. 7:18–20)

> For out of Jerusalem will come a remnant, and out of Mount Zion a band of survivors. The zeal of the LORD Almighty will accomplish this. Therefore this is what the LORD says concerning the king of Assyria: "He will not enter this city or shoot an arrow here. He will not come before it with shield or build a siege ramp against it. By the way that he came he will return; he will not enter this city," *declares the* LORD. "I will defend this city and save it, for My sake and for the sake of David My servant." (Isa. 37:32–34)

In effect, once the abomination of desolation has occurred, the Antichrist's quest is over. It is immediately followed by the seven bowls of judgment.

Just before the rapture occurs, John records, "And I heard a voice from heaven, saying 'Write, Blessed are the dead who die in the Lord from now on!'"[1216] These are the overcomers whose spirits and souls are released and raptured just before the bowl judgments.

The next several verses give a warning about false Christs and prophets that do many signs and wonders so as to lead astray, if possible, even the elect.[1217] The signs and wonders will be so convincing that if your name is not written in the Lamb's Book of Life, you will be deceived. The confidence we have and the assurance we are given that these are all false Christs and prophets is given in verse 27 when Christ says, "For as the lightning comes forth from the east and shines as far as the west, so also will be the coming of the Son of Man." Anyone that proclaims to be Christ and does not meet this criterion is a false Christ.

Verse 30 gives us the sign asked for by the disciples: Christ returning on a cloud.

Christ further explains to his disciples that no one except God knows the time, the day nor the hour for these events (verse 36). However, in verse 32–33 he tells us that just as we know spring is coming by the buds on the trees, we will be able to recognize that He is near by the signs we observe. These signs or buds are the events Christ has already told his disciples about— the beginning of birth pangs. What we watch for is the signs increasing in frequency and intensity as we get closer to the end of human history—wars and rumors of wars, famines, earthquakes, persecution, deliver you to affliction and killing you, you will be hated by all nations for my name's sake, false prophets, lawlessness, and love will grow cold. "This gospel of the kingdom shall be preached in the whole world, as a testimony to all the nations, and then the end will come."[1218]

The rest of chapter 24 takes on a tone of warning and council. It no longer corresponds to the timeline; however, the information is important to our general understanding. Verse 34 mentions, "This generation will not pass away until all of these things have occurred." and that "heavens and the earth will pass away, but My words shall not pass away."

There is also a reference in verse 37 that "just as in the days of Noah, they did not understand until the flood came and took them all away; so shall the coming of the Son of Man be." One thing to keep in mind about this reference to Noah is the commonality that it has with Lot at Sodom and Gomorrah and the Hebrews in the exodus from Egypt. Noah and his family were protected from the flood waters, but they did have to go through the ordeal.[1219] "He who endures to the end will be saved."[1220] The birth pangs are the best indication we have for the appointed time of the day of the Lord, and one additional bud of spring is "but they continually mocked the message of God, despised His word and scoffed at His prophets, until the wrath of the Lord arose against his people, until there was no remedy."[1221]

The final warnings are about what Christ finds you doing when he returns. Those living in accordance with his commandments will be rewarded, and those living in disobedience, the master will "cut him in pieces and assign him a place with the hypocrites."[1222]

James tells us that faith without works is dead.[1223] Your behavior should demonstrate that you are a person of faith, obedient to the Lord's commandments. "A tree is known by its fruit."[1224]

Daniel gives us a warning of one of the buds of spring when he foretells us that "and he [Antichrist] will make a firm covenant with the many."[1225] It is assumed by current traditional thought that this covenant will be a peace treaty signed by the Antichrist with Israel and will set in motion the beginning of the seven-year tribulation. However, if it is to be a peace treaty with Israel, I think Scripture would say that. The word *covenant* in this context in the Hebrew means a confederacy; we will get to this a little later.

THE FOUR HORSEMEN OF THE APOCALYPSE

As human history nears its conclusion, everything will unfold as is prophesized in the Bible. Satan sends the Antichrist out in an attempt to control everything in provisional reality. The Antichrist will need to form a military to remove the opposition in his quest for world domination.[1226] In this manner, Satan believes he can accomplish his five "I wills."[1] The ensuing events of the tribulation are portrayed in three separate sets of judgment: the seals, the trumpets, and the bowls. Each of the sets of events includes seven judgments that will devastate the world and humanity.

The first series of events to occur are the seal judgments set in motion by Christ breaking the seven seals of the scroll handed to him by God.[1227] The first four seals release the four horses of the apocalypse; with this, the tribulation begins. Also, as prophesied, the man of lawlessness is revealed, and he is the rider of the white horse. We know the Holy Spirit's restraint has been removed, otherwise Satan would have begun this evil reign of terror long before the first seal was broken.

The rider on the first horse, the white horse, is the Antichrist. His actions will result in the death of many Jews and Christian martyrs.

> Then I saw when the Lamb broke one of the seven seals, and I heard one of the living creatures saying as with thunder, "Come." I looked, and behold, a white horse, and he who sat on it had a bow, and a crown was given to him, and he went out conquering and to conquer. (Rev. 6:1–2)

The second seal brings war.

> When He broke the second seal, I heard the second living creature saying, "Come." And another, a red horse, went out; and to him who sat on it, it was granted to take peace from the earth, and that men would slay one another, and a great sword was given to him. (Rev. 6:3–5)

The fourth seal predicts the death of many.

---

[1] *A Brief History of the Bible*, chapter 3.

> When the Lamb broke the fourth seal…And I saw and behold, a pale green horse, and the name of the one sitting on it was death; and Hades followed after him. And authority was given to them to kill over the fourth of the earth with sword, and with famine, and by the wild beasts of the earth. (Rev. 6:7–8, IGNT)

The four horsemen are given authority to kill over the fourth of the earth. Who are these people that are killing the inhabitants of a fourth of the earth? And who are they killing?

There are riders on two white horses mentioned in the book of Revelation. In chapter 19, the rider is identified as Christ. "And on His robe and on His thigh He has a name written, "KING OF KINGS AND LORD OF LORDS.""[1228] The rider of the white horse in chapter 6 is unidentified; however it is clear from the context of the text that this is the Antichrist. We can look to the writings of Islam to confirm the identity of the rider of the first white horse.

The Muslims believe that the rider of the white horse in chapter 6 is the Mahdi, their Messiah. When the Mahdi returns on the white horse, he will usher in the Islamic version of the end-times.

Islam teaches that in the end time, one of their former religious leaders, who disappeared, will return as the Mahdi, a messianic figure. The Mahdi is purported to be a direct descendant of the prophet Muhammad. He chose not to have a successor and will return when commanded to do so by Allah. Upon the return of the Mahdi, he will rule for seven years and bring about unprecedented prosperity and justice to Islam and rid the world of all its evils. Daniel refers to this unprecedented wealth. "In a time of tranquility he will enter the richest part of the realm, and he will accomplish what his fathers never did, nor his ancestors; he will distribute plunder, booty, and possessions among them, and he will devise his schemes against strongholds, but only for a time."[1229]

The Hadith, which means "tradition," is a collection of the deeds, sayings, and teachings of Muhammad written two centuries after his death. The arbitrary authority of the Hadith was used to replace the Qur'ān in forming the basis of Shari'ah Law.

There are two branches of Islam: Sunnis, with over a billion adherents, and Shias, about two hundred million, primarily in Iran, Iraq, Lebanon, Azerbaijan, and Bahrain. Sunnis believe Muhammad's successors, called caliphs, should be chosen by consensus. Shias believe Muhammad's successors, called imams, should be a bloodline descendant of Muhammad. Both sects believe the final messenger from Allah to usher in the end-times is the Mahdi.

Ka'b al-Ahbar is viewed among Muslims as a trustworthy transmitter of Hadith. Ka'b al-Ahbar is supported in his view that this description of the rider on the white horse as found in the book of Revelation is indeed the Mahdi by two well-known Egyptian authors, Muhammad ibn Izzat and Muhammad Arif in their book *Al Mahdi and the End Times*. Izzat and Arif quote Ka'b al Ahbar as saying, "I find the Mahdi recorded in the books of the Prophets. For instance, the book of Revelation says, 'And I saw and behold a white horse. He that sat on him…went forth conquering and to conquer.'" Izzat and Arif then go on to say; It is clear that this man is the Mahdi who will ride the white horse and judge by the Qur'ān.

The Mahdi will proclaim his arrival and unite all of the Muslim nations under his rule. Just before we started this subchapter, Daniel 9:27 was referenced, where it reads that the Antichrist will "make a covenant with the many." This is brought to fruition by the Mahdi as he unites the nations of Islam, under Islamic beliefs only the Mahdi can declare a Caliphate. The covenant in this context is not a peace treaty with Israel. Covenant in the Hebrew in this application means a confederacy. The covenant will be a confederacy of Muslim nations, the United Arab States of Islam, the new Caliphate, as the Antichrist begins his Islamic quest for world domination. The Qur'ān teaches, "Fight with them until all religion is for Allah. Strive against them with a mighty striving."[1230] The Mahdi will unite Muslims under the sign of the crescent moon and with their creed; "There is no God but Allah and Mohammad is his prophet." The crescent moon is the sign of Islam and represents the new moon, moving to fulfillment as the full moon. Islam is both a government and a religion. The Mahdi will attempt to establish a one-world order under a one-world government/religion, namely Islam under Shari'ah law. The Mahdi has a bow but no arrows; this is a conquest without a war, and he is given a crown and authority by Christ. All things are under Christ's sovereign control. The Mahdi uniting the Muslim nations is the conquering and to conquer. It is uniting the Muslim nations "over a fourth of the earth." There are 1.6 billion Muslims, and they are a majority in forty-nine countries of the 196 countries in the world, or 25% with a Muslim majority. The Sunnis and Shias will put aside their differences at the command of the Mahdi because God has decreed it. "These have one mind, and their power and authority they shall give up to the beast."[1231] The quest for world domination is the war of the second horseman, the red horse, as he proclaims a worldwide jihad against all non-Muslim nations and people. "Authority was given to them over a fourth of the earth to kill with the sword."[1232]

The Mahdi and his minions in provisional reality will think their strategies are working, unaware that all of the events are being orchestrated by God.

"For God gave into their hearts to do His mind, and to act in one mind, and to give their kingdom to the beast, until the words of God shall be fulfilled."[1233] God started the whole enterprise into motion by removing the Holy Spirit's restraint, allowing Satan to proceed and sending the grand delusion. A one-world order was tried once before at the Tower of Babel.[1234] God did not allow it to succeed then; there is no reason to think he will allow it to succeed this time either.

Daniel also made other predictions about the Antichrist. "He will speak out against the Most High and wear down the saints of the Highest One, and he will intend to make alterations in times and *in law*; and they will be given into his hand for a time, times and half a time." ¹²³⁵ The Mahdi will establish a moral system of laws from which all superstitious faiths will be eliminated. Satan's focus will be primarily against Christians rather than any other religion as only Christ offers true salvation and eternal life. The alterations in law, God's natural laws, are the implementation of Shari'ah law, the moral code and religious law of Islam.

> And there is salvation in no other One, for neither is there any other name under Heaven having been giving among man by which we must be saved. (Acts 4:12, IGNT)

> Jesus said to him, "I am the Way, and the Truth, and the Life. No one comes to the Father except through Me." (John 14:6, IGNT)

The Mahdi arrives riding on the white horse of the apocalypse as the messiah for Islam. The messiah of Islam is the Antichrist of Christianity—the destroyer.[1236] Al-Mumeet is one of the ninety-nine names for Allah in the Qur'ān, and it means "destroyer."

The Qur'ān, the holy book of Islam, is the precise blueprint that Satan and the Antichrist (Mahdi) will need to follow to bring about all that is prophesied in the Scriptures of Christianity. The Qur'ān is the perfect vehicle for Satan to use in his ill-fated attempt to accomplish his five "I wills" in provisional reality.[1237]

> Those who disbelieve from among the people of the book and the idolaters will be in the fire of hell, abiding therein. They are the worst of creatures. (Qur'ān 98:6)

> And any that say, "The Messiah is the son of Allah," Allah's curse be on them! (Qur'ān 9:30)

The Qur'ān further states that "Allah is only one God. Far be it from His glory to have a son."

"Who has not taken to Himself a son and who has not a partner in the kingdom."

"It beseems not Allah that He should take to Himself a son."

"And it is not worthy of the Beneficent that He should take to Himself a son."

"Allah has not taken to Himself a son, nor is there with Him any other god. He, Whose is the kingdom of the heavens and the earth, and Who did not take to Himself a son."[1238]

Islam teaches that the Bible had been corrupted by so many human authors that God gave a final version to Muhammad.[1239] Christians believe that the Bible is the inspired word of God, and that every word is God-breathed.[1240] The Bible is not man's interpretation, but the words are from the Holy Spirit.[1241] The Bible also warns against anyone adding to the Bible or taking away from it.[1242] The Qur'ān, the holy book of Islam, was written by Muhammad with the aid of an angel. Muhammad both took away from and added to the holy Scriptures of Christianity as he relied heavily on the Bible in the creation of the Qur'ān.

The Bible explicitly tells us:

> Beloved do not believe every spirit, but test the spirits to see whether they are from God;...By this you know the Spirit of God; every spirit that confesses that Jesus Christ has come in the flesh is from God; and every spirit that does not confess Jesus is not from God; this is the spirit of the antichrist, of which you have heard that it is coming, and now it is already in the world. (1 John 4:1–3)

This does not necessarily mean that the Antichrist is in the world today; however, the spirit of the Antichrist is in the world today and is prevalent within the Qur'ān and Islam. The Qur'ān specifically denies the Sonship of Jesus Christ; it denies his incarnation and his deity.

Who is the liar but the one who denies that Jesus is the Christ. This is the antichrist. (1 John 2:22–23)

The Mahdi will wage a holy war, the jihad, until "all nations must surrender to Islamic rule, if not its faith, then its government, if not willingly then by force" (Qur'ān 61:9). The Qur'ān also specifies that all able-bodied men must participate in the jihad (Qur'ān 25:52).

There may be unwilling participants; however, the Mahdi has ordered the participation of all able-bodied men and quotes from the Qur'ān:

> Fighting is enjoined on you though it is disliked by you; and it may be that you dislike a thing while it is good for you, and it may be that you love a thing while it is evil for you; and Allah knows while you do not. (Qur'ān 2:216)

> And fight them until there is no persecution, and religion is only for Allah. (Qur'ān 2:193)

John gives us a warning:

> They will put you out of the synagogue, but an hour is coming that everyone killing you will think to bear a service before God. And they will do these things to you because they do not know the Father nor Me. (John 16:2–3)

The Qur'ān refers to Christians as polytheists because we believe in a triune God: God the Father, Christ the Son, and the Holy Spirit.

The Qur'ān addresses polytheists:

> Allah will chastise the polytheistic men and women, the entertainers of evil about Allah, and Allah is wroth with them and

has cursed them and prepared hell for them; and evil is the resort. (Qur'ān 48:6)

The Mahdi will fulfill the role of the messenger for Allah to the followers of Islam. The role of the messenger is also addressed in the Qur'ān. "Whoever obeys the messenger, he indeed obeys Allah."[1243]

The Antichrist (Mahdi) will proclaim that he is the messenger, "the warner," sent from Allah to inform the people. The Qur'ān teaches that appointed messengers would be sent from time to time and that Muslims are to obey Allah and his messengers; in fact, they are to obey the messenger as if his commands are coming directly from Allah. "Obey Allah and obey the messenger., you are responsible for the duty imposed on you, and the messenger's duty is only to deliver the message plainly."[1244] If someone does disobey Allah, "And whoever disobeys Allah and his messenger, surely for him is the fire of hell, to abide therein for ages."[1245] Allah commands, and the messenger will command jihad against Jews, Christians, atheists, and all other religions. Muslims will have no choice but to obey, go to hell, or denounce their faith. If you are a Muslim and denounce your faith, the punishment is death. With these three choices, Muslims, and some non-Muslims, will be deluded into participating in the jihad. It is also important to keep in mind that the Mahdi is no ordinary man.

> That is, the one whose coming is in accord with the activity of Satan, with all power and signs and false wonders, and with all the deception of wickedness for those who perish, because they did not receive the love of the truth so as to be saved. And for this reason God will send upon them a deluding influence so that they might believe what is false, in order that they all may be judged who did not believe the truth, but took pleasure in wickedness. (2 Thess. 2:9–12)

The delusions, miracles, and false wonders will work together to convince people of the deity of the Antichrist.[1246] It will also firmly establish in the minds of Muslims that the Mahdi is their messiah. With the delusions and false wonders there will not be any moderate Muslims, all will answer the call of jihad.

As the Antichrist (Mahdi) preaches from the Qur'ān, "O you believe, obey Allah and obey the messenger [Mahdi]; then if you quarrel about anything refer it to Allah and the messenger, if you believe in Allah and the last day" (Qur'ān 4:59).

This is a closed-loop system. All will be instructed to obey the messenger; if anyone disagrees, they are to ask the messenger what they shall do. The messenger, of course, will say obey the messenger. "And we sent no messenger but that he should be obeyed by Allah's command."[1247] "Whoever obeys the messenger he indeed obeys Allah."[1248]

> And whoever obeys Allah and the messenger, they are those whom Allah has bestowed favors from among the prophets and the truthful and the faithful and the righteous, and a goodly company are they. (Qur'ān 4:69)

> So let those fight in the way of Allah who sell the world's life for the hereafter. And whoever fights in the way of Allah, be he slain or be he victorious, we shall grant him a mighty reward. And what reason have you not to fight in the way of Allah. (Qur'ān 4:75)

> Those who believe fight in the way of Allah, and those who disbelieve fight in the way of the devil. (Qur'ān 4:76)

In essence, if you do not fight for Allah, you are a not a believer, and your final destiny will be in hell. Muslims are to sell this world's life in exchange for life in paradise; die fighting for Allah, and be assured that you won't go to hell. The willingness of a soldier to die for his/her cause provides a tremendous motivation and is an extremely powerful weapon.

The Qur'ān condemns Jews and Christians because "the Jews rejecting Jesus, a prophet of God, as a liar, and doing their utmost to slay him and the Christians raising a mortal prophet to the dignity of Godhead."[1249]

We now know who is committing this genocide—the Mahdi, the Antichrist of Christianity, the messiah of Islam and the Muslim followers of the faith as they conduct their jihad against non-Muslims, peoples, and nations. To understand Islam you have to view their religion from their perspective. Those who speak for Islam say it is a religion of peace and that Islam is opposed to terrorist attacks on the innocent. In the fulfillment of Islam, the full moon, all non-Muslims will have been killed, converted or subjugated, therefore there will be peace. Terrorist's attacks are only perpetuated against Islam, hence they are against them. What we consider terrorist attacks by Muslims against non-Muslims they see as jihad, or Allah's will, and therefore they are not considered terrorist attacks.

Continuing with Revelation 6, we come to verse 9:

> And when He opened the fifth seal, I saw under the altar the souls of those having been slain for the word of God, and for the witness which they had maintained. And they cried with a great voice, saying. Until when, holy and true Master, do You not judge and take vengeance for our blood, from those dwelling on the earth? And there was given to each one a white robe. And it was said to them that they should rest yet a little time, until might be fulfilled also the number of their fellow-slaves and their brothers, those being about to be killed, even as they. (Rev. 6:9–11, IGNT)

There is a lot to consider in these passages thus far in chapter 6. Both the Greek New Testament and the Hebrew Bible have the same word for *saint* and it is rendered as *holy one*. The saints under the altar are the Christians and messianic Jews that have been slaughtered by the Mahdi and his jihadists. This genocide will start unexpectedly with the advent of the Mahdi and so many believing Satan's deception that Islam is a religion of peace. Daniel's warning was "And he will destroy many while they are at ease."[1250] The most unsuspecting, unarmed, and least able to defend themselves will be Christians and Jews living in Muslim nations; these will be the first to be killed, those under the altar, as the Mahdi moves to unite Islam. There will also be many deaths from the radicalized Muslim cells that have been planted in other nations, especially in Eastern Europe, to arise and fight with the announcement of the worldwide jihad.

The saints under the altar ask God when their deaths will be avenged. Situations or acts are only avenged when a wrong has been committed, the shedding of innocent blood[1251] in this case.

The wealth or the booty that the Mahdi spreads around will be from the possessions confiscated from the saints, Muslim-viewed apostates, and nations that offered resistance. "In a time of tranquility he will enter the richest part of the realm, [Saudi Arabia] and he will accomplish what his fathers never did, nor his ancestors; he will distribute plunder, booty, and possessions among them, and he will devise his schemes against strongholds, but only for a time."[1252]

There are thirteen nations with the death penalty for not believing in Allah, being an atheist, or converting from Islam: Iran, Afghanistan, Pakistan, Qatar, Saudi Arabia, Somalia, Sudan, United Arab Emirate, Yemen, Malaysia, Maldives, Mauritania, and Nigeria. There will also be booty from the counties the Mahdi subdues.

Additionally, the Antichrist has been unleashed as the rider on the white horse, and he has been given authority to kill. Some or most of those killed are the saints under the altar. There are Christians that take up arms, however—"and that men would slay one another"[1253]—to defend themselves, their families, and prevent the shedding of innocent blood.[1254] The saints under the altar were killed for the word of God and the witness they had maintained;[1255] in short, they would not convert to Islam. We do know, however, from the book of Daniel and the book of Revelation that the Antichrist is given authority to wage war against the saints and to overcome them.

> I kept looking, and that horn [Antichrist, Mahdi] was waging war with the saints and overpowering them. (Dan. 7:21)

> And his (antichrist – Mahdi) power will be mighty, but not by his own power (it will come from Satan), and he will destroy to an extraordinary degree and prosper and perform his will; he will destroy mighty men and the holy people. (Dan. 8:24)

> And it was given to him to make war with the saints and to overcome them; and authority over every tribe and people and tongue and nation was given to him. (Rev. 13:7)

We are in an age of tolerance—tolerance for anything except Christianity. The saints are slain by Muslims who think they are doing the bidding of Allah. These will be the birth pangs of persecution in full force. There are only two kinds of people that can commit such horrific acts as those depicted in the activities of the conquest of the four horses of the apocalypse. They are people that are godless and are under the influence of Satan or those that have been deceived into thinking they are doing the work of their god or Allah.[1256] The United States has been involved in its fair share of wars, and occasionally very small minorities of US soldiers commit acts of atrocity. However, the news chooses not to report the daily and horrific atrocities committed by our godless enemies, fascists, communists, the Japanese in WWII, and Muslims today. Mainstream media in the US only report the atrocities of America's enemies when some other country has already broken the story, and even then the slant will support their agenda. A soldier that does not think he has to stand before God in judgment for his conduct is capable of horrendous acts as a normal course of soldiering. For the most part, American soldiers bear a much heavier burden in warfare because we know we will report to a higher authority. "He has told you, O man, what is good; And what does the Lord require of you, But to do justice, to love kindness, And to walk humbly with your God."[1257]

There are many references in Scripture about Christians being persecuted for their faith. We are seeing some of these birth pangs today. The Muslim Brotherhood has even invented a word, Islamophobia, to try and demonize people who speak the truth about Islam. "Then they will deliver you up to affliction, and will kill you; and you will be hated by all nations for My name's sake. And then many will be offended, and they will deliver up one another, and will hate one another."

Islam has to be recognized for the real threat that it poses to non-Muslims. Everyone will have three choices: convert to Islam,[1258] put your head on the chopping block, or fight, unless, of course, we have lost our Second Amendment rights. Any representative or senator that has voted or will vote against our Second Amendment right should be voted out of office. It is obvious they do not understand the rights of "We, the People," nor do they understand the Constitution, which they have sworn an oath to defend against all enemies, foreign and domestic.

Stalin had twenty-six million of his unarmed citizens killed.[2] Mao had twenty-five million of his unarmed citizens killed. It was the same for the unarmed citizens of Hitler, Pol Pot, Hussein, Idi Amin, Kim Jong, Ho Chi Minh, and countless other dictators.

Islam has already decaled war on the United States, the great Satan, and our politicians appear to be blind to this threat. WWI and WWII were the result of continual appeasement to an aggres-

---

[2] Estimates are as high as fifty million.

sor until baby Godzilla was allowed to grow into a monster. For the most part politician's desires to maintain the status quo in order to be reelected are incapable of brining change or fighting evil.

Our advice and counsel for how to respond to this grievous situation is given to us from the book of Daniel.

"And by smooth words he will turn to godlessness [atrocities] those who act wickedly toward the covenant [his confederation], but the people who know their God will display strength and *take action*."[1259]

Turning the other cheek is how Christians are told to respond in seeking peace with all men.[1260] However, turning the other cheek is not the only response for Christians; we are to protect the innocent, insure justice prevails, and prevent the spilling of innocent blood.[1261] In Isaiah we are told, "Learn to do good, seek justice, reprove the ruthless, defend the orphan, and plead for the widows."[1262] We are also told, "Cursed be the one who does the Lord's work negligently, And cursed be the one who restrains his sword from blood."[1263] There is tremendous evil in the world, and that is why governments are given the power of the sword.[1264] Scripture says we are to love our enemies; however, we are not to love God's enemies.[1265] The conquest of the Hebrews into the Promised Land was to exact God's judgments on the pagan nations that reside where Israel was to be established[1266] and mercy on other nations.[1267] We know from Scripture that God cannot do evil[1268] and that there is no wickedness in Him.[1269] Therefore, when God commands the Hebrews to utterly destroy the inhabitants of a land, it must be because of their incredible evil. David, the greatest king and warrior in Israel, fought God's battles. Because my lord is fighting the battles of the Lord."[1270] Spiritual battles of foundational reality fought out through people and weapons in provisional reality. Moses, Joshua, Saul, David, Cyrus the Great,[1271] Nebuchadnezzar,[1272] Assyria,[1273] America, divine intervention,[1274] slings, stones, spears, and bow and arrows.[1275] "For the battle is the Lord's, and He will deliver you up into my hands."[1276] "When I saw their fear, I rose and spoke…to the people, "Do not be afraid of them; remember the Lord who is great and awesome, and fight for your brothers, your sons, your daughters, your wives and your houses."[1277] Christ warns against anyone causing a child to stumble. Muslims of Islam by direction of the Qur'ān cut the heads off children when they won't convert. A tree is known by its fruits.

Scripture also says:

And He said to them, "Because of the littleness of your faith, for truly I say to you, if you have faith the size of a mustard seed, you will say to this mountain, Move from here to there, and it will move; and nothing will be impossible to you." (Matt. 17:20)

We know that we cannot pick up a mountain and move it, but we can understand from this that we will be able to do the seemingly impossible because through faith and the power of Jesus Christ, nothing will be impossible for us.[1278] There is also a scriptural understanding that a mountain symbolically represents a kingdom.[1279] From this we can know that a person can make a significant difference in the affairs of men. God has always and will continue to work through people. Revelation 6:4 says, "And that men would slay one another," that implies an opposition of forces.

When Christ bid to Peter to come to him on the water, Peter stepped out of the boat, then his faith floundered, and he began to sink. It is then recorded, "Immediately Jesus stretched out his hand and took hold of him, and said to him, 'You of little faith, why did you doubt?'"[1280] To do the impossible, Peter did that; he walked on water. How much faith did it take? Faith the size of a mustard seed. Peter was able to do the miraculous even with just a little faith. But he doubted. James tells us, "But let him ask in faith without any doubting, for the one who doubts, let not that man expect that he will receive anything from the Lord."[1281]

And I saw when He opened the sixth seal. And behold a great earthquake occurred. And the sun became black as sackcloth made of hair, and the moon became as blood; and the stars of the heaven fell to earth…And the heaven departed like a scroll being rolled up. And every mountain and island were moved out of their places. And the kings of the earth, and the great ones, and the rich, and the commanders and the powerful ones. And every slave and freeman hid themselves in caves and in the rocks of the mountains. And they said to the mountain and to the rocks, fall on us, and hide us from the face of the One sitting on the throne, and from the wrath of the Lamb, because the great day of His wrath has come; and who is able to stand. (Rev. 6:12–17)

The saints under the altar are given robes and told to rest awhile until the rest of their brothers and sisters are also slain. Up to this point in time, all of the carnage has been caused by man. With the opening of the sixth seal, continuing events take on a supernatural power—earthquakes, the sun becomes dark, the moon like blood, and the stars begin to fall from heaven. Everyone on earth now understands that all that is happening is out of their control. There is a God, He is in control, and is now exerting His power over all of his creation. We are under God's authority, whether we submit to it or not. All of those on earth that are without faith in God, in Christ, and the Holy Spirit run and hide in complete and total fear. "Because the great day of His wrath has come, and who is able to stand?"[1282]

And now we know who is being killed: non-Muslims that will not acquiesce to the demands of the Antichrist and who maintain the testimony of Jesus Christ.

When Christ breaks the seventh seal, there is silence in heaven for a half an hour. An angel appears with a golden censer, and the smoke of the incense mixes with the prayers of the saints and ascends to God. The angel then casts the censer to earth, which is accompanied by peals of thunder, flashes of lightning, and an earthquake.[1283]

TOM NEWMAN

THE JUDGMENTS OF THE SEVEN TRUMPETS

The role of prophecy is strictly to glorify God in two ways. God uses prophecy so that he can make humanity aware of future events so that when they do occur, people will understand that God is the Creator and that everything is under his sovereign control.[1284] Second, God uses prophecy to warn his people that they should take heed of his commandments, statutes, and dictates to ensure their place in his eternal kingdom.[1285] As situations unfold, they will provide the missing elements to make the meaning of the prophecy self-evident to all who witness these events.[1286]

We must stay very close to a scriptural understanding when trying to comprehend prophecy lest we add too much of our own thinking and present false doctrines. The very nature of biblical prophecy is unformulated and not meant to be explicit until the events transpire.

The Old Testament begins with Adam and Eve in the garden of eden, individuals living in direct communication with God. God would come and walk in the garden with Adam in the cool of the day.[1287] Paradise was that perfect existence foiled by the influences of Satan,[1288] man's inherent weakness to restrain himself against the temptations of evil,[1289] and man's proclivity to do his will rather than God's.[1290] Our penchant for weakness comes from our fallen nature, which is made obvious by our unwillingness to follow the commandments and statutes of God. We would all rather be in charge of our own destiny, exerting our own will. As ridiculous as that really is, "man's steps are ordained by the Lord, who can understand his way?"[1291] When we are in charge of the decisions in our life, invariably we will choose to sin. When we are indwelt by the Holy Spirit, we are able to obey God, and we are able to resist evil.[1292] The indwelling Holy Spirit gives us the power to overcome temptation; however, we can still make a free-will choice to sin. Obedience is also a free-will choice to walk in the ordained steps

THINGS TO COME

God has laid out for our life. The Bible ends with creation of a new heaven and a new earth,[1293] with Christ as the government[1294] and individuals in direct communication with God. However, in this second beginning, instead of the introduction of Satan,[1295] it will be the destruction of Satan and all of his minions.[1296] The culmination of the battle between good and evil that has lasted for the entire existence of humankind will have come full circle. Christ will return to God that which he set out to create in the first place: a redeemed world.[1297] A world filled with people who conduct themselves worthy of their calling,[1298] keeping the way of the Lord in all that they do, which is living in righteousness and justice, loving-kindness, and walking humbly with their God.[1299] Very much unlike how most of us live our lives today, we will have to be transformed in order for this to come about.

God first created the angels, the heavens, the earth,[1300] and then man.[1301] Adam and Eve failed in their ability to honor God's requirement of them. They did not obey his commandment, honor his sovereignty, or obey his will. The issue was whether they would let God determine what was good or evil, or should they make that decision and disregard what God had said. Simply put, not to eat from the tree of knowledge of good and evil.[1302] The simplicity of the lesson is so that everyone can understand, if not in wisdom, then by example. Because of their disobedience, God expelled them from the garden of eden and removed their immortality.[1303] In God's justice for disobedience, "For in the day that you eat from it you will surely die." Adam and Eve paid the price for their sin. "For the wages of sin is death."[1304] He is the God of love! He is also the God of justice.

God did not cause the death of Adam and Eve; in their free-will choice for disobedience, they made the decision to die. They were expelled from the garden not only as punishment but for their protection. They proved they could not be trusted, so they were expelled least they also eat from the tree of eternal life and live in their sin, without redemption, forever.

> See, I have set before you today life and prosperity, and death and adversity; in that I command you today to love the LORD your God, to walk in His ways and to keep His commandments and His statutes and His judgments. But if your heart turns away and you will not obey, but are drawn away and worship other gods and serve them, I declare to you today that you shall surely perish. I call heaven and earth to witness against you today, that I have set before you life and death, the blessing and the curse. So choose [free will] life in order that you may live, you and your descendants, by loving the LORD your God, by obeying His voice, and by holding fast to Him; for this is your life and the length of your days. (Deut. 30:15–20)

Why do we think it is any different for us? Life for death because of disobedience that is the measure of justice.

> "I, the Lord, have spoken, it is coming and I shall act. I shall not relent, and I shall not pity, and I shall not be sorry, according to your ways and according to your deeds I shall judge you," declares the Lord God. (Ezek. 24:14)

> And there you will remember your ways and all your deeds, with which you have defiled yourselves; and you will loathe yourselves in your own sight for all the evil things that you have done. Then you will know that I am the Lord when I have dealt with you for My name's sake, not according to your evil ways or according to your corrupt deeds. (Ezek. 20:43–44)

God's judgment resumes with the seven trumpets. The first trumpet brings hail mixed with fire and blood, which will burn up a third of the earth's vegetation.[1305] The second trumpet brings something like a great burning mountain that crashes into the sea, and a third of the seas turn to blood, and this kills a third of the creatures in the sea and destroys a third of the ships.[1306] The question arises, is this a meteor or some metaphysical occurrence? The answer is yes. The point is not to be sidetracked with nonessential issues.[1307] God says he will do it, so we can rest assured that it will be done.[1308] How he does it is really not our concern, just as soldiers in battle know little of what the generals are planning.[1309] However, Satan would like us to spend time on nonessential issues[1310] that keeps us from working on our own sanctification and doing God's work, which is evangelizing to the yet-to-be-saved.[1311] "Save others, snatching them out of the fire,"[1312] which will bring glory to God.

The third trumpet causes a great star to fall from heaven, burning like a torch, which falls on the rivers and streams. The star is called Wormwood, and it makes a third of the earth's water bitter. It is not revealed what causes the water to taste bitter; however, many people will die after they drink the bitter water.[1313]

The fourth trumpet judgment dims the sun, moon, and stars by a third of their brightness. An eagle soars in the sky giving an ominous warning of "woe, woe, woe"[1314] to all who remain on earth because of the remaining three trumpet blasts.

The fifth trumpet, the first woe, releases from the abyss locusts that have the power of scorpions. The locusts are allowed to torment everyone that does not have the seal of God on their forehead (the 144,000[1315] and the overcomers[1316]). However, they are not allowed to kill anyone.[1317] The people that are tormented by these locusts are in incredible pain that will last for five months. Those stricken will try to kill themselves but all efforts will fail.[1318] One could reason that the 144,000 with a seal on their foreheads are Messianic Jews with their names written in Christ's book—the remnant of Israel.

The sixth trumpet, the second woe, releases four angels who have been prepared for this hour, day, month, and year, and they will kill a third of mankind.[1319] The four angels of the sixth trumpet release a supernatural army of two hundred million spiritual entities on horseback that breath fire, smoke, and brimstone, which are called plagues, and kill the third part of man.[1320]

This is a very significant event; aside from the absolute carnage, Scripture says that "the rest of mankind, who were not killed, did not repent of their works, and did not repent of their murders, nor of their sorceries, nor of their immorality nor of their thefts."[1321] Those killed by this supernatural army are by reason saints, former pseudo-Christians. Because they did repent, those remaining after this onslaught were those who have not yet repented "of their murders [slaying Christians and Jews], sorceries [witchcraft], fornications [sex slaves], and thefts [booty]," nor have they come to faith in Jesus Christ (Muslims).

We do not know of those that were killed during the tribulation were beheaded by the jihadist of the Mahdi because they would not convert to Islam, worship the beast, or take its mark.[1322] We do know that a third of the remaining population will also die of the plagues of the supernatural army, of starvation in the famine, and by wild beasts.

This brings us to the third woe in chapter 12; however, there is some other information we need to consider in chapters 10 and 11 first.

> And I saw another strong angel coming down out of heaven…having a scroll…and he cried with a great voice…and when he cried, the seven thunders spoke their sounds…and a voice out of heaven said to me, Seal what things the seven thunders spoke and do not write these things…and the voice out of heaven told me to go and take the scroll and eat it…Take and eat it up, and it will make your belly bitter, but it will be sweet as honey in your mouth…And it was sweet in my mouth; and when I ate it, my belly was made bitter. And he said to me, You must again prophesy before peoples and nations and tongues and many kings. (Rev. 10:1–11)

John is asked to eat the scroll that is sweet in his mouth and bitter in his stomach. This is exactly what the to-be-saved saints and the

overcomers will be experiencing during the tribulation. The sweet is the victory in that justice is finally being meted out on all the evil, Satan and wicked people on the earth that have caused so much pain and suffering and death. Yet, the carnage will make us nauseous, bitter in our stomach. "Vengeance is mine and retribution , In due time their foot will slip; for the day of their calamity is near, and the impending things are hastening upon them."[1323] The third woe:

> And the seventh angel trumpeted. The kingdoms of the world became our Lord's, even of His Christ; and He shall reign forever and ever, and the twenty-four elders said, We thank You, Lord God Almighty, the One who is, and who was, and who is coming, because You took Your great power and reigned. And the nations were full of wrath; and Your wrath came, and the time of the judging of the dead, and to give the rewards to Your slaves the prophets, and to the saints, and to the ones fearing Your name to the small and to the great and to destroy those destroying the earth. And the temple of God in Heaven was opened, and the ark of His covenant was seen in His temple and lightnings, and earthquakes, and a great hail occurred. (Rev. 11:15–19)

> And war occurred in heaven, Michael and his angels making war against the dragon. And the dragon and his angels made war, but they did not have strength, nor was a place yet found for them in Heaven. And the great dragon was cast out, the old serpent being called the devil and Satan, he deceiving the whole habitable world; was cast out onto the earth, and his angels were cast with him. Then I heard a loud voice in heaven, saying, "Now has come the salvation, and power, and the kingdom of our God and the authority of His Christ, because the accuser of *our brothers* is thrown down, the one accuses them before our God day and night. And *they overcame him* because of the *blood of the Lamb* and because of the *word of their testimony*, and they *did not love their soul even until death*. Because of this, be glad, the heav-

ens and you who dwell in them. Woe to the ones dwelling on the earth and in the sea, because the devil has come down to you, having great anger, knowing that he has a little time... And the dragon was enraged over the woman, and went away to make war with the rest of her seed, *those keeping the commandments* of God, and having the testimony of Christ Jesus. (Rev. 12:1–17)

The portion of Scripture above that reads "and they did not love their soul even until death"[1324] means, just like Christ, Christians were willing to sacrificially throw down their life in obedience, suffering for others. Satan is still warring with the saints—those keeping the commandments.

Additionally, the verses that reads" they overcame him because of the blood of the Lamb and because of the word of their testimony" is to be understood that we do not have power on our own. John 15:5 quotes Christ saying, "For apart from Me, you can do nothing." In the word of our testimony we are professing our faith in Christ; in our faith we have access to the power in the name of Christ and in his shed blood. The Antichrist receives his power from Satan; we receive ours from Christ, the Holy Spirit, and the ministering spirits (angels)[3], sent out to render service to those about to inherit salvation.[1325]

The Antichrist will demand that everyone in his United Arab States of Islam will take the mark of the beast on the hand or on their forehead[1326] so that they may be identified as followers of the beast. It will be mandated that all commerce will be conducted by these marks so that those without the mark will be forced to receive the mark or will no longer be able to work, to buy, or to sell. It will then be decreed that all must worship the beast; those refusing will be killed.[1327] The design of this entire enterprise is so that Satan can rid the world of the remaining Christians, Jews and anyone else that will not worship him. This is persecution at the

---

[3] *Strong's Dictionary* defines spirits in this application as "angels sent out to aid those about to inherit salvation."

extreme end of the birth pangs; "They will make you outcasts, an hour is coming for everyone who kills you to think he is offering service to God."[1328]

THE RAPTURE OF THE SAINTS

Christ makes a statement in Revelation that we had better take very seriously. The three woes are going to be perpetuated on those remaining on earth. The first woe is for those who do not have the seal of God on their forehead.[1329] We can go as far ahead as Revelation 13 and find that the saints are still on the earth, that they have not been raptured.

> And it was given to him to make war with the saints and to overcome them; and authority over every tribe and people and tongue and nation was given to him. (Rev. 13:7)

The Christians that are overcomers, are in the tribulation, sword in hand, evangelizing to all that have not committed their life to Christ and to the pseudo-Christians.[1330] "This gospel of the kingdom shall be preached in the whole world as a testimony to all the nations, and then the end will come."[1331] The overcomers are being protected. The words *keep* and *kept* in the original Greek usage in the New Testament mean "to guard" and "to protect."[1332] "Because you have *kept* the word of My perseverance, I also will *keep* you from the hour of testing, that is about to come upon the whole world, to test those who dwell upon the earth."[1333] The overcomers are doing that which Christ has commanded us to do: spread the word of the gospel. "I am the way, and the truth, and the life; no one comes to the Father but through Me."[1334] Scripture has told us that it is God's desire that none should perish. "God our Savior, who desires all men to be saved and to come to a knowledge of the truth."[1335] This protection is specific to overcomers and specific to the tribulation period. "Now to Him who is able to do exceeding abundantly beyond all that we ask or think, according to the power that works within us."[1336] Pseudo-Christians and non-Christians will have to endure the tribulation until they are purified and come to a saving faith, at which time they will be taken as they are killed.[1337]

Christ in his explanation of the parable of the soils defines the difference between pseudo-Christians, nonbelievers, and overcomers.

> When anyone hears the word of the kingdom, and does not understand it, the evil one comes and snatches away what has been sown in his heart. This is the one on whom seed was sown beside the road. And the one on whom seed was sown on the rocky places, this is the man who hears the word, and immediately receives it with joy; yet he has no firm root in himself, but is only temporary, and when affliction or persecution arises because of the word, immediately he falls away. And the one on whom seed was sown among the thorns, this is the man who hears the word, and the worry of the world, and the deceitfulness of riches choke the word, and it becomes unfruitful. And the one on whom seed was sown on the good soil, this is the man who hears the word and understands it, who indeed bears fruit, and brings forth, some a hundredfold, some sixty and some thirty. (Matt. 13:19–23)

Daniel talks about the overcomers as believers with insight, and they give understanding to the many during these perilous times. "And those who have insight among the people will give understanding to the many [pseudo- and non-Christians]; yet they will fall by sword and by flame, by captivity and by plunder, for many days [pseudo- and non-Christians]. And some of those who have insight will fall, in order to refine, purge, and make them pure, until the end time because it is still to come at the appointed time."[1338] Daniel explains that there are those that will be purified, made worthy of heaven through their suffering, just as Christ was perfected in his suffering, and he was sinless.[1339] How much more will we have to be purified to be Christ lke? There are others that will continue in their unbelief.

> Many will be purged, purified and refined, but the wicked will act wickedly, and none of the wicked will understand, but those who have insight will understand. (Dan. 12:10)

The overcomers are the people that have lived a committed Christian life—solidly grounded in their faith.[1340] The people that know "and He dies for all, that they who live should no longer live for themselves, but for Him who died and rose again on their behalf,"[1341] and that is how they live their life. These will be qualified as overcomers and take action evangelizing and take action against those shedding innocent blood, the ones who do not restrain their sword from blood. "Your rod and Your staff, they comfort me."

> Go in through the narrow gate, for wide is the gate, and broad is the way that leads to death. And many are the ones who go through it. For narrow is the gate, and constricted is the way that leads to life, and few are the ones who find it. (Matt. 7:13, IGNT)

Psalm 91 is considered by the soldiers in the US military to be the soldier's psalm, and it will be the overcomer's psalm during the tribulation.

TOM NEWMAN

He who dwells in the shelter of the Most High
Will abide in the shadow of the Almighty.
I will say to the Lord, "My refuge and my fortress,
My God, in whom I trust!"
For it is He who delivers you from the snare of the trapper
And from the deadly pestilence.
He will cover you with His pinions,
And under His wings you may seek refuge;
His faithfulness is a shield and bulwark.

You will not be afraid of the terror by night,
Or of the arrow that flies by day;
Of the pestilence that stalks in darkness,
Or of the destruction that lays waste at noon.
A thousand may fall at your side
And ten thousand at your right hand,
But it shall not approach you.
You will only look on with your eyes
And see the recompense of the wicked.

For you have made the Lord, my refuge,
Even the Most High, your dwelling place.
No evil will befall you,
Nor will any plague come near your tent.
For He will give His angels charge concerning you,
To guard you in all your ways.
They will bear you up in their hands,
That you do not strike your foot against a stone.
You will tread upon the lion and cobra,
The young lion and the serpent you will trample down.

"Because he has loved Me, therefore I will deliver him;
I will set him *securely* on high, because he has known My name.
"He will call upon Me, and I will answer him;
I will be with him in trouble;
I will rescue him and honor him.
"With a long life I will satisfy him
And let him see My salvation."

This is being *kept* from the hour of testing by divine intervention and protection.[4]

The pseudo-Christians—Christians in name only—and non-Christians who are perishing during the tribulation have not lived their life in obedience to the commandments of the Holy Trinity. They come to a saving faith as they are evangelized to by the overcomers while being purged and purified by their suffering through the tribulation. All that have not come to a knowledge of the truth will be purified; those who do not will be purged.

> Then the Lord said, "Because this people draw near with their words And honor Me with lip service, But they remove their hearts far from Me, And their reverence for Me consists of tradition by rote." (Isa. 29:13)

For anyone to have to endure any part of the duration of the tribulation seems extremely severe. However, that is because we cannot comprehend God.[1342] Whenever we try to understand God, we try to bring him down to our level. We can simply not understand the degree of God's infinite holiness from the restrictions of provisional reality, yet alone the dimensions of an eternal kingdom. It is not just a matter of our sinfulness; it is also a matter of our disobedience to what he requires of us. We can only try by attempting to understand what he reveals to us in his word. "Every tree that does not bear good fruit is cut down and thrown into the fire."[1343] This purification process is justified because in God's eyes. "There in not one without sin, no not one."[1344] Why is there no one without sin? Verse 18 explains, "There is no fear of God before their eyes." We simply do not understand his purity and absolute holiness from our fallen state; we have to take God at his word. "For as the heavens are higher than the earth, so are My ways higher than your ways,

---

[4] I understand full well about being kept, see Just War by Tom Newman which accounts my experiences with the 101st Airborne in Vietnam in 1968, where we sustained 97% casualties and fatalities.

And My thoughts than your thoughts."[1345] Our understanding of God, our reverence, our fear of him is a mere shadow of what it actually should be.[1346] The best we can do is be submissive to his will and his word because we cannot possibly understand what is the mind and plan of one who is infinite and has infinite knowledge.[1347] Our attitude toward God is to be submissive with fear and reverence; that is not our position toward the outside world. Our counsel for our conduct towards the outside world is, "Only be strong and very courageous."[1348] "Cursed be the one who does the Lords work negligently, and cursed be the one who restrains his sword from blood."[1349]

> As it is written in the law of Moses, all this calamity has come on us; yet we have not sought the favor of the Lord our God by turning from our iniquity and giving attention to thy truth. Therefore, the Lord has kept the calamity in store and brought it on us; for the Lord our God is righteous with respect to all His deeds which He has done, but we have not obeyed His voice. (Dan. 9:13–14)

Christians will struggle trying to understand this. How can a God of love allow all of this carnage to befall mankind? Is it any different than what man has done and is doing to his fellow man? The only difference is that God only acts out of justice; man acts out of greed, lust, and his inherent evil nature. James says; "From where do wars and fighting among you come? Is it not from this your lust…? How is this justice? It is recompense for our noncompliance.[1350] We make the same decisions as did Adam and Eve. What have we been asked to do? To love the Lord with our heart, mind, and soul—to be perfect and to be holy.[1351] Have we done all of these things? What has Christ asked us to do? If you love Me, obey My commandments. Have we done this? Do we obey the Ten Commandments? "Remember the Sabbath day, to keep it holy, in it you shall not do any work."[1352]To put a finer line on the Sabbath: "Turn your foot from doing your own pleasure, the holy day of the Lord honorable, and honor it, desisting from your own pleasure."[1353] God says He will not be "mocked; for whatever a man sows, this he will also reap,"[1354] and God's words will not come back empty.[1355]

A pre-tribulation rapture position predisposes Christian to complacency, which plays right into the hands of Satan by buying into his deception and making provisions for him to succeed. Thinking when all hell breaks loose we will be raptured before the tribulation begins so all that is occurring right now is really not a concern for us is a false doctrine. This is a rationalization straight from Satan. We as Christians will be held accountable for what happens in provisional reality. We have been given stewardship over the earth and of the morality of others.[1356] The rapture—who withdraws their army before the fight?

> As they have chosen their *own* ways, And their soul delights in their abominations, So I will choose their punishments And will bring on them what they dread. Because I called, but no one answered; I spoke, but they did not listen. And they did evil in My sight And chose that in which I did not delight. (Isa. 66:3–4)

> The earth mourns *and* withers, the world fades *and* withers, the exalted of the people of the earth fade away. The earth is also polluted by its inhabitants, for they transgressed laws, violated statutes, broke the everlasting covenant. Therefore, a curse devours the earth, and those who live in it are held guilty. Therefore, the inhabitants of the earth are burned, and few men are left. (Isa. 24:4–6)

> Woe to those who call evil good, and good evil; Who substitute darkness for light and light for darkness; Who substitute bitter for sweet and sweet for bitter! Woe to those who are wise in their own eyes And clever in their own sight! Woe to those who

are heroes in drinking wine And valiant men in mixing strong drink, Who justify the wicked for a bribe, And take away the rights of the ones who are in the right! For they have rejected the law of the LORD of hosts And despised the word of the Holy One of Israel. On this account the anger of the LORD has burned against His people, And He has stretched out His hand against them and struck them down. (Isa. 5:20–25)

Therefore, listen to me, you men of understanding. Far be it from God to do wickedness, And from the Almighty to do wrong. For He pays a man according to his work, And makes him find it according to his way. Surely, God will not act wickedly, And the Almighty will not pervert justice. (Job 34:10–12)

You shall love the LORD your God with all your heart and with all your soul and with all your might. These words, which I am commanding you today, shall be on your heart. You shall teach them diligently to your sons and shall talk of them when you sit in your house and when you walk by the way and when you lie down and when you rise up. (Deut. 6:5–7)

Have you not done this to yourself. By your forsaking the Lord your God, When He led you in the way? (Jer. 2:17)

But this is what I commanded them, saying, 'Obey My voice, and I will be your God, and you will be My people, and you will walk in all the way which I command you, that it may be well with you. Yet they did not obey or incline their ear, but walked in their own counsels and in the stubbornness of their evil heart, and went backward and not forward. (Jer. 7:23–24)

Thus says the Lord to His people, "Even so they have loved to wander; they have not kept their feet in check. Therefore the Lord does not accept them; now He will remember their iniquity and call their sins into account." (Jer. 14:10)

> The heart is more deceitful than all else. And is desperately sick: Who can understand it? "I, the Lord, search the heart, I test the mind, Even to give to each man according to his ways, According to the result of his deeds. (Jer. 17:9–10)

> Now the end is upon you, and I shall send My anger against you; I shall judge you according to your ways, and I shall bring all your abominations upon you. For My eye will have no pity on you, nor shall I spare you, but I shall bring your ways upon you, and your abominations will be among you; then you will know that I am the Lord. (Ezek. 7:3–4)

> And you should not fear the ones killing the body, but not being able to kill the soul. But rather fear Him being able to destroy both soul and body in Hell. (Matt, 10:28, IGNT)

He is a God of love and compassion and equally a God of justice and wrath. God demonstrated His love for us by sending His Son to die for us while we were yet sinners. We accepted that gift and continued in our sins without accepting the due responsibility for the gift of salvation we have accepted. We think because He is a God of love, we have a free pass. The endurance of these events in provisional reality is only perceived as heart-wrenching, if you do not have an understanding of foundational reality. "About those who are asleep, so that you will not grieve as do the rest who have no hope."[1357] Although, He asked us to reciprocate that love by obedience to His commandments, we chose to rebel. Even the overcomers will be purified; we are all given a measure of faith.[1358] To whom much has been given, much will be required.[1359] And we still have our job to do, to "go into all the world preaching the gospel."[1360] As the overcomers preach the gospel, people come to faith in Jesus Christ primarily because of all of the carnage that is going around them everywhere.[1361] As they come to faith, they are killed, to be relieved of any more suffering, because now their eternal life has been secured. All that die in their iniquity are subject to the second death.

What would society look like today if we had adopted and enforced just three of God's commandments and held them as sacred?

> But if in the field the man finds the girl who is engaged, and the man forces her and lies with her, then only the man who lies with her shall die. But you shall do nothing to the girl; there is no sin in the girl worthy of death, for just as a man rises against his neighbor and murders him, so is this case. (Deut. 22:25–26)

> Then the man who lay with her shall give to the girl's father fifty *shekels* of silver, and she shall become his wife because he has violated her; he cannot divorce her all his days. (Deut. 22:29)

> When you make a vow to the LORD your God, you shall not delay to pay it, for it would be sin in you and the LORD your God will surely require it of you. You shall be careful to perform what goes out from your lips, just as you have voluntarily vowed to the LORD your God, what you have promised. (Deut. 23:21–23)

The implications of these three laws for society would be capital punishment for the crime of rape. Capital punishment is not revenge killing; it is not meant to be a deterrent. It is punishment, pure and simple.

If a man has intercourse with a virgin, he must marry her and cannot divorce her because he has violated her.

The vows we make to God during the wedding ceremony are until death do we part—no divorces.[1362] Without divorce, we are forced to work through our challenges and not just give up for personal selfish reasons.

We can see the inherent good in obedience to God's commandments. However, man has put himself above God and condones what God condemns.

THINGS TO COME

If your child was spinning out of control and headed for certain death, as a parent with your love for your child, wouldn't you do whatever was necessary to save them from certain destruction? Why should it be any different for us than it was for Jews when they were under the curse for their lack of faith and disobedience? "Jesus Christ is the same yesterday and today, yes, and forever."[1363] I was a pseudo-Christian before my refining war experience and returned a committed Christian. I will again have to go through the refining process as an overcomer to be worthy of entrance to heaven because even on my best day, I am still a loathsome sinner. I am forgiven when I repent, but that still does not change who I am. We are not sinners because we sin; we sin because we are sinners.

We now come to chapter 14, finally, our reprieve. First we have the fulfillment of the requirement that the gospel be preached to the whole world referenced in Matthew 24:14. We understand that this has been the responsibility of the 144,000 to the Jews and the fourth of the world. It has been to the overcomers to minister to the other nations of the world. However, God brings to fruition the requirement of Mattew 24:14.

> And I saw another angel flying in mid-heaven, having an everlasting gospel to proclaim to those dwelling on the earth, even to every nation and tribe and tongue and people, saying in a great voice, Fear God, and give glory to Him, because the hour of His judgment has come; also, Worship Him who has made the heavens, and the earth, the seas, and the fountains of water. (Rev. 14:6–7)

People like to speculate that we live in the end-times because with TV and the internet, we are now in a time that the gospel can be preached to the whole world. That qualification has always been met; God will do it, and he will have an angel preach the gospel to the whole world from above the earth where everyone can hear, and because of the carnage, they will be very attentive.

Another angel, a third one, follows the first and proclaims that:

> If anyone worships the beast and his image, and receives a mark on his forehead or upon his hand he also will drink of the wine of the wrath of God, which is mixed full strength in the cup of His anger, and he will be tormented with fire and brimstone in the presence of the holy angels and in the presence of the Lamb. And the smoke of their torment goes up forever and ever, and they have no rest day and night. (Rev. 14:9–11)

The fate of the Mahdi and all of his followers is sealed by the Lamb.

> Here is the patience of the saints; here are the ones keeping the commands of God, and the faith of Jesus. And I heard a voice out of Heaven saying to me. Write; Blessed are the dead, the ones dying in the Lord from now. Yes, says the Spirit, they shall rest from their labors, and their works follow with them. (Rev. 14:12–13)

"Blessed are the dead, the ones dying in the Lord from now, they shall rest from their labors and their work, eternal fruit follow with them." This is the rapture, the death of the overcomers. However, only the bodies die; the souls and spirits of the overcomers are changed in the twinkling of an eye. They are raised imperishable,[1364] and they are with the Lord forever.[1365]

> And I saw; and behold, *a white cloud*, and on the cloud One sitting, like the Son of man. Having on His head a golden crown, and in His hand a sharp sickle. And another angel went forth out of the temple, *crying in a great voice* to the One sitting on the cloud, Send Your sickle and reap, because Your hour to reap came because the harvest of the earth was dried, And the One sitting on the cloud thrust His sickle onto the earth, and the earth was reaped. (Rev. 14:14–16)

The saints that are the overcomers endure until the end,[1366] professing their faith, preaching the gospel, and giving witness by their testimony. They are the ones that will be raptured. These activities define Daniel's "the people who know their God will display strength and take action" along with taking up the sword as jihadist and Christians "slay one another."[1367] "Then we the living, remaining, will be caught up in the clouds to a meeting of the Lord in the air, and so always with the Lord we will be." Rest from our labors of "save others, snatching them out of the fire." We were told in Revelation 3 all that is entailed in being an overcomer. Enduring this peril was not in vain; we will eat from the tree of life and receive a crown of life. We will not be hurt by the second death. We will be given a new name. We will be given authority over the nations and to rule them with an iron fist so the earth will never again see the inhumanity and evil that consumes our world today. We will be acknowledged by Christ before the Father. Our name will not be blotted out from the Book of Life, from which all will be judged in the final judgment. We will be clothed in white. And we will be with Christ in heaven on His throne. Christ is our example, and we are told He endured all that He did for the joy and the glory that awaited Him. This is our example: to endure for the joy and glory that awaits us in foundational reality.

> Fixing our eyes on Jesus, the author and perfecter of faith, who for the joy set before Him endured the cross, despising the shame, and has sat down at the right hand of the throne of God. (Heb. 12:2)

> Be glad in that day and leap for joy, for behold, your reward is great in heaven. (Luke 6:23)

We will be held accountable for the state of the world. Scripture tells us that "the eyes of the Lord are in every place watching the evil and the good."[1368] Because we will be held accountable, the rapture will occur in the timing of Revelation 14:14 after the death of billions of people as God brings His justice onto the earth and all its inhabitants. Christians love to say, "We will be outta here." Joel says, "Let all the inhabitants of the land tremble, For the Day of the Lord is coming; Surely it is near, A day of darkness and gloom, A day of clouds and thick darkness."[1369] The tribulation is to render justice on the world and to purge, purify, and refine pseudo-Christians, nonbelievers who convert, and Christians alike.[1370] The appointed time[1371] of the end has been set; it will be unfortunate for those who must endure the tribulation. No less so than for the Jews that were alive during the Holocaust.

Many profess that Christians will be raptured before the tribulation begins; however, the only verse that declares that Christ is coming on a white cloud to rescue his saints does not occur until Revelation 14:14. I put more credence in what the Scripture actually says than the speculation of others that cannot be supported by Scripture.

The significance and importance of what we do in provisional reality has its ultimate fulfillment in eternity—forever in foundational reality. God's wrath will also fall on those who have had the opportunity of a free-will choice to believe in Jesus Christ as their Lord and Savior and have not.[1372] All that endure the judgments of God on humanity realize that all that is written in the Bible is true.[1373] They witnessed the events of Revelation unfolding precisely as they were foretold two thousand years ago.

The church has not safeguarded the truth by teaching the whole Gospel they have led many believers into their half-truth, which is the same as teaching a false doctrine or apostasy.

We are drawn to and hang on too tightly to this idea of life in provisional reality. God tries to warn us that we are a vapor, a mist, a blade of grass that withers; we are as sheep to the slaughter.[1374] Christ asked His disciples to evangelize to the world, and the world hated them because as Christ warned, "They hated Me, they will also hate you."[1375] Why? Because Christ brought the light, the truth, and it revealed that their deeds were evil. They loved the darkness rather than the light[1376] because they did not want their evil deeds revealed, so they hated the light. And they killed the light; they also killed the disciples. All but John died as martyrs, and even John they tried to kill, numerous times, but God kept him.[1377] People would rather kill the source of light than change their ways—self-will over God's will. It is the same path that the Hebrews took rebellion rather than obedience to the point of killing Christ. The victory for Christ and the victory of Christ were not realized in provisional reality. His glory and victory were realized in foundational reality; the victory is eternal. Everything of earth, of provisional reality, is temporary, of no lasting value. We should attach very little significance of anything that is temporary, including our lives, here in provisional reality. Our victory will be in foundational reality, just as Christ's was.

> While we look not at the things which are seen, but at the things which are not seen; for the things which are seen are temporal, but the things which are not seen are eternal. (2 Cor. 4:18)

> Do not love the world, nor the things of the world. If anyone loves the world the love of the Father is not in him. (1 John 2:15)

We will be slaughtered,[1378] however, only our bodies die, as they are temporary; our spirit and souls are eternal. We will fulfill our destiny in foundational reality—in eternity. Scripture provides our encouragement.

> For momentary, light affliction is producing for us an eternal weight of glory far beyond all comparison. (2 Cor. 4:17)

> For I consider that the sufferings of this present time are not worthy to be compared with the glory that is to be revealed to us. (Rom. 8:18)
>
> Things which eye has not seen and ear has not heard, And which have not entered the heart of man, All that God has prepared for those who love Him. (1 Cor. 2:9)
>
> But we do not want you to be uninformed, brethren, about those who are asleep, that you may not grieve, as do the rest who have no hope. For we believe that Jesus died and rose again. (1 Thess. 4:13–14)

When I suffered from anaphylactic shock and flatlined, my body stayed behind because that was its reality; my spirit and soul went into foundational reality because that is their realm.[1379] When I was in foundational reality, I was fully conscious, and I was still very much the person I am now. We do not die; we are transformed from physical to spiritual, and we continue after death. There will be a lot to endure during the tribulation. We are best served by maintaining a perception on all of this from foundational reality. Our bodies are formed from dust; our spirit and soul are God-breathed. We should not expect what befalls the body to be the same fate as the spirit and soul. They have different origins—one physical, one spiritual. They are made out of different stuff, and they will have different fates.[1380]

> Jesus said to her, I am the resurrection and the life, he who believes in Me shall live even if he dies, and everyone who lives and believes in Me *shall never die.* Do you believe this? (John 11:25–26)
>
> It is sown a natural body, it is raised a spiritual body. If there is a natural body, there is also a spiritual body. (1 Cor. 15:44)

> Behold, I tell you a mystery, we shall not all sleep, but we shall all be changed, in a moment, in the twinkling of an eye. For this perishable must put on the imperishable, and this mortal must put on immortality. (1 Cor. 15:51–53)

> Although he was a son, he learned obedience from the things which he suffered. And having been made perfect, he became to all those who obey him the source of eternal salvation. (Heb 5:8–9)

We too will have to be made perfect through our suffering. Even Christ had to be made perfect, and he was without sin. How many have been obedient to "therefore you are to be perfect, as your heavenly Father is perfect"[1381] and "but like the Holy One who called you, be holy yourself in all your behavior"?[1382] Because it is written, "You shall be holy, for I am holy."[1383]

Christ's death on the cross pays the penalty for all repented sins of all believers so that we are forgiven and may have eternal life. But even after I am forgiven, I have not changed; I still am a fallen creature and must be purged, purified, and refined because of who I am. The tribulation, whether for a pseudo-Christian or an overcomer, is still a refining process to qualify a person to enter heaven. I have to be completely submitted to God before I enter heaven, or I too may rebel in foundational reality as did Satan and a third of the angels. Even though I am forgiven, as Paul says, I still do the things I do not want to do.[1384] Even though I am indwelt by the Holy Spirit and have the power to overcome sin, I still choose to sin. There is a plethora of benefits available to the Christian—forgiveness, grace, imputed righteousness, justification, the indwelling Holy Spirit, eternal life—but it still does not change my fallen nature. My soul, who I am as a person, will go into heaven; however, my soul has to be fundamentally transformed, and that will happen through the refining process. "Through many tribulations we must enter the kingdom of God."[1385]

Why is all of this necessary—the slaughter of billions and the complete elimination of evil? Let's say you are a truly committed Christian and have put your faith in Jesus Christ as your only means of salvation, and through the grace of God have been granted salvation. What assurances do you have, or does anyone have, that once you are in foundational reality (heaven), you will not choose to rebel like Satan and his minions? We need to be fundamentally transfigured; this purging and purifying process of the tribulation will produce that change and ultimately curtail our free-will choice to rebel. "Giving thanks to the Father, who has qualified us to share in the inheritance of the saints in Light. For He rescued us from the domain of darkness, and transferred us to the kingdom of His beloved Son."[1386]

What about the people that have already died and do not go through this process? People that have a good understanding of foundational reality will see the inherent necessity of this process. For those still stuck in provisional reality, let me offer an illustrative example. Scripture tells us that God, the Trinity, created angels in numbers too high to count. Scripture also tells us about Satan.

> You had the seal of perfection, Full of wisdom and perfect in beauty. You were blameless in your ways. From the day you were created. Until unrighteousness was found in you. You were internally filled with violence, And you sinned. You corrupted your wisdom by reason of your splendor. (Ezek. 28:12, 15–17)

Satan rebelled. At the time of the creation of angels, there was no evil; if there was no evil, none of the angels would have known what evil was or is. Satan said he wanted to be like the most high (the five "I wills".)[1387] The other angles, not knowing evil, thought, *Okay, that's a good thing. He wants to be as good and as righteous as God.* God identified his true motives when he saw inequity in the heart of Satan. A third of the angels sided with Satan, and they too made a free-will choice to rebel. In heaven with God, witnesses to all God's splendor, majesty, holiness, omniscience, and omnipotence, they chose to rebel. God thought, *Okay, they did not know what evil was, what evil looked like. I will have to show them how evil starts, grows, and destroys everything. Let's make man in our own image and give him free will as well.* Three times in the book of Daniel it says the angels are watching, we can speculate, along with all of those that have already died. "This sentence is by the decree of the angelic watchers. And the decision is a command of the holy ones, In order that the living may know That the Most High is ruler over the kingdom of men."[1388]

Evil must run its course to its full consummation so that all will understand evil—that it only ultimately destroys everything—so that in eternity, all free-will choices will be made for good, to honor and give glory to God in complete obedience as was demonstrated by Christ in his life and on the cross, obedience unto death. Whether we go through the tribulation or watch the process with the angelic watchers, this experience will fundamentally change our very soul so that once in heaven, we will never choose to rebel against God; we will exist in eternity in complete submission and obedience.

We are told in Scripture that Christ will return on a cloud for the rapture of the saints. In Scripture, that does not happen until Revelation 14. The exegesis texts for our understanding thus far are as follows:

- With the clouds One like the Son of Man was coming. (Dan. 7:13)

- What will be the sign of Your coming and of the end of the age? (Matt. 24:3)

- Unless those days were cut short. [The tribulation will be cut short. It is the 1,335 days of Daniel 12:12]. (Matt. 24:22)

- The sign of the Son of Man and the end coming on the clouds. (Matt. 24:30)

- Then we who are alive and remain will be caught [harpazo] together with them in the clouds. (1 Thess. 4:17)

- He is coming with the clouds, and every eye will see Him. (Rev. 1:7)

- Because you have kept the word of My patience, I also will keep you out of that hour of trial which is about to come upon the whole habitable earth to test those who dwell on the earth [keep, kept, to guard and protect]. (Rev. 3:10)

- Four horses of the apocalypse and it was granted to them to take peace from the earth and that men should slay one another. Authority was given to them over a fourth of the earth, to kill with sword. (Rev. 6:1–8)

- Underneath the altar the souls of those who had been slain because of the word of God [saints slaughtered, not raptured], (Rev. 6:9)

- And each was given a white robe; and they were told to rest for a little while longer, until the number of their fellow servants…who were to be killed even as they had been, should be complete [more saints to be killed]. (Rev. 6:11)

- The great day of His wrath. (Rev. 6:17)

- White robes—these are the ones who come out of the great tribulation—serve Him day and night. (Rev. 7:14)

- And a third of mankind was killed by the plagues. [The saints are still on the earth. Those that were killed, repented; those that did not repent, continue.] (Rev. 9:18)

- The rest of mankind who were not killed did not repent. (Rev. 9:20)

- The nations were raged, Your wrath came and the time came for the dead to be judged, reward for Your slaves, prophets and saints and those who fear Your name and to destroy those who destroy the earth. (Rev. 11:18)

- War in heaven, and the dragon is thrown down. (Rev. 12:7)

- The dragon enraged with the woman and went to make war with the rest of her children, who keep the commandments and hold to the testimony of Jesus [the saints that are still on the earth]. (Rev. 12:17)

- It was also given to it to make war with the saints and to overcome them [the saints that are still on the earth]. (Rev. 13:7)

- The many that did not worship the beast are to be killed [the saints that are still on the earth]. (Rev. 13:15)

- An angel flying in heaven with an eternal gospel to preach then the end will come. (Rev. 14:6)

- Here is the patience of the saints who keep the commandments. (Rev. 14:12)

- Behold a white cloud, and sitting on the cloud was one like a son of man. And an angel cried out, "Put in your sickle and reap the harvest of the earth is ready." [The rapture, coming on the clouds to reap the elect. This is the only reference to Christ returning to earth on the clouds for His elect. Scripture says this is when the rapture happens.] (Rev. 14:14)

Hitler killed six million unarmed Jews and five million Christians; no one raised a hand or an army to stop the genocide. Christians are persecuted today in America and killed in other counties; no one raises a hand or an army to stop the persecution and the killings. Birth pangs and buds of spring.

Revelation 14:14, the rapture, occurs after the seven seals and the seven trumpet judgments have occurred. It is reasonable to assume that the abomination of desolation occurs immediately after the rapture when all of the Christians are removed, that the antichrist (Mahdi) would declare himself as god. Daniel tells us that the abomination occurs 1,290 days after the onset of the tribulation.[1389]

Chapter 14 continues with a second reaping; this time it is for those destined for God's wrath.

> And another angel came out of the temple which is in heaven, and he also had a sharp sickle. Then another angel, the one who has power over fire, came out from the altar; and he called with a loud voice to him who had the sharp sickle, saying, "Put in your sharp sickle and gather the clusters from the vine of the earth, because her grapes are ripe." So the angel swung his sickle to the earth and gathered *the clusters from* the vine of the earth, and threw them into the great wine press of the wrath of God. And the wine press was trodden outside the city, and blood came out from the wine press, up to the horses' bridles, for a distance of two hundred miles. (Rev. 14:17–20)

> If anyone worships the beast and his image, and receives a mark on his forehead or on his hand, he also will drink of the wine of the wrath of God, which is mixed full strength in the cup of His anger. (Rev. 14:9–10)

Keep in mind that as far as the Scripture is concerned, Israel is the center of the world,[1390] God's chosen people in a chosen land. Everything in Scripture revolves around Israel, and later in biblical history, the church, or the family of believers, becomes involved.

The rapture scenario as portrayed here is the only view that makes sense of Christ's parable of the tares and the wheat.[1391]

In the book of Daniel, there are a number of dreams and visions to which Daniel gives the reader an understanding of

THINGS TO COME

their interpretation. In King Nebuchadnezzar's dream of the great statue,[1392] there is a lot of speculation that the ten toes of the statue represent a revival of the Holy Roman empire. This understanding comes from Daniel 9:26, which reads, "The people of the prince who is to come will destroy the city and the sanctuary." Because the Roman army destroyed Jerusalem and the temple in AD 70, it is assumed that the Antichrist will come from the remnant of the old Roman empire. This speculation was fueled by the creation of the European Economic Community, which began with six members and grew to a membership of twelve. The EC has since grown to twenty-seven countries.

However, when the Roman army took land by conquest, it would draft men from the indigenous population into its ranks and make them part of their legions. When Vespasian abandoned his conquest for Jerusalem to travel from Egypt to Rome to become the new emperor, he sent his son Titus to capture Jerusalem. Titus sailed from Alexandria in Egypt and launched his attack on Jerusalem from Syria.[1393] Titus used the Fifth and Tenth Legions that were already in Judah. He also employed the Fifteenth Legion from Turkey and the Third from Syria. The geography of Turkey and Syria represent the people who the prince (the Antichrist) is to come from. It may not be his country of origin, but it is where his seat of power will be.

Revelation 17 reads, "Here is the mind which has wisdom. The seven heads are seven mountains [kingdoms] on which the woman sits, and they are seven kings; five have fallen; [the Assyrian Empire of Sennacherib,[1394] the Babylonian Empire of Nebuchadnezzar,[1395] the Medes and Persians of Cyrus the Great,[1396] the Hellenistic Dynasty of Alexander the Great,[5] and the Seleucids of Antiochus][1397] one is [John was living in the time of the Roman empire, the sixth.] the other has not yet come; and when it comes, he must remain a little while. The beast which was and is not, is himself also an eighth and is one of the seven, and he goes to

---

[5] Alexander's rule occurred after the writings of the Old Testament.

destruction."¹³⁹⁸ The seventh conquers of the Middle East were the Mongols under Genghis Khan. There was much infighting after the death of Khan, and the empire broke into four parts. The eastern portions were subjugates by the eighth and final empire, the Ottoman Turkish empire, which converted the Mongols to Islam. The Ottoman empire was defeated and disbanded by the allies in WWI. The Ottoman Turkish empire, the beast, which was and is not, was the eighth. The beast is himself also an eighth and is one of the seven. The Ottoman Turkish empire was the eighth, and because they subjugated the Mongols and converted them to Islam, the seventh meets the criteria of "an eighth and is one of the seven." The beast is the revival of the Turkish Ottoman Empire, the caliphate, not a revival of the Roman empire.

The dynasties of old ravaged the Middle East and parts of Europe, overwhelming villages and towns and killing and subjugating the unarmed populations. The strategy of rapid surprise attacks on smaller and weaker armies was usually successful. The raids were aided by poor or no source of communication for help. Their quest was to wrest control of the resources of other lands, plunder their wealth, and to subjugate the population into slave labor because they could not afford to pay laborers to build the edifices they wanted to create. The conquests were driven by greed, power, and lust.¹³⁹⁹ This was all changed by providence when the largest military in the world, Great Britain, was unable to best a much smaller force of an armed citizenry with a resolve: the American revolution and the anointing of One Nation Under God. America was also the nation that brought an end to the slave labor industry.

Satan deceives by turning the truth into a lie and by turning lies into deceptions of truth. Christ came to earth and performed miracles by the power of God, and the Jews accused him of having satanic powers.¹⁴⁰⁰ The Antichrist will use satanic powers to perform his miracles, and he will be worshiped as a god.¹⁴⁰¹ The coming onto the scene of the Antichrist (Mahdi) is said to be according to the work of Satan and in all power, signs, wonder, and falsehood, and in all deceit of unrighteousness for those who are perishing.[1402]

Scripture tells us that Satan will confer the rule of the world on to the Antichrist,[1403] who is identified as the Mahdi of Islam. History records many instances where it is not difficult to believe that Satan was guiding the action and destiny of certain governments—the dynasties of old, Nazi Germany, Stalin, Mao, Hussein, Ho Chi Minh, Kim Jong, and Calles. It is evidently true that some governments are run independent of God.

America is the only nation founded under the principle of "One Nation Under God." We have been richly blessed for the last 239 years as no other nation has because of that declaration, from ox carts to a man on the moon in 200 years. However, even we have gone astray as we override God's law with man-made laws. Divine permission is given to Satan, and he gives the kingdoms to whoever will follow his dictates.[1404] This is within the sovereign purpose of God. God, being infinite, is infinitely good. Satan, being finite, is evil to the extent of his resources, means, and the restrictions imposed on him by the Holy Spirit until he is taken out of the midst. It is also true. "So that the living may know that the most High rules in the kingdom of men, and gives it to whomever He will."[1405]

Satan, from foundational reality, will direct all of the Antichrist's behavior and will attempt to rule provisional reality. Satan's evil nature and undertakings reach beyond our ability to comprehend based on our limited understanding of the interplay between foundational and provisional reality.

Christians, indwelt by the Holy Spirit, need to be serious about their study of Scripture in an attempt to understand these very complicated and vastly important issues. How else will we come to understand the holiness of God and what he requires of us?[1406]

Misconceptions about the true identity of Satan are more prevalent then the truth. "And men loved the darkness rather than the light; for their deeds were evil,"[1407] and the light would have exposed them. People like to believe that ignorance is bliss and that they cannot be held accountable for the things they do not know. However, Scripture reveals that we all know about God because God has innately embedded within us the knowledge or an awareness of who he is.[1408] This is why nonbelievers will be held accountable and punished for their nonbelief. Additionally, "And the Holy Spirit also testifies to us; for after saying, This is the covenant that I will make with them After those days, says the Lord; I will put My laws upon their heart, and on their mind I will write them,"[1409] How do we know we have this innate and internal knowledge? The Holy Spirit bears witness to us through our conscience. "In that they show the work of the law written in their hearts, their conscience bearing witness and their thoughts alternately accusing or else defending them."[1410] If we are not well versed in Scripture to help us interpret the Holy Spirit's bearing witness to us, we can justify just about any behavior. God has also sent us His Son. "And He is the radiance of His glory and the exact representation of His nature, and upholds all things by the word of His power."[1411] Because of who Christ is, we know God, "I in You and You in Me."[1412] When we are in Christ, others may come to know Him through us.

When we do not respond to this innate information and deny, suppress, or ignore the truth, we are mimicking the rebellion of Satan. Just like in any civilization, ignorance of the law is no excuse. Citizens are obligated to understand the laws and abide by them.

THE SEVEN BOWLS OF WRATH

All of the Christians have been removed from the earth before the bowl judgments begin. The overcomers have endured to the end to the rapture, the appointed end of their suffrage. Christ warned in

Matthew 24 that after the sign of His coming on the clouds, we would come the end of the age. The bowl judgments are against all of those that would not repent and put their trust in Christ for their salvation. The pseudo-Christians and nonbelievers that became true Christians have come to a saving faith and have been removed during the tribulation. The fate of those remaining is, "For they poured out the blood of saints and prophets, and Thou hast given them blood to drink. They deserve it."[1413] Everyone is accountable to God, whether they want to acknowledge that or not.[1414] "At the name of Jesus, every knee will bow, of those who are in heaven and on the earth, and under the earth."[1415]

The fate of the Mahdi and the jihadists for the spilling of innocent blood come in the bowl judgments. "Thou dost hate all who do iniquity, Thou dost destroy those who speak falsehood; The Lord abhors the man of bloodshed and deceit…And the one who loves violence His soul hates. The wicked will return to Sheol, even all the nations who forget God."[1416]

The first bowl leaves all that have the mark of the beast with a loathsome and malignant sore.[1417]

The second bowl turns the seas to blood and everything in the seas die.

The third turns the rivers and springs to blood, as well.[1418] "Blood to drink, they deserve it."

The fourth angel pours out his bowl on the sun, and it turns up the heat so that the heat from the sun scorches the earth's inhabitants like fire.[1419]

The fifth bowl plunges the kingdom of the Mahdi into complete darkness, and they gnaw their tongues because of the pain, and they blasphemed God.

The sixth angel's bowl has the ability to dry up the Euphrates River so that the kings from the rising of the sun will be unhindered as they advance to participate in the battle of Har-Magedon.[1420]

The seventh bowl is poured out, there are flashes of lightning and peals of thunder, and a voice is heard saying, "It is done." Huge hailstones come down from heaven to the men below.[1421] The bowl judgments exact justice on the Antichrist (the Mahdi), all of his followers (the jihadists), and all those remaining on the earth.

It is now time for the battle before the millennium kingdom is established by Christ. Christ returns, now at his second coming, riding on a white horse with an entire army riding on white horses with him. "And from His mouth comes a sharp sword, so that with *it*, He may smite the nations; and He will rule them with a rod of iron; and He treads the wine press of the fierce wrath of God, the Almighty. And on His robe and on His thigh He has a name written, KING OF KINGS AND LORD OF LORDS."[1422]

We don't really think that Christ has a physical sword in His mouth; what he has is a command for his army to smite the nations. The word *it* in this verse is referencing how Christ will smite the nations; in the original Greek, *it* is rendered here as "other persons." Paul says in Ephesians 6 that "the sword of the Spirit, which is the word of God." With this understanding, this verse is rendered "and from His mouth comes a sharp command, so that with the command *the other persons with Him* may smite the nations."[1423] This battle is prophesized by the prophet Ezekiel, and the details are found in chapter 38 to 39, and Christ orchestrates the entire battle.[1424] All of the nations that are mentioned are today Muslim countries. Gog of the land of Magog (Turkey), the prince of Rosh, Meshech, and Tubal (Turkey through Azerbaijan). *Strong's Dictionary* defines Gog as symbolically referencing a future Antichrist. Magog, Tubal, and Gomer are all today known as Turkey. Gomer as a part of Turkey includes Syria and Lebanon. Torgamah is modern-day Iraq, Persia is today Iran, parts of Iraq, and Afghanistan. Put is Libya; Meshech is Azerbaijan. Ethiopia is the same as today and may include Sudan.[1425] "These nations will know the wrath of the Almighty." Christ, in his warning to the church in Pergamum, where the throne of Satan is, said that if they did not repent, he would "make war against them with the sword of My mouth."[1426]

The next occurrence is that an angel descends from heaven and binds Satan in chains and casts him into the abyss where he is to remain for a thousand years.[1427] This is our prima facie evidence that the cosmic battle has never been between God and Satan. It has always been Satan against man to achieve his five "I wills" within the framework of the permissive will of God. God was never challenged by Satan as is evidenced by the fact that he is disposed of by a mere angel, and *mere* is used only in the sense of a comparison to God.

If we hold to a strictly provisional view of these events, we can wonder how God could have let so much suffering and pain exist. However, if we view things foundationally, we understand that events of this life are not really significant in light of our eternal existence. To put this in perspective, because we struggle with eternity, let's say our life of seventy-odd years is equivalent to one second in a year of 31,000,001 seconds. What happens in the one second of our life is inconsequential compared to the other thirty-one million seconds as long as we made the right decisions and heaven is our final abode. This is the very reason Scripture tells us we are a vapor,[1428] a breeze.[1429] "All flesh is like grass, it withers and dies."[1430] Circumstances and events seem paramount from within provisional reality; however, the whole point of faith is a trust in the benevolence of God and faith in his sovereignty in the things not seen.[1431] Christ endured all that he did for the joy that awaited him.

This is in and of itself proof of our eternal existence because a God of love, compassion, and mercy would not have allowed all of the suffering if it were not for a greater reward that will make all suffering pale in comparison.

> For I consider that the sufferings of this present time are not worthy to be compared with the glory that is to be revealed to us. (Rom. 8:18)

> For momentary, light affliction is producing for us an eternal weight of glory far beyond all comparison. (2 Cor. 4:17)

All flesh is like grass; life in provisional reality is really inconsequential—a vapor, a breeze, a mist. What really matters is the life we have in foundational reality—our eternal existence in the presence of God, Jesus Christ, the Holy Spirit, other saints, and the entire celestial hosts—forever. How foolish are all of those who gave up eternity for the fleeting pleasures of provisional reality or those that think their salvation depends on them being a good person and gave up everything for a vapor. And this is why it is so important that we try to reach the lost, and they are lost because they have no idea where they are heading, and they are going to miss their eternal destination of rewards, joy, rest, and peace.

Once Satan is confined to the abyss, Christ begins his thousand-year rule on the new earth.[1432] All of those that were beheaded during the tribulation because of their faith and refusing to worship the beast will be brought back to life[1433] and rule with Christ for a thousand years. After the thousand years, Satan is released from the abyss so that he may once again deceive the nations of the world.[1434] Okay, I'll let you see this unrepressed evil and rebellion one more time so that you never forget that evil always leads to destruction. "A spectacle to the world, both to angels and to men, so that all may learn."[1435] How many times did God in the Old Testament tell the Hebrews to remember?

Upon Satan's release from the abyss after the thousand years, he gathers his army together and surrounds the camp of saints at Jerusalem. As the enemies of God assemble to make war against Christ and his army of followers, he and his army are destroyed by fire from heaven.[1436] Finally, Satan is cast into the Lake of Fire for all eternity.[1437]

The only survivors of the great tribulation were the remnant of Israel. The earth was repopulated during the millennium reign of Christ. Even after the second destruction of the entire earth,

THINGS TO COME

the flood, and the great tribulation, the progeny of the remnant chooses to rebel against God. Mankind must be fundamental transformed from their fallen state before they can enter heaven free of flesh, purged, purified, and refined.[1438]

The underpinnings of God's divine plan are his covenants: man's stewardship of the earth,[1439] man's fallenness,[1440] man is to suppress sin and violence,[1441] the Promised Land,[1442] his chosen people,[1443] the grafting of the gentiles,[1444] and redemption through his Son and His resurrection.[1445] Scripture refers to Israel as the land of the blessing and the curse.[1446] This description comes from the understanding that God will bless the nations that help Israel. God, in like manner, will curse the nations that bring harm to Israel. This idea of the blessing and the curse is also extended to the chosen people for their obedience to God, which will be blessed, and their disobedience will be cursed.[1447] Thus stated, we see God's plan unfold in both foundational and provisional reality. Provisionally, there is constant strife between Israel and the Muslim nations over the land of Israel.[1448] Foundationally, Satan uses the nations of the Middle East to continue his attacks against the Jews, God's plan, and the Christians. It has been Satan's constant vendetta to destroy the Holy People of Israel, to destroy the lineage of Jesus Christ, and to seek his own status as God.

In order for Christ to complete his required tasks, it was necessary for him to shed himself of his deity, to not do his will, but instead become completely obedient to God, obedient to the point of death.[1449] We are told to "have this attitude in yourselves which was also in Christ,"[1450] and follow the example of Christ in order for us to perform our assigned tasks, to shed ourselves of ourselves.

Christ prayed to the Father:

> I have given them Thy word; and the world has hated them, because they are not of the world, as I am not of the world. I do not pray You take them out of the world, but that You keep them from the evil. They are not of the world even as I am not of the

world. Sanctify them in Your truth; Your word is truth. As You send Me into the world, I also sent them into the world. (John 17:14–18, IGNT)

As God sent Christ into the world, Christ has sent us into the world. God sent Christ into provisional reality for some very specific reasons; we are to continue the work Christ was sent to accomplish.

- For the Son of Man has come to save that which was lost. (Matt. 18:11)

- Just as the Son of Man did not come to be served, but to serve, and to give His life as a ransom for many. (Matt. 20:28)

- He said to them, "Let us go somewhere else to the towns nearby, so that I may preach there also; for that is what I came for."(Mark 1:38)

- I did not come to call righteous ones, but sinners to repentance. (Matt. 9:13)

- The Spirit of the Lord is upon Me, because He anointed Me to preach the gospel to the poor [poor in spirit]. He has sent Me to proclaim release to the captives, and recovery of sight to the blind, to set free those who are oppressed. (Luke 4:18)

- For the Son of Man did not come to destroy men's lives, but to save them. (Luke 9:56)

- I have come to cast fire upon the earth; and how I wish it were already kindled. (Luke 12:49)

- This is the will of Him who sent Me, that of all that He has given Me I lose nothing, but raise it up on the last day. [The Holy Spirit puts people in your life for this very reason.] (John 6:39)

- For judgment I came into this world, so that those who do not see may see, and those who see may become blind. (John 9:39)

- Now My soul has become troubled; and what shall I say, "Father, save Me from this hour"? But for this purpose I came to this hour [purged, purified, and refined]. (John 12:27)

- For this I have been born, and for this I have come into the world, to testify to the truth. Everyone who is of the truth hears My voice. (John 18:37)

- The Son of God appeared for this purpose, that He might destroy the works of the devil.(1 John 3:8)

- Do not think that I came to bring peace on the earth; I did not come to bring peace, but a sword. (Matt 10:34)

Christ's incarnation was the exact representation of God so that through Christ, we may come to know God.[1451]

"Not everyone who says to Me Lord, Lord will enter the kingdom of heaven. But the one who does the will of My Father who is in heaven."[1452] "He said to them, indeed the harvest is much, but the laborers are few. Therefore, pray to the Lord of the harvest, that He send out workers into His harvest."[1453] Jesus affirms that believer's prayers contribute in the fulfillment of God's plan. The gospel is the eschatological announcement that precedes judgment and urges people to repent and put their trust in Christ. Jesus does not yet command his disciples to go into the harvest but to pray. No one can do their work of the harvest without being chosen, called, and equipped by God.

One of the parables from Christ has a very appropriate application. It is found in Matthew 25:14–30. I have referenced this parable before, so I'll be brief. A man is going on a journey [Christ]; he calls his three servants together and *entrusted his possessions to them* [the earth and all it contains, including souls]. To one he gave five talents, spiritual gifts and a calling, another two, and to the last, one. The one with five doubled his to ten, the one with two doubled his to four. The third slave accomplished nothing with what he had been given. When the master returned he cast out the worthless slave into the outer darkness; in that place, there shall be weeping and gnashing of teeth. We too will be held accountable for how much fruit we bore. "Well done, good and faithful slave. You were faithful over a few things, I will set you over many, [ten and four talents]" or "Evil slothful slave, throw the worthless slave out into the outer darkness [one talent]." Our talents are the gifts and opportunities provided to us by God.

THE PROSTITUTE RELIGION

Islam will profess that God and Allah are different names for the same God. "Our god and your God is One."[1454] Worship will be directed to the Antichrist, who is the false god established by Satan. However, once Satan has obtained dominance over the Muslim nations and started his conquest for the rest of the world, he will destroy the prostitute religion of Islam[1455] he has established to ensure worship falls to him.[1456] This is 1,290 days into the tribulation,[1457] and the Antichrist (Mahdi) will enter the holy temple in Jerusalem, and halt the sacrifices. He will then demand that he be worshipped. This act will be the abomination of desolation,[1458] to which God will respond with the seven bowl judgment to utterly destroy all that remain on the earth. This is also where the Jewish remnant is told to flee to the mountains.[1459]

The beginning of Revelation 17 describes the mystery and the adulterations of the prostitute religion.

> And one of the seven angels who had the seven bowls came and said to me, "Come, I will show you the punishment of the great harlot, sitting on many waters, [water is biblically symbolic for humanity] with whom the kings of the earth committed fornication and the ones inhabiting the earth became drunk with the

wine of her fornications." [Prostitute as she supports and justifies the beast and not the God of Christianity.] Then the angel carried me away in the Spirit into a desert. And I saw a woman sitting on a scarlet beast [the Antichrist] filled with the names of blasphemy having seven heads and ten horns. The woman was clothed in purple and scarlet, and gilded with gold, precious stones and pearls, having a golden cup in her hand, filled with the abominations and unclean things of her fornication. (Rev. 17:1–4, IGNT)

And on her forehead was a name having been written; MYSTERY BABYLON THE GREAT THE MOTHER OF THE HARLOTS AND OF THE ABOMINATIONS OF THE EARTH. I saw that the woman was drunk with the blood of the saints, the blood of those who bore testimony to Jesus. [Indicative of Islam's role in the murder and terrorism and of the saints killed during their persecution, during the tribulation, and today.] When I saw her, I was greatly astonished. (Rev. 17:5–6, IGNT)

"When I saw her, I was greatly astonished." John is taken to the desert to see the harlot. Most translation say John was taken to the wilderness; however, the original Greek says desert. Mecca in the desert is the birthplace of Islam. "The woman whom you saw is the great city, which reigns over the kings of the earth."[1460]

The book of Revelation explains Babylon's destruction. "I heard a voice from heaven, say come out of her, so that you will not participate in her sins, for her sins have piled up. Pay her back double according to her deeds. To the degree that she glorified herself and lived sensuously."[1461] The original Greek does not use the word *sensuously* but rather *luxuriated*.

The ultimate justification for Islam is that the Qur'ān says, "Islam is the only true religion,"[1462] and the only occupants of heaven will be the believers of Islam.[1463] Islam declares that reforming the earth should be the primary responsibility of humanity. Man is also to achieve a state of being sinless while here on earth.

The state of being sinless is accomplished through prayer to Allah and by the perfect suppression of all evil tendencies.[6]

Scripture tells us that conditions on earth and evil men will continue to go from bad to worse, deceiving and being deceived.[1464] The only real remedy for the earth will be for Christ to usher in the new heaven and the new earth.[1465] Perfection on earth will only be under the rule of Christ after the defeat of Satan, and humankind will live in a redeemed world.[1466] The Bible is the documentation of human history and man's inability to achieve a sinless state, which only Christ has achieved. However, if man is able to achieve a sinless state, as the Qur'ān suggests, then there would have been no reason for Christ to come to earth as the redeemer for mankind. This deception is also a part of Satan's strategy; if we do not need a redeemer, there is no need for Christ. The emphasis on the jihad in Islam gives Satan the ability to oppress and kill any that will not worship the Antichrist (Mahdi). The solution for godless people and governments has always been the same strategy, as history has demonstrated; when your system is completely false, whenever the system is scrutinized, and the opposition cannot be silenced, kill them, unless, of course, they are armed. Then, you must disarm them first.

The Qur'ān specifies exactly what the duties of a Muslim are: read the Qur'ān, observe daily prayer to Allah, pay the poor rate, offer Allah a goodly gift, ask for forgiveness, and participate in the jihad.[1467] Muslims are instructed to fight against people of the book and those who do not believe in Allah until they pay the tax and are in a state of subjection.[1468] Islamic law also states that all nations must surrender to Islamic rule—if not its faith, then its government, if not willingly, then by force.

Verse 25:52 of the Qur'ān reads, "So obey not the disbelievers, and strive against them a mighty striving with it." The footnote for this verse explains its meaning: "This verse affords a clear proof of the significance of the word *jihād*, as used in the Holy Qur'ān.

---

[6] Qur'ān commentary to chapter 76 titled "The Man"

THINGS TO COME

Every exertion to spread the truth is, according to this verse, a *jihād*; nay, it is called the *jihād kabīr* ("mighty striving") or the *great jihād*. Fighting in defense of religion received the name *jihād* because under the circumstances, it became necessary for the truth to live and prosper; if fighting had not been permitted, truth would surely have been uprooted. It should be noted that the greatest *jihād* that a Muslim can carry on is one by means of the Qur'ān, to which the personal pronoun *it* at the end of the verse unquestionably refers because it must be carried on by *every* Muslim under all circumstances."[1469] All Muslims must participate in the jihad; it is the only way of preserving the truth in Islam—silence the opposition. Any that do not believe are to be converted or killed. And this is a religion of peace?

All adult males and able-bodied Muslims are expected to take part in hostile jihads against non-Muslim neighbors and neighboring lands.

Since its beginning, Islam has been spread through the imperial conquest of its Christian neighbors. The nine Crusades of AD 1095 to AD 1291 were fought by the church of Rome to stop the spread of Islam and retake Jerusalem. Muslim armies had conquered Europe as far as Spain, the Balkans, and into France, waging 548 battles of genocide against Christian cities and states over the course of 1,300 years. The majority of the Middle East was Christian, from Morocco to Turkey and Iraq prior to Islam. The Islamic onslaught was stopped at the Battle of Tours in France where the Muslims were defeated. The second major defeat of Islamic invasion into Europe occurred on September 11th 1683 at the battle of Vienna. Islam and the Qur'ān offer the perfect opportunity for Satan and the Antichrist (Mahdi) to rally the followers of Islam to act as pawns while Satan orders the destruction of all remaining Christians and Jews.

"O you who believe, fight those of the disbelievers who are near to you and let them find firmness in you, And know that Allah is with those who keep their duty."[1470] Then Satan can command all of Islam and the new converts, to worship him, and Satan will have accomplished his five "I wills;" however, it will only be within provisional reality, and his only followers are those destined for the second death in the lake of fire.

A follower of Islam has no assurance that they are going to paradise, as heaven is referred to in the Qur'ān. Their admittance to heaven is strictly based on the decision of Allah, and his decision is made contingent on good deeds outweighing bad deeds.[1471] In the final analysis, the only sure way to get into heaven is to die as a martyr fighting for the spread of Islam against any of the nonbelieving peoples or nations,[1472] in other words, fighting to eliminate Christianity and the Jews. The Qur'ān teaches that "fighting is prescribed for you" and that Muslims should "fight the polytheists [Christians] all together as they fight you altogether. And know that Allah is with those who keep the duty."[1473] "So when the sacred months have passed, slay the idolaters, wherever you find them, and take them captive and besiege them and lie in wait for them in every ambush."[1474] The Qur'ān states that all Muslims that die in this fashion automatically become martyrs of the faith and are awarded special privileges in heaven.[1475] "Surely Allah loves those who fight in this way."[1476] There are those that will reason that not all Muslims are extremists, all Germans were not Nazis either.

Christ taught us to "love your enemies and pray for those who persecute you."[1477] The Qur'ān teaches to "fight with them until all religion is for Allah. Strive against them with a mighty striving."[1478] The Bible tells us that Christ will return to destroy the works of Satan.[1479]

God has sovereignty over all of the nations of the world.[1480] The appearance of dynasties have come and gone since the beginning of time, but the word of God lives forever.[1481] Only the Jews and the Jewish nation have prevailed and maintained their existence, culture, and religion, even after a 1,900-year absence.[1482] God has a chosen people so that every nation and tribe will know of his sovereignty.[1483] All that he has covenanted to Israel has come about. Satan has tried repeatedly to destroy the people of Israel, the Jewish nation, to discredit God, and to cause those in provisional reality to question and lose faith. More importantly, Satan first tried to prevent the birth of Christ.[1484] Then he tried to wipe out the proof of the lineage of Christ by repeated attempts to eliminate the Jewish race. This is the continuing effort of Satan to rid the world of the Jews. Satan tempted Christ in the wilderness and tried to convince him to forgo his deity.[1485] Satan had King Herod kill all of the newborn males in Bethlehem[1486] in an effort to have Christ killed. Satan was only able to get Christ killed through Judas, the Pharisees, and the Sadducees. God turned the murder of Christ into good as he does with everything.[1487] When all else failed, Satan created the religion of Islam to rid the world of the Christians and the Jews so that he can be worshipped. However, all of the enemies of Christ will be annihilated by Christ. He is the one true God and cannot be defeated.[1488] Any religion or government that attempts or threatens to annihilate the Jews or eradicate the state of Israel are agents of Satan. Satan always has the same objective; he just finds new players and develops new strategies. However, as with the Abrahamic covenant, the Jews are the only peoples that God has made a promise to.

In Judges we read:

> Now these are the nations which the Lord left, to test Israel by them that is all who had not experienced any of the wars of Canaan; only in order that the generation of the sons of Israel might be taught war, those who had not experienced if formerly These nations are; the five lords of the Philistines (today the southern portion of the Gaza Strip) and all the Canaanites (today the northern portion of the Gaza Strip and the West Bank) and the Sidonians (today the Golan Heights, Syria) and the Hivites who lived in Mount Lebanon, from Mount Baal-hermon as far as Lebo-hamath. They were for testing Israel. (Judg. 3:1–4)

Israel has had to fight seven wars since 1948 to maintain its independence, all of which they have won. Just months after the UN declared Israel a nation and established a two-nation state with the Palestinians, Israel was at war. The Arab nations rejected the idea of a two-nation state. Egypt, Jordan, Syria, Iraq, and Lebanon—all with standing armies, artillery, tanks, and war planes—attacked Israel. The newly formed Israel had thirty thousand militia, thirteen thousand rifles, and two pieces of artillery. All five attacking nations were defeated. These are the same nations that again attacked Israel in 1967 and again were defeated, this time in six days. People had better understand who they are fighting when they engage Israel. None of the Muslim nations will grant Palestinians citizenship as they desire to keep Israel engulfed in conflict. This also appears to be by God's design to maintain Israel's fighting edge.

The battle has always been between good and evil, a cosmic battle, the powers of the spiritual forces of evil, against God, his angels, and all those who believe that Jesus Christ is Lord.[1489] "For our struggle is not against flesh and blood, but against the rulers, against the powers, against the world forces of this darkness, against forces of wickedness in the heavenly places."[1490]

God's eternal plan is not about countries and governments within provisional reality; they are merely unwitting participants in this cosmic battle. There are two philosophies of life: that of the Triune God of Christianity and the obedience to his commandments, and the diametrically opposed philosophy of Satan and his rebellion. Although Jews do not believe that Christ was the Messiah, they believe he is yet to come. They will believe when they witness Christ coming on the clouds as recorded in Revelation 14:14. Their lamentation upon this realization is recorded in Isaiah 53.

The Islamic absolute statement of commitment to their faith is, "There is no god but Allah and Muhammad is his prophet." The Christian statement of absolute faith is, "For God so loved the

THINGS TO COME

world that He gave His only begotten Son, that whoever believes in Him should not perish, but have eternal life."[1491] Christianity believes in a Triune God, a God that is the Father, the Son, and the Holy Spirit. The god of Islam is strictly a singularity. "Allah has not taken to himself a son, nor is there with him any other god."[1492]

The basic tenants of the two religions are also very different. In the Qur'ān, Abraham is told in a dream to sacrifice Ishmael,[1493] not Isaac, as is recorded in the Bible of Christianity.[1494] This difference sets both religions on very separate paths. Ishmael has the Arabs being the promised people with a promised land, and Isaac has the Jews as God's chosen people to occupy Israel forever. Ishmael's descendants, the Arabs, have always persecuted Isaac's, the Jews, then as today, just as nonbelievers have always persecuted believers. The path of Isaac leads to Christ, the redeemer of all mankind by his sacrificial death. "The Father and I are One."[1495] The path of Ishmael leads to a system of works where you must be good enough to enter heaven, and there are no specific criteria; it is an arbitrary system left in the hands of a capacious entity. Christ died so that men might be saved. Allah wants everyone to die for him; Christ died for everyone. Satan the destroyer[1496] wants to destroy all life. Who do you want to spend eternity with?

The Qur'ān disavows the deity of Christ and the existence of the Holy Spirit. The Qur'ān also states that Allah does not have a Son and that the assertion that he did is "an abominable assertion" and "anyone who says he is God besides Allah will be recompensed in hell."[1497] The Islamic religion teaches that Christ existed and that he was the son of Mary.[1498] However, the Qur'ān states that Christ was not the Son of God because "Allah begets not."[1499] Further, the Qur'ān states, "The Messiah, Jesus, the son of Mary, is only a messenger of Allah and his word. Allah is only one God. Far be it from His glory to have a son."[1500] Christ was created just as Adam was, from dust.[1501] In the Qur'ān 3:6, the title reads, "Jesus Cleared of False Charges." The footnote explains: "But the word is used here really to show that the Jewish plans to cause Jesus' death on the cross would be frustrated and that he would afterwards die a natural death."[1502] Consequently, Christ was not crucified, and he did not die on the cross as the salvation for humanity.

> And for their disbelief and for their uttering against Mary a grievous calamity. And for their saying; We have killed the Messiah, son of Mary, the messenger of Allah, and they killed Him not, nor did they cause His death on the cross but He was made to appear to them as such…and they killed Him not for certain. (Qur'ān 4:156–157)

Instead, the Qur'ān states Christ died in old age of natural causes. There is a latter passage in the Qur'ān that references Christ. "O Jesus, son of Mary, thou spokest to the people in the cradle and in old age…"[1503] Qur'ān 9:5 is titled "Islam Will Triumph in the World." Here we are told that "those who say the Messiah is the Son of Allah will receive the curse of Allah, and that Islam will prevail over all religions in spite of the polytheists."[1504] With all of these significant differences ,God and Allah are not different names for the same God, yet the Qur'ān makes this claim. But then again, Satan is the father of lies. They are different names for different entities. One is the true Triune God of Christianity; the other is a false god.

The supreme objective of Islam is world domination of its government/religion. Any sin a Muslim commits—lying, killing, betrayal, bribes, rape, beheading, suicide bombings, killing innocent women and children—are excused as long as they were committed for the purpose of advancing Islam. If they are committed for selfish motives, then they are sin. That is why there is so much uncertainty about how Allah will view their actions. What are a man's true motives?

THE EVOLUTION OF MANKIND

During the millennium kingdom, the thousand-year reign of Christ,[1505] Satan will be in chains in the abyss.[1506] There is no clearer evidence of Satan being the author of pain, suffering, and evil than the scriptural understanding that while Satan is confined to the abyss, all wars cease. War immediately resumes upon his release from the abyss.[1507]

In Peter's second epistle, he dialogues about the three phases of the earth's evolution. First is the world before the flood, or "the world that was." Second is the heavens and the earth, which is the state of provisional reality today. The third is "the new heaven and the new earth, which occurs after the rapture of the saints and the culmination of the great tribulation.[1508]

When God creates the new heaven and the new earth, it will be a new beginning. Har-Magedon is the end of human history; it is also a new beginning. The earth will be so decimated by the havoc from the tribulation period it will be spent and in need of a new creation. Man's claim of global warming and futile attempts to offer solutions are a clear demonstration of man's complete arrogance.

The evolution of humankind is supernatural, from human to spiritual, mortal to immortal, and corporal to incorporeal. Our evolution has nothing to do with changes and mutations in our DNA and has everything to do with a transformation from one dimension of existence to another. The process of our sanctification is the provisional process that guides this evolution—or better yet, this transformation—from a being that lives in provisional reality to one that lives in foundational reality, flesh to spirit. God, Jesus Christ, the Holy Spirit, and faith drive humankind's transformation. This is the only process of evolution for man.

> It is sown a natural body, it is raised a spiritual body. If there is a natural body, there is also a spiritual body. For this perishable must put on the imperishable, and this mortal must put on immortality. (1 Cor. 15:44, 53)

Satan, his minions, and all nonbelievers are cast away forever. They will exist in whatever kind of a reality the outer darkness and the fiery lake of burning sulfur[1509] represents because it has been ordained by God. The real torment of the outer darkness and the second death are an eternal existence separated from God, Christ, and the Holy Spirit.

Without the Holy Spirit's restraint on Satan, his ruthless evil would have ended the human experience a long time ago, as is evidenced by the catastrophic evil unleashed by the four horsemen of the apocalypse.

A word about the second death. As humans, our first death is our physical death of the body. Our first death can result in an eternal life, as promised by the Triune God for believers.[1510] When someone's lifestyle and lack of faith prevents them from entering heaven, they are denied eternal life, which is life after death, so they experience the second death in the lake of fire.[1511] When believers pass from this life, from provisional reality, we are reborn into foundational reality and into paradise. The second death is not a rebirth; it is a second death. Instead of the opportunity for rebirth, there is death. Both states are for eternity—one in eternal glory and one in eternal damnation.

> He who believes in the Son has eternal life; but he who does not obey the Son shall not see life; but the wrath of God abides on him. (John 3:36)

The time Christians spend in provisional reality is a lifelong process of our sanctification. Our process of becoming holy as our faith and relationship with the Trinity continually matures. Our maturity as

Christians will be manifested in faith, our values, and our behavior. This is precisely the reason we do not know the time, the hour, or the day. We have to be righteous all of the time, not just before the event. Sanctification should be a lifelong process of purging, purification, and refinement, as it will be during the tribulation. "And everyone who has this hope fixed on Him purifies himself, just as He is pure."[1512] It should be the prayer of all of us that our process of sanctification be completed before we pass over the threshold; that is the wrong time to find out we are lacking.

> I urge you therefore, brethren, by the mercies of God, to present your bodies a living and holy sacrifice, acceptable to God, which is your spiritual service of worship. And do not be conformed to this world, but be transformed by the renewing of your mind, that you may prove what the will of God is, that which is good and acceptable and perfect. (Romans 12:1–2)

The process of sanctification is God's will for our lives.[1513] Remember, God considers this serious business. He tells us to "work out our salvation with fear and trembling"[1514] and to "conduct yourselves in fear during the time of your stay upon the earth."[1515] In essence, we are all less than holy; in fact, God says that there is not one of us without sin—not even one.

> There is none righteous, not even one; There is none who understands, There is none who seeks for God; All have turned aside, together they have become useless; There is none who does good, There is not even one. (Rom. 3:10–12)

Why? Verse 18 tells us, "We have no fear of God at all."

We are called out from our sinful state[1516] by God to become one of his children so that we may share an inheritance in heaven and a relationship with the Triune God.[1517] God has known from the beginning of time who he will call out to be his children.[1518]

"God has chosen you from the beginning for salvation through sanctification by the Spirit and faith in the truth."[1519] In the process of sanctification is an understanding about the need to change our behavior. We need to possess moral excellence[1520] because of the precious and magnificent promise of what will be our nature for an eternity, first as angels,[1521] then "when He appears, we shall be like Him."[1522] We change our behavior now out of gratitude for this eternal gift,[1523] never because we think we can earn our salvation. It is a free gift.[1524] Scripture teaches that while salvation is by grace, judgment is according to works. Works are not the bases of our salvation; they are the evidence of it. When James says, "Faith without works is dead,"[1525] he means that if our behavior has not changed, we do not have true faith. "As a result of the works, faith was made complete."[1526] "You see then that a man is justified by works and not by faith only."[1527] "For as the body is dead apart from the Spirit, so also faith is dead apart from works."[1528] Christ died for you; you must live for him.[1529] If our behavior does not conform to God's expectations, we will never accomplish the work that the Trinity has designed for us to do before time began during our brief stay in provisional reality.[1530]

Christ has given us the example of how to live. Christ emptied himself of his deity so that he would "do the will of Him who sent Me"[1531] and do only that which was pleasing to His Father.[1532] Just as we are to empty ourselves[1533] of self, our ego, and do only the Father's will. And what has God asked of us? To love him with all of our heart, soul, and strength, to keep his commandments in our hearts,[1534] to live justly, love kindness, and to walk humbly with him.[1535] That is why we are told not to love the things of the world but rather to seek his kingdom and righteousness.[1536] Life is temporary;[1537] our inheritance is for an eternity. Empting ourselves means forgoing our ego in humility so we do the things that are pleasing to God, and not do the things that are pleasing to us. This is being who God wants us to be and doing what he wants us to do for his plan and his glory.

What are the characteristics of a true Christian, one of the overcomers?

> I am the true vine, and My Father is the vinedresser. Every branch in Me that does not bear fruit, He takes away; and every *branch* that bears fruit, He prunes it so that it may bear more fruit. You are already clean because of the word which I have spoken to you. Abide in Me, and I in you. As the branch cannot bear fruit of itself unless it abides in the vine, so neither *can* you unless you abide in Me. I am the vine, you are the branches; he who abides in Me and I in him, he bears much fruit, for apart from Me you can do nothing… My Father is glorified by this, that you bear much fruit, and *so* prove to be My disciples. Just as the Father has loved [social or moral sense] Me, I have also loved [social or moral sense] you; abide in My love [benevolence]. If you keep My commandments, you will abide in My love [benevolence]; just as I have kept My Father's commandments and abide in His love [benevolence]. These things I have spoken to you so that My joy may be in you, and *that* your joy may be made full. (John 15:1–11)

We are to love others in a social and moral sense, to do no harm to others, obeying the teachings of Christ and the commandments, statues of God, and thereby we receive their benevolent love.

> Do not be anxious about anything, but in everything by prayer and supplication with thanksgiving let your requests be made known to God. And the peace of God, which surpasses all understanding, will guard your hearts and your minds in Christ Jesus. Finally, brothers, whatever is true, whatever is honorable, whatever is just, whatever is pure, whatever is lovely, whatever is commendable, if there is any excellence, if there is anything worthy of praise, let your mind dwell on these things. What you have learned and received and heard and seen in me—put these things into practice, and the God of peace will be with you. (Phil. 4:6–9)

That you may walk worthy of the Lord, fully pleasing to him, bearing fruit in every good work, and increasing in the knowledge of God, being strengthened with all power according to his glorious might, for the display of all endurance and patience; while joyfully giving thanks to the Father, who has qualified you to share in the inheritance of the saints in the light. (Col. 1:10–12)

Then put to death your members which are on the earth: fornication, uncleanness, passion, evil lust, and covetousness, which is idolatry, on account of which things the wrath of God is coming upon the sons of disobedience, among whom you also walked at one time, when you were living in these. But now, you also put off all these things: wrath, anger, malice, evil speaking, shameful words out of your mouth. Do not lie to one another, having put off the old man with his practices, and have put on the new, having been renewed in full knowledge according to the One creating him; where there is no Greek and Jew, but Christ is all and in all. (Col. 3:5–11, IGNT)

Therefore, as the elect of God, holy and dearly loved, clothe yourselves with heartfelt compassion, kindness, humility, gentleness, and patience. Bear with one another and forgive each another, should anyone have a complaint against another. As the Lord has graciously forgiven you, so also you must forgive. And cover all these virtues with love, which is the bond that leads to perfection. And let the peace of Christ be the ruling principle in your heart, to which indeed you were called in one body. And be thankful. Let the word of Christ dwell in you richly as you teach and admonish one another with all wisdom. (Col. 3:12–17)

Everyone who believes that Jesus is the Christ has been born of God, and everyone who loves the Father loves his child. By this we know that we love the children of God: whenever we love God and obey His commandments. For this is the love of God: that we keep His commandments. And His commandments are not burdensome, because everyone who has been born of God conquers the world. And this is the victorious power that has conquered the world—our faith. (1 John 5:1–4)

Who is wise and understanding among you? By his exemplary conduct let him show his works done in the gentleness born of wisdom. But if you have bitter jealousy and selfish ambition in your heart, do not be arrogant and tell lies against the truth. This is not the wisdom that comes down from above, but is earthly, unspiritual, and demonic. For where jealousy and selfish ambition exist, there you will find disorder and every evil practice. But the wisdom from above is first of all pure, then peaceable, gentle, open to reason, full of mercy and good fruits, free from prejudice and hypocrisy. And a harvest of righteousness is sown in peace by those who make peace. (James 3:13–18)

Now this is the message that we have heard from Him and are proclaiming to you: God is light, and there is absolutely no darkness in Him. If we say that we have fellowship with Him but continue to walk in darkness, we lie and are not putting the truth into practice. But if we walk in the light, as He is in the light, we have fellowship with one another, and the blood of Jesus His Son cleanses us from all sin. If we say that we are without sin, we are deceiving ourselves and the truth is not in us. If we confess our sins, He is faithful and just and will forgive us our sins and cleanse us from all unrighteousness. If we say that we have not sinned, we make Him a liar and His word is not in us. (1 John 1:5–10)

Now the works of the flesh are obvious: sexual immorality, impurity, debauchery, idolatry, sorcery, quarrels, strife, jealousy, fits of rage, selfish rivalries, dissensions, divisions, envying's, drunkenness, orgies, and things like these. I warn you, as I warned you before: those who practice such things will not inherit the kingdom of God! By contrast, the fruit of the Spirit is love, joy, peace, patience, kindness, generosity, faithfulness, gentleness, self-control; against such things there is no law. And those who belong to Christ Jesus have crucified the flesh with its passions and desires. Since we live by the Spirit, let us also be guided by the Spirit. (Gal. 5:19–25)

There is personal suffering in this life partly because when we are suffering, we will not sin,[1538] and partly because we are fallen and prone to sinning, which causes our own pain and suffering. Suffering is also caused by the evil deeds of others, our carelessness, incapacity, neglect, and the consequences of an inherently dangerous world. The discipline of the Lord can cause us pain as can the ramifications of Satan who roams the earth seeking whom he might destroy. Christ achieved perfection through his suffering,[1539] which is the effect suffering should have on us. That is why James tells us to count it all joy when we encounter suffering.[1540]

"For we are His workmanship, created in Christ Jesus for good works, which God prepared beforehand so that we would walk in them."[1541] All of the experiences we have in this life are orchestrated by the Holy Spirit and are designed to equip us for our preordained work. God does have a plan for our life; however, it is not for us per se. We are to accomplish our preordained work as it is a thread in the tapestry that God is weaving for this time in history, a subset of His overall plan. Once we are equipped, we must be open to the guidance of the Holy Spirit to now accomplish our preordained good work. This is God's will for your life, and if you are obediently in compliance, you are doing God's will. In this we are producing our good fruit, the only good fruit is fruit that is eternal. "My Father is glorified by this, that you bear much fruit, and so prove to be My disciples."[1542] We are told in Scripture not to love the world because the demonic influences will distract us from our preordained responsibilities and from becoming who God wants us to be.[1543] The fundamental difference between committed Christians and pseudo-Christians is whose will are you pursuing, God's or yours? All of our problems and all of their solution are theological.

Whatever this life brings to us will pale in comparison to what is the experience of eternal life.[1544] Because our faith is small, we put too much emphasis on life. There are 48,000 deaths in America every week. Death after all is inevitable, and without death of the body, we cannot be transformed into our eternal state. "Just as we have borne the image of the earthly, we will also bear the image of the heavenly."[1545] Not all of our experiences or concepts about life are easily definable until we have experienced them for ourselves. However, it is not possible to experience everything, so we rely on the testimony of others—people who have been where we have not and experienced something different from our experiences. Christ was begotten and has his origins in foundational reality. He has been with the Father since before time.[1546] His words to his disciples on his impending death were, "Rejoice, because I go to the Father."[1547] God's first priority in our life is where we spend eternity; the second is accomplishing our predetermined good works.

We know that Christ has gone to prepare a place for us. There are those that do not come to a saving faith during their life, and they will not come to faith as they endure the terrors of the tribulation.[1548] Some are destined to an eternity in hell[1549] because of their stubborn, rebellious, and unrepentant sinful behavior. When a person becomes a Christian, their name is entered into the Book of Life.[1550] All whose name is found there will be partakers in the eternal inheritance provided for by the death of Christ[1551] and the grace of God.[1552] In fact, it is such a joyous occasion that when a name is entered into the Book of Life, there is rejoicing in heaven at the conversion of every sinner.[1553]

The Bible is addressed to Christians, so we are to read it as a personal conversation from God to us. Christians are taken to God's house at the rooms that Christ has prepared for us, those that were predestined by God to be his children,[1554] and any who wish may come. The lost did not love God enough to keep his commandments and statutes even though Scripture says, "Whoever may call on the name of the Lord will be saved."[1555] They did not rely on the testimony of Jesus Christ[1556] for their salvation. The unredeemed think they can accomplish salvation themselves by being a good person. Works and good deeds are all meaningless without faith.[1557] All of the works and miracles performed by Christ were done so that God could be glorified. Our works are to glorify God, not ourselves.

There are two philosophies of life: that of Christ and his teachings and the demonic spirit of Satan—good and evil. Your thoughts and actions will reflect one of these two philosophies. You willingly exhibit behaviors in obedience to Christ or in obedience to Satan. It's not as if Satan is attacking you when you're indwelt by the Holy Spirit; if you sin, you are yielding to the temptations of Satan's influences by your free-will choices. These are the satanic influences and deceptions, the mere existence of evil, thoughts, and behaviors provide temptation. Whether you sin or not is your choice. "Greater is He who is in you than he who is in the world."

THE FINAL JUDGMENT AND THE BOOK OF LIFE

> Then I saw thrones, and they sat on them, and judgment was given to them. And I saw the souls of those who had been beheaded because of their testimony of Jesus and because of the word of God, and those who had not worshiped the beast or his image, and had not received the mark on their forehead and on their hand; and they came to life and reigned with Christ for a thousand years. (Rev. 20:4)

The next event is the great day of judgment. "And they were judged every one of them according to their deeds."[1558] Everyone is judged, believers and nonbelievers alike. However, the deeds and works of believers are judged for the assignments of crowns, duties, rewards, and responsibilities.[1559] "But store up for yourself treasures in heaven."[1560] "There is therefore now no condemnation for those who are in Christ Jesus."[1561] Nonbelievers are judged for their evil deeds and for their commission of the unpardonable sin.[1562] The sin of rejecting the ministry of the Holy Spirit and rejecting Jesus Christ as the incarnate Son of God and the sole means of our salvation through his sacrificial death. Our salvation is summed up by faith alone, in Christ alone, and by grace alone.

The essence of conforming to God's will is obedience to that will. Adam and Eve rebelled against God's sovereignty. The covenants set up the blessing and the curse for obedience and disobedience for God's chosen people, the only people God has ever made a promise to. The seeds of rebellion are planted by the perception, real or not, that an authority is either capricious or arbitrary. God is neither, but these are the flaming arrows that fill men's mind with doubt where faith is lacking. Worship is only true worship when it is a free-will choice. The advent of Jesus Christ brought obedience by example and obedience by faith as a free-will choice out of gratitude for that which we receive in God's system of grace—eternal life.

There are many illustrations in the Bible as to how God will separate the faithful from those lacking faith:[1563] the sheep from the goats,[1564] the chaff from the wheat,[1565] and the good fish from the bad fish.[1566] Scripture is very specific about who will and who will not be saved. Those that do not honor God as God or acknowledge the Lordship of Jesus Christ but put more credence in man or their own conception of what is right and wrong are the goats, chaff, and the bad fish.[1567] People that will not inherit the kingdom include; those that are fornicators, adulterers, idolaters, abusers, homosexuals, thieves, drunkards, revilers, swindlers, and people that are covetous.[1568] Sins of immorality are heinous because they are sins of the body, and the body is the temple for the Holy Spirit.[1569] When people engage in sins of the flesh, they are engaging the Holy Spirit in their sins as well. We are told to flee from immorality.[1570] It is reasonable to consider that if we engage in sexual immorality or the use of narcotics, the Holy Spirit may choose to cease his indwelling ministry in us. With the withdrawal of the Holy Spirit's restraining ministry a person is much more vulnerable to demonic activity.[1571] This is why sexual immorality and the use of narcotics leads to increasing decadence. Additionally, Paul warns of immorality, impurity, sensuality, idolatry, sorcery, jealousy, and those who exhibit outbursts of anger, or cause dissention, strife, or disputes.[1572] In the book of Revelation, John also warns that those headed for the second death are people that are cowardly, unbelieving, abominable, murderers, immoral persons, sorcerers, idolaters, and all liars.[1573] Simply stated, we all need Christ as our redeemer. We know this because God has said that none of us is without sin.

When people died prior to Christ's resurrection, they would go to either hell or to what was referred to as Abraham's bosom.[1574] Wicked, evil, and people lacking faith descended into hell, and the righteous went to Abraham's bosom. The righteous people that died before Christ's resurrection will be judged on their faith in God and by their obedience.[1575] After Christ was crucified, he descended into hell[1576] to preach the gospel,[1577] to give everyone in Abraham's bosom angelic forms, and brought them to heaven.

There are no judgments or punishments for all of the believers.[1578] In the culmination of God's eternal plan, there are no sins to punish any Christian for; all sins have been forgiven through the death of Christ on the cross.[1579]

This is the culmination of the battle of good and evil. There is a new heaven and a new earth under the rule of Christ. God will wipe away every tear, and there will no longer be any death, mourning, crying, or pain.[1580] All of that has passed away with the destruction of Satan. Christ will return to God what he set out to create in the first place a redeemed world populated with people that are living according to his will and are living in a manner that is worthy of their being called[1581] a holy people.

The simple fact from the Qur'ān is that all religion is to be for Allah. Everyone will be given a chance to convert to Islam, and if not, Allah says you are to be killed.

The simple truth from the Bible is, as much as everyone hopes for a pre-tribulation rapture, that position is not supported by Scripture. Christ returns on a white cloud; however. it does not occur until Revelation 14:14, after many of the earth's inhabitants have been killed, at least 2.5 billion (Rev. 9:15) by the two hundred million supernatural army. There is also the great multitude which no one could count who come out of the great tribulation.[1582]

Christians must endure the horror of the tribulation so that we may be purged, purified, and refined because we have failed so miserably at what God has asked us to do. "There is none without sin, no, not one." This purging and purification process is so that we may be qualified to enter heaven;[1583] it has nothing to do with the forgiveness of sins. Be holy and perfect. We already are in God's eyes as He sees us through the blood of Christ; however, we are still fallen and will have to experience a fundamental change in who we are.

> For this reason also, since the day we heard of it, we have not ceased to pray for you and to ask that you may be filled with the knowledge of His will in all spiritual wisdom and understanding, so that you will walk in a manner worthy of the Lord, to please Him in all respects, bearing fruit in every good work and increasing in the knowledge of God; strengthened with all power, according to His glorious might, for the attaining of all steadfastness and patience, joyously giving thanks to the Father, who has qualified us to share in the inheritance of the saints of Light (Col. 1:9–12)

Scripturally speaking, Christ said, "Then they will deliver you to affliction and will kill you, and you will be hated by all nations because of My name."[1584] John says, "I saw underneath the altar the souls of those who had been slain because of the word of God, and because of the testimony which they had maintained."[1585] Daniel says, "I watched and that horn made war with the saints and overcame them."[1586] John adds, "It was given to him to make war with the saints and to overcome them."[1587] Daniel says, "Those who have insight among the people will give understanding to the many; yet they will fall by sword and by flame, by captivity and by plunder for many days."[1588] "Many will be purged, purified, and refined."[1589] Christ said, "Unless those days had been cut short, no life would have been saved; but for the sake of the elect those days will be cut short."[1590] Daniel says, "From the time that the regular sacrifice is abolished and the abomination of desolation is set up, there will be 1,290 days. How blessed is he who keeps waiting and attains to the 1,335 days!"[1591] The disciples asked, "Tell us, when will these things happen, and what will be the sign of Your coming, and of the end of the age?[1592] Christ said,

"And then the sign of the Son of Man will appear in the sky, and then all the tribes of the earth will mourn, and they will see the Son of Man coming on the clouds of the sky with power and great glory."[1593] Paul says, "Then we who are alive and remain will be caught up together with them in the clouds to meet the Lord in the air, and so we shall always be with the Lord."[1594]

After all of this, after the seal and trumpet judgments, we have the rapture for the remaining overcomers. John writes, "Then I looked, and behold, a white cloud and sitting on the cloud was one like the Son of Man, having a golden crown on His head and a sharp sickle in His hand. And another angel came out of the temple, crying out with a loud voice to Him who sat on the cloud, 'Put in Your sickle and reap, for the hour to reap has come, because the harvest of the earth is ripe.' Then He who sat on the cloud swung His sickle over the earth, and the earth was reaped."[1595]

THINGS TO COME

There is a lot of speculation about the role of America in the end-times. Most seem to think that America is not mentioned in the Bible. After the destruction of Jerusalem and the temple in AD 70, the whole of the Jewish population was spread throughout the rest of the habitable world, known as the great diaspora.[1596] Many Jews were routed to Europe, Germany, and Russia, and many married outside of their faith. The Jews of the diaspora are commonly referred to as the ten lost tribes of Israel.

It was the belief of many of the founding fathers and the clergy during the 1600s and 1700s that America was the new promised land, and the Americans were the new chosen people. They saw many similarities between the Jews' exodus from Egypt and pharaoh and their own exodus from Europe under the restrictive rule of George III and the church of state. Both groups were in search of religious and personal freedom. The founding fathers considered individual freedom as essential in allowing a person to make a free-will choice to believe in Jesus Christ as Savior. Islam was spread by imperialistic conquests, convert to Islam, subjugation, or die. The Catholic Church tortured people and held inquisitions that resulted in death for many deemed heretics. Religions that force compliance are not religions of faith but institutions of slavery. Martin Luther began the Protestant reformation. Let people have a Bible of their own and decide for themselves. George Washington refused a third term as president and refused to be made king. As Mosed did also, Washington supported a country ruled by natural law and God and not ruled by man. Scripture reads; "For the Lord is our judge, The Lord is our lawgiver," "For a child will be born to us, a son will be given to us; And the government will rest on His shoulders."

At President Washington's first inaugural address, he stated, "No people can be bound to acknowledge and adore the invisible hand, which conducts the Affairs of men more than the People of the United States. Every step, by which they have advanced to the

character of an independent nation, seems to have been distinguished by some token of providential agency."

At his farewell address, Washington remarked, "And let us with caution indulge the supposition, that morality can be maintained without religion. Reason and experience both forbid us to expect that national morality can prevail in exclusion of religious principles."

Thomas Jefferson said, "God, who gave us life, gave us liberty. And can the liberties of a nation be thought secure when we have removed their only firm basis, a conviction in the minds of the people that these liberties are of the gift of God?"

John Quincy Adams said. "The highest glory of the American Revolution was this: it connected in one indissoluble bond the principles of civil government and the principles of Christianity."

In 1787, Ben Franklin addressed Washington at the Constitutional Convention by suggesting, "I have lived, sir, a long time, and the longer I live, the more convincing proofs I see of this truth, that God governs in the affairs of men. And if a sparrow cannot fall to the ground without His notice, is it probable that an empire can rise without His aid? We have been assured, sir, in the sacred writings, that 'except the Lord build the house they labor in vain that build it.' I firmly believe this, and I also believe that without His concurring aid, we shall succeed in this political building no better than the builders of Babel. I therefore beg leave to move that henceforth prayers imploring the assistance of heaven and its blessings on our deliberations be held in this assembly every morning before we proceed to business."

That God governs in the affairs of men would seem to be explicit in that God has used America in the past to bring Hitler to justice as well as the emperor of Japan, Mussolini, and more recently, Manual Noriega and Saddam Hussein.

Daniel says the Antichrist "will take actions against the strongest of fortresses with the help of a foreign god [Satan]."[1597] America is certainly the strongest of fortresses,[1598] if we can stem

THINGS TO COME

the current efforts to dramatically reduce the size of our military. Our navy and air force remain the strongest in the world.

When Scripture speaks of the nation's bringing justice on the Antichrist, it says in Ezekiel:

> So the Lord Jehovah says this; Because you have given your heart as the heart of gods, therefore, behold, I will cause to come on you awesome strangers of the nations (America). And they shall draw their swords against the beauty of your wisdom, and will profane your splendor. They shall cause you to go down to the pit, and you shall die the deaths of the slain in the heart of the seas. Will you still say, I am of the gods, before Him who strikes you? But you are a man, and not God, in the hands of Him who pierces you. (Ezek. 28:6–9, IHOT)

> Our laws and our institutions must necessarily be based upon and embody the teachings of The Redeemer of mankind.
> It is impossible that it should be otherwise; and in this sense and to this extent our civilization and our institutions are emphatically Christian. This is a religious people. This is historically true. From the discovery of this continent to the present hour, there is a single voice making this affirmation. We find everywhere a clear recognition of the same truth. These, and many other matters which might be noticed, add a volume of unofficial declarations to the mass of organic utterances that this is a Christian nation.
>
> —*Church of the Holy Trinity*
> *v. United States*, 1892

The addendum contains a legal brief presented to the US Supreme Court by fellow Christian Chris Gates, which they have not acted upon. It will only be acted upon if enough pressure can be exerted upon Congress and the US Supreme Court from "We the People."

THE ALPHA AND THE OMEGA

Christ was the first and only one to exist as both man and God. He was the first in that he was present at creation, the first to be resurrected, the prototype for humanity, the Alpha. Christ is also the end, the Omega, as in him is the end of man's captivity and condemnation to sin. Moreover, he will usher in the end of human history and create a new heaven and a new earth. Christ is the new covenant that brought us from the law to a personal relationship for the sake of our eternal salvation.

THE NEW COVENANT

Christ taught the essentials of the meaning of life, for provisional reality, for foundational reality, and for us individually. In one particular instance, he gave us to understand these essentials by speaking analogously about bread. "My food is that I should do the will of Him who sent me, and that I may finish His work."[1599] Finishing God's work is bringing as many people as possible to the salvation offered by Jesus Christ. Our sinful nature is complicated by the intervening influences of the spiritual warfare.[1600] Adding to this complication is the necessity of God granting us free will. "And Jehovah repented that He had made man on the earth; and He was angered to His heart. I regret that I have made man."[1601] The creation of a redeemed world, God's original design, will only be accomplished by the return of Christ and the establishment of his rule for the new heaven and the new earth.[1602] God is omniscient. He foresaw every contingency. He wove into the fabric of his plan all of the variables of human disobedience, Satan, and free will. Every contingency precipitated the occurrence of the next predetermined part of God's divine plan. Christ, like us, had free will, yet he used his free will to follow God's will and to be obedient.[1603] For Christ, doing the will of God was as necessary and as life-sustaining as eating is to us.

> Do not labor for food that perishes but for the food, which endures to everlasting life. Which the Son of Man will give to you for the bread of God is the one coming down out of heaven and giving life to the world. I am the bread of life. The bread, which I will give you, is My flesh, which I will give for the life of the world. The one partaking of My flesh abides in Me and I in he. (John 6:27, 35, 48, 51, 56 IGNT)

> The one partaking of My flesh and drinking from My cup reaffirms their commitment to the new covenant and has everlasting life, and I will raise him up on the last day. The one partaking of my flesh and drinking My blood abides in Me, and I in him. Even as the living Father sent Me, and I live through the Father, also, the one partaking of Me, even that one will live through Me. (John 6:54–57 IGNT)

"The bread also which I will give for the life of the world is My flesh."[1604] The flesh, which was Christ incarnate, God in human form. He came into provisional reality so that he could take on himself the sins of all humanity. Then the flesh, his life, would be sacrificed as atonement for the sins of everyone in provisional reality. "Those partaking of My flesh abide in Me and I in him." Anyone that believes this to be true partakes of the flesh of Christ, symbolically represented as the bread of communion. Christ's sacrificial death was sufficient for the atonement of sin because Christ is and was the requirement of God for the salvation of man. Moreover, we have life, eternal life, through his death and our belief that we as fallible beings are unable to meet the requirements of God. We need Christ to make us worthy to receive God's grace and the promise of everlasting life.

JESUS CHRIST

When God makes a covenant, it is ratified when both sides meet their obligation. As when Abraham accepted the covenant from God, in obedience left the Ur Valley, and went to the land that God would show him. Once ratified, no one sets the covenant aside or adds conditions to it.[1605] The law was given as a teacher to lead us to faith in Christ so that we may be justified by faith.[1606] In the time before Christ appeared in the flesh, righteousness was rewarded with a long and prosperous life.[1607] The sons of Israel were unsure what would become of them after death other than that they would go to Sheol. Strong's dictionary defines *Sheol* as "the world of the dead, grave, hell and pit."[1608]

The Old Testament is vague about what transpired after death. The Pharisees believed in a resurrection after death; the Sadducees did not. We have a view of Abraham's bosom recorded in Luke where some that die are in torment, and others are in a much better place. They are separated by a great chasm where they wait for judgment day.[1609] This is more than likely where the concept of purgatory originates. The chosen people in their rejection of

Christ were not able to bring salvation to the world.[1610] The ministry of Christ revealed the mystery of faith and the promise of salvation. There was a partial hardening of the heart of Israel so that they would not believe and ultimately would reject Christ as their Messiah.

The mystery that is now revealed is that the hardening of the Jews was done so that the Gentiles could come to faith in Jesus Christ.[1611] The promise of salvation belongs to all who believe Jew and Gentile alike.[1612] We as believers are all sons of God through our faith in Jesus Christ.[1613] Moreover, if we belong to Christ, then we are Abraham's descendants. As his descendants, we are heirs according to the promise[1614] of everlasting life through faith in Jesus Christ. "While we were still helpless, at the right time Christ died for the ungodly."[1615] "And God demonstrated His own love toward us, in that while we were yet sinners, Christ died for us." [1616]

> Attaining to all the wealth that comes from the full assurance of understanding, resulting in a true knowledge of God's mystery, that is Christ Himself in whom are hidden all the treasures of wisdom and knowledge. (Col. 2:2–3)

> And when the fullness of the time came, God sent forth His son, born of a woman, born under the law so that He might redeem those under the law, that we might receive the adoption as sons. (Gal. 4:4–5)

The angel Gabriel appeared to Mary to bring her good tidings of great comfort and joy,[1617] and he said to her,

> Hail, one having received grace, the Lord is with you. You are blessed among women. Do not fear Mary, for you have found favor from God. And behold you will conceive in your womb and bear a Son, and you will call His name Jesus. This One will be great and will be called Son of the Most High. And the Lord

God will give Him the throne of His Father David. And He will reign over the house of Jacob forever, and in His kingdom there will be no end. (Luke 1:30–33 IGNT)

The Holy Spirit will come upon you, and the power of the Most High will overshadow you and for this reason that holy One being born of you will be called Son of God. For nothing is impossible with God. And Mary said, behold, the slave of the Lord! May it be to me according to your word? (Luke 1:34–38 IGNT)

The coming of the Messiah had long been predicted in the Old Testament.[1618] He was to be the perfect king.[1619] He would restore the nation of Israel and free its people from the oppression of the Roman Empire. The Jews were expecting a king to be born as a direct descendant of the line of David.[1620] They did not expect a teacher born by some obscure distant relative—a girl of perhaps sixteen and her husband a carpenter. Mary, with a genetic lineage of King David, and Joseph, as a legal descendant, were the perfect fulfillment of prophecy in the Old Testament.[1621]

The Jews were expecting a reprieve from provisional reality. They were not expecting Christ, the true Messiah, who would bring salvation to all of humanity, everlasting freedom for everyone. They could not break out of an empirical perception of reality. They were unable to recognize the truth of foundational reality. Jesus, born of Mary, is legitimately human, born of a human and being flesh, mind and soul, a human personality. However, had Christ been the child of Mary and Joseph, there would have been no legitimate claim to Jesus's deity. He would have been wholly human, and it could be reasoned that he was like any other man and could not make the claim that he is the Son of God. However, being fathered by the Holy Spirit and born of a woman,[1622] Christ is the perfect solution, a combination of humanity and deity. He was a combination of provisional and foundational reality.

> For in Him all the fullness of deity dwells in bodily form. And in Him, you have been made complete, and He is the head over all rule and authority. Having been buried with Him in baptism, in which you were also raised up with Him through faith in the working of God who also raised Him from the dead. Even when you were dead in your sins, He made you alive, with Him having forgiven us all our sins, having canceled out the certificate of debt, having taken it out of the way, having nailed it to the cross. (Col. 2:9–10, 12–14)

If Christ had just supernaturally appeared, he would have had no human qualities, and whatever occurred in his life could not be guaranteed to be an experience that we as mortals would share. The reality of his death and resurrection[1623] demonstrated his and our ability to pass from provisional reality into foundational reality. Christ becoming flesh shared in our human experience and to demonstrate his power over death[1624] and the reality of a resurrected everlasting life.[1625] Faith would require that the Messiah would be a demonstration of a human existence, followed by a spiritual, resurrected existence. Jesus Christ is the prototype for humankind, the Alpha. God's provision for man's inability to conquer his own sin nature was to send his Son so that we as believers could obtain salvation. We are incapable of securing our own salvation through our merit; it is obtained through our faith in Jesus Christ, and in Christ alone. This is accomplished solely by God's grace as he deems with absolute sovereignty that Christ will be the propitiation for our sins.[1626] This absolute truth is the foundation of our faith.

> God rescued us from the domain of darkness and transferred us to the kingdom of His Beloved Son in whom we have redemption, and the forgiveness of our sins, Christ is the image of the invisible God, the first born of all creation. For by Him all things were created both in heaven and on earth, visible and invisible whether throngs or dominion or rulers or authorities all things

THINGS TO COME

have been created through Him and for Him, He is before all things, and in Him all things hold together. He is also head of the body, the church, and He is the beginning the first born from the dead, so that He Himself will come to have first place in everything, "The Alpha." For it was the Father's good pleasure for all the fullness having made peace through the blood of His cross, through Him, I say whether things on earth or things in heaven reconciled you in His fleshy body through death in order to present you holy and blameless. (Col. 1:13–20, 22 IGNT)

THE CONUNDRUM OF FREE WILL

God's ultimate plan for humanity was to have a world populated with people that would meet his requirements for righteousness. "What does the Lord require of you? To act justly and to love mercy and to walk humbly with your God."[1627] To walk humbly means to live in obedience to God's will. That means that we obey him and that we love one another. It must be remembered that God orchestrates everything that affects his divine plan for humanity.[1628] The only caveat is the gift of God for us to have free will. Without free will, we would not be able to make a free-will choice to honor and obey God.[1629]

God's plans may seem to have been frustrated by man's free will; however, none of what has transpired in human history has been unknown by God, and his plan cannot be reversed.[1630] The advent of Christ as the salvation for humanity is repeatedly foretold in prophecy in the Old Testament.[1631] It is revealed as an absolute truth in the New Testament.[1632] God's will is a very idiosyncratic phenomenon. Adam and Eve failed in their attempt for many reasons, because of Satan, a supernatural influence, preaching a false doctrine. "Surely you will not die" and "You will be like God."[1633] Contributing to their failure was their lack of obedience to God, their lack of faith in God's truth, and their desire to do their will instead of God's. This was all possible because of their free-will ability to choose not to honor or to obey God. It is because of these criteria, we refer to man as having a fallen nature.

The population that followed did not deviate from the path taken by Adam and Eve. "That every intent of the thoughts of his heart was only evil continually."[1634] There were other complications here with "the angels that keep not their first estate."[1635] Therefore, God destroyed the world with a flood that covered the entire earth.[1636]

The next phase of the redeemed world plan would be a chosen people, the nation of Israel. God called out a righteous man, Abraham, to establish his holy people, the people chosen of God.[1637] It was God's desire that a chosen people would live a godly life, and in turn, God would richly bless and protect them.[1638] All of the people of the world would either witness or hear about the chosen people living reverently and being richly blessed and protected by God. Then they too would seek out the God of the nation of Israel.[1639] However, God's chosen people, like Adam and Eve and every generation since, would not honor God or obey his commandments. "The spirit is willing, but the flesh is weak."[1640]

The nation of Israel alternated between God's blessings and his curse—[1641] blessings for obedience, and the curse for disobedience. The just discipline administered by God is referred to as a curse because that is how it is viewed from people within provisional reality.

In the continual unfolding of God's divine plan—"at the right time, Christ died for the ungodly"[1642]—God introduced his Son. Christ is the one solution that could overcome the evil in provisional reality.[1643] God in the flesh could now establish a relationship with his people. From a provisional perspective, it is easier for us to make a free-will choice to something that exists in our touch-and-feel reality. Now it would be easier for us to understand that he will bear our sins, overcome death, offer salvation

THINGS TO COME

for all humanity, and produce a redeemed world. God being holy cannot overlook our sin as that would compromise his perfect holiness.[1644]

According to God's perfect plan, when the fullness of the time came, he sent his only begotten Son into provisional reality.[1645] According to Old Testament prophecy, he was born from a virgin.[1646] He was born under the law so that he might redeem those under the law, that we would receive the adoption as sons.[1647] A man of flesh, born a descendent of David, declared the Son of God, with power, would overcome death by resurrecting himself first and then all believers.[1648] The gospel is the power of God for salvation to everyone who believes, for in it the righteousness of God is revealed through faith. As it is written, "But the righteous man shall live by faith."[1649] The appearance of Christ in the history of man was to secure salvation for all that choose to believe, and by his appearing, many have come to know God and believe in the gospel of Jesus Christ.[1650]

Since the appearance of Christ and his short ministry of three years, over the last two thousand years, hundreds of millions of people have come to faith in God through Jesus Christ and have received salvation.

In Christ's first thirty years, he experienced our everyday lives and the experiences of a man from birth into adulthood within provisional reality. Christ appearing as a man also let us know that God understands firsthand our trials and struggles, our sorrow, and our joy. We are also to understand that we are able to overcome temptations and the evil that exists in provisional reality as Christ had done. Christ knows all of our vulnerabilities, the behaviors, and attitudes that have caused men to fail in the past, continue to fail today, and will continue into the future. After his thirty-year experience in provisional reality, Christ began his three-year ministry and preached the remedy: "Do not love the things of the world,"[1651] "Love your neighbor as yourself."[1652] "Love the Lord your God with all of your heart, with all of your strength, and with all of your might."[1653] That is what it will take to overcome evil and control our free will. Most importantly, he taught, "I am the way, and the truth, and the life, no ones comes to the Father except through Me."[1654]

The very people Christ came to redeem rejected him, which was also a part of God's plan. Christ's death not only served as the perfect sacrifice, it was a demonstration of eternal life. If Christ, a man, died and rose from death, the same will be true for all of us. "By His power God raised the Lord from the dead, and He will raise us also."[1655] Christ taught that the kingdom of heaven was at hand,[1656] and it was; he was the kingdom. However, he was referring to foundational reality, and the nation of Israel did not understand that. They were looking for another King David to free them from the oppression of Rome.[1657]

The chief priests and Sadducees ignored the message of Christ until they saw he was developing a following. Then, out of fear of losing their power, prestige, and wealth, they began to plot against Christ and discredit his message.[1658] This is the same pride and the same sin we saw in Satan.[1659] It is also the same pride that prevents us from having complete faith and confidence in God.[1660] Pride prevents us from turning the control of our life over to God. We are reluctant to abandon our will for our life and adopt God's will as the primary focus for the direction of our life. We resist the "seeking His kingdom first" kind of orientation.[1661]

The advent of Christ was not a new direction for God's divine plan as it was the ultimate solution, a part of the continual unfolding of God's plan. Man is incapable of securing his own redemption, and we need, every one of us, a Savior, someone to secure our salvation. We, as believers, realize that we owe our life to Christ because he gave up his life for us. He introduced an individual, personal relationship between man and God. God's chosen people rejected Christ, and in that rejection, the focus shifted from a chosen people to anyone that exercised their free-will choice to believe that Jesus Christ was the Son of God.[1662] Moreover, that

Christ is the only hope we have of being accepted by God through our faith that Christ is our only salvation. Christ died on the cross for our salvation. He was resurrected so that we would have a hope and know that the same glory of a resurrection awaits any who choose to believe the message of the gospel.[1663] I have decided to follow Christ, forsaking all others and forsaking everything in this temporal existence. I forgo everything in provisional reality for the only true enduring reality, that of foundational reality.

THE MYSTERY OF FAITH

Because of the relationship between God and Christ and our relationship with Christ, we have a relationship with God.[1664] The base of our relationship with God is because of our faith in Christ and our belief that because of his sacrificial death for the atonement of our sins, our sins are forgiven by God.

We cannot approach God on our own merit because we are not perfect as God has asked us to be;[1665] we are also not holy as he has requested.[1666] For God to accept us as we are would require that he compromise his perfect holiness, which he cannot do and still maintain his perfect holiness. The very essence of God is absolute purity, absolute truth, absolute perfection, and absolute holiness.[1667] If God were to compromise and overlook our sin, then God would not be what God is: unchangeable. Because he is unchangeable, we can have faith in God and know that all he has said will never change, and all that he has promised will come to pass. His truth will always be the truth; if he changed, then nothing would be absolute. Because God is the creator of everything,[1668] he is the absolute authority, and his truths are absolute truth.[1669]

Just as Moses interceded for the sons of Israel,[1670] Christ intercedes for all Christians.[1671] This is why Scripture reveals that no one may come to God except through his Son, the only redeemer of humanity, Jesus Christ. "No one can come to Me unless the

Father who sent Me draws him; and I will raise him on the last day."[1672] Therefore, the fruition of God's plan, a redeemed world, will come about upon Christ's return. He will cast Satan, the rebellious angels, and all nonbelievers into the lake of fire.[1673] He will govern all of humanity, with everything at his command in the new earth.[1674] God has requested that we all are to be perfect and holy, yet not one of us is able to accomplish this degree of perfection because of our proclivity for sin that exists within our fallen nature. Individuals left to their own free will to guide their destiny ended in the great flood, Sodom, Gomorrah,[1675] and countless other examples.[1676] God's wrath destroyed peoples, cities and nations because their every thought was evil. A holy people, singled out by God to be a living example of God's grace, rejected God. For the most part, since creation, man has either rejected God or put his own will above God's will. Man's default is self-will and rebellion, not God's will and obedience.

THE FIRST MYTH: IF I AM ONLY GOOD ENOUGH

There are two widely held misconceptions about Christianity and salvation. The first is that some believe that when they die, they will stand before Christ, all of their lives sins will be placed before God, and they will be held accountable. The consensus seems to be that if the good in their lives outweighs the bad, they will get into heaven. This misconception is one of the reasons people think that being a good person will earn them salvation.[1677] Christ tells us, "I am the way, and the truth and the life, and no one comes to the Father but through Me."[1678] This statement by Christ is very explicit. The "good person" concept comes from the teachings of the law of Moses and incidentally Islam. In the Old Testament, there is so much emphasis placed on behavior, all of the dos and don'ts. They were intended to identify that which was sinful and that which was righteous behavior. The law was never intended to prepare anyone for salvation; it was meant to prepare the world for Christ.[1679] God gave humankind many chances at redemption, and we just could never get it right.[1680]

The law presented the concept that good behavior is rewarded with blessings, and wrong behavior is met with punishment, the curse.[1681] For those that think salvation can come through being a good person. This is where their confusion comes from. In the Old Testament, people lived under the law, the old covenant, and God said in essence, "Do as I say, and things will go well for you here on earth."[1682] When people followed the law, they were demonstrating their faith in God and attempting to be righteous or a good person. The law also proved that man could not uphold God's standards and that salvation for humanity would have to come from God himself.

The New Testament also addresses behavior and goes into great detail about behavior that finds favor with God and behavior that is characterized by people that will not inherit the kingdom.[1683] The Old Testament had behavior as a prerequisite to God's grace. However, Christ brings a new covenant, and if we believe in salvation through Jesus Christ, we are no longer under the law.[1684] Moreover, our behavior becomes characteristic of one who has received salvation, and in like fashion, we walk according to our calling, and walk worthy of one who has been accepted by God.[1685] The law outlined behavioral constraints and liberties before the fact: do this, and you are righteous; disobey, and experience my justice. The new covenant in Christ puts the focus on behavior after the fact. Believe in Jesus Christ and salvation through his death, and you will then behave righteously out of gratitude for being saved from the wrath of God. We also express gratitude[1686] because we have the promise of eternal life. Christ secured our salvation through his death. Even though we are imperfect and sinful by our very nature, Christ died for us.[1687]

> We should all have as our ambition, to be pleasing to our Lord, for we must all appear before the judgment seat of Christ, so that each may be recompensed for his deeds while in the body, according to what he has done, whether good or bad. (2 Cor. 5:9–10)

The case can be made that behavior or being a good person has a lot to do with our eternal state. Being a good person has nothing to do with us obtaining eternal life; our behavior, however, does determine our rewards in heaven. More importantly, however, being a good person is how God wants us to live our life here in provisional reality. God gives us parameters for righteous behavior only because it is right and not because it brings us salvation. "And there is salvation in no one else; for there is no other name [Jesus Christ] under heaven that has been given among men by which we must be saved."[1688] The absolute truth remains that no one will enter heaven without being a follower of Jesus Christ. When Christ is in glory before God, he will not acknowledge non-Christians, those who have not acknowledged Christ before men.[1689] For these individuals there is a different fate and a different eternity.[1690]

The question is, what about the day of judgment and the Scriptural reference to everyone standing before Christ to be judged?[1691] Nonbelievers, because of their lack of faith, will be judged for the sins they have committed because they do not have Christ to intercede on their behalf. Christ has not taken away their sins, and they will be held accountable and punishable for all of their own sins. "And they were judged every one of them according to their deeds."[1692] Because they have resisted the Holy Spirit and denied Christ, there is no pardon for their sins, and they will have to bear the burden of their own punishment. "And if anyone's name was not found written in the book of life, he was thrown into the lake of fire."[1693] When a person becomes a believer in Jesus Christ and believes that Christ is the Son of God and that he was sent for the redemption of all of our sins, Christ enters their name in the book of life, and there is rejoicing in heaven.[1694]

Christians are judged as well; however, we are judged as good and faithful servants. Our judgment is an evaluation of how well we executed the will and call of God for each of us individually in our life.[1695] Furthermore, we are judged by how effectively we used the spiritual gifts we were given and if we accomplished the predetermined work that we were to do.[1696] Our judgment is to determine our rewards for our faithful execution. "Rejoice and be glad, for great is your reward in heaven."[1697] "Rejoice in that day and leap for joy, because great is your reward in heaven."[1698] It is through Jesus Christ that we are able to know the glory of God.[1699] Through faith, we know that he who raised the Lord Jesus will also raise us.[1700] If we think that by being a good person, we can earn our own salvation, we are presupposing that we can accomplish more than God can and we are ignoring the sacrificial work of Christ on the cross.

> And the nations were full of wrath; and Your wrath came, and the time of the judging of the dead, and to give the reward to Your slaves the prophets, and to the saints, and to the ones fearing Your name—to the small and to the great. (Rev. 11:18)

IS IT EVER TOO LATE?

Scripture seems to indicate that there is a hierarchy or a ranking of order for the citizens of heaven. Just to put aside any thoughts that everyone in heaven is the same of equal rank, for our position is awarded by our works, some to positions of authority and responsibility, and some to lesser roles. "Truly not has arisen among those born of a woman any greater than John the Baptist. But the least in the kingdom of heaven is greater than he."[1701] This clearly indicates that not all are equal in heaven. Christ also tells us that upon his return that "My reward is with Me, to render to every man according to what he has done."[1702]

There is much consideration given to when a person becomes a Christian. Can people really be saved on their deathbed? Matthew 20 tells the parable of the workers and the landowner. The landowner goes out early in the morning and hires laborers to work in his vineyard all day for one denarius. He also goes out at the third hour, the sixth hour, and the ninth hour and hires more laborers. When evening came, the landowner called all of the laborers together to receive their pay. All received one denari, and those that worked all day grumbled because they thought it was not fair that all received the same reward for differing amounts of time spent at their task. To which the landowner responded,

> Friend, I am doing you no wrong, did you not agree with me for a denarius? Take what is yours and go, but I wish to give to this last man the same as to you. Is it not lawful for me to do what I wish with what is my own? Or is your eye envious because I am generous? So the last shall be first and the first last. (Matt. 20:13–16)

We can equate this to those that have been Christians all of their lives and those who became a Christian in the third, sixth, or ninth hour of their life. What is it to us if Christ is generous with what is his? He has paid the price. Shall the pot say to the craftsman, "Why have you made me thus?"[1703]

There is not much we can really understand about foundational reality with our empirically based understanding from provisional reality. That is why only God and Christ can judge and forgive sins, as they are sovereign over their creation. Moreover, their thoughts are higher than our thoughts,[1704] and their ways are not the same as our ways.[1705] Christ tells us, "Do not judge, so that you will not be judged; do not condemn and you will not be condemned, pardon and you will be pardoned."[1706] He tells us that if we do judge others, he will hold us to the same criteria.[1707] The point Christ makes is to forgive others seven times seventy times,[1708] just

as we have been forgiven, because if we do not forgive, we will not be forgiven.[1709] The point is this: it is a matter for the righteous judgment of Christ. We also know that as humans our judgment process is flawed. Our judgments are faulty, they are circumstantial, sometimes wrong, hasty and revengeful, and often prejudicial. "Then the Lord saw that the wickedness of man was great on the earth, and that every intent of the thoughts of his heart was only evil continually."[1710]

What is the fate of a murderer? Scripture tells us that a murderer cannot inherit the kingdom of God. "Everyone hating the brother is a murderer, and you know that every murderer does not have everlasting life abiding in him."[1711] Christ also said, "Not everyone who says to Me, 'Lord, Lord' will enter the kingdom of heaven."[1712] Another question is, what about the last-minute conversion of people on death row? Are they sincere in their faith or is it an "I've got nothing to lose" frame of mind? There are some issues that we, as fallible humans, cannot possibly understand enough about absolute truth to be able to make a determination. Speculations about these inconclusive topics serve no purpose for our salvation. In fact, they can distract us from that very path as Scripture warns us not to spend time on empty speculations.[1713] There are important differences between murder and taking someone's life. Murder is the unjust termination of life. There are legitimate actions that result in the death of another human being. Capital punishment is sanctioned in Scripture as a means of executing justice.[1714] Capital punishment is not revenge killing, or a deterrent, or getting even; it is punishment. Killing is also justified in a just war. There are also times when representatives of governments may need to use extreme force to enforce the law. There are also provisions for self-defense. Empirical speculations that run contrary to the word of God are the doctrines of deception.[1715] Christ repeatedly warned his disciples and us about deception and false teachings.[1716] False teachings as when the murder of abortion is regulated to a discussion about when life begins, as if that changes the definition of murder. Once again, it is our will, our choice (pro-choice) over God's will. Scripture says, "Trust in the Lord with all your heart, and do not lean on your own understanding."[1717]

The Interlinear Bible, Hebrew Translation of Psalm 139:15–16 reads, "My bones were not hidden from You when I was made in secret; when I was woven. Your eyes saw my embryo."

embryo em·bry·o (ĕm'brē-ō')

an embryo is:

1. An organism in its early stages of development, especially before it has reached a distinctively recognizable form.
2. An organism at any time before full development, birth, or hatching.

God weaves us in the womb, and that process begins at conception, in the embryonic state, from day 1.

Believers are controlled by the love of Christ,[1718] because he died for everyone's sake that those who live should no longer live for themselves but instead live for the one who died and rose again on their behalf,[1719] Christ who has given us the promise of eternal life.

THE SECOND MYTH: ONCE SAVED, ALWAYS SAVED

The second misconception about Christianity and salvation is that some people believe that if you are once saved, you are saved forever—once saved, always saved. Two verses that give us this confidence are found in John.

> This is the will of the Father who sent Me, that all He has given me I should lose none of it, but should raise it up at the last day. For this is the will of Him who sent Me, that everyone who beholds the Son and believes in Him may have everlasting life; and I Myself will raise him up at the last day. (John 6:39–40)

> My sheep hear My voice, and I know them, and they follow Me; and I give eternal life to them, and they will never perish; and no one will snatch them out of My hand." My Father, who has given them to Me, is greater than all; and no one is able to snatch them out of the Father's hand. "I and the Father are one. (John 10:27–30)

All of the conditions for our salvation have been met on the cross.[1720] There are two separate acts involved in the crucifixion. Christ as God was nailed to the cross as a sacrifice for all, and he took the sins of the world onto himself. His death was the result of the burden of all of the sins of humanity. He was the perfect sacrifice, as he was holy and blameless during his entire stay on earth.[1721] The death of Christ is the atonement for all of man's sins—past, present, and future. We were washed clean of all of our sins by his blood.[1722] Then he was resurrected and raised in everlasting glory.[1723]

Christ was crucified and died on the cross as a sacrifice for the atonement of our sins, period. Then he was raised from the dead to everlasting life. These are the provisions for our salvation, and these two acts can never be undone. Believing means we understand that we cannot attain a state of holy perfection on our own. We need Christ to intercede on our behalf. We only attain eternal life because Christ has taken our sins upon himself. Human history has demonstrated that we always stumble over our sinful nature. Understanding this is how we receive our eternal salvation. Out of gratitude for Christ's sacrifice, we reciprocate the love that he demonstrated to us. "No greater love has a man than this than to lay down his soul for others." "If you love Me, obey My commandments." How do we know what Christ requires of us unless we become students of the Scripture? Christ died and was raised from the dead. He is now at the right hand of God, interceding on our behalf.

> In all these things, we overwhelmingly conquer through Him who loves us. (Rom. 8:37)

> When Christ, who is our life, is revealed, then you also will be revealed with Him in Glory. (Col. 3:4)

The crucifixion of Jesus Christ and his resurrection can never be undone. Once Christ died on the cross, the provision for anyone who believes has been secured forever.[1724] This does not mean that for us once saved, always saved, but rather all of the conditions for our salvation have been met on the cross once and for all. The provision for being able to be saved is set and secure, but not our salvation.

Several verses lead us to understand that our condition is not once saved, always saved; if we do not have a true saving faith, our salvation is not secure.

> For if we go on sinning willfully after receiving the knowledge of the truth there no longer remain a sacrifice for sins. (Heb. 10:26)

> For those being once enlightened and having tasted of the heavenly gifts, and becoming partakers of the Holy Spirit and having tasted the good word of God, and the works of power of a coming age, and falling away, it is impossible for them again to renew to repentance. For they again will be crucifying to themselves the Son of God, and putting Him to open shame. (Heb. 6:4–6)

THINGS TO COME

In the book of Jonah, he warns Nineveh that if they don't repent and follow God's ways they will be destroyed; they repent, and the people of Nineveh believed God. And God relented. Nahum was written 150 years later; it is about the utter destruction of Nineveh because they returned to their evil ways.

BALANCING THE BOOKS

The role of judging humanity falls to Christ and to Christ alone.[1725] We will be held accountable for how we judge others. "As we have judged others so to will we be judged."[1726] We are to have discernment so that we can identify doctrines, theories, laws, policies, and other religions that are contrary to that which we know to be true.[1727] The absolute truth is the gospel of Jesus Christ. There is a difference between discernment and judgment. Scripture tells us that our judgments are faulty, and as such, our judgments are untrustworthy. Our role is to forgive others so that we too may be forgiven.[1728] We should only be concerned with judging ourselves so that we continue to improve and so that we will not be judged.[1729] When we judge ourselves, we repent and make changes in how we do things. This continues our process of sanctification and may spell us from future various trials,[1730] which usually is corrective discipline from the Lord.[1731]

Therefore, if anyone is a believer in Christ, they are a new creation, and the old sinful ways are put behind us.[1732] We exemplify the character and righteousness of Christ, and we are a new creation—[1733] we are born again.[1734] A loving God that did not want to condemn everyone because all have sinned[1735] sent his Son to reconcile our sinfulness.[1736] God reconciled us to himself through Christ, specifically that God was in Christ reconciling provisional reality and not counting our trespasses against us.[1737] In accounting, when you reconcile the books, you balance the entries. For every entry in the minus column, there is an entry in the plus column. This same principle applies here, except Christ's side of the balance sheet has provisions for the sins of all believers, past, present, and future. All sins that are repented (recorded) are reconciled in the books. "But He having offered one sacrifice for the sins for all time sat down at the right hand of God."[1738] The sacrificial death of Christ earned him his place at the right hand of God so that he may continue to intercede on our behalf, as the high and holy priest. Jesus, because He continues forever, holds His Priesthood permanently. Therefore He is able also to save forever those who draw near to God through Him, since He always lives to make intercession for them.[1739]

> For we have a High Priest that is able to sympathize with our infirmities, one having been tried in all respects according to our likeness, apart from sin. Therefore let us draw near with confidence to the throne of grace, that we may receive mercy, and we may find grace for help in time of need. (Heb. 4:15)

As noted above, Christ having taken human form understands the human condition. In our likeness in the same environment, he remained sinless. The person seeking to be a good person as their source of salvation is trying to fulfill the law; they do not seek Christ, and as such, they have fallen from the grace of God.[1740] Christ is the Alpha, the beginning of our faith, and the Omega, the ultimate goal of our faith. "I press on after the mark, for the prize of the high calling of God in Jesus Christ."[1741] We are to run the race while present on earth, and the finishing line is Christ, the ultimate Perfector of our faith.[1742]

"MY LORD AND MY GOD"

As Christians, when we start to become more obedient, we make ourselves more accessible to the Holy Spirit, who will help us[1743] as he begins his perfect work in us.[1744] He takes us through the

successive stages of our developmental process of sanctification, thereby assisting us in perfecting our faith.

The law of Moses does not apply as universally today as it did to the nation of Israel. It is still the same Ten Commandments, and a lot of what is written in the law of Moses[1745] has solid and sound application for today. We have to understand the culture and historical settings of the times. We probably would not stone a stubborn and rebellious son that is also a glutton and a drunkard[1746] as is suggested. However, it is still good counsel to not take a bribe or distort justice,[1747] to move your neighbor's boundary marker,[1748] or for a woman to wear a man's clothing and a man to wear a woman's clothing.[1749] Christ brought a new covenant, and our guidelines are the teachings of Christ in the New Testament. The law of Moses still serves the same purpose to help us make righteous decisions. Righteous behavior prepares us for the Holy Spirit, and he has a desire to indwell every believer. This begins a building cycle; the more the Holy Spirit is able to direct our lives, the more righteous we become and the more righteous we become the more direction we have from the Holy Spirit. This is possible because the Holy Spirit gives us the ability to overcome evil.[1750]

We begin to read Scripture because we want to know or at least understand more about our relationship with God, his Son, Jesus Christ, and the Holy Spirit. Then we have access to the enlightenment and illumination of the Holy Spirit as we read the Word of God. The indwelling Holy Spirit guides our understanding, and he reveals things to us about our behavior, our thoughts, and our relationship with Christ and the very truths of God.[1751] We have been rescued from our former life of darkness.[1752] We now respond to the guidance of the Holy Spirit, who guides us through our conscience with impressions he forms in our mind.[1753] This is the beginning of our personal relationship with Christ and with God. We understand that we were lost; we were not within God's grace. We also understand that God first loved us[1754] as was demonstrated by his action in sending his Son, Jesus Christ, to die as the bearer of all of our sins. "Greater love has no man than to lay down his soul for his fellowman."[1755] Moreover, by this, we know we are loved by both the Father and the Son. It was God who was crucified on the cross.[1756]

After all that the disciples had been through with Christ, all they had seen and witnessed, they still did not understand that Christ and God were one. Thomas was the first one to get it right. However, even Thomas did not get it until after Christ had died. Thomas did not get it until he could see and feel. "Then He said to Thomas, 'Reach here with your finger, and see My hands; and reach here your hand and put it into My side; and do not be unbelieving, but believing.'"[1757] "My Lord and My God"—Thomas finally saw that Christ was God.[1758] God's plan was to create humans and celestial beings for a reciprocal love relationship. God gives to us, and we in turn worship his goodness and holiness. We cannot make the free-will choice to be involved in this relationship unless of course, we have what appears to us in provisional reality to be free will. He also gives us the ability to make choices for our will instead of God's will. Free will gives us the options for choices—choices for good or evil. Christ is the antidote for all of the poor free-will choices made by man, angels, you, and me.

All good healthy relationships are based on unselfish love.[1759] When we acknowledge the love that was expressed to us from God and his Son, we reciprocate that love to others in service and to God and his Son in obedience. In like manner, we should love our neighbor as we love ourselves.

> Teacher, which is the great commandment in the Law?" And He said to him, "You shall love the Lord your God with all your heart, and with all your soul, and with all your mind. This is the great and foremost commandment. The second is like it, you shall love your neighbor as yourself. On these two commandments depend the whole law and the prophets. (Matt. 22:36–40)

A PERSONAL RELATIONSHIP WITH CHRIST

"If you love Me, obey My Commandments." It is through willing obedience that we reciprocate God's love. It is by the free-will demonstration of our obedience that we become righteous and heirs of the promise of eternal life. When we attain that personal relationship with God through Jesus Christ, we are obedient out of love and no longer out of a sense of duty or a fear of punishment. God and Jesus as parts of the holy Trinity are One.[1760] Christ expressed it as "I in you and you in Me, Father."[1761] Love is the basis of any personal relationship. This is how we attain a personal relationship. We already know that God first loved us;[1762] now we in turn reciprocate that love to God through free-will obedience, which is our expression of love.[1763] Moreover, we are to love him with all of our hearts, minds, and souls.[1764] This means we bring all of our personal agencies to bear in our obedience. If we are successful, then we do love God with all of our hearts, minds, and souls. Our hearts, minds, and souls are all contributors of our free will. The key factor in understanding God's love for us is that he does not love us for who we are in our decadence; he loves us because of his tremendous capacity to love. If we are using our hearts, minds, and souls in obedience to God as a demonstration of our love, then we are overcoming evil and expressing our love to God and we are not being willfully disobedient to God.

We have gone from the law to a personal relationship. We understand God first loved us and sent his Son to die as the only means by which we may obtain salvation and eternal life. Covenants are God's promises. He establishes the requirements on both sides. We obey, and he delivers on the promise of eternal life. We have a promise of an inheritance, and we obey out of a reciprocation of his love. Both sides are demonstrating their love for one another. In this, we have a personal intimate relationship with God through his Son, Jesus Christ. A personal, intimate knowledge of our God is what sets Christianity apart from any other religion. Pagans have to guess what their gods require, and in some instances, they were driven to sacrificing their newborn babies.[1765]

AND I MYSELF WILL RAISE HIM UP

Christ lives through the Father, and believers will live through Christ. The work that Christ was sent to do, the will of his Father, was to provide the means by which our sins may be atoned. Through Christ we would become sons, heirs of God's kingdom. "This is the will of Him who sent Me, that of all that He has given Me I lose nothing, but raise them up on the last day. For this is the will of My Father, that everyone who beholds the Son and believes in Him, may have eternal life, and I Myself will raise him up on the last day."[1766] Those that are given to Christ are God's elect—his chosen ones from before time began.[1767] All who know Christ and have an innate[1768] understanding of God are his elect, or those that are called. "No one can come to Me, unless the Father who sent Me draws him, and I will raise him up on the last day."[1769] All that are children of God have a desire to know him and to develop a relationship with him.

Christ brought a new covenant and made that announcement at the last supper when he said, "This is My cup, which I shed for you, take and drink, for this is the new covenant." The new covenant is that Christ died for our sins to secure the means of our salvation because we are unable to be sinless on our own. History demonstrates the inability of God's chosen people to abide in his decrees and statutes in spite of the blessings bestowed on them by God. He gave them fair warning in his decrees of the consequences of rebellion. The Hebrews rebelled anyway, in spite of all the miracles they had witnessed in their exodus from Egypt. Any of us that remain in the wilderness will also perish.

THINGS TO COME

Believe in God, believe also in Me." In My Father's house are many dwelling places. But if it were not so, I would have told you. I go to prepare a place for you! If I go and prepare a place for you, I will come again, and receive you to Myself, that where I am you may be also. (John 14:1–3)

I AM the way, and the truth, and the life. No one comes to the Father except through Me. If you had known Me, you would have known My Father. (John 14:6–7)

This is the message we have heard from Him and announce to you, that God is Light, and in Him there is no darkness at all. If we say we have fellowship with Him and yet walk in the darkness, we lie and do not practice the truth; but if we walk in the Light, as He Himself is the Light, we have fellowship with one another, and the blood of Jesus His Son cleanses us from all sin. If we say we have no sin, we are deceiving ourselves, and the truth is not in us, He is faithful and righteous that He may forgive us the sins, and may cleanse us from all unrighteousness. If we say that we have not sinned, we make Him a liar and His word is not in us. (1 John 1:5–10)

THAT YOU MAY HAVE JOY

Jesus knew from the beginning who would not believe.

"For this reason I have told you that no one is able to come to me except it is given to him from My Father."[1770]

Remain in Me and I in you. As the branch is not able to bear fruit of itself, unless it remains in the vine, so neither can you unless you remain in Me. I am the vine you are the branches. He that remains in Me and I in him, this one bears much fruit. For apart from Me you are not able to do anything. (John 15:4–5)

TOM NEWMAN

If you remain in Me, and My words remain in you, whatever you desire you will ask, and it will happen to you. In this My Father is glorified, that you should bear much fruit, and you will be My disciples. As the Father loved Me, I also love you, continue in My love. If you keep My commandments, you will continue in My love; as I have kept My Father's commandments and continue in His love. I have spoken these things to you that My joy may abide in you, and your joy may be full. This is My commandment that you love one another as I have loved you. (John 15:7–11)

Greater love than this has no one, that anyone should lay down his soul for his friends, you are My friends if you do whatever I command you. You have not chosen Me, but I chose you out, and planted you, that you should go and should bear fruit, and your fruit remains. (John 15:13, 16)

Anyone who has seen Me has seen the Father. How can you say, `Show us the Father'? Don't you believe that I am in the Father, and that the Father is in Me? The words I say to you are not just My own. Rather, it is the Father, living in Me, who is doing His work. Believe Me when I say that I am in the Father and the Father is in Me; or at least believe on the evidence of the miracles themselves. I tell you the truth, anyone who has faith in Me will do what I have been doing. He will do even greater things than these, because I am going to the Father. And I will do whatever you ask in My name, so that the Son may bring glory to the Father. You may ask Me for anything in My name, and I will do it. If you love Me you will keep My commandments. (John 14:9–15)

THINGS TO COME

ONE SHEPHERD, ONE FLOCK

One of the most endearing portrayals of Christ is as the shepherd and his followers as sheep, which is perfectly illustrated in Psalm 23. The sheep hear his voice, and he calls his own sheep by name, and he will lead them out. When he puts forth his own sheep, he goes out in front of them, and the sheep follow him because they know his voice, and because they are his sheep, they never follow a stranger.[1771]

> The Lord is my Shepherd, I shall not want. In pastures of green grass He makes me lie down; He leads me to waters of rest. He restores my soul. He guides me in the path of righteousness for His namesake. Even though I walk through the valley of the shadow of death I will fear no evil, for You are with me; Your rod and Your staff, they comfort me. You prepared before me a table before my enemies. Thou hast anointed my head with oil; my cup runs over. Surely goodness and mercy shall follow me all the days of my life; and I will dwell in the house of Jehovah for the length of days. (Ps. 23:1–6 IHOT)

The Lord is our shepherd, and we are his sheep. He provides for us, and he restores our souls. A shepherd leads his sheep along the safest and most secure route. As long as the sheep follow, they are kept from harm. Our life on earth is in the valley of the shadow of death, and it is filled with peril. However, Christ has overcome death in his resurrection, and so all that remains for the Christian is the mere shadow of death, not death. A shadow is not real; it only represents something, and a shadow is only made possible by the presence of light. Godly intervention and God's holy angels will intercede for us in this life for reasons only specifically known by God.[1772] However, we can be sure the cause for intervention has very little to do with provisional reality and has everything to do with foundational reality. The whole cosmos system in provisional reality is under the control of Satan,[1773] the enemy. For now, our place is in Satan's cosmos system—"prepared a place for me in front of my enemy."[1774] We, however, have been anointed by God and have more than we need to overcome evil. God's goodness and mercy will follow us all the days of our life in provisional reality as long as we remain in the guidance of the shepherd. Then we will dwell in the house of the Lord in foundational reality forever.

"I came that they may have life and have it abundantly." "I am the good shepherd, and I know those that are mine. And I Am known by the ones that are mine. Even as the Father knows Me, I also know the Father, and I lay down My soul for the sheep. And I have other sheep, [Gentiles] which are not of this fold [Jews]. I must also lead those, and they will hear My voice [gospel] and there will be one flock."[1775] The one flock will be comprised of all believers Jews and Gentiles alike, and one shepherd, Jesus Christ.

> For this reason My Father loves Me, because I lay down My soul [crucifixion], that I may take it up again [resurrection]. No one takes it from Me [Satan], but I lay it down from Myself [My own free will], I have authority to lay it down, and I have authority to take it up again. [In His resurrection death was overcome] I received this commandment from My Father. (John 10:10–18)

> The works, which I do in the name of My Father, these bear, witness about Me. How could I do these things if I Am not who I say that I Am? But you do not believe, for you are not My sheep. My sheep hear My voice, and I know them, and they follow Me. And I give eternal life to them, and they shall never perish. And no one will take them out of My care, My Father who has given them to Me is greater than all, and no one is able to take them out of My Father's care either. I and the Father are one. (John 10:25–30)

Adam and Eve could have lived eternally in paradise in the garden of eden. Not only was there a tree of good and evil, there was also a tree of eternal life.[1776] Perhaps after a period of time of faithful obedience they would have been offered eternal life just as we are. However, their disobedience ended the covenant relationship with God. Satan's bidding, "Surely you will not die," was a complete lie. Satan brought death to humanity. Through the resurrection of Jesus Christ, death was defeated, and the offer of eternal life is made available to everyone who will believe.

"I give a new commandment to you, that you love one another, just as I have loved you."[1777] "My teachings are not Mine; they are from My Father who sent Me."[1778] "My witness is true, for I know from where I came and where I go."[1779] "For unless you believe that I am He, you will die in your sins."[1780] "The One sending Me is true, and what I heard from Him, these things, I tell the world."[1781] "The Father did not leave Me alone, for I always do the things pleasing to Him."[1782] "If you continue in My word, you are truly My disciples, and you will know the truth, and the truth will set you free."[1783] "Truly, truly, I say to you, he who hears My word, and believes Him who sent Me, has eternal life, and does not come into judgment, but has passed out of death into life."[1784] "Truly, I say to you, if anyone keeps My word he shall never see death."[1785] "If you do not believe Me, believe My miracles, that you may perceive and may believe that the Father is in Me, and I in Him,[1786] otherwise how else could I do these things. I and the Father are One."[1787]

> Who has saved us and called us with a holy calling, not according to our works, but according to His own purpose and grace, which was granted us in Christ Jesus from all eternity. But now has been revealed by the appearance of our Savior Christ Jesus, who abolished death and brought life and immortality to light through the gospel. (2 Tim. 1:9–10)

> The Lord knows those who are His and everyone who names the name of the Lord is to abstain from wickedness. (2 Tim. 2:19)

> What does the Lord require of you? To act justly and to love mercy and to walk humbly with your God. (Mic. 6:8)

THE UNPARDONABLE SIN

There is a caveat. It is not the will of your Father who is in heaven that one of these little ones perish[1788] and that he wishes for all to come to repentance and to be saved.[1789] However, "no one can come to Me unless the Father who sent Me draws him; and I will raise him up on the last day."[1790] It is unfortunate that some people struggle with the concept that the only way to eternal life is through faith in Christ. Those who do not understand this are the children of wrath,[1791] those who practice the deeds of darkness.[1792] They will try to earn their own salvation, which is impossible, and they are destined to eternal damnation. Not believing in the gospel of Jesus Christ, which is eternal life made possible by his sacrificial death. To reject the belief that no one gets into heaven except through Jesus Christ[1793] is the unpardonable sin,[1794] in which there is no salvation. Unbelief is the ultimate abomination to the Lord. This position calls God a liar and attempts to negate the sacrificial death of Jesus Christ. When God says it is his will that none of these shall perish, that means that if you, as one of God's elect, resist the call of God in your life, he, God will stop at nothing to redeem you. The calling of God for you is irrevocable.[1795] God cares little of the things of provisional reality. "Do not love the world; he who loves the world cannot love God."[1796] Remember, Christ spent thirty years gaining an epithetical understanding of this life and shared in the experiences that are common to us all.

Often what we see as tragedies in this life can be misconstrued. There is nothing God will not do to ensure that his elect are heirs of eternal life. He has already given his word that "none of these will perish."[1797] Moreover, he has already sent his Son to die that we might be saved.[1798] If he sent his Son to die for us, we can understand that he will stop at nothing in terms of his involvement in our life, to bring us into a right relationship with him. "Although He was a Son He learned obedience from what He suffered and being perfected He became the author of eternal salvation to all those obeying Him."[1799] It is unfortunate that so many of us do not seek God of our own accord, but rather we need to be prodded by his intervention. We usually do not respond in a positive fashion to his blessings because when we are blessed, we think we have brought all this good fortune on ourselves and that it has happened by our own doing.[1800] We respond to God more attentively during our trials and tribulations, as they have a way of making us focus on God. For God, however, it is not about provisional reality; it is all about foundational reality. If we of our own free will make the decision to establish a relationship with God, we may be able to forgo much of the pain and suffering we endure in life.

As we are ambassadors of Christ,[1801] we too are to do the will of the Father and see that none of these, the elect, perish.[1802] The message here is that just as Christ's confidence and faith in his Father was such that he only did the Father's will,[1803] not his own, and that he only did that which was well pleasing to his Father,[1804] we are to be like-minded.[1805]

God sent Christ to earth because of man's inability to refrain from sin. Our course left unaltered would have all of humanity perishing in the lake of fire, which is the second death.[1806] Christ was the antidote to our inevitable sinfulness and for our inability to honor God's requirements. "No man is without sin."[1807] Without a savior to take our sins on himself, there would be no redemption for humankind.

TOM NEWMAN

THE RETURN OF THE ALPHA AND THE OMEGA

The return of Jesus Christ as the King of kings and the Lord of lords is referred to as the second coming of Christ. "I am the Alpha and the Omega, the first and the last, who is and who was and who is to come, the Almighty."[1808] Christ was there at the beginning, at creation, working with God to create provisional reality and humanity.[1809] Christ will be there at the end, and he will usher in the culmination of provisional reality and human history. The creative forces of the universe—God the Father, Christ the Son, and the Holy Spirit—also created all of the celestial beings, including Satan and his minions, who introduced evil into the world. God, being perfectly holy, is not able to commit evil that had to be left to one of his creations. Christ is King of kings and Lord of lords over all of provisional reality, past, present, and in the new heaven and the new earth.[1810] God is sovereign over both realities, over all that he has caused to be in existence, in all eternity, and in all infinity. Satan is a part of God's divine plan and always has been. Otherwise, we would have not had the perfect evolution of God's plan. God's plan could only have evolved exactly as he willed it to unfold. God, being omniscient, omnipotent, and omnipresent, could never be thwarted in his endeavors or in the conclusive execution of his perfect plan.

We sometimes make too much of the events of this life. The only real act of any significance in provisional reality is our free-will choice of faith. This choice will guarantee that we have an eternal existence with Jesus Christ, God, the Holy Spirit, fellow saints, and the celestial beings in paradise. "I am the way, the truth and the life, and no one comes to the Father except through Me."[1811]

Christ will bring an end to evil with the destruction of the beast, the false prophet, Satan, and all his minions. They will all be inhabitants in the lake of fire.[1812] Christ was the first and the last and the only one that has ever existed as both God and man. Christ was the first resurrection, and he will resurrect all of

humanity—some to punishment, and some to eternal glory.[1813] He is the first and the last, the beginning, and the end.[1814] Everything has a beginning, a state of being and an end. This is God's life cycles for everything in provisional reality. However, everything in foundational reality has an eternal existence. Humanity had its birth at creation in the garden of eden with Adam and Eve. The culmination of humanity will occur at the second coming of Jesus Christ. Foundational reality is comprised of beings created by God and Jesus Christ that have an eternal existence. The second birth is a continuing state of evolution, a transformation from one dimension of existence into another.[1815] The precipitating event for this transformation for the individual is death.

Those that stood their entire life without Christ now they will face judgment without Christ.

> And the dead were judged from the things which were written in the books according to their deeds. (Rev. 20:12)

Those that are judged from the things written in the books according to their deeds apply to all that died prior to the advent of Jesus Christ. They are judged on the demonstration of their faith or their lack of faith. Their faith was manifested in the degree of their obedience to the law of Moses. In the Old Testament, obedience to the law was rewarded with blessings; those that were disobedient received a curse. In the New Testament, everything gets personal. We develop a personal relationship with Christ, we as the sinner and he as our Savior. This relationship, however, is still grounded in obedience, and even more so, it is grounded in love. "He first loved us." "If you love Me, obey My commandments." We have always had to have guidelines for our behavior because of our ability to exercise our free-will choices and our proclivity to seek our own path and ignore God. The ability for us to be able to express free-will choices is imperative for us to be able to choose to believe or not to believe. We also choose to obey or not to obey, to inherit the kingdom or not. For those who died since Christ's ministry: "And if anyone's name was not found written in the book of life, he was thrown into the lake of fire."[1816] This includes both those that never believed in Jesus Christ as Savior and those who have had their name blotted out from the book of life by God.[1817] It also includes those that minimized the death of Christ on the cross by thinking they could earn their way into heaven by being a good person. At Christ's return, we will all be transformed into an eternal state, some to a state of incomprehensible peace and joy, and others to a state of incredible anguish. The earth and heavens will be replaced by a new heaven and a new earth.[1818] In this new state of existence, there will not be any pain, suffering, crying, or death.[1819] This new form of government will be administered by Christ.[1820]

There is a divine plan for humanity's existence as mortals, and there is a continuation of that plan for our existence into eternity. As mortals in provisional reality, we tend to see everything with an end state. It is hard for us to envision infinity or eternity. Yet that is exactly what has been promised to us by God and by his Son, Jesus Christ.[1821] "And we have beheld and bear witness that the Father has sent the Son as Savior of the world. Whoever confesses that Jesus is the Son of God, God abides in him and he in God."[1822] Moreover, Christ will declare, "I am making everything new again."[1823] "It is done; I am the Alpha and the Omega."[1824] The new Jerusalem will descend out of heaven.[1825] The tabernacle of God will be among men.[1826] Moreover, the city has no need of the sun or of the moon to shine upon it for the glory of God will illuminate it and its lamp is the Lamb.[1827] In Christ's second return, he comes as King of kings and Lord of lords, as a ruler, a warrior, and a king. In his second coming, he will free the world of oppression, evil, tyranny, and the effects of Satan. In Christ's first ministry, he offered everyone the opportunity for eternal life, Jew and Gentile alike. If the Jews had not rejected Christ as their king, the way would not have been open for the redemption of all. Redemption is based on our free-will choices to accept, reject, and believe or not to believe. Christ came offering eternal life in foundational reality, and because his solution was not for provisional reality, he was rejected.

The God of truth cannot lie.[1828] The God who is omniscient,[1829] omnipresent,[1830] and omnipotent[1831] cannot error or be mistaken in what he says or does.[1832] A completely holy God cannot deceive because there is no evil in him.[1833] Therefore, God is either telling us the truth and we have an inheritance with him in eternity, or it is not true, and God's truth is not true. The resurrection is true, and so is eternal life. If Christ did rise from the dead as he said he would,[1834] then he is God, and all that he says is true and that is absolute truth because his truth will outlive humankind and provisional reality. It is absolute truth because his truth survives our reality; the proof for truth is in the resurrection of Jesus Christ. Who in his resurrected state appeared to over five hundred people in a forty-day period.[1835] "I am the truth and the life. The Father and I are One."[1836] Their truth is absolute because they have created everything. Jesus Christ was the prototype for humankind. Humankind, whether individually or collectively, as a chosen people, were not able to maintain their righteousness. Christ was not only sent for our salvation, but also as a perfect example of how we are to live our lives. Christ the Son of God and we as believers are also sons;[1837] we have one Father who has an inheritance for all of his children.

> For let this mind be in you which also was in Jesus Christ, although He existed in the form of God, He did not regard Himself as God. He emptied Himself taking the form of a man…and became obedient to the point of death, even death on a cross. Therefore God highly exalted Him and bestowed the name, which is above every name. So that at the name of Jesus every knee will bow, in, on and under the earth. And that every tongue will confess that Jesus is Lord, to the glory of God the Father. (Phil. 2:5–11)

"Work out your salvation with fear and trembling for it is God who is at work in you, both to will and to work for His good pleasure."[1838] "Be blameless and harmless, as children of God, without fault in the midst of a crooked and perverse generation, shine as lights to the world."[1839] "He who began a good work in you; conduct yourself in a manner worthy of the gospel."[1840] Christ never had his own interests in mind, only God's, even beyond self-preservation. After his death and because of his complete obedience, he was exalted. We received salvation and the prospect of eternal life through faith in Christ's work and God's grace. As Christ emptied himself and conformed to the will of God, we are to do the same. We should make more free-will choices to be indwelt, to adopt the teaching of Christ, and to overcome evil. Of the utmost importance, we should consistently make free-will choices to do God's will and not our will.

AT THE APPOINTED TIME

If we look at how time is used in the Bible, we can get a real sense that human history unfolds by God's timetable, and it will end according to his timing as well. What is interesting to note is the specific mention that the timing of events has to be right for so many things that occur. In Genesis, we have the beginning of earth and human life. We also find the first mention of things occurring at an appointed time when God explains to Abraham that his people will be interned as slaves for four hundred years.[1841] Then the fourth generation of his people will return when the iniquity of the Amorites is complete.[1842] In Genesis 21, we learn that the birth of Isaac[1843] occurred at the appointed time. The Psalmist tells us that God will have compassion on Zion at the appointed time.[1844] In the book of Daniel, Gabriel the angel is interpreting a dream for Daniel and tells him, "Behold I am going to let you know what will occur at the final period of the indignation, for it pertains to the appointed time of the end."[1845] Further on in the book of

Daniel, when Gabriel is explaining future events to Daniel, he talks about all kinds of alliances and strategies that will be taking place; however, it is all for naught as Gabriel finishes with, "But it will not succeed, for the end is still to come at the appointed time."[1846] This concept of the end coming at the appointed time, when all of the criteria has been met and God will end provisional reality, appears repeatedly throughout the Bible.[1847] "Until the end because it is still to come at the appointed time." Also in Habakkuk 2:3, the Lord said, "For the vision is yet for the appointed time, it hastens toward the goal, and it will not fail." God's involvement in the history of mankind is reaffirmed when he says, "In those days and at that time I will cause a righteous branch of David to spring forth."[1848] To give us a sense of what this means, God also tells us that the day and night occur at their appointed time.[1849]

The concept of events being pre-established in time is continued into the New Testament. Christ was traveling by Gadarenes where he came across two men that were demon possessed. When they saw Christ, they yelled out, "What do we have to do with You, Son of God? Have You come to torment us before the time"?[1850] Matthew also records that when the disciples asked Christ where he wanted them to prepare the Passover, he responded with "Go into the city to a certain man and say to him, The Teacher says, 'My time is at hand; I am to keep the Passover at your house with My disciples.'"[1851] Christ also tells his brothers twice that there are things he is not ready to do "because His time has not yet come"[1852] or "My time has not yet been fulfilled."[1853] The book of Romans, which is a theological snapshot of the Christian faith, records that Christ died at the right time for the ungodly.[1854] Paul also tells us that Christ was born when the fullness of the time had come in.[1855] Other time-sensitive events are the predictions regarding the end times;[1856] "take heed you do not know the appointed time because He has fixed a day in which He will judge the world in righteousness."[1857] All the celestial beings, all of humankind, and all of human history are subject to God's timetable.

TOM NEWMAN

WALK WORTHY OF YOUR CALLING

A central theme throughout the Bible is that of obedience. The basic tenant of obedience is a conscious, free-will choice to make righteous decisions and to do the will of God. Moreover, the will of God for you in your life is to stay constantly focused on the process of your sanctification.[1858] Obedience means obeying to the letter God's Ten Commandments and obeying the spirit of the law of Christ's teachings. "He who has My commandments and keeps them is the one who loves Me; and he who loves Me will be loved by My Father, and I will love him and will disclose Myself to him."[1859]

Faith is all about choices, choices for righteousness and not for evil, choices of obedience and not disobedience. In disobedience, we are made sinners; in obedience, we are made righteous.[1860] Christian obedience is not forced or legalistic; it is willingness on the part of the believer to love and honor God just as Christ did. "If you keep My commandments, you will abide in My love; just as I have kept My Father's commandments and abide in His love."[1861] "And this is love that we walk in obedience to His commandments."[1862] "For the law was given through Moses, grace and truth were realized through Jesus Christ."[1863] Those that are obedient and who please God are blessed; our blessings come in many forms. By being obedient to God's will, we can be confident before God that anything we ask in accordance with his will, believing we will receive.[1864]

More importantly, those who are obedient live in him, and he lives in those who are obedient. We know this to be true because he has given the Holy Spirit to us, and the Holy Spirit dwells within us.[1865] The law is still a guiding principle in the life of a believer. It is not a means of salvation; it is rather a moral and ethical code of conduct. We exhibit obedience as an expression of our love for God.[1866] We are able to be obedient by the power of the Holy Spirit,[1867] who is given to all who believe.[1868] Through obedience, we come to know Christ,[1869] and God's love is made complete in us.[1870] As children of God, we are cautioned about conforming to the evil desires of the world.[1871] These are the evil desires we had before we came to know Christ and before we became obedient because the God who has called us is holy, and we too are to be holy.[1872] The very fact of the obedience of Christ is that which accredited him to be the compensation (propitiation) of our sins.[1873] Christ's perfect obedience and his ability to remain sinless is the very reason he is the salvation of all humanity.

THE TEMPTATION OF CHRIST

One of the reasons Christ came to earth was so that we would have a new standard to follow for our behavior; as such, we should take our cues from him.[1874] In reality, we cannot just assume how Christ would behave. We must become like him in thought, in perceptions, in word and in motivation. Then we will respond as he may have. You have to know Scripture so well that you know what he would do.

When Satan confronted Christ in the wilderness with his threefold temptation, Christ rebuked Satan and responded to him by quoting from Scripture. Christ defeated Satan and was able to resist temptation because he was obedient to the will of his Father, took counsel from Scripture, and was steadfast in his faith. In the first instance, Satan attempted to break down the separation, which Christ had preserved between his deity and his humanity.

> And the tempter came and said unto Him, If thou art the Son of God, command that these stones become bread. But He answered and said, it is written, Man shall not live by bread alone, but by every word that proceeds out of the mouth of God. (Matt. 4:3–4)

The second test involved a shortcut for Christ to receive all of the kingdoms of provisional reality without enduring the horrendous suffering that awaited him at his trial and crucifixion. Had Christ acquiesced to Satan's temptation, there would have been no salvation for humanity. Satan's temptation had no influence on Christ; he was steadfast in his devotion to the plan God had for him. This is a paramount example and truth for us to follow as well. The second test demonstrates the necessity of doing God's will.

> Then the Devil takes Him to the holy city; and he set Him on the wing of the temple. And he said to Him, If You are the Son of God, throw yourself down: for it has been is written; He shall give His angels charge concerning You: and they shall bear You on their hands, lest You strike Your foot against a stone. Jesus said unto him, Again it has been written; You shall not tempt the Lord your God. Again, the devil takes Him to a very high mountain, and he showed Him all the kingdoms of the world, and all their glory. And he said to Him, I will give all these things to You if falling down You will worship me. Then Jesus said to him, Go Satan! For it has been written: You shall worship the Lord your God, and shall serve Him only. Then the devil left Him. And behold! Angels came near and served Him. (Matt. 4:5–11 IGNT)

The encounter between Christ and Satan is completely supernatural. Satan took Christ up on a mountaintop where they could see all of the kingdoms of the earth.[1875] There is, of course, no place in provisional reality where this could have taken place. All of the kingdoms of earth cannot be viewed from a single location. Christ remains steadfast; God does not tempt, and he cannot be tempted.

Satan introduced a philosophy of life that is directly opposed to the revealed will of God. It is a lie in the sense that self-will contradicts God's will, and God's will is infinitely true because God is infinitely holy and infinitely perfect. God as the Creator of everything that exists is the author of what is and what is not truth.

Recorded in the book of Matthew, Jesus asks his disciples who they think he is. Peter answers, "Thou art the Christ, the Son of the living God." Jesus replied with, "Blessed are you, Simon Barjona, because flesh and blood did not reveal this to you, but My Father who is in heaven."[1876] It is through the Holy Spirit that we receive communication directly from God. This is a perfect example of how the Holy Spirit imparts truth to believers. A mere five verses later, we see a different Peter when Christ tells his disciples what fate awaits him at his crucifixion and death. Peter says, "God forbid it, Lord! This shall never happen to You." Christ responds with, "Get behind Me, Satan! You are a stumbling block to Me; for you are not setting your mind on God's interests, but man's."[1877] You are concerned with provisional reality, not foundational reality. In one instance, we see Peter receive a truth from the Holy Spirit, and in the next minute, we see him being influenced by Satan. God's influences will always be about foundational reality; Satan's will always be about provisional reality.

Christ was offered everything he could want if he would just denounce God as Satan had done. In obedience to God, Christ refused. In response to Satan, four times Christ said, "It has been written."[1878] All Christ needed to do to refute Satan was to rely on Scripture, the Word of God, and a willful decision to remain steadfast to the will of God. In resisting the temptation of Satan, Christ proved that man could resist Satan, all of his works and all of his ways.[1879]

Christ, in his obedience, demonstrated his sinless nature and his qualification to be the perfect sacrifice. "Being found in appearance as a man He humbled Himself and became obedient to His death, even death on the cross."[1880] "Although He was a Son, He learned obedience from what He suffered, and once made perfect, He became the source of eternal salvation for all who obey Him."[1881] Sin separates us from God[1882] and the conviction from the Holy Spirit,[1883] and suffering brings us closer to God.[1884] We have a very simple process to follow, and the steps are clearly outlined in Scripture. "Submit to God, resist the Devil and he will flee from you. Draw near to God and He will draw near to you. Cleanse your hands, you sinners; and purify your hearts."[1885] The onus for this entire process is on us; submit, resist, and draw near to God.

There are considerations that because Christ was the Son of God, it is no wonder he could remain sinless. However, Christ emptied himself of his deity.[1886] He told his followers that with the aid of the Holy Spirit, "They would be able to do more than these things."[1887] The idea of complete obedience gives us the ability to have relationships that are more significant with fellow followers of Christ. If we are always obedient then in our relationships, we are able to love one another fervently from the heart.[1888] We do not have to worry about our relationship being compromised by temptation or sin. Obedience is straightforward; to put a finer point on it, we are told that God will punish those who do not obey. When Christ returns, "He will punish those who do not know God and do not obey the gospel of our Lord, Jesus Christ."[1889] Simply put, this is why we must evangelize, "Am I my brother's keeper?"[1890] The answer to that question is supposed to be yes. Obedience is a true measure of one's faith; faith without works is dead.[1891]

People can know about God and the saving work of Christ and still not believe. Knowing is not the same thing as believing. You may know how to swim but still not be able to swim. The true measure of one's faith is reflected in their behavior. Through faith, one's behavior conforms to the will of God, the measure of that conformity, or the degree to which one's behavior conforms to God's behavioral expectations is a measure of one's faith. There are two kinds of obedience: obedience out of love and obedience out of fear. We can have a healthy fear of God;[1892] however, our willingness to change our behavior should be done out of respect, love, and gratitude toward God for what he has done in grace. We can say we are Christians, that we have faith in Jesus Christ, but is that reflected in our behavior? We can say anything about ourselves as to who we are, but what does our behavior reveal about who we are? We will know a tree by its fruits.

> Therefore as you have received Christ Jesus the Lord, so walk in Him. Having been firmly rooted and now being built up in Him and establishing, in your faith, and overflowing with gratitude. See to it that no one takes you captive through empty deception and philosophy, according to the tradition of men, and elementary principles of the world, rather than according to Christ. (Col. 2:6–8)

REJOICE AND BE GLAD FOR GREAT IS YOUR REWARD IN HEAVEN

God's mercy, which comes to us through Christ, will obtain for us a reward richer than our wildest imagination. "Rejoice and be glad, because great is your reward in heaven."[1893] Sin is a very idiosyncratic phenomenon; whatever is in your life that prevents you from being obedient to God is sin.

> What does the Lord your God require of you, but to fear the Lord your God, to walk in all His ways and love Him, and to serve the Lord your God with all your heart and with all your soul, and to keep the Lord's commandments and His status which I am commanding you today for your good? (Deut. 10:12–13)

When we walk humbly with God, we are submissive to his will. Our behavior obediently conforms to God's behavioral expectations. We are to be as children; we are children of God. This is no different from the healthy relationship between a child and their earthly father. It is much like raising our kids; we think we understand the whole process, but our theory is different from their reality. We are supposed to be the commensurate role models for our kids. We can say anything; however, it is our behavior over time that reveals what is important to us. "For where your treasure is, there your heart will be also."[1894] Our children will learn their values from our behavior. To a lesser extent from what we say, unless, of course, our words are substantiated by our behavior. One of the most important things we can teach our children are godly principles for life and a solid practice of regular Scripture reading. The godly principles are of course, found in the Bible, and the Holy Spirit will guide them in all truth, so everything is not always coming from us, the parents. So if you want your children to be good students of Scripture, how often do you model that behavior? If you want your kids to read the Bible, let them see you constantly reading the Bible, and then they will know how important it is.

When I began the process of writing this book I would get up at 5:00 a.m. every morning to spend an hour reading Scripture before I started my daily routine. After I had been doing this for about ten years, my son got up one morning at five with his Bible. He sat next to me on the couch, and I asked him what was up. He said, "If you get up at five every morning to read the Bible, I better figure out why it is so important." He got up at five with me for the next three years; that's how long it took him to read the complete Bible. It is imperative that we teach our children about Christ so that they may have the aid of the Holy Spirit before they become corrupted by Satan's influences in the cosmos world system.

The seeds of adolescent rebellion are not as easily explained away by the sudden onslaught of hormones, and someone is just going through a phase. The origins of teenage rebellion are twofold. One is the physiological change in the adolescent's mind, which imparts them with the ability for abstract thought. The ability to think abstractly gives our youth the epiphany that there are different ways of looking at things, not just our way. They not only cease to take everything that we say as absolutes, they in fact begin to analyze not only what we are telling them but also what we have taught them. Moreover, they begin to look for the consistency between our words and our behavior as they try to find where they fit into the grand scheme of things. If there is a high degree of correlation between what we say and what we do, there is less of a chance that there will be rebellion. This time of transition in the adolescents' thought process is less tumultuous if they have a good understanding of God's absolute truths to use as a foundation and the basis of their moral fiber.

Second, the seeds of rebellion are always found in hypocrisy and arbitrary rule. None of which is to be confused with the distancing most adolescents orchestrate as they seek to gain their independence and learn to stand on their own. The more pull we exert, the more push we will feel. As Christ once said when he was surrounded by children, "Unless you change and become like little children you will not enter the kingdom of heaven."[1895] His point was as children comply with the dictates of their parents without question, well, from the ages of two or three until they become spotted by the cosmos system, we too should exhibit this same level of unquestioning compliance. Children conform to their parent's wishes and decrees, in a sense, in blind obedience. That is exactly how we are to approach our relationship with God—in blind obedience. Faith after all is blind because we put our confidence in the things not seen—in foundational reality, not in provisional reality.[1896] This is possible because of the supernatural elements of our composition and because of the witness of the Holy Spirit.[1897] We know the elements of our faith are true as long as we are not suppressing the Holy Spirit. Children obey out of love for their parents, and parents, out of love for their children, teach them right and wrong.[1898] We want them to be productive members of society. We want them to experience joy, we want their life to turn out well, and we want them to spend eternity in heaven. For the parents, the adolescence quest for independence is a time of heartache and concern. Concern because on their own we wonder if things will go well without our being there to guide them and counsel them. If we have raised our kids to be good Christians, they leave our care and go into God's care. We struggle with turning our kids over to God as much as we struggle with turning our own lives over to God. As earthly fathers love and care for their children, it is no different with God. He desires that we have a life characterized by prosperity and hope.[1899] However, more importantly from a foundational perspective, God's concern for us is that we experience eternal life in his presence. "Love the Lord your God with all your heart and with all your soul and with all your mind. This is the first and greatest commandment."[1900]

"He who began a good work in you will perfect it until the day of Jesus Christ." "Be sincere and blameless until the day of Christ."[1901] "Conduct yourself in a manner worthy of the gospel, for to you it has been granted for Christ's sake, not only to believe in Him, but also to suffer for His sake."[1902] "Do nothing from selfishness or empty conceit, but with humility of mind regard one another as more important than yourself. Do not merely look out for your own personal interests, but also for the interests of others."[1903] "Have the same attitude as Christ did, which was, although He existed in the form of God, He did not regard Himself as God. He emptied Himself, taking the form of a man, and became obedient to the point of death, even death on the cross. For this reason, God highly exalted Him and bestowed on Him the name, which is above every name. So that at the name of Jesus every knee will bow, in, on and under the earth and that every tongue will confess that Jesus Christ is Lord."[1904] We are to work out our salvation with fear and trembling;[1905] salvation, the narrow gate and the constricted way, is not the easy path, and there are those on the broad path that will not inherit the eternal kingdom of God.[1906]

> For it is God who is at work in us, both to will and to work for His good pleasure, do all things without grumbling or disputing so that you will prove yourself blameless and innocent, children of God, above reproach in the midst of a crooked and perverse generation among whom you appear as lights to the world. (Phil. 2:13–15)

Everyone remaining in Him does not sin. Everyone sinning has not seen Him nor do they known Him. The one practicing righteousness is righteous, even as that One is righteous. The one practicing sin is of the devil, because the devil sins from the beginning. For this, the Son of God was revealed, that He undo the works of the devil. Everyone who has been begotten of God does not sin, because His seed abides in Him, and he is not able to sin, because he has been born of God. By this, the children of God and the children of the devil are revealed. Everyone not practicing righteousness is not of God; also the one not loving his brother. Because this is the message that you heard from the beginning, that we should love one another. (1 John 3:6–11)

See what manner of love the Father has given us, that we may be called children of God. For this reason, the world does not know us because it did not know Him. But we know that if He is revealed, we shall be like Him, because we shall see Him as He is. And everyone having this hope will purify himself. (1 John 3:1–2)

Righteousness through faith in Christ, the righteousness which comes from God on the basis of faith. That I may know Him, know the power of His resurrection and fellowship of His sufferings, being conformed to His death in order that I too may be resurrected from the dead. Not that I have already obtained it, or have become perfect, but I press on so that I may lay hold of that for which also I was laid hold of by Christ. I press on toward the goal for the prize of the upward call of God in Christ Jesus. Keep living by that same standard to which we have attained. (Phil. 3:9–16)

Righteousness from faith comes from God. We are righteous not out of our own accord but rather through our relationship with Christ, the source of our imputed righteousness. Christ's suffering was part of his human experience, and it was in demonstration for us. Christ always did the will of his Father, regardless of the cost. We too must do God's will despite the cost and remain faithful. Christ suffered as an example to and for us; there will be suffering in provisional reality.[1907] Our suffering is not unique to us. "Knowing that the same experiences of suffering are being accomplished by your brethren who are in the world."[1908]

PERFECTION IN FAITH, NOT PERFECT

We will have to suffer many times to attain perfection—not perfection as people, but perfection in our faith. The entire time Christ was in provisional reality, he remained obedient and faithful. We are enabled by the Holy Spirit to accomplish the same degree of faithfulness. "Because everything having been born of God overcomes the world; and this is the victory that has overcome the world—our faith. Who is the one who overcomes the world, but he who believes that Jesus is the Son of God."[1909] "He who is in you [the Holy Spirit] is stronger than he who is in the world [Satan]."[1910] Obey as I have obeyed. "If you keep My commandments, you will continue in My love; just as I have kept My Father's commandments and continue in His love."[1911]

> Rejoice in the Lord; beware of evildoers, put no confidence in the flesh, worship in the Spirit of God and Glory in Christ Jesus. I lost everything and because I gained Christ I consider everything I lost rubbish. (Phil. 3:1–3, 8)

"The Lord knows those who are His and everyone who names the name of the Lord is to abstain from wickedness."[1912] "The power of God who has saved us, through Christ, and called us, His elect, with a holy calling, not according to our works, but according to God's own purpose and grace which is granted to us in Jesus Christ for all eternity. It is Jesus Christ, who abolished death and brought life and immorality to light through the gospel."[1913] "Retain the standard of sound words, which you have heard; Guard, through the Holy Spirit who dwells in us, the treasure, which has been entrusted to you."[1914] "Not everyone who says, 'Lord, Lord,' will enter the kingdom of Heaven."[1915] We must genuinely be followers of Christ, in body, mind, and actions.

"He who believes in Me, does not believe in Me but in Him who sent Me. He who sees Me sees the One who sent Me."[1916]

> Jesus who rescues us from the wrath to come. (1 Thess. 1:10)

> The commandments we gave to you by the authority of Jesus Christ. For this is the will of God, your sanctification that you abstain from sexual immorality, that each of you know how to posses his own vessel in sanctification and honor not in lustful passion like those who do not know God. And that no man transgresses and defrauds his brother in the matter because the Lord is the avenger in all these things. For God has not called us for the purpose of impurity but in sanctification. So, he who rejects this is not rejecting man but the God who gives His Holy Spirit to you. (1 Thess. 4:2–8)

THE MEASURE OF A CHRISTIAN

The law was written as specific commandments: things to do, and things not to do. The law is broad-based advice and counsel about how we should live our life and conduct ourselves in our relationships with God and with others. The teachings and statutes of Christ are more in the nature of the spirit of the law and profess an attitude. "Because you have been raised up with Christ, keep seeking the things above, where Christ is, set your mind on the things above, [foundational reality] not on the things that are on earth [provisional reality]."[1917] "When Christ is revealed, then you also will be revealed with Him in glory. Therefore, consider yourself dead to immorality, impurity, passion, evil desire, and greed, which amount to idolatry. For it is because of these things that the wrath of God will come upon the sons of disobedience as you once were."[1918] God was performing his miracles through Christ so that through Christ, we are able to know God. This is possible because of their relationship. Christ teaches us that we too will be able to do miraculous things when he, in like manner, works through us. This is all done for the glory of God. "In this My Father who is in heaven is glorified."[1919] However, the really important work that we do is to be for God's glory not ours, actions benefiting foundational reality, not provisional reality.

All too often, we have the wrong motives in what we seek.[1920] "Everyone who believes that Jesus is the Christ has been born of God. Everyone loving the Father loves also the One having been born of Him. By this we know that we are the children of God."[1921] We demonstrate our love for God by keeping his commandments and overcoming evil with good. We hold in check our sinful nature and love our brothers and sisters in Christ. As humans, we have biases and prejudices. We can even just be plain wrong about some things. We live in a society that teaches us to look out for number one. Even Christians rely on secular solutions first. For the most part, because of whom we are, and our fallen nature, we do not respond to others as we should. We tend to think that we live our everyday lives as we have to and rely on God in those extreme situations when we are overwhelmed. However, this kind of thinking is backward. Most of the Bible is God's communication about how we should behave toward our fellow man. His counsel is not for us to respond in kind; we as Christians should take the lead, responding in kind is our natural tendency. If you treat me abruptly, I do the same; if you are friendly toward me, I respond in kind and am friendly toward you. However, as Christians we are to follow

God's expectations and Christ's example for our behavior toward one another. The Spirit of God is in us, and we are in the Father and the Son, which means we live through Christ. We live toward foundational reality, not provisional reality, because "the flesh does not profit anything."[1922]

If we abide in Christ and He in us, then he is a part of everything we do.[1923] We control Satan's influences and accept God as part of our everyday lives in all of our experiences. As Christians, we lay aside our former manner of life; we lay aside the old man, which was corrupted. And we put on the new man, which in the likeness of Christ has been created in righteousness and holiness and truth.[1924] The "old man" is who we are before we are in Christ; the "new man" is who we are when we are obedient to Christ's commandments. "Therefore, laying aside falsehood, speak truth each one of you with his neighbor, be angry, yet do not sin, do not give the devil an opportunity. Do not grieve the Holy Spirit of God, by whom you were sealed for the day of redemption. Let all bitterness, wrath, anger, clamor, and slander be put away from you, along with all malice. Be kind to one another, tenderhearted, forgiving each other, just as God in Christ also forgave you."[1925] "He jealously desires the Spirit which He has made to dwell in us. He gives a greater grace. Therefore it says, 'God is opposed to the proud, but gives grace to the humble." Submit therefore to God. Resist the devil and he will flee from you. Draw near to God and He will draw near to you."[1926] "As obedient children, do not be conformed to the former lusts which were yours in your ignorance, but like the Holy One who called you, be holy yourselves also in all your behavior." "Since you have in obedience to the truth purified your souls for a sincere love of the brethren, fervently love one another from the heart."[1927] "For I am confident of this very thing, that He who began a good work in you will perfect it until the day of Christ Jesus. And this I pray, that your love may abound still more and more in real knowledge and all discernment so that you may approve the things that are excellent, in order to be sincere and blameless until the day of Christ. Only conduct yourself in a manner worthy of the gospel of Christ."

"Do all things without grumbling or disputing so that you will prove yourself to be blameless and innocent, children of God above reproach in the midst of a crooked and perverse generation, among whom you appear as lights in the world."[1928] "See to it that no one takes you captive through philosophy and empty deception, according to the traditions of men, according to the elementary principles of the world, rather than according to Christ. Devote yourself to prayer, keeping alert in it with an attitude of thanksgiving. Whatever you do, do your work heartily, as for the Lord rather than for men, knowing that from the Lord you will receive the reward of the inheritance. It is the Lord Christ whom you serve."[1929] "Do not be conformed to this world, but be transformed by the renewing of your mind." This renewing takes place through prayer and Scripture reading, which helps level the playing field. "So that you may prove what the will of God is, that which is good, acceptable, and perfect. For through the grace given to me I say to everyone among you not to think more highly of himself than he ought to think; but to think so as to have sound judgment, as God has allotted to each a measure of faith. Therefore, accept one another, just as Christ also accepted us to the glory of God."[1930] "For whatever is born of God overcomes the world; and this is the victory that has overcome the world—our faith. Who is the one who overcomes the world, but he who believes that Jesus is the Son of God."[1931] "Do not judge and you will not be judged, and do not condemn, and you will not be condemned, pardon, and you will be pardoned. Give and it will be given to you, for by your standard of measure it will be measured to you in return."[1932] "He has told you, O man, what is good; And what does the Lord require of you but to do justice, to love mercy and to walk humbly with your God."[1933] "For the love of Christ controls us, having concluded this, that one died for all, therefore all died; and He died for all, so that they who live might no longer live for themselves, but for Him who died and rose again on their behalf."[1934]

THINGS TO COME

WHAT IS JUSTIFICATION?

Some of the terms in Christian doctrine seem a little obscure.

In the Old Testament, during the period between Adam and Christ, forgiveness was sought and granted on the premise of obedience to the law, repentance, and animal sacrifices. All of the sins of the Hebrews would be transferred to a goat. The goat would then be sent over a cliff or out into the wilderness, taking all of their sins with him—the scapegoat. Since the crucifixion of Christ, salvation is through faith alone, in Christ alone, by grace alone.

Faith was measured by keeping the Mosaic law, all six hundred and thirteen commandments, which means to do what is good, do what the Lord requires, to love mercy, and walk humbly with God. In essence, men were just because of their own deeds or works.[1935] Their obedience to these six hundred statues showed their willingness to conform to God's expectations. However, the bar was too high, and humankind was too weak. No one was able to accomplish all that was required. It is impossible for man to become holy by our own devices. Additionally, man distorted the law with his own rules, traditions, and interpretations.[1936] Let us just say there were all sorts of problems with a system that relied so heavily on man with free will.

Man continually asserts self-will over the will of God. God has preordained all that has and will come to pass. The next step was part of the continual unfolding of God's eternal plan. With the advent of Christ, everything about the old system changed. However, a remnant remains that still thinks their salvation is contingent upon their good behavior and their good works. It does not; Scripture is very clear on this point: salvation lies solely on faith in Jesus Christ.[1937]

> And there is salvation in no one else; for there is no other name under heaven that has been given among men by which we must be saved. (Acts 4:12)

Justification means that we are just in the sight of God. Moreover, we are just because of the death of Christ. When Christ died as the perfect sacrifice, our sins were and are forgiven, and we became just, or justified. No one is actually justified until one believes in Jesus Christ as his or her Savior. Conditionally, the reason for which they could be justified when they do believe was secured once and for all by Christ in his death.

Justification has been secured forever by the death of Christ; this does not mean that Christians once saved are saved forever. It means that the provisions for salvation, the death of Christ, has been accomplished and cannot be undone.

Therefore, after Christ died on the cross, he was raised from the dead. The death of Christ is an act unto itself; after the completion of that act, then Christ arose from the dead. These are two completely separate phenomena with each having their own major significance in the course of events for humankind. Through Christ's death, we are justified; through his resurrection, we receive salvation and eternal life.

WHAT IS IMPUTED RIGHTEOUSNESS?

Another elusive doctrine is imputed righteousness. No one is righteous on his or her own merit in God's eyes, so righteousness must come from somewhere else. Our righteousness comes from the death of Christ. The connection between Christ's death and our righteousness is the indwelling Holy Spirit. Because Christ was righteous, and we, through faith, are united with him.[1938] His righteousness is transferred to us.

God does not assert that sin does not exist. God states that he, having covered sin with redeeming blood, does not see or take into account our sins. He also does not account the accusations Satan makes about us when he is before God.[1939] That God does not mark iniquity is possible only through redemption and is never a matter of mere graciousness. God is just, and he is merciful; these are not the same thing. If I speed breaking the law, and I get a ticket, that is justice. If I speed, breaking the law, and the officer gives me a warning, not a ticket, that is mercy. God will be merciful to believers and just with nonbelievers, and this is the essence of true justice.

In Christ's death, we as sinners are justified, which means we are spared from what we deserve. In imputed righteousness, we are given that which we did not earn. Forgiveness in the Christian's existence is the subtraction of that which has been sinful.

The act of accepting Christ as Savior is one act, yet it results in many specific benefits; among these are forgiveness, righteousness, and justification. These benefits are solely contingent on the relationship between the believer and Christ. Justification is the official divine recognition of our righteousness. The absolute righteousness of God is made available through Christ and is imputed, or credited, to all believers. All believers are equally righteous in the sight of God. God considers the believer righteous because of the believer's faith and the relationship with Christ. Imputed righteousness is the believer's standing or covering and has nothing to do with the believer's own righteousness. God is said to be just when he justifies a sinner who does no more than to believe in Jesus.[1940] The chief end of man is to glorify God. All of us will be either a demonstration of his grace in all its perfection[1941] or a display of his wrath[1942] in all the ages to come. It should be understood that when we talk about being saved, we are being saved from the wrath of God that will deliver every unrepentant sinner to eternal damnation. Satan, on the other hand, because of his self-righteousness, has never been able to reconcile himself to the doctrine of imputed righteousness.

All of the work necessary to ensure our salvation has been accomplished by Christ on the cross. All that remains to be done is for us to believe that it is all true. To have faith in God and Jesus

Christ and trust that everything is as it has been revealed to us in Scripture. When we conduct ourselves in accordance with the behavioral parameters in Scripture—walking in the light, putting on the new man—we establish a relationship with both God and Christ through the Holy Spirit. With the work that Christ has accomplished on the cross, and with our asking for forgiveness of our sins, we are in a state of constantly being cleansed from our sins, being made white as snow.[1943] In addition, this perpetuates our relationship with God and his Son. Walking in the light is responding to and being guided by the Light, and God is Light. In a practical way, it means that when the light, which is God, shines into the heart and reveals sin or darkness that is there, it is judged and put away by his grace and power. "If we confess our sins, He is faithful and just to forgive us our sins, and to cleanse us from all unrighteousness."[1944] Our part in this process is to diligently work on our sanctification, which is doing God's will as he has commanded us.

> For this is the will of God, your sanctification; that is, that you abstain from sexual immorality. For God has not called us for the purpose of impurity, but in sanctification. (1 Thess. 4:3,7)

> Lead a tranquil and quiet life in all godliness and dignity. This is good and acceptable in the sight of God our Savior, who desires all men to be saved and to come to the knowledge of the truth. (1 Tim. 2:2–4)

The Christian is not only different in his ideals, his manner of life, and his outward relationships; in reality, he is a new creation in Jesus Christ.[1945]

> and be kind one to another, tenderhearted, forgiving each other, even as God also in Christ forgave you. (Eph. 4:32)

THINGS TO COME

> For if you forgive men their trespasses, your heavenly Father will also forgive you. But if you do not forgive men their trespasses, neither will your Father forgive your trespasses. (Matt. 6:14–15)

FAITH IS AN ATTITUDE

In gaining deliverance from the power of sin, the believer's responsibility is faith and faith alone, which yields oneself unto God. It is an attitude of faith, which is renewed and pursued, in every succeeding day. To walk by means of, or a dependence on, the Spirit is to be delivered from the lust of the flesh.[1946] The conflict is not between the indwelling Spirit and the flesh; it is rather a conflict between the new "I" and the old "I." The new "I" is the regenerated man. Scripture tells us that the child of God can resist sin even though we will be plagued in this life by our own rebellious tendencies and Satan's constant influences. The power we have to resist is through the power of the indwelling Holy Spirit.[1947] No word of the Scripture sanctions the notion that any Christian ever attains to a place where he is not able to sin. Sin, however, does lose its power over the believer, though the presence of sin and temptations are never gone. Their influence, however, is greatly reduced as a believer's motivation turns from pleasing self to pleasing God. This transformation is from the natural or unregenerate state to a regenerated or a spiritual state. The battle has always been between the flesh and the spirit. As we become more spiritual, we become more engaged in foundational reality, although we are still in provisional reality.

> That in the ages to come He might show the exceeding riches of His grace in kindness toward us in Christ Jesus: for by grace we have been saved through faith; and that not of yourselves, it is the gift of God; not of works, that no man should boast. For we are His workmanship, created in Christ Jesus for good

works, which God prepared beforehand so that we should walk in them. (Eph. 2:7–10)

The grace of God cannot be manifested except as there are fallen creatures in existence. Who, because of the corruption of sin, are objects of grace and the demonstration of divine grace, the inestimable glory of which is observable not in time but in eternity. This is all accomplished for the glory of God and Jesus Christ.

THE MEANING OF LIFE

The tribulation and the rapture begin the conclusion of provisional reality and human history. The great tribulation is a period of unprecedented upheaval that will affect the eternal destiny of everyone. The great tribulation is the culmination of the spiritual battle between good and evil. Satan's evil rebellion and his philosophy are crushed by Jesus Christ. Satan and his minions are cast into the lake of fire for an eternity of damnation, which is the second death.

God wanted to establish for himself a holy people. People that would get to know him so that he could develop a relationship with them. It is no different for us than it was for the Jews. He wants us to honor and worship him, and he will provide for our salvation. God would also bless these people so that the entire world would know about the supreme God of the blessed people. God even knew who these people would be before they were born.[1948] A prerequisite of salvation was that his people would have a free-will choice. Most choose not to abide by his decrees and commandments. The predestined and nonpredestined alike were unable to abide in God's will; humankind would not be faithful. God continued with his divine plan and provided for a Savior that would take away the sins of the world.[1949] This was necessary so that an absolutely holy God would not have to compromise his holiness when he extends eternal salvation to less than holy people. "The Spirit is willing, but the flesh is weak."[1950]

The process initiated by God in provisional reality will continue until evil has run its course and all of the saved are saved. This means that all of the predestined Gentiles and Jews have been born again and are saved.[1951] God caused the stubbornness in the Jews so that the offer of salvation would be extended to everyone else. When all of the predestined to be saved have been saved,[1952] God will save all of Israel when he brings to a close the experience of provisional reality. The Jews will accept Christ at his second coming as their Messiah.[1953] In God's infinite wisdom, this all comes full circle. The Jews were looking for a Savior in provisional reality, a king that would save them from Rome's domination and their worldly challenges. They rejected the king of foundational reality. At his second coming, the Jews will see Christ as the Savior in provisional reality and accept his kingship for foundational reality. God first chose the Jews as He also predestinated his elect to be saved. No one comes to Christ unless drawn by the Father.[1954] People are only saved through faith in Jesus Christ. Everyone that makes a free-will choice to believe once drawn by the Father are those that are predestined to be saved.[1955] It is God's desire that none should perish.[1956] He makes his offer to everyone. He knew from before time began who would accept and who would reject his offer. All of those that accept are the predestined because in God's foreknowledge, he knew who would accept. Although the offer is made to all, there are many who do not accept.[1957] "Enter by the narrow gate; for the gate is wide, and the way is broad that leads to destruction, and many are those who enter by it. For the gate is small, and constricted is the way, that leads to life, and few are those who find it."[1958]

As we view the history of humanity in retrospect, we see that the battle of good and evil has always been within ourselves. We have always had the power to choose, and we ultimately are in charge of our own destiny. "I have put before you a choice of life and death, choose life."[1959]

If we fail to respond to God's calling, and we are one of his children,[1960] he will continue to challenge us in life's situations until he has us firmly on our path to sanctification.[1961] Our calling is irrevocable.[1962] There is a pattern in God's grand scheme of things, and we must pay close attention to the details.

We look for the meaning of life in our everyday experiences; however, we do not realize the most important events of our lives when they happen. The meaning is not known until many years later when we understand the long-term consequences, both good and bad, of our experiences. The only way to avoid this conundrum is to know that the Holy Spirit is guiding us and that He is orchestrating the events in our lives today.[1963] We need to be cognizant of that, and based on that knowledge, we need to examine our life's experiences from within this context. Then we are able to see the Holy Spirit at work in our lives and the execution of the idiosyncratic plan he has for the life of every believer. The question is never "Why is God frustrating the plans I have for my life?" It is "What have I done to frustrate the plan God has for me?"

Faith is the way through our life's challenges.[1964] This very realization gives a new dimension of significance to our lives. The meaning something or some event has for us is tied to its worth. Our life can have two outcomes: an eternal damnation, which obviously has no worth, or an eternity in heaven. We are unable to assign a value to heaven because of the limitations of our empirical thinking style and our limited provisional experiences. However, Scripture tells us that an eternal life in heaven will exceed all of our expectations.[1965] The meaning or the value of our life will be tied to the outcome. The meaning of the events in our life will be determined by our ultimate destination.[1966] The more we realize the significance of the events in our life, the more meaning there is to our life. Sometimes it is difficult to understand that there is a reality beyond provisional reality that we are involved in every day. God's reality, or foundational reality, is not just a reality we visit with prayers when we are in trouble or hurting. For many, that is all we choose to acknowledge of foundational reality until we are able to look at life from a kingdom perspective and seek[1967] what is beyond the limitations of our empirical cognitive style of thinking and experiencing. The more we realize the significance of the events in our life, the more meaning there is to our life. It is not so much our experiences in provisional reality as it is the implications of these experiences in foundational reality. "The God who made the world and everything in it is the Lord of heaven and earth. He gives all men life and breath and everything else. From one man He made every nation of men, that they should inhabit the whole earth." God has determined when each of us should live, where exactly we should live, what country, and who our parents should be. In this manner, God orchestrates our DNA and our lives learning and experiences. Scripture tells us that God forms us in the womb. God did this so that men would seek him and perhaps reach out for him and find him, though he is not far from each one of us. For in him we live, move, and have our being.[1968]

THE ABSOLUTE TRUTH

Faith in God and in his grace and the belief that Jesus Christ is the redeeming savior of humanity so that through his sacrificial death we may have an inheritance is the essence of our eternal life.[1969] When we fully appreciate the reality of this situation, we realize that it is an incredible gift—a gift to pass on, and one that costs us nothing. The more people that we share this reality with the more we increase our "crop yield." We all have an opportunity for faith, but we are all tempted by sin and do sin. We all experience the trials and tribulations of life as well as the joys, love, and relationships afforded to us in the human condition.

In the final analysis, the battle has been within ourselves, and that is why we are held accountable. We have it within our power to prevail over evil; in spite of our challenges, we have God's Word, his providence, the Holy Spirit, and our Lord and Savior.[1970]

We find meaning to the events in life by how we understand them. Ultimate truth can only come from God through faith. God is the author of all that transpires. He has created everything, and he orchestrates the events in all that he has created. Only by looking at things from God's perspective do we find an understanding to the events of life. Left to our own understanding, we struggle with the meaning of life.[1971] Our understanding through faith defines most of life's events; for those that remain unresolved, we have faith in an omniscient God who is in control of all things and has our best interests in mind, which will always be reflected in his actions.

Death is the gateway of transformation; death is our birth into foundational reality. When believers stand before God, he will say: "Well done, good and faithful servant, you have run the race, and kept the faith."[1972] "You have been faithful with a little you will be given much."[1973] Our faith in Christ and our obedience to God will determine where we spend eternity. What we accomplish in life, our deeds and works, will determine what we will do in eternity. To whom much has been given, in terms of our talents, abilities, and blessings from God, much will be required. Our God given talents and spiritual gifts are the tools God gives us to accomplish the work he has preordained for us.[1974]

Everyone will be a perfect fulfillment of what God has planned for each of us in our life and in eternity. As one of God's elect, he will complete the perfect work he has begun in you.[1975]

If you witnessed an accident where someone was injured and you knew what needed to be done, would you stand by and watch without helping? Alternatively, would you do what you could? If you have the knowledge that gives eternal life, will you keep that to yourself?

In the *Star Trek* TV series, the crewmembers would use the ship's hologram for training and occasionally for recreation. Once in the hologram, the program would run knowing the crewmembers' strengths and weaknesses. The individual crewmembers would respond to the situations as they evolved. Different levels

of difficulty would increase skills and abilities. Life is analogous to the hologram; it is God's program, and we are required to do our best in the situations that are presented to us and all situations designed by God are completely tailored to our individual needs, whether we are aware of that or not.

At the end of the day, God wants us in heaven regardless of what it takes. We want a purposeful, meaningful life filled with good times, which is possible within the parameters of God's permissive will. The guidelines and expectations for our behavior are explicitly spelled out for us in God's Word. What determines the outcome is our response, and our response is determined by the meaning our perception of reality has for us. If I am firmly planted in my faith, then I understand that everything that happens in my life is either ordained or permitted by God and orchestrated by the Holy Spirit. To seek his kingdom first and his righteousness means that I have a perception of provisional reality that is tempered by the understanding that provisional reality exists within foundational reality. The meaning for events in my life comes from foundational reality, not provisional reality. Regardless of the events that transpire in provisional reality, I know that all things work for the good of those who love the Lord. I also understand that there will be things or events in this life that I will not understand because of the differing characteristics of the two realities.[1976] This is complicated by my inability to comprehend God or foundational reality. However, because of my faith, I trust God[1977] that all things are for the best and that I can blindly put my faith in his providence for my life.[1978] I trust the things not seen. I also understand that although I do not completely understand foundational reality, ultimately, foundational reality has more bearing on my life and plays a more significant role in my life's experiences than events within provisional reality.[1979]

The single most important thing that determines our ultimate destination is our faith. When our faith is the most important thing in our life, it defines the meaning of events in our life, which in turn dictates our behavior.

When the material things in life are the most important things to us, then they determine how we interpret events, and they give a materialistic meaning to our life. God is the one true thing that endures forever. Our possessions can be gone overnight, and that is why Christ tells us not to put our faith in our possessions.[1980] If we perceive our worth to be tied up in what we have, when it is gone our worth, our self-worth is gone as well. Our fortune is something we really do not control anyway. Moreover, it is the same for work, our children, and our marriage; everything here on earth is tenuous. It is our faith in God which gives us our worth. As a child of God, our worth is tied up in that eternal relationship. Our worth is in being counted worthy by God[1981] and his acceptance of us into his eternal kingdom.[1982] Some people feel they can never achieve a status of being accepted by God, so they do not even try. It is safer to have standards of their own, and then they can never miss. However, to be able to be accepted by God is the precise role that Christ plays in concert with the grace of God.

By believing that Jesus Christ is the Son of God and has died for the removal of our sins, with our repentance, there is the promise of eternal life. Christ's sacrifice was enough to remove all sin, individually and collectively for all humanity—past, present, and future. We also believe that God is gracious enough to forgive all that we have done, and that is all that is required. What are we to do about all of the behavioral parameters, all of the dos and don'ts, found in Scripture? They are all guidelines for our behavior. They are indicators of where we are in our process of sanctification. Moreover, we know if we love God by the nature of our behavior. If our behavior conforms to God's will expressed in his dos and don'ts, we honestly have faith in God and his Son, Jesus Christ. Even if at first we have to force ourselves to conform to God's guidelines, and because we are forcing ourselves, our behavior does not seem genuine. As our process of sanctification matures, so does our faith, and soon our behavior is righteous because we are appreciative of all that God has done for us, and we want to do that which is good and well pleasing to him. If our behavior does not conform to God's expectations, we are still immature in our personal process of sanctification. We are children of God. We as parents discipline and correct our children because we want them to have a happy and fulfilling life. God the Father corrects and disciplines us, his children, with the same motivation. He uses the events and circumstances of our life because he wants us to have a happy and fulfilling life in eternity.

I can sometimes look at the suffering in the world and be absolutely moved beyond words. That compassion in me is the presence of Christ.[1983] One of the greatest things we can ever accomplish in this life is to ease the human condition and safeguard the world's children. And for the rest, as Jude says, "Save others, snatching them out of the fire."[1984]

EPILOGUE

He who has My commandments and keeps them is the one who loves Me; and he who loves Me will be loved by My Father, and I will love him and will disclose Myself to him. (John 14:21)

This is the great and foremost commandment. You shall love the Lord your God with all your heart and with all your soul, and with all your mind. The second is like it, you shall love your neighbor as yourself. (Matt. 22:37–39)

Love is patient, love is kind and is not jealous; love does not brag and is not arrogant, does not act unbecomingly, it does not seek its own, is not provoked, does not take into account a wrong suffered, does not rejoice in unrighteousness, but rejoices with the truth; bears all things, believes all things, hopes all things, endures all things. Love never fails. (1 Cor. 13:4–8)

BIBLIOGRAPHY

Unless otherwise noted all Bible references are from the New American Standard Bible, published by Zondervan.

Biblica: The Bible Atlas, Global Book Publishing, Lane Cove, NSW 2066, Australia.

The Interlinear Bible, Hebrew to English, volumes 1 through 3, published by Hendrickson Publishers.

The Interlinear Bible, Greek to English, volume 4, published by Hendrickson Publishers.

Strong's Complete Dictionary of Bible Words, by James Strong, published by Thomas Nelson Publishers.

The Holy Qur'ān Arabic text with English translations, by Maulana Muhammad Ali, published by Ahmadiyya Anjuman Isha'at Islam Lahore Inc. U.S.A. Ohio, U.S.A.

NOTES

1. John 20:19
2. Luke 4:30
3. John 8:59
4. Matt 8:27
5. Matt 15:31
6. John 11:23–45; Matt 9:18–19, 23–25; Mark 5:22–24, 38–42; Luke 7:11–15, 8:41–42, 49–56
7. John 6:21
8. Mark 9:2–8
9. Luke 6:8
10. Mark 1:24, 5:7
11. John 16:7–10, 13
12. Luke 1:35
13. 1 Cor 13:9–12
14. Heb 11:1
15. 2 Cor 4:18
16. Psalm 90:10
17. Matt 6:33
18. Romans 8:28
19. 1 Cor 15:39–53
20. Psalm 46:10; Romans 15:13; Deut 4: 39; Job 38
21. Isa 41:10; Jer 29:11
22. 1 John 2:15–17; Matt 6:19–21
23. 1 Peter 1:15–16
24. Heb 11:3
25. Job 38:4–38
26. John 4:24; 2 Cor 3:17
27. John 1:14, 18, 3:16, 16:27–28; Luke 1:35; Acts 13:33; Heb 1:5, 1 John 4:9
28. Hebrews 5:5; Psalm 2:7
29. Gen 12:1–4
30. *Strong's Complete Dictionary of Bible Words* defines "Gentile" as a foreign nation; any nation other than Israel
31. Gen 12:1–3
32. Romans 5:15–19
33. Rev 5:9
34. Matt 1:1
35. Isaiah 40:9–11, 42:1–4, 52:13–15, 53:1–12, 61:1–2; Dan 9:26; Micah 5:2–4; Jer 23:5; Psalm 110:1–7
36. Deut 29:12–13
37. Gen 9:9–10, 17:7; Exodus 6:4, 19:5–6; Psalm 33:11–17; Isa 40:8; Romans 9:4; 1 Peter 1:24–25
38. Gen 12:3; Psalm 24:1, 127:1; Prov 16:33; Isa 14:24–28, 15:1, 14, 43:13
39. Gen 9:12, 17:7; Jer 33:20–21, 25; 2 Chron 6:14–15, 17
40. Psalm 37:23, 33:11; Eph 1:11, 22
41. Gen 12:1–4
42. John 14:21, 15:10; 1 John 5:3, 2 John 1:6
43. Rev 1:3
44. John 3:15–16
45. 1 Tim 2:3–4
46. Gen 6:6, *The Interlinear Hebrew–Aramaic Old Testament*–Hendrickson Publishers 1985
47. Gen 7:17–24
48. Deut 4:32–40, 14:2, 21, 26:18–19, 28:9; 1 Peter 2:9; Eze 44:23–24
49. Gen 12:1
50. Gen 12:2
51. Gen 12:3

52. Joshua 8:33–35
53. Gal 3:8–9
54. Gen 13:14–18, 17:8
55. Gen 17:1–8, 16, 24:1
56. Deut 4:27, 28; 64–68
57. Gen 12:3; Deut 11:26–28, 23:5, 30:1, 19; Josh 8:34; Psalm 37:22; Nehemiah 1:4–11, 9:5–37
58. Psalm 83:4
59. 2 Tim 2:10–13
60. Gen 13:14
61. Gen 13:15
62. Gen 15:18–21
63. 2 Tim 3:15
64. 1 John 4:9–16
65. Matt 16:21, 27:50–53; Mark 8:31, 15:22–34; Luke 9:22, 24:25–26
66. Heb 9:28; John 10:11; Luke 24:50–52
67. John 20:17
68. Matt 25:46; John 3:15–16, 36, 4:14, 5:24, 6:40, 47, 54, 10:28, 11:25–26, 40, 14:3, 6, 17:3; Romans 5:21, 6:23; Titus 1:2, 3:7; 1 John 2:25, 5:11–13
69. Rev 21:3–4, Mark 10:30, Luke 18:30
70. Micah 6:8; 1 Kings 2:3; Prov 21:3; Isa 56:1; Eze 18:19–21
71. Exodus 3:14
72. Deut 7:6–9
73. Deut 10:12
74. Lev 19:18; Matt 22:37–39; Mark 12:33; Romans 13:9
75. Jer 29:11
76. Gen 13:15; Exo 6:8, 33:1; Lev 26:42; Deut 1:8, 6:10
77. Luke 21:20
78. Rev 21:2–3
79. Rev 19:11–21
80. Rev 19:16
81. Rev 21:1, 10
82. Eze 5:8–17, 28:25–26; Deut 4:27, 28:64; Neh 1:8; Jer 9:16
83. Eze 37:1–14; Deut 30:1–5; Zech 10:9–12; Jer 50:19–20, 23:1–4, 31:1–9
84. Zech 8:1–15; Psalm 37:22; Romans 11:5–11
85. Zech 8:13
86. Eze 28:24–26; Jer 30:7, 10–11; Psalm 14:7; Isa 49:8, 13
87. Ex 32:13; Eze 37:25; Josh 14:9; 1 Chron 28:8; 2 Chorn 20:7
88. Joel 3:2
89. Gen 12:3; Eze 28:24–25
90. Gen 26:5
91. Romans 4:1–12
92. Gen 16:15, 21:1–3
93. Gen 17:20, 21:12–13
94. Gen 25:31–33, 43:33; 1 Chron 5:1
95. Gen 17:18–19
96. Qur'ān Ch 2, v 127, 143
97. Gen 22:2, 12
98. Qur'ān Ch 2: v 133, 125, 127,
99. Ch 2, v 120
100. Qur'ān Ch 2, v 122–124
101. Qur'ān Ch 5 v 13
102. Qur'ān Ch4 v 46
103. Qur'ān Ch 5 v 72
104. Qur'ān Ch3 v 85
105. Qur'ān Ch 3 v 19
106. Gen 17:5
107. Gen 36:7–9
108. Gen 25:22
109. Gen 25:23
110. Gen 25:24–25
111. Gen 27:27–29
112. Gen 25:29–34
113. Gen 27:35–36

THINGS TO COME

114. Gen 21:2
115. Gen 16:2
116. Gen 27:41
117. Gen 32:24–32, 35:10–12
118. Gen 28:13
119. Rev 19:14–21
120. Psalm 139:13–15; Jer 1:5, Job 31:15; Ecc 11:5; Isa 44:2, 24
121. Psalm 139:16
122. Matt 26:41
123. Romans 9:13
124. Romans 9:15–18
125. Jer 44:23; Deut 28:47–49, 30:1; Joel 2:26; Hosea 2:1–23; Amos 3:1–2, 14; Judges 3:7–8
126. Deut 30:19; Jer 3:12–13, 4:1–2, 5:23–25, 14:10, 18:1–17, 26:13; Isa 14:1–3
127. Gal 39:1–4
128. Gen 41:54–57, 42:1–8
129. Exodus 1:15–16, 22
130. Exodus 2:2–3
131. Exodus 3:1–9
132. Exodus 3:10
133. Exodus 7:8–12:36
134. Exodus 13:21–22
135. Exodus 14:16
136. Exodus 14:27–28
137. Exodus 14:31
138. Exodus 13:5, 33:3; Lev 20:24; Num 13:27
139. Exodus 19:1–3, 20:1–20
140. Exodus 19:5–8
141. Exodus 19:3, 20–21, 34:1–4
142. Psalm 105:16–17, 24–25
143. Romans 9:17
144. Exodus 32:7–8 *The Interlinear Hebrew–Aramaic Old Testament*–Hendrickson Publishers 1985
145. Exodus 32:21–24
146. Gen 3:12
147. Gen 3:13
148. Exodus 32:14
149. Jer 26:3
150. 1 Tim 2:5; Heb 9:15, 12:24
151. Heb 10:10; 1 John 2:1–2; Heb 9:22–28
152. Heb 9:15
153. Exodus 32:31, 33–35 *The Interlinear Hebrew–Aramaic Old Testament*–Hendrickson Publishers 1985
154. Rev 20:15
155. John 9:31
156. Gen 18:16–33; Exodus 32:7–18 *The Interlinear Hebrew–Aramaic Old Testament*–Henderson Publishers 1985
157. Psalm 33:11
158. Exodus 19:1–4
159. Exodus 33:13
160. Ex 24:3
161. Deut 12:8; Judges 17:6; Philip 2:21
162. Romans 3:23–26, 28
163. Gal 3:23–27
164. Exodus 19:5–8; Romans 2:12–20, 7:7–8:18
165. Deut 12:8
166. Deut 11:26–28
167. Deut 4:5–8
168. Matt 15:1–9; Isa 29:13–16
169. Matt 23:2–36, 13:11–17
170. Exodus 20:1–26; Deut 5:6–21; Exo 31:12–18
171. Exodus 20:13–*The Interlinear Hebrew–Aramaic Old Testament*–Hendrickson Publishers 1985, also see Gen 9:6
172. Exodus 20:1–17 *The Interlinear Hebrew–Aramaic Old Testament*–Hendrickson Publishers 1985

391

173. Exodus 21:12 *The Interlinear Hebrew–Aramaic Old Testament*– Hendrickson Publishers
174. Exodus 21:18–19
175. Exodus 21:23–24 *The Interlinear Hebrew–Aramaic Old Testament*– Hendrickson Publishers 1985
176. Exodus 22:16
177. Exodus 23:8
178. Exodus 24:3–8
179. Exodus 25:2
180. Exodus 25:8
181. Exodus 25:10–22
182. Gal 3:19–29
183. Gal 3:6–18
184. John 6:32–40
185. Romans 3:21–26; Heb 2:17; 1 John 2:1–2, 4:9–10
186. John 16:13; Acts 4:8, 31, 28:25; 1 Thess 1:5; Heb 10:15; 1 Peter 1:12
187. Exodus 19:5–6; Deut 7:6, 14:2, 33:27–29; 1 Peter 2:9–10
188. Gen 2:15–17, 3:14–21, 9:1–16, 12:1–3; Exo 19:5–8; Deu 29:10–15, 30:11–20; 2 Sam 7:4–17; Jer 31:31–34; Luke 22:17–20
189. Deut 31:24, 26
190. Acts 7:2–53
191. Gen 15:13
192. Exodus 3:10, 12:41
193. Joshua 21:45; 1 Kings 8:56; Isa 40:8, Psalm 33:11, Matt 5:18, 24:35
194. Exo 3:10, 18:16, 32:7–14, 30, 33:5–11; Num 14:11–24, 16:1–3, 21–22, 41–50,
195. 1 Tim 2:5
196. Exodus 12:12–13; John 3:14–16
197. Exodus 7:20–25, 8:1–6, 16–19, 20–24, 9:1–7, 8–11, 12–17, 18–26, 10:1–7, 21–23, 11:4–10, 12:1–32
198. Exodus 14:19–20
199. Exodus 14:21–31
200. Exodus 15:22–25, 17:5–6
201. Exodus 16:2–4
202. Exodus 17:6–16, 34:11, 40:34–38; Num 14:31
203. Deut 1:26–35; Num 14:11, 16:1–35; Acts 7:39; Psalms 106:21–46
204. Num 13:25–33
205. Num 14:1–11
206. Numbers 14:26–38
207. Exodus 32:1–10; Deut 1:26, 43, 9:12; Num 25:1–2
208. Numbers 32:13, 20:1–13, 25:1–11
209. Numbers 14:30
210. Ex 12:37
211. 2 Thess 1:8–10
212. Col 1:10–14; Eph 4:1–7; Rom 12:1
213. Heb 12:1–3; 1 John 5:1–5; Rom 6:1–11; Eph 4:17–5:21
214. 1 John 1:5–10, 2:12
215. John 3:15–16; 1 John 1:7, 4:9–16; Heb 10:1–18
216. Heb 10:38–39; 1 John 2:28–29, 5:3; 1 Pet 3:12, 4:18; Luke 1:6; 1 Tim 1:9; 2 Tim 4:8
217. Gen 2:15–17
218. Gen 3:14–21
219. Gen 9:1–19
220. Gen 1:28–31
221. Gen 2:16–17
222. Duet 11:26–28, 28:1–14; Gen 22:18; Luke 11:28
223. Lev 26:1–13, 14–39; Eph 5:6
224. Gen 1:28
225. Gen 3:14–15
226. Gen 3:14
227. 2 Thess 2:7
228. Gen 3:15
229. Gen 3:15, 1 John 3:8

THINGS TO COME

230. Gen 3:16, *Interlinear Hebrew-Aramaic Old Testament*-Hendrickson Publishers 1985
231. Gen 3:17–19
232. Gen 6:5
233. Gen 6:6
234. Gen 9:1–3
235. Gen 9:14–15
236. 2 Peter 3:10
237. Joshua 23:14; Isa 40:8
238. Gen 12:1–3, 17:4–11
239. Gen 17:19
240. Gen 27:27–30; Lev 26:42; 2 Kings 13:23
241. Deut 5:1–33, 6:1–25, Deut 16–25
242. Deut 7:1, 30: 3–5; Gen 17:7–8, 26:3–4, 35:11–12; Lev 26:42–45; Jer 16:14–15
243. Deut 28:1
244. Deut 4:1, 7:12–13, 8:6, 10:12, 11:1; Romans 7:21–25
245. Deut 1:1–4:43
246. Deut 5–11
247. Duet 12–16
248. Duet 16:18–26:19
249. Deut 27–34
250. 2 Samuel 7:10
251. 2 Samuel 7:11
252. 2 Samuel 7:13, 16
253. Matt 1:1
254. Jer 31:31
255. Jer 31:33
256. John 14:26
257. Heb 8:7–13,
258. Luke 22:20; Heb 9:15–23
259. Matt 26:27–28; Mark 14:24; Luke 22:20; Romans 3:24–25
260. Jer 31:34; John 3:15, 5:24, 6:40, 6:47, 10:28; Rom 6:23; 1 Tim 1:16; 1 John 5:11–13, 20; Jude 1:21
261. Exo 32:9, 33:3–5, 34:9; Romans 10:21
262. Romans 3:10–12
263. Jer 31:34
264. Acts 2:22–23, 3:13–18, 10, 11:16–18, 22:1–21, 26:16–17; John 10:16
265. John 6:37–40, 15:1–11; Romans 5:1; 1 John 2:12
266. John 3:16
267. Lev 26:44; Deut 4:31
268. Numbers 14:11
269. Romans 3:10–12; Psalm 14:1–3, 143:2
270. Matt 26:28
271. 2 Tim 3:16
272. Matt 13:34; Mark 4:33–34; Luke 8:9–10
273. John 3:34
274. John 14:16–17
275. John 14:26
276. 1 Thess 1:5
277. Romans 8:27; 1 Cor 2:9–13
278. 2 Thess 2:7
279. John 14:6
280. Matt 16:16–17
281. 2 Cor 4:3–4
282. Matt 28:5; Luke 1:13, 30, 2:10; Rev 1:17
283. Matt 14:25–27; Mark 6;48–51; John 6;19
284. Mark 5:35–42; Matt 9:24–26; Luke 7;13–15, John 11;40–44
285. Acts 10:44, 11:15, 20:23
286. John 14:26, Luke 2:26, 12:12, 1 Thess 1:5; Heb 10:15
287. Matt 28:5; Luke 1:13, 30, 67, 2:10; Rev 1:17; Acts 1:16, 19:6, 28:25; 2 Peter 1:21
288. 2 Tim 1:14; Acts 2:4, 13:52; John 14:17; James 4:5

289. 1 Cor 12:4–11; Eph 1:17; Heb 2:4
290. 2 Thess 2:6–7
291. Acts 9:31, 20:28
292. Gal 5:22–23
293. Heb 10:15
294. Romans 8:26; Jude 1 :20
295. Acts 1:8, 4:31; Romans 15:13; Mic 3:8; 1 Peter 1:12
296. Romans 5:5
297. John 16:13
298. John 16:12–15
299. 1 Cor 6:19
300. 1 Cor 12:3–11
301. Job 1:6–12
302. John 16:7
303. Acts 9:31
304. Gal 5:22–23
305. Heb 10:15; John 15:26; Romans 8:16
306. John 16:8–10
307. 1 Cor 2:10–16
308. 1 Cor 2:14
309. 1 Cor 2:10
310. Romans 1:19
311. 1 Chron 28:9, Acts 15:8
312. Romans 8:26
313. 1 John 4:1–4, 5:4
314. Romans 8:26–28
315. Matt 7:11
316. Acts 4:8; Eph. 5:18
317. Eph. 2:10
318. John 6:44
319. John 8:12
320. 2 Cor 5:17–19; 1 Peter 1:15
321. 1 Peter 1:16
322. Matt 9:37
323. Heb 12:1
324. 1 Tim 1:18; 2 Tim 4:7
325. 1 John 1:7
326. Romans 6:4
327. 2 Tim 3:17
328. Romans 1:19
329. Matt 24:31
330. 1 Peter 1:15; 2 Peter 1:3; Jude 1:1
331. Acts 28:26–28; Romans 11:24–25
332. John 10:16
333. 2 Pet 3:9
334. Psalms 37:23, 127:1–2; Proverbs 5:21, 15:10, 23:13; 1 Cor 11:32
335. John 6:44
336. Eph 2:18
337. 2 Cor 3:16; 1 Pet 2:21
338. 1 John 3:8
339. 1 John 3:5
340. John 3:17
341. Matt 1:23
342. 2 Cor. 4:11; Romans 12:1
343. Matt 5:48
344. 1 Peter 1:16
345. 1 Cor 8:6
346. 1 Peter 4:18; Eph 2:5, 8
347. Mark 2:7; Luke 5:21
348. Romans 10:9
349. Acts 4:12
350. James 2:14, 17
351. James 1:14
352. Romans 10:13; 1 Tim 2:4; John 3:15
353. 2 Tim 3:17
354. Gal 5:22–23
355. Rom 8:4–15
356. John 14:27
357. 2 Tim 2:24
358. Phil 4:6
359. 1 Peter 5:7
360. Phil 2:4, *Interlinear Hebrew–Aramaic Old Testament*–Hendrickson Publishers 1985

361. Romans 8:28
362. Proverbs 3:5
363. James 1:27
364. 1 Tim 5:14–15
365. Gen 2:18–25; Eph 5:30–31
366. Romans 7:2–3
367. 1 Cor 7;2–4, Solomon 1;13
368. Proverbs 5:18–19
369. 1 Thess 4:3
370. 1 Cor 6:18
371. Rev 21:8; 1 Cor 6:9–10; Gal 5:19–21; Romans 1:18–2:16; 1 Thess 4:3
372. 2 Cor 5:9
373. James 4:7–8
374. Rom 11:29
375. Luke 22:3
376. Matt 16:23
377. Acts 5:3; 1 Chron 21:1; Luke 13:16, 22:3, 31; 1 Thess 2:18
378. 2 Cor 11:14
379. Deut 18:10–12
380. 3 John 1:3
381. Rom 8:29–30; 1 Cor 2:7; Eph 1:5
382. John 13:18; Luke 1:77; Acts 4:12; Romans 1:16; 1 Thess 5:9
383. Romans 12:2
384. Matt 7:1–2
385. 1 John 1:9
386. Amos 3:3
387. Rom 1:16; Eph 1:13; Phil 1:7
388. Romans 5:3–5; Psalm 7:9; 2 Cor 1:6
389. James 1:3–4
390. Matt 25:14–30
391. Matt 25:21
392. Matt 25:26
393. Matt 25:41
394. Gen 2:7; John 6:63
395. Gen 3:19
396. Job 33:4
397. Romans 8:16
398. Matt 26:41; Rom 8:4–6; Gal 5:17, 6:8
399. Matt 22:30; Luke 20:36
400. 1 John 3:1–3
401. Matt 16:26
402. 1 Peter 1:17, Romans 7:24
403. Gen 3:19; Psa 103:14
404. Prov 16:32
405. Prov 25:28
406. Matt 26:41
407. Hos 4:12
408. Dan 5:20
409. 1 Peter 3:4
410. Isa 30:1
411. Eccl 7:9; Prov 19:19
412. James 4:7
413. James 2:26; Job 33:4; Ezek 37:14
414. 1 Peter 2:11
415. 1 Cor 15:44
416. Romans 8:6
417. Romans 8:11
418. Gal 5:16–21
419. Rom 1:13
420. Acts 20:22
421. Romans 8:6
422. Eph 2:2
423. Deut 29:29; Matt 10:26; Mark 4:22
424. Heb 9:14–15
425. Romans 13:4
426. Acts 23:1, 24:16; Romans 9:1; 1 Cor 8:12
427. 2 Cor 1:12
428. Romans 2:15; Heb 9:14; 2 Cor 3:2–3
429. 1 Tim 1:5

430. Heb 13:18
431. Romans 5:12, 6:7
432. Luke 10:19
433. Jude 1:19
434. 1 Cor 8:7, 12
435. John 8:11; Luke 13:3; Acts 3:19
436. Matt 26:41
437. 2 Cor 10:5
438. Romans 2:14–15
439. Titus 1:15
440. Heb 10:22
441. John 8:9
442. 1 Tim 4:2, 1:5, 19, 3:9
443. Rom 9:1
444. Romans 1:21, 13:5, Acts 19:9, 2 Cor 3:14
445. 1 Thess 5:19
446. John 10:30, 17:3; Matt 26:38, 42, 56; Luke 22:44; Isa 52:14
447. Romans 8:29–30
448. Heb 13:2
449. John 16:12–13
450. Romans 8:18
451. Psalm 40:8
452. Matt. 12:30; Acts 26:18; 1 Tim 5:15
453. 1 John 4:4
454. Phil 2:13; John 8:29; 2 Cor 5:9
455. Eph 6:10–12
456. Eph 6:12
457. John 4:34, 5:30, 6:38–39
458. Eph 5:11
459. Luke 10:19
460. John 10:30
461. John 17:15–Most modern translations say "evil one," however, the original reads, "keep them from evil."
462. Romans 8:9–17
463. Rev 20:10
464. Rev 21:1
465. Rev 21:3
466. Rev 20:12, 15; Col 2:8
467. John 15:5–6
468. John 8:12, 12:35; Acts 26:18; Eph 5:8; 1 John 1:6
469. James 1:6–7
470. James 4:8
471. Eph. 4:1; 1 Thess. 2:12,
472. Matt 3:10; 7:19; Luke 3:9; John 15:6
473. Eph 5:18
474. Rev 3:16
475. Gal 6:8; Phil 3:3; Matt 26:41; Rom 8:4
476. Gen 3:1; 2 Cor 2:11; John 8:44, 13:2, 27; 1 Pet 5:9
477. James 1:27; Matt 13:22, 38; John 14:17
478. John 14:20
479. Rev. 14:15–20
480. 2 Tim 3:16
481. 2 Cor 2:11
482. Rev 12:9
483. Job 1:7; 1 Peter 5:8
484. 2 Tim 2:26
485. Psalm 148:1–6; Col 1:15–17; Eph 3:9
486. Ezek 28:12–19; Luke 10:18; Rev 12:4–17
487. Matt 25:41
488. 2 Thess 2:7
489. John 8:44
490. 2 Cor 4:3–4
491. Matt 26:28; Rom 5:9; Eph 2:13; Heb 9:14, 22, 10:19; Rev 1:5
492. 1 Cor 15:40, 48–54
493. Rev 5:11
494. Heb 2:6–8

THINGS TO COME

495. 1 Cor 6:3
496. Eze 28:15
497. Isa. 14:12–16
498. Luke 19:14
499. Rom. 9:21; Isa 29:15–16
500. John 3:19
501. Gen 3:5
502. Gen 3:22, 2:17
503. Gen 2:7
504. Gen 3:1–7
505. Gen 6:1–4; Jude 1:6
506. Gen 6:12–7:5
507. Matt 1:18–25
508. Luke 2:1–20
509. Matt, Mark, Luke, John
510. Matt 27:33–54
511. Matt 28: 1–7
512. John 14:16–17; Rom 8:11; Acts 9:17
513. John 21:25, 2:1–11, 4:46–54, 5:1–17, 6:1–25, 9:1–11, 11:1–46, 21:1–11; Matt 8:1–15, 8:23–34, 9:1–8, 18–37, 12:10–29, 14:15–36, 15:21–39, 17:1–18, 24–27, 20:29–34, 21:18–22; Mark 1:23–28, 5:1–17, 7:31–37, 8:22–26; Luke 5:4–11, 7:11–15, 13:11–17, 14:1–5, 17:11–21, 22:47–53
514. Proverbs 16:9, 33, 20:24; Psalm 11:4, 24:1, 33:13–17, 47:2, 57:11, 65:5, 68:19, 89:11, 103:19, 119:90–91; Job 42:1–2; Isa 44:24, 45:12
515. Gen 3:21
516. Gen 3:7, 10
517. Gen 2:15–17, 3:8–13
518. 1 John 5:19
519. 2 Cor 4:4
520. 1 John 3:20; Proverbs 8:12–21; Matt 11:27, 12:25
521. Psalm 139:7–12; Jer 23:24; Heb 4:13
522. 1 John 3:20; Jer 32: 17, 27; Psalm 103:19; Isa 40:26–31
523. 1 Peter 2:22; Titus 1:2
524. Job 1:7
525. 1 Pet 5:8
526. Heb 2:5–10
527. 1 Cor 6:3
528. Acts 17:24–28; Dan 2:19–23, 4:17; Eph 1:3–7, 10–11; 1 Chron 16:30; Exo 9:23–26; 1 Tim 1:17; Isa 40:12–17, 26, 45:6, 48:3, 64:8; Job 38:1–41; John 19:10–11; Psalm 139; Rom 8:28–30, 9:11–21; Proverbs 16:4, 9, 33
529. Eph 2:10
530. Rev 12:9
531. 2 Cor 4:4; Acts 26:18; 2 Cor 2:11, 11:14; Rev 2:24, 12:9
532. 2 Cor 4:4
533. John 8:44
534. Rev 12:4, 9; Matt 25:41
535. Eph 6:10–18
536. John 8:44
537. Gen 3:1–7; Acts 5:3, 13:10
538. 2 Cor 11:14; Rev 12:9; John 8:44; Acts 13:10
539. 1 John 2:13, 3:12, 5:19; John 17:15; Eph 6:16; 2 Thess 3:3
540. James 4:7
541. 1 Sam 16:14
542. Job 2:7; Acts 10:38
543. Rev 12:4, 9, 12
544. Isa 14:12
545. Isa 14:12–20
546. Rev 20:7–9
547. Matt 4:1–11; Mark 1:12–13; Luke 4:1–13
548. Luke 22:3; John 13:2, 27
549. 2 Cor 4:4
550. Matt 13:19; Mark 4:15
551. Heb 2:14

397

552. Mark 4:15
553. Job 2:7; Matt 16:23; Luke 22:31; Rev 2:10
554. John 8:44
555. 1 Sam 16:14
556. 1 John 5:19
557. Job 1:7, 2:2; 1 Thess 2:18, 1 Peter 5:8
558. Heb 13:8
559. Isaiah 45:9; Job 41:10–11
560. 1 Cor 2:9; Isaiah 65:17; Jer 29:11; John 14:2
561. Rev 20:14–15
562. 1 Peter 2:11; Psalm 112:7; Prov 11:19; 1 Cor 15:58; Col 1:23; Heb 6:19
563. Rom 12:2; James 4:4
564. John 8:29
565. 1 John 2:15–16
566. 2 Thess 2:6–8
567. John 3:19–21; Rom 1:25; 1 John 2:6, 3:7–9, 5:12; Acts 26:18
568. Rev 11:15, 12:10; Matt 6:8–13
569. John 8:44; 2 Thess 2:6–12; Gen 3:1–4; Mark 4:15; Luke 22:3; 2 Cor 2:11, 11:14; Rev 12:9, John 13:2, 20:10; Acts 13:10; 2 John 1:7
570. Luke 10:19–20
571. Acts 1:8; Eph 3:20; 2 Tim 1:7
572. Acts 26:18
573. John 5:30
574. Eph 6:10–17
575. Eph 6:18
576. 2 Cor 2:11
577. Gen 3:12
578. Gen 3:13
579. James 4:4
580. Matt. 9:37
581. Heb 1:13–14; Psalm 91:11, 103:20–21, 109:11; Luke 4:10
582. 2 Thess 3:3
583. Rom 4:21; Isa 48:3, stands forever
584. 2 Cor 1:21
585. 2 Cor 5:20
586. 2 Tim 4:7 The Interlinear Greek-English New Testament
587. Phil 2:15
588. Rev 20:10
589. 2 Tim 4:1–2
590. Dan 11:36–45; Matt 24:15–26, 2 Thess 2:8–10; Rev 12:9, 13:4–18
591. 1 John 2:17
592. John 10:27–29, Rev 17:14, 21:3, 27, Deut 7:6–9, Isa 62:12, 1 Pet 2:9, Matt 22:14
593. James 2:19
594. Matt 8:29
595. 2 Cor 2:11
596. Eph 6:16
597. Job 1:7; 1 Peter 5:8–9
598. Heb 5:13–14
599. 1 John 4:1–6; 2 John 1:7
600. 1 John 2:22
601. 1 Tim 4:8
602. John 14:6
603. 2 Cor 11:14–15
604. Rev 13:15
605. Matt 24:32
606. 2 Tim 3:1–5, 13
607. 2 Tim 3:1
608. 2 Tim 2:14–26
609. Matt 24:24
610. Heb 11:1, 3, 7; 1 Cor 2:9; 2 Cor 4:18
611. Mark 2:7
612. John 8:7; Rom 3:23
613. John 3:15, 14:6; Rom 3:24, 8:23; 1 Cor 1:30; Eph 1:7; Col 1:14; Heb 9:15
614. 1 Pet 1:16

615.	Matt 5:48		649.	1 John 4:4
616.	Heb 11:3		650.	Phili 2:13
617.	Jude 1:6		651.	Deut 7:9; Heb 13:8
618.	Gen 6:2		652.	Rom 11:33; Job 11:7
619.	Gen 6:4		653.	2 Cor 10:5
620.	John 8:44		654.	Phil 4:8
621.	1 John 3:10		655.	Gal 5:22–23
622.	Gen 6:6		656.	Eph 4:22
623.	Gen 6:7–8		657.	James 4:7–8
624.	Jude 1:6 - 7		658.	Gal 5:19–21; Romans 13:13; 1 Cor 6:9
625.	Romans 8:1–15, Gal 5:16–26		659.	Rom 8:28
626.	1 John 5:19		660.	Heb 12:11; 1 Peter 1:6
627.	2 Cor 4:3–4		661.	1 Thess 1:3–5, 5:8–9
628.	John 12:40; Romans 1:28; Jer 17:5		662.	2 Cor 4:4
629.	2 Cor 10:5		663.	1 Cor 1:18
630.	James 4:7–8		664.	Isa 59:2
631.	Rom 1:32		665.	1 Peter 5:8
632.	Psalm 25:10; Gen 18:25; Rev 15:3–4; Neh 1:5, 9:31; Psalm 51:1; Dan 9:9, 18; Mic 7:18, 2 Cor 13:11; Eph 2:4		666.	Job 1:12
			667.	Job 1:16, 19, 2:7
			668.	Job 1:12, 2:6
633.	Titus 1:2		669.	1 Cor 5:5; 2 Cor 12:7; 1 Tim 1:20
634.	Ezek 28:12		670.	John 19:15
635.	John 8:44		671.	Heb 11:1–3; 2 Cor 4:18
636.	Psalm 139:16		672.	Matt 25:14–30
637.	Psalm 116:15		673.	Matt 25:1–13
638.	Psalm 139:13–15; Isa 44:2, 49:5; Jer 1:5		674.	John 3:36, 5:24, 8:24; Col 3:25; 2 Thess 1:8–10, 2:10
639.	Exo 31:3, 35:31		675.	James 1:12
640.	Psalm 139:13–16		676.	Eph 1:7; Col 1:21–23; Heb 9:14, 22, 10:26, 11:6; 1 Cor 6:9–11; Acts 4:12; 2 Peter 2:20–21
641.	Acts 17:26			
642.	Psalm 91:11		677.	Heb 10:26–31, 2 Tim 2:20–21
643.	Romans 8:29–30		678.	Isaiah 59:2; Zachariah 7:13; Psalm 66:18; John 9:31; James 4:3
644.	Romans 8:28			
645.	1 Cor 13:9			
646.	John 10:25–30, 11:25, 14:6; Eph 2:8		679.	Isa 55:8–9
			680.	1 Cor 2:14–15
647.	2 Cor 2:11		681.	James 1:2
648.	Eph 6:16			

682. Romans 8:28
683. Rev 5:8–10, 20:6; 2 Tim 2:10, 12; 1 Cor 6:3
684. James 1:2–4; 1 Peter 1:6–7; 2 Thess 1:5
685. 1 Peter 1:3–9; Psalm 29:11; John 14:27; Philippians 4:7
686. Matt 8:27
687. Rom 11:33; Job 5:9, 11:7–8
688. Luke 19:14
689. Deut 12:7–9; Prov 12:15, 16:9, 33, 21:2; Philippians 4:6
690. Col 3:23–24; Eph 6:6–8
691. 1 Tim 5:8; Num 14:27; Philippians 2:14
692. Gal 6:9–10; Col 3:17
693. 1 Peter 5:7
694. Psalm 145:13; Deut 10:13–15, 17, 20–21
695. Philippians 4:6; Isaiah 41:10
696. Matt 6:33
697. James 4:3
698. Isaiah 46:9–11; John 15:7; James 1:6–7
699. John 11:4, 15, 25
700. 1 John 5:14–15
701. Matt 8:12; Ecc 12:14; Matt 11:20–24, 12:36; John 5:24–26; Romans 2:2–6; 2 Cor 5:10; 2 Peter 2:4–10
702. Rev 20:2, 10
703. 1 Cor 6:9–11; Gal 5:19–21
704. Matt 25:30
705. Matt 24:16, 21–22, 25:31–46; Rev 7:4, 9, 14
706. Psalm 77:13; Isaiah 5:16
707. John 3:16
708. Isaiah 45:18; Rev 4:11
709. 1 Cor 13:9
710. Matt 8:12
711. 2 Thess 1:5–10; John 3:36
712. John 3:19–21
713. Exo 34:6; Deut 4:31; Neh 9:17, 31; Job 8:5; Psalms 51:1, 116:5; Dan 9:9; Joel 2:3; Jonah 4:2
714. John 3:36; Romans 1:18, 8:3–8, 13:4; Eph 5:6; Job 34:12; Psalm 37:28; Prov 2:8; Isa 30:18; Luke 7:27–30, 18:6–8; Jer 10:10; Nah 1:2; Rev 16:1, 19:15
715. 1 John 4:4
716. Deut 4:40, 6:17–18, 10:13
717. Phili 2:12
718. Romans 3:9, 23; John 6:39–40; 1 Tim 2:5
719. Deut 10:12, 30:15–16; Micah 6:8
720. 1 John 5:19; Matt 18:7; John 12:31; 1 Cor 5:9–10, 11:32; Gal 1:4; Eph 2:2, 12, 6:12; 1 John 2:16; Rev 12:9
721. Gen 3:5; Isa 14:12–14; Deut 9:27; Jer 5:23, 13:10; Deut 12:8
722. Isaiah 14:12–14
723. Gen 3:4
724. Gen 3:3–4
725. Rev 20:10, 14, 15
726. Eph 2:1–2
727. Gen 6:5
728. Psalms 139:13, 104:30
729. Matt 11:28–30; Psalms 71:3–17, 119:169–176
730. Isaiah 14:13–14
731. Romans 5:12–14
732. Gen 4:8
733. Gen 6:5
734. Gen 6:6
735. Rev 12:3–4
736. Gen 5:27
737. Prov 21:2
738. 2 Peter 2:5
739. 1 Kings 2:3; Isaiah 30:21
740. Col 1:16–20; Rev 4:11
741. Rom 9:20–21

742. 2 Tim 2:21; Col 1:10
743. Eph 4:1
744. Eph 4:1; 1 Tim 2:12, 2 Tim 1:11
745. Eph 2:7
746. John 10:30, 17:21–22
747. 1 Pet 1:12
748. 3 John 1:11
749. Matt 4:9
750. John 8:29
751. Matt 7:14
752. Romans 1:19
753. Rev 17:14
754. John 8:29
755. Romans 2:8
756. John 5:24, 6:39
757. Rev 4:5–11
758. 2 Peter 3:13; Rev 21:1
759. Rev 5:4–10
760. Matt 25:41; Rev. 20:10
761. Phil 4:6
762. Psalms 118:8, 146:3; 2 Cor 1:9
763. Romans 12:2; Col 3:2
764. John 16:22
765. 1 Cor 15:6
766. 1 Cor 15:42
767. 1 Cor 15:51
768. Matt 25:41; Rev 20:10
769. Isaiah 55:9
770. Deut 10:14
771. Job 10:12
772. 1 Pet 2:21
773. Jer 31:33
774. Deut 4:40
775. Deut 10:12–13, 11:1; Romans 15:4
776. James 4:17
777. 1 John 5:18–20
778. Rev 20:12–15, 21:27, 13:8
779. Romans 3:10
780. Psalm 14:3, 54:3; Romans 3:10, 12
781. Deut 4:39–40; 1 Sam 2:6–8
782. Romans 8:11
783. Romans 8:32
784. Romans 6:23; Luke 13:3
785. Romans 9:14–15
786. Heb 10:26
787. Ish 41:10, 48:17, 64:8; Jer 18:4–6; Romans 9:21
788. Gen 25:21–26
789. Gen 25:23
790. Romans 9:17
791. Exodus 14:18
792. Prov 20:24
793. Jer 10:23
794. Romans 8:28–30
795. Acts 10:1
796. Acts 10:2
797. Acts 10:3–8
798. Acts 10:9–12
799. Acts 10:13–14
800. Acts 10:15–17
801. Acts 10:31–48
802. Acts 10:44
803. Ezk 36:26–27
804. 2 Tim 1:13–14, 19–26
805. 1 Thess 2:10–14
806. James 4:7–8
807. Isaiah 59:2
808. Matt 6:24; Luke 16:13 *The Interlinear Greek-English New Testament*
809. Eph 6:16; 1 Thess 4:1–7; 2 Thess 2:13–17; Romans 6:19–22; Heb 12:14
810. Prov 23:17; Matt 27:17–19; Mark 7:20–23; Romans 1:28–30; Titus 3:1–11; Eph 5:1–6; Col 3:1–11

811. Romans 2:4–11; 1 Peter 2:1–5; James 3:13–18; Mark 7:20–23; Gal 5:16–26
812. Gen 17:1; 2 Chr 20:6, 25:8; Jer 32:17; Dan 2:20; Matt 22:29; Mark 12:24; Acts 2:24; 1 Cor 4:20, 6:14; Rev 11:17, 12:10, 16:9, 19:1
813. Isa 40:12–18; Exo 8:10; Romans 11:33; Col 2:2–3; Job 5:9, 11:7
814. Jer 23:23–24; 1 Kings 8:27; 2 Chron 2:6; Isa 66:1; Matt 18:20, 28:20
815. Romans 1:20; Job 12:7–10
816. John 1:1–5
817. Gen 1:2–5
818. Gen 1:1
819. John 1:3, 10; 1 Cor 8:6; Col 1:15–17; Heb 1:2
820. Romans 1:20
821. Luke 18:16–17; Matt 18:3, 19:14
822. 1 John 2:15; Romans 12:2; James 1:27
823. James 4:4
824. Matt 6:33
825. 1 Pet 1.17, 2.11
826. Dan 8:26, 12:8–9; Romans 11:24–29; 1 Cor 2:4–13, 15:50–51; Eph 3:8–10, 5:31–32; 2 Thess 2:7; 1 Tim 3:9; Rev 1:20, 10:1–7, 17:1–13
827. John 16:23; 2 Cor 12:2–4
828. John 14:26; 1 Cor 2:9–10
829. Rev 15:3–4
830. 1 Peter 1:16; Lev 11:44, 19:2
831. 1 Tim 1:16; 1 Peter 2:21; Col 2:5–7; Phili 2:4–5, 1 John 2:5–6
832. Matt 19:17; John 14:15, 15:10; 1 John 2:3, 5:3; Rev 14:12
833. Matt 28:18–20
834. Matt 9:37
835. 2 Sam 22:31; Isaiah 40:8; Psalm 33:11, 100:5, 103:17, 136 ; Heb 1:10–12, 13:8
836. Rev 4:1–2
837. Rev 4:3, 6, 7
838. Luke 16:22–25; Jude 1:13; Rev 14:11, 20:10
839. Matt 25:34–50; Romans 3:22–26, 5:1–2, 15–21; Eph 1:4–10, 2:4–10
840. John 12:44–47, 14:6; Acts 4:12
841. Lev 18:4–5, 26:14–17; Deut 4:39–40, 28:12–15; Judges 10:13; 1 Sam 7:3, 12:15; 1 King 3:14
842. Amos 9:15; Exodus 19:5; Lev 26:1–13; Eze 36:22–24
843. Deut 28:64; Lev 26:14–39; Eze 36:19, Psalm 78:56–60, 81:11–16, 89:30–34
844. Hosea 3:1–5, 5:15, 6:1–2
845. Acts 7:51–53; Rom 9:31–32; Matt 23:37
846. Exo 15:23–24, 32:1, 8, 33:2–5
847. Isaiah 44:6, 45:5–7, 46:11; Dan 2:21–22, 4:17
848. Mark 13:27; Matt 24:31; Luke 18:7; Romans 8:28–32
849. John 10.14–18; Romans 11:29; Phili 1:6; 2 Tim 1:9
850. John 10:1–5, 11–16, 25–30
851. John 10:16
852. Acts 17:28; Job 12:10; Dan 5:23
853. Psalm 12:6–7; Romans 9:6; Heb 4:12
854. Rom 8:28
855. Matt 10:22; 1 Tim 1:5; Heb 12:2; 1 Cor 15:58
856. Luke 1:37
857. Jer 29:11
858. James 1:17
859. John 14:2
860. John 3:36, 14:6; Acts 4:12, 16:31; Rom 10:9, 13
861. Matt 3:16–17, 28:19; 1 Cor 12:4–6; 2 Cor 3:17, 4:4, 13:14, 2 Thess 2:13; 1 Peter 1:2

THINGS TO COME

862. Matt 22:37; Deut 10:12; Mic 6:8
863. Dan 8:26, 12:4, 9; Rev 10:4
864. Psalm 103:15–18
865. James 4:14
866. Romans 11:33; Job 11:7–8, 33:14; Isa 55:8–9; Job 26:5–14, 42:1–3
867. Matt 6:33
868. Psalm 90:10
869. 1 Pet 1:17
870. 1 Cor 15:38, 40, 44, 53
871. 1 Cor 15:49
872. 1 Cor 15:53–54
873. 1 Cor 2:9
874. Matt 5:14, 16
875. Matt 5:15, Luke 8:16
876. 2 Tim 4:2
877. James 1:8
878. Eph 6:16
879. Matt 10:19–20
880. Luke 23:43; 2 Cor 12:3–4; Rev 2:7
881. John 14:1–6, 28, 16:22
882. 2 Tim 1:10; Matt 28:10–20; Acts 1:11; John 20:26–29
883. 1 Cor 15:50–58; 1 John 5:11–13; John 14:1–6
884. Luke 23:43; Rev 2:7
885. Psalm 116:15
886. 1 Thess 4:13
887. Rev 6:10–11
888. 2 Tim 1:9–10; John 1:10, 8:23, 17:13–21, 18:36; Acts 17:24–28; 1 John 4:9, 14; Romans 12:2, 1 Cor 2:12; Rev 4:1–2
889. Rev 1:17–18; 1 Cor 39–58
890. 1 Tim 6:12; 2 Tim 4:7
891. Rom 2:5; Heb 10:27; Rev 14:7, 16:5
892. Jer 25:30–38; Romans 2:2–6, 8:22–23
893. 1 Tim 2:4
894. Matt 8:26–27; Joshua 10:12–13; Job 38:1–41, 39:1–30
895. Deut 30:15–20; 1 Tim 6:11; 2 Tim 2:19; 1 Thess 2:12–13, 5:21–22
896. John 14:15; 2 John 6
897. John 14:15, 21, 23, 15:10
898. 1 John 2:3–4, 3:24, 5:3
899. John 1:14; 1 Peter 3:17–18; 1 John 1:1–4; 2 Thess 2:4–7; Eph 2:4–10; Romans 5:14–21
900. Matt 20:28; Mark 10:45; 1 Tim 2:6
901. 1 Cor 15:42, 44, 49–51
902. 1 Peter 1:6–11; 2 Cor 4:18
903. 1 John 3:18–19; Matt 7:15–20, 12:33–37; Luke 6:43–45
904. Romans 1:20
905. Romans 1:18–19
906. Romans 8:28
907. Deut 23:4–6; Philippians 1:12–20; Romans 8:18; 2 Cor 1:7; 2 Thess 1:5; Heb 2:9; 1 Peter 1:11
908. Philippians 4:6; Isaiah 41:10; Matt 6:25
909. 1 Peter 5:6–7
910. Heb 12:2–3; James 1:2–4; Philippians 3:11–21
911. Matt 6:33
912. Joshua 10:13–14
913. Job 2:10, 5:17, 8:18; Philippians 2:13; Isaiah 48:10, 17; Eph 1:11; Eze 34:11; James 1:5; Jer 1:5
914. Rev 4:8
915. James 4:7–8
916. Jam 1:4, 12; Rom 5:3
917. 1 Cor 9:24; Heb 12:1
918. 1 Tim 6:12
919. James 5:11
920. 2 Cor 4:17

921. James 1:2
922. Luke 12:48
923. Matt 26:53–54
924. Matt 25:26–30
925. James 1:5; Col 1:9
926. James 1:5
927. Philippians 2:12
928. Philippians 1:6
929. 1 Pet 2:20; 1 Cor 13:9–12; 2 Cor 4:16–18, 5:6–8; Philippians 3:13–21
930. John 3:16; Deut 32:4; Isa 5:16; Gen 18:25; Psalm 97:2; Rom 5:8; Eph 1:5–7; 1 John 4:8, 18; Rev 15:3–4; Zeph 3:17
931. 1 Peter 3:9
932. 1 Peter 2:21
933. 2 Cor 4:4
934. Romans 8:29–30
935. Matt 24:31; Luke 18:7; Romans 8:33–39
936. John 6:40, 12:37–43; Romans 10:16–21; 2 Thess 2:8–16; Titus 1:13–16; Jude 1:4–5
937. Romans 6:23, 9:17–33; 1 John 5:11–12; 1 Cor 6:9–10
938. 2 Peter 2:1–10, Jude 1:5–8
939. 1 Peter 4:18
940. 1 Cor 1:18
941. Prov 3:5–7; Phili 3:1–12; Matt 16:26
942. Romans 8:28
943. 2 Cor 11:14
944. 2 Cor 10:5
945. Eph 4:14
946. John 8:31–36; Romans 6:16–22; Gal 4:4–9
947. Romans 12:1–2, 14:10–13, 1 Peter 1:15–17, Matt 12:35–37
948. Rom 2:6–10, Deut 30:19
949. Luke 11:23
950. Eph 4:11–16
951. Phil 3:13–16, Matt 26:41, 1 Tim 6:8–12
952. 2 Tim 1:9
953. John 8:44; Rom 1:22–25; 1 John 3:8
954. Luke 11:23, James 1:5–8, Rev 3:16
955. Matt 6:24; Romans 6:16, 23; 1 Cor 8:6
956. 1 Pet 2:21–23; 1 Cor 11:1; 1 Tim 1:16
957. Matt 26:39
958. John 14:6
959. Rev 13:1–18
960. 1 John 3:8
961. Eph 2:5–8; Acts 15:11; Romans 3:24, 5:15
962. 1 Peter 1:6–7, 4:13
963. James 1:2
964. Col 1:10–15; 1 Sam 2:2–10; Ezek 34:11–31; Gen 50:20; Isaiah 41:10,13; Job 10:8–17; Psalm 91:1–16; Prov 3:6, 5:21, 16:9, 33
965. Psalm 37:23–24; Ezek 36:27; Job 11:7, 22:21, 32:8, 33:14–18; John 14:26; Eph 6:12–17; 1 John 4:4; John 14:23, 15:4
966. James 1:12
967. Eph 3:20
968. 1 Peter 1:6–9
969. 2 Cor 13:9; Rom 4:20–22; Eph 3:16; Exo 15:2; 1 Chr 16:11; Psalm 20:6, 28:7, 140:7; Isa 12:2
970. Job 36:26–31, 37:5; 1 Cor 14:2; Luke 8:25; Eph 4:13; Heb 11:1–3, 11:29
971. Job 28:28; Psalm 111:10; Prov 9:10
972. Acts 14:22
973. 1 Peter 1:17
974. Philippians 2:12
975. 1 Peter 4:18

THINGS TO COME

976. 1 Cor 10:13
977. Heb 13:5
978. 1 Cor 2:9; Romans 8:18; 1 Peter 4:12–14, 19
979. James 1:12
980. 1 Tim 2:4; John 3:16–17, 4:10; Titus 2:11; 2 Peter 3:9; Deut 30:19
981. John 15:13; Romans 5:8, 8:38–39; 1 Cor 2:9, Eph 2:4, 3:19; Col 3:12; 1 Thess 1:4; Rev 1:5
982. Romans 3:25, 9:14; Job 34:12; Psalm 45:6; Isa 5:16, 30:18
983. John 8:32
984. James 1:2
985. 1 Peter 5:7
986. Jer 29:11
987. Gal 1:4; Eph 2:8; 2 Tim 1:1, 3:15; 1 Peter 1:9; 1 Cor 1:21
988. Eph 1:2–13
989. Eph 1:9–23, 2:6, 8; Deut 30:19
990. Eph 2:10; Heb 11:3
991. Romans 11:33
992. Isaiah 55:8–9
993. 1 Tim 2:4
994. James 1:2
995. James 1:3–4
996. James 1:12
997. Matt 7:14
998. Philippians 1:6
999. Luke 15:7
1000. James 1:3–4; Matt 5:48; John 3:19–21; Eph 4:1, 5:8–18; Col 1:10–12; 1 Thess 2:12–13
1001. Isaiah 44:24; Psalm 139
1002. Prov 20:24
1003. 1 Peter 2:21, 4:1
1004. Acts 14:22; John 16:33; Rev 1:9
1005. James 1:2–7; Isa 30:21; Psalm 25:8–10
1006. Prov 17:3; Ezek 13:9
1007. 1 Peter 4:12–14, 19, 5:10; 1 Cor 10:13
1008. Eph 2:10
1009. Philippians 1:6
1010. Luke 2:11; John 3:15; 1 Tim 4:10; 2 Tim 3:15; Gal 2:20
1011. Rom 11:29
1012. Rom 6:16; John 3:36, 14:15; Acts 5:29, 32; Romans 6:16; 2 Thess 1:8; Heb 5:8
1013. Rom 9:20; Jer 10:23–24, 18:6; Isaiah 44:2, 24
1014. Prov 21:31
1015. Psalm 139:13; Isaiah 44:24; Jer 1:5
1016. Psalm 139:13–15
1017. Psalm 139:16
1018. Jonah 1:2
1019. Jonah 1:3
1020. Jonah 1:17
1021. Proverbs 15:10
1022. Heb 12:9
1023. Proverbs 6:23; Deut 8:5; Psalm 118:18; Prov 3:11; 1 Cor 11:32; Heb 12:5–6
1024. Job 7:17–18
1025. 1 John 4:16–19; Prov 3:12, 13:24; 1 Cor 11:32; Heb 12:6, 9–11; Rev 3:19
1026. 1 Tim 2:2–6, 4:10; 2 Peter 3:9; Titus 2:11
1027. Romans 1:1–7, 8:28–30, 9:24; 1 Cor 1:2, 24, 7:17; Eph 4:4; Phil 3:14; 1 Tim 6:12; Heb 9:15; 1 Peter 1:15; Rev 17:14
1028. Romans 1:20; Eph 6:1; Col 3:20; 1 Tim 5:4; Job 12:13–25; Psalm 19:1–6
1029. John 8:11; Mark 1:4; Acts 2:38, 3:19, 17:30; Rev 2:21–22
1030. 1 Peter 4:1; 2 Cor 7:9–10

1031. 1 Tim 4:7; Prov 13:18, 15:32, 19:27; Heb 12:7–11; Rev 3:19
1032. Heb 12:5–6
1033. Prov 19:20; Isa 30:1
1034. 1 Cor 11:32
1035. Heb 12:7–8, 11; Job 5:17; Prov 3:11, 19:20, 27
1036. 1 Peter 2:21
1037. Micah 6:8; 1 Kings 2:3; Deut 11:1; 2 Cor 10:5
1038. Philippians 3:12–16
1039. Gal 5:22–26
1040. 1 Cor 10:13; 2 Peter 2:9; Deut 8:5
1041. Philippians 1:6
1042. Job 9:3, 14, 13:3, 15, 40:2
1043. Matt 13:1–23
1044. Matt 13:20–21
1045. Matt 13:22 The Interlinear Greek-English New Testament
1046. Matt 13:19
1047. Prov 3:5; Deut 1:31–33; Psalm 78:21–22, 146:3; Isa 42:17; Jer 48:7
1048. Job 5:17; Proverbs 3:11
1049. 1 Cor 7:17
1050. Matt 7:13–14; Luke 13:24
1051. Romans 8:29–30
1052. Rom 11:29
1053. Isaiah 46:9–11
1054. Eph 2:10
1055. John 14:15, 21, 34
1056. 3 John 11; Psalm 37:27; Prov 11:27; Isa 5:20; Amos 5:14–15; Rom 7:14–25
1057. Eph 4:24–31, 5:3–4
1058. Eph 4:32
1059. Eph 5:5; Jude 15–16; 1 Cor 6:9–10
1060. John 15:1–11
1061. John 15:2
1062. Luke 12:48
1063. Matt 25:21
1064. Matt 25:26
1065. John 15:16
1066. Mal 3:2–3; Zec 13:9
1067. Gal 2:20, 3:2–5; Col 1:23; 1 Tim 6:12; 2 Tim 4:7
1068. John 15:5, John 15: 1–11
1069. John 15:4–5, 8
1070. John 15:4
1071. John 15:2
1072. Gal 5:16–26
1073. 1 Pet 1:7; Zec 13:9; James 5:3; Mal 3:2; Rev 3:18
1074. Mal 3:2
1075. Col 1:12
1076. Psalm 32:3–5; Job 42:7; Jer 7:20, 25:15; Eze 20:33; Nah 1:2; John 3:36; Romans 1:18, 2:5, 9:22; Eph 5:6; Rev 14:10
1077. Heb 12:28, 13: 15, 21; Col 1:12,
1078. Revelation 3:10, Interlinear Greek New Testament
1079. Revelation 19:11–16
1080. *Strong's Complete Dictionary of Bible Words*, p. 586
1081. Daniel 8:17–19; 2 Timothy 3:1
1082. 2 Peter 3:2–13; Jeremiah 23:20; Psalm 75:2; Daniel 8:19, 11:27; Mark 13:33
1083. Romans 9:27; Isaiah 10:22; 1 Peter 3:18
1084. Matthew 25:46
1085. 1 Thessalonians 5:1–5
1086. 1 Thessalonians 5:9
1087. Matthew 24:13
1088. 2 Timothy 3:16, Interlinear Greek New Testament; Matthew 4:4
1089. Romans 15:4; John 14:26
1090. Revelation 10:4
1091. Daniel 8:26

1092. John 16:13–15, 14:26, 1 Corinthiansinthians 2:10–13
1093. Acts 1:9
1094. Acts 1:11
1095. Revelation 19:11
1096. Matthew 26:64; Mark 13:26; Luke 21:27; 1 Thessalonians 4:17; Daniel 7:13; Mark 8:38; Matthew 16:27
1097. John 14:16
1098. 2 Thessalonians 2:7, Interlinear Greek New Testament
1099. Isaiah 19:1–3
1100. John 18:37
1101. 1 Timothy 3:15
1102. 1 Timothy 2:3–4, Interlinear Greek New Testament
1103. Matthew 24:6–8, 1 Thessalonians 5:3
1104. 1 Thessalonians 1:10, Interlinear Greek New Testament
1105. 1 Thessalonians 5:9
1106. Romans 3:25; Hebrews 2:17; 1 John 2:2, 4:10
1107. Revelation 6:17, Interlinear Greek New Testament
1108. 1 Thessalonians 1:10, Interlinear Greek New Testament
1109. John 3:36
1110. Revelation 3:10, interlinear Greek New Testament
1111. Psalm 5:5
1112. Matthew 4:17
1113. Matthew 15:3
1114. Matthew 15:9
1115. Matthew 23:19
1116. Matthew 23:23
1117. Revelation 3:10
1118. John 4:21-23
1119. Ephesians 4:1; 2 Thessalonians 1:11; 2 Corinthians 5:15
1120. 2 Corinthians 5:15
1121. 1 Timothy 3:15
1122. Ephesians 3:10
1123. Galatians 5:4
1124. Romans 15:19; Acts 24–28, 26:14–23
1125. Psalm 5:5–6, 7:11–12, 11:5
1126. Exodus 19: 4–5, 11–13, 16, 20:18–21
1127. Exodus 20:20
1128. 2 Chronicles 19:2; Ezra 8:22; Malachi 2:1–2, 7–9
1129. John 14:15
1130. Matthew 18:15
1131. 1 Timothy 2:4
1132. 2 John 1:9
1133. Gen 19:16, 43:14
1134. John 1:9
1135. Colossians 3:12; Mark 1:41, 6:34, 8:2
1136. Ezekiel 36:26
1137. Ezekiel 36:26–27, Interlinear Hebrewsrew Old Testament
1138. Amos 1:11
1139. Matthew 26:36–46
1140. Hebrews 12:1–3
1141. John 3:16
1142. 1 John 3:16
1143. 1 John 4:10
1144. 1 John 5:3
1145. Psalm 111:10
1146. Romans 11:33–36
1147. Isaiah 6:5
1148. Matthew 27:46; Psalm 22:1–2
1149. Mark 9:7
1150. Luke 18:16
1151. Romans 11:34
1152. Matthew 22:37–39
1153. Galatians 6:2

1154. Deuteronomy 4:24; Hebrews 12:29
1155. Genesis 22:1–19
1156. Hebrews 10:31
1157. 1 John 4:8, 16
1158. Genesis 42:18; Exodus 1:17, 9:29–30,18;21, 20:20; Leviticus 19:14,32; Matthew 10:28; 2 Corinthians 7:1; Romans 3:18
1159. Leviticus 18:22; Romans 1:24–32
1160. Leviticus 18:22
1161. Revelation 2:16
1162. Revelation 19:15
1163. Deuteronomy 23:3
1164. Matthew 18:15–20
1165. Matthew 16:7–12
1166. 2 John 7; 1 John 4:2–3
1167. Galatians 1:7–8
1168. John 14:6
1169. Ephesians 2:8–9
1170. Acts 4:12
1171. 1 Corinthians 10:31
1172. 2 Timothy 3:13
1173. 1 Timothy 3: 1–13
1174. Matthew 13:24–30
1175. *American Historical Documents*, The Harvard Classics, ©1938
1176. Romans 1:21–27; 1 Corinthians 6:9–10; 1 Timothy 1:9–10; Deuteronomy 5:17; Psalm 127:3, 139:13–16; Ecclesiastes 11:5; Isaiah 49:1; Jeremiah 1:5
1177. Ephesians 4:28
1178. Ezekiel 36:3–6, 22
1179. Job 21:14–15
1180. 2 Peter 2:6; Jude 5–9
1181. Exodus 20:7
1182. Exodus 20:2–17; Isaiah 58:13
1183. Mark 7:20–23
1184. Luke 19:14
1185. Luke 11:35
1186. Romans 5:1–11
1187. 1 Corinthians 15:5–8
1188. Matthew 24:4
1189. 2 Timothy 3:16
1190. Matthew 24:12–13, Interlinear Greek New Testament
1191. 1 John 4:4
1192. Hebrews 1:14; Psalm 34:7
1193. www.worthynews.com, wwwopendoorsusa/christian–persecution/world–watch–list
1194. Ezekiel 33:2–9
1195. Psalm 5:6
1196. Psalm 11:5
1197. 2 Thessalonians 2:12
1198. 2 Kings 25:8–9; 2 Chronicles 36:19
1199. Ezra 1:1–5
1200. Haggai 1:3–4
1201. Ezra 6:13–15
1202. Nehemiah 2:8
1203. Nehemiah 6:15
1204. 2 Chronicles 36:22–23
1205. Isaiah 45:1
1206. Zechariah 4:14; Haggai 2:22–23
1207. Colossians 1:16
1208. Daniel 9:27
1209. Daniel 8:11, 9:27
1210. Daniel 12:12
1211. Matthew 24:22, Interlinear Bible Greek New Testament
1212. Revelation 3:10; 2 Kings 19:31; Jeremiah 32:40–43, 46:28; Joel 2:18, 3:1–3; Daniel 12:1–4; Micah 4:1–3; Zephaniah 2:4–13
1213. Revelation 12:6
1214. Daniel 12:1–4
1215. Isaiah 46:13
1216. Revelation 14:13
1217. Matthew 24:24

1218. Matthew 24:14
1219. 2 Peter 2: 4–11
1220. Matthew 24:13; Mark 13:13, Interlinear Greek New Testament
1221. 2 Chronicles 36:16
1222. Matthew 24:51
1223. James 2:20, Interlinear Greek New Testament
1224. Matthew 12:33
1225. Daniel 9:27
1226. Revelation 6:4, 13:8, 15
1227. Revelation 5:1–2, 7, 6:1
1228. Revelation 19:11, 13, 15–16
1229. Daniel 11:24
1230. Qur'ān Ch 25:52, 8:39
1231. Revelation 17:13, Interlinear Greek New Testament
1232. Revelation 6:8
1233. Revelation 17:17, Interlinear Greek New Testament
1234. Genesis 11:1–9
1235. Daniel 7:25
1236. 1 Corinthians 10:10
1237. Isaiah 14:12–20
1238. Qur'ān 4:171, 17:111, 19:35, 92, 23:91, 25:2
1239. Qur'ān 2:75–79, 4:82, 6:34
1240. 2 Timothy 3:16
1241. 1 Thessalonians 1:5–6; 2 Peter 1:20–21
1242. Revelation 22:18–19; Deuteronomy 4:2
1243. Qur'ān 4:80
1244. Qur'ān 24:54
1245. Qur'ān 72:23
1246. Revelation 13:13–14
1247. Qur'ān Ch 4:4
1248. Qur'ān Ch 4:80
1249. Qur'ān, "The Opening"
1250. Daniel 8:25
1251. 1 Samuel 19:5
1252. Daniel 11:24
1253. Revelation 6:4
1254. Nehemiah 4:10–14
1255. Revelation 6:9
1256. John 16:2
1257. Micah 6:8
1258. Matthew 10:32–34
1259. Daniel 11:32
1260. Luke 6:29
1261. Proverbs 6:16–19, 31:9; Isaiah 1:16
1262. Isaiah 1:17
1263. Jeremiah 48:10
1264. Romans 13:4
1265. Psalm 139:19–22
1266. Deuteronomy 20:16–18
1267. Deuteronomy 20:10–15
1268. Psalm 5:4
1269. Job 34:10
1270. 1 Samuel 25:28, 17:20–47
1271. Isaiah 44:28, 45:1
1272. Jeremiah 27:6, 32:28; Ezekiel 30:10; Daniel 4:31
1273. Ezekiel 23:9; Micah 5:6
1274. 2 Kings 19:35; Isaiah 31:8, 37:35; Exodus 18:10; Ezekiel 23:9; Jeremiah 22:25; Jude 6:9, 10:7
1275. Acts 13:22, 36
1276. Deuteronomy 31:5; Jude 2:16, 7:9; 1 Samuel 17:47; 2 Samuel 3:18; 1 Chronicles 12:18, 14:15, 21:16; 2 Chronicles 21:16
1277. Nehemiah 4:14
1278. Philippians 4:13
1279. Revelation 17:9–10
1280. Matthew 14:28–31
1281. James 1:6–7
1282. Revelation 6:17
1283. Revelation 8:1–5

1284. 1 Timothy 6:15–16; Psalm 103:19; Daniel 7:27
1285. Luke 16:16; Acts 28:23; Zechariah 1:6; 2 Chronicles 24:19
1286. John 14:29
1287. Genesis 3:8
1288. Genesis 3:1, 3–5, 13
1289. Romans 5:12–14; 1 Peter 5:8
1290. Psalm 14:3, 53:3
1291. Proverbs 20:24; Jeremiah 10:23
1292. 1 John 2:13–14, 4:4
1293. Revelation 21:1
1294. Revelation 21:3
1295. Genesis 3:1
1296. Revelation 20:10
1297. Revelation 5:9–14, 21:1–6
1298. 2 Thessalonians 1:4–12; Revelation 21:7; 1 Corinthians 6:9–11; Galatians 5:19–25; Deuteronomy 33:3
1299. Genesis 18:19; Deuteronomy 10:12–13; Micah 6:8
1300. Genesis 1:1
1301. Genesis 1:26:27, 2:7
1302. Genesis 2:17
1303. Genesis 3:10–24
1304. Romans 6:23
1305. Revelation 8:7
1306. Revelation 8:8–9
1307. Titus 3:9
1308. Isaiah 14:27, 37:26, 46:11; Numbers 23:19
1309. 2 Timothy 2:4
1310. 1 Timothy 1;4–7
1311. Mark 16:15
1312. Jude 1:23
1313. Revelation 8:10–11
1314. Revelation 8:13
1315. Revelation 14:1
1316. Revelation 3:12
1317. Revelation 9:4–5
1318. Revelation 9:6–10
1319. Revelation 9:15
1320. Revelation 9:16
1321. Revelation 9:13–21
1322. Revelation 20:4
1323. Deuteronomy 32:35
1324. 1 John 3:16; Matthew 10:38–39
1325. Hebrews 1:14
1326. Revelation 13:16–17
1327. Revelation 13:15
1328. John 16:2
1329. Revelation 9:4
1330. Matthew 7:21–22; Luke 6:46; Isaiah 29:13; Ezekiel 33:31
1331. Matthew 24:14
1332. Revelation 3:10; 2 Thessalonians 3:1–3; Ezra 8:31; Psalm 34:19; Isaiah 40:28–31, 42:13,
1333. Revelation 3:10
1334. John 14:6
1335. 1 Timothy 2:3–4
1336. Ephesians 3:20; Psalm 4:8, 60:11–12; Proverbs 2:7–8; Isaiah 41:10; Jeremiah 15:20–21
1337. Titus 2:14; Psalm 107:10–15; Isaiah 30:1; Daniel 11:33–35; Revelation 7:14, 9:15, 20, 13:15, 14:13
1338. Daniel 11:33, 35
1339. Hebrews 5:8–10
1340. 2 Corinthians 5:15; Romans 14:7–9; 1 Chronicles 28:9; 2 Chronicles 19:7; Proverbs 6:16–19; Jeremiah 17:9–10, 32:19; Hosea 14:9; Malachi 3:16–18
1341. 2 Corinthians 5:15
1342. Romans 11:33; Job 5:9, 11:7–8
1343. Matthew 7:19
1344. Romans 3:12
1345. Isaiah 55:8–9

THINGS TO COME

1346. Psalm 33:13–15, 99:1–9, 139:2; Isaiah 6:2–5, 44:8, 46:9–10; Habakkuk 1:13; Malachi 3:16–18; 1 John 1:5
1347. Hebrews 10:36–38
1348. Joshua 1:6, 7,9, 18, 10:25; Deuteronomy 31:23, 31:6, 7; 1 Chronicles 22:13, 28:20; 2 Chronicles 37:7, 15:7
1349. Jeremiah 48:10
1350. Ezekiel 21:3–7
1351. Deuteronomy 6:5, 11; Matthew 5:48; Leviticus 19:2
1352. Exodus 20:8
1353. Isaiah 58:13
1354. Galatians 6:7
1355. Isaiah 14:24, 26, 27, 45:5–7, 55:11; Jeremiah 4:18, 23:20, 30:24; Lamentations 3:37–38; Ezekiel 20:43–44, 24:14; Daniel 4:34–35; 2 Kings 22:13; 2 Chronicles 36:16; Psalm 76:7, 77:9; Ecclesiastes 11:5,
1356. Genesis 1:26; Ezekiel 3:16–21
1357. 1 Thessalonians 4:13
1358. Ephesians 4:12–13
1359. Luke 12:48
1360. Mark 16:15
1361. Psalm 78:34; Hosea 5:15; Joel 1:15, 2:2; Amos 5:18, 20
1362. Numbers 30:1–2
1363. Hebrews 13:8
1364. 1 Corinthians 15:51–52
1365. 1 Thessalonians 4:17
1366. Matthew 10:22; James 1:12; 1 Peter 1:4–6, 5:10–11
1367. Revelation 6:4
1368. Proverbs 15:3
1369. Joel 2:1–2; Ezekiel 9:4–6; Zephaniah 1:14–17
1370. Daniel 12:10; Titus 2:14
1371. Daniel 8:19 11:27, 35; Matthew 8:29
1372. Matthew 25:41–46; Mark 3:29; 1 Corinthians 6:9–10; Romans 2:5–12; Galatians 5:19–21; John 3:36; 1 John 3:15; 2 Thessalonians 1:8–9; Jude 7; Revelation 21:8
1373. 1 King 8:56
1374. James 4:14; Job 7:7; Psalm 39:5, 44:22
1375. John 15:18
1376. John 3:19
1377. 2 Corinthians 11:23–27
1378. Romans 8:36
1379. 1 Thessalonians 5:23
1380. Genesis 2:7; Psalm 104:29–30
1381. Matthew 5:48
1382. 1 Peter 1:15
1383. 1 Peter 1:16
1384. Romans 7:14–21
1385. Acts 14:22
1386. Colossians 1:12–13
1387. Isaiah 14:12–20
1388. Daniel 4:13, 17, 23
1389. Daniel 12:11
1390. Ezekiel 38:12
1391. Matthew 13:24–30
1392. Daniel 2:31–35
1393. Flavius Josephus, *The Wars of the Jews*, Book IV, Chapter 11
1394. 2 Kings 15–20; Zephaniah 2:13–15
1395. 2 Kings 24, 25; 2 Chronicles 36; Jeremiah 33,39,40,52
1396. Isaiah 40–55; 2 Chronicles 36; Ezra 1, 3–6; Haggai, Nehemiah
1397. First and Second Maccabees
1398. Revelation 17:9–11
1399. 1 John 2:16; Mark 7:20–23
1400. Matthew 12:24

1401. 2 Thessalonians 2:4, 8–10; Daniel 7:25, 8:23–25; Revelation 13:13–14; Matthew 24:22
1402. 2 Thessalonians 2:9–10
1403. Revelation 13:1–10; Daniel 8:23–25
1404. Luke 4:6
1405. Daniel 4:17 Interlinear Hebrew Old Testament
1406. Romans 12:2
1407. John 3:19–21
1408. Romans 1:19; John 1:9
1409. Hebrews 10:15–16
1410. Romans 2:15
1411. Hebrews 1:3
1412. John 14:20
1413. Revelation 16:6
1414. Romans 3:19
1415. Philippians 2:10–11
1416. Psalm 5:5–6, 11:5, 9:17
1417. Revelation 16:2
1418. Revelation 16:3–4
1419. Revelation 16:8–9
1420. Revelation 16:12–16, Interlinear Greek New Testament
1421. Revelation 16:17–21
1422. Revelation 19:15–16
1423. Psalm 149:6–7; Jeremiah 48:10; Joel 3:9–17; Zechariah 12:1–5, 6–12, 14:5, 9, 11
1424. Revelation 17:17
1425. Ezekiel 38:1–7
1426. Revelation 2:15–16
1427. Revelation 20:1–2
1428. James 4:14; Ecclesiastes 6:12
1429. Psalm 78:39
1430. 1 Peter 1:24; Isaiah 40:6–8
1431. 2 Corinthians 4:18
1432. Revelation 20:1–6
1433. Revelation 20:4
1434. Revelation 20:7–8
1435. 1 Corinthians 4:9; Daniel 4:13, 17, 23
1436. Revelation 20:9
1437. Revelation 20:10
1438. Daniel 11:35, 12:10
1439. Genesis 1:28
1440. Genesis 3:14–21
1441. Genesis 9:1–19, 19:5–8
1442. Genesis 12:2, 15:7, 18
1443. Genesis 12:1–3, 19:5–8; Deuteronomy 29:10–15, 30:11–20
1444. Romans 11:15–27
1445. 2 Samuel 7:4–17; Jeremiah 31:31–34; Acts 2:22–24, 32–33, 36, 38–40, 4:27–30
1446. Genesis 12:3
1447. Deuteronomy 30:19–20; Joshua 8:34
1448. Genesis 25:22–23
1449. Philippians 2:5–11
1450. Philippians 2:1–2
1451. Hebrews 1:3
1452. Matthew 7:21
1453. Luke 10:2, Interlinear Greek New Testament
1454. Qur'ān Ch 29:46
1455. Revelation 17:15–18
1456. Daniel 11:31, 12:11; Revelation 13:4, 8
1457. Daniel 12:11
1458. Daniel 9:27; Matthew 24:15; Mark 13:14–23
1459. Matthew 24:16–22
1460. Revelation 17:18
1461. Revelation 18:4–7
1462. Qur'ān Ch 3:19
1463. Qur'ān Ch 3:85
1464. 2 Timothy 3:13
1465. Revelation 21:1–5

THINGS TO COME

1466. Revelation 22:1–5
1467. Qur'ān Ch 73:20; 25:52; 22:39–40
1468. Qur'ān Ch 9:29
1469. Qur'ān Ch 25:52
1470. Qur'ān Ch 9:123
1471. Qur'ān Ch 45:23
1472. Qur'ān Ch 4:74, 77; Ch 47: 4–7
1473. Qur'ān Ch 9:36
1474. Qur'ān Ch 9:5
1475. Qur'ān Ch 4:74; 22:58
1476. Qur'ān Ch 61:4
1477. Matthew 5:44
1478. Qur'ān Ch 25:52, 8:39
1479. 1 John 3:8
1480. Isaiah 40:23, 41:2, 43:10–13, 46:9–11; Daniel 2:21, 4:17; Psalm 83:18
1481. 1 Peter 1:25
1482. Ezekiel Ch 36
1483. Deuteronomy 7:6; Exodus 33:16; 1 Chronicles 17:21
1484. Revelation 12:4
1485. Matthew 4:1–11
1486. Matthew 2:16
1487. Romans 8:28; Genesis 50:20
1488. 1 Corinthians 15:20–28; John 17:2; Acts 17:30–31
1489. Ephesians 6:10–17; 2 Corinthians 10:3–5
1490. Ephesians 6:12; Colossians 1:12–14; Mark 4:15; Acts 26:18; 1 Timothy 5:15
1491. John 3:15
1492. Qur'ān Ch 23:91; 4:171; 17:111; 19:35, 92; 23:91; 25:2; 112:3; 37:152; 39:4
1493. Qur'ān Ch 37:102–112
1494. Genesis 22:2
1495. John 10:30
1496. 1 Corinthians 10:10
1497. Qur'ān Ch 21:29
1498. Qur'ān Ch 2:87
1499. Qur'ān Ch 112:3
1500. Qur'ān Ch 4:171
1501. Qur'ān Ch 3:59
1502. Qur'ān Ch 3:6
1503. Qur'ān Ch 5:110
1504. Qur'ān Ch 9:33
1505. Revelation 20:4
1506. Revelation 20:2–3
1507. Revelation 20:7–9
1508. 2 Peter 3:5–13
1509. Revelation 19:20; Matthew 25:30
1510. John 17:3, 3:16, 36
1511. Revelation 20:15
1512. 1 John 3:3
1513. 1 Thessalonians 4:3
1514. Philippians 2:12
1515. 1 Peter 1:17
1516. 1 Peter 2:9
1517. 2 Peter 1:10–11; John 14:2–3; 2 Timothy 4:18
1518. Ephesians 1:4, 11
1519. 2 Thessalonians 2:13
1520. 2 Peter 1:4–8; Colossians 1:10; 1 Thessalonians 2:12; 1 Peter 4:6–10
1521. Mark 12:25
1522. 1 John 3:2
1523. Hebrews 12:28–29
1524. Ephesians 2:8–9
1525. James 2:20
1526. James 2:22
1527. James 2:24
1528. James 2:26
1529. 2 Corinthians 5:15; 1 Peter 4:1–2
1530. Ephesians 2:10
1531. John 4:34; Matthew 26:39

1532. John 8:29
1533. 1 John 2:6
1534. Deuteronomy 6:5–9
1535. Micah 6:8; Titus 2:12
1536. 1 John 2:15–16; Matthew 6:33
1537. James 4:14; Psalm 78:39; Ecclesiastes 6:12
1538. 1 Peter 4:1
1539. Hebrews 5:8
1540. James 1:2–4, 12
1541. Ephesians 2:10
1542. John 15:8
1543. Romans 12:2
1544. Romans 8:18; 1 Corinthians 2:9; 2 Corinthians 4:17
1545. 1 Corinthians 15:49–58
1546. John 1:1–5
1547. John 14:28
1548. Daniel 12:10
1549. Revelation 20:15, 21:8, 27; Matthew 13:48, 25:32–36, 41–46; 2 Thessalonians 1:8; Romans 9:15–25; Psalm 69:27–28; Galatians 5:19–21
1550. Philippians 4:3; Revelation 3:5, 13:8; 20:15: 21:27
1551. Matthew 20:28; 1 Timothy 2:6
1552. Ephesians 2:8; 2 Thessalonians 2:16; Titus 2:11; Romans 3:24
1553. Luke 15:7
1554. John 1:12, 14:2–3; Romans 8:29–30
1555. Romans 10:13, Interlinear Greek New Testament; 1 Timothy 2:4; John 3:15
1556. Romans 1 :18–32
1557. Romans 3:28, 9:30–32, 11:6; Galatians 2:16
1558. Revelation 20:13
1559. Revelation 22:12
1560. Matthew 6:20
1561. Romans 8:1
1562. Matthew 12:31–32
1563. Matthew 25:34, 41
1564. Matthew 25:32–33
1565. Matthew 3:12
1566. Matthew 13:48–50
1567. Romans 1:18–32
1568. 1 Corinthians 6:9–10
1569. 1 Corinthians 6:13–19
1570. 1 Corinthians 6:18
1571. 1 Samuel 16:14
1572. Galatians 5:19–21
1573. Revelation 21:8, Interlinear Greek New Testament
1574. Luke 16:19–31
1575. Hebrews 11:1–12; Romans 1:17, 4:16; James 2:14–26; Galatians 3:8–9
1576. Ephesians 4:9
1577. 1 Peter 3:18–20; 4:6
1578. John 5:24
1579. Colossians 1:22; 1 Peter 2:24; 3:18
1580. Revelation 21:4; Micah 4:1–3
1581. Colossians 3:12–17; Revelation 21;27
1582. Revelation 7:9, 14
1583. 2 Thessalonians 1:4–12
1584. Matthew 24:9–14; Luke 21:10–19
1585. Revelation 6:9
1586. Daniel 7:21
1587. Revelation 13:7
1588. Daniel 11:33
1589. Daniel 12:10
1590. Matthew 24:22
1591. Daniel 12:11–12
1592. Matthew 24:3
1593. Matthew 24:30
1594. 1 Thessalonians 4:17
1595. Revelation 14:14

THINGS TO COME

1596. Ezekiel 36:19
1597. Daniel 11:39; Isaiah 13:3–5
1598. Isaiah 13:3–5; Jeremiah 6:22; Ezekiel 28:6–10; Nahum 1:2–3, 6, 9
1599. John 4:34
1600. Eph 6:12, 2:1–10, 3:8–11; John 12:31; Acts 26:18; Col 1:13
1601. Gen 6:6–7 *The Interlinear Hebrew–Aramaic Old Testament*– Hendrickson Publishers 1985
1602. Rev 21:1–7
1603. Matt 26:39, 52–54; John 4:34, 5:30, 6:29, 38–40
1604. John 6:51
1605. Gal 3:15
1606. Gal 3:24
1607. Jer 7:23; Deut 4:40; 1 Kings 2:3
1608. *The New Strong's Complete Dictionary of Bible Words*, James Strong, by Nelson Publishing; word 7585 pg. 525
1609. Luke 16:19–31
1610. Isa 26:18; Romans 11:1–15
1611. Romans 11:25; Acts 26:22–23; Luke 2:31–32
1612. Eph 3:3–6
1613. Gal 3:26–28
1614. Gal 3:29
1615. Rom 5:6
1616. Rom 5:8
1617. Luke 2:10
1618. Isaiah 9:6–7, 11:1–2, 52: 13–15, 53:1–12, 61:1–2; Luke 4:16–21; Jer 23:5, 30:9; Daniel 9:24–27; Psalm 2:7–9
1619. Isaiah 11:1–10, 19:20; Micah 5:1–5; Dan 7:13–14; Psalm 45:6–7
1620. 1 Chronicles 17:11–14; Isaiah 9:6–7
1621. Isaiah 9:1–7; Micah 5:2, 4
1622. Luke 1:30–38, 42, 46–49; John 1:14
1623. Romans 6:5, 9; 1 Cor 15:20–22; John 20:9, 26–29; Matt 28:5–7
1624. Acts 2:22–24
1625. Acts 17:30–32
1626. 1 John 4:10
1627. Micah 6:8; Deut 10:12–13
1628. Isa 14:24, 37:26, 46:11; Num 23:19; Job 23:13; Acts 2:23, 4:28
1629. Deut 30:15–19, 12:8, Joshua 25:15, Job 34:4, 33, Prov 1:29, Isa 7:15–16, 56:4, II Cor 9:7, Gal 3:24
1630. Isa 14:26–27, many translations say frustrate, however the original Hebrew text says, "who can reverse it," a rhetorical question meaning no one or nothing can reverse God's plan.
1631. Gen 3:15; Isa 7:14, 9:6, 40:9–11, 42:1, 62:10–11; Jer 23:5–6; Zec 9:9; Psalm 110:1
1632. John 17:1–12; Eph 4–9; Acts 2:22–24, 32–36, 4:12, 13:26–31
1633. Gen 3:4
1634. Gen 6:5
1635. Jude 1:6, also see Chapter 3; The Cosmos p. 89
1636. Gen 6:6–7, 12–13, 7:11–24
1637. Deut 7:6
1638. Deut 7:9–16
1639. Isa 12:1–6, Deut 4:31–37
1640. Matt 26:41
1641. Gen 12:3, 27:12, 29; Deut 11:26, 30:1; Num 24:9; Joshua 8:34; Dan 9:11
1642. Romans 5:6
1643. 1 John 3:5, 8; John 12:31; 1 Peter 3:18–22
1644. Eze 20:43–44, 36:22–23, 39:7; Lev 22:32; Rev 15:4

1645. 1 John 5:1; John 1:14; Heb 1:5–13
1646. Isa 7:14
1647. Gal 4:4–5
1648. Rom 1:3–5
1649. Rom 1:17
1650. John 17:1–21
1651. 1 John 2:15
1652. Mark 12.30
1653. Luke 10:27; Matt 22:37; Mark 12:33
1654. John 14:6
1655. 1 Cor 6:14
1656. Matt 10:7; Luke 10:9
1657. Isa 9:6–7
1658. Matt 12:14, 22:15; John 11:47–53, 12:42–43
1659. Isa 14:12–15; Prov 8:13, 16:18
1660. Proverbs 3:5, 8:13, 16:18
1661. Matt 6:33
1662. John 3:15, 10:9; Matt 7:7–12; Acts 17:27–31
1663. John 3:36, 6:39–40, 44, 54, 11:25–26; 1 Peter 1:3–5
1664. John 6:65, 10:30, 14:21–23, 17: 11, 21; Romans 5:1–2, 6:23; 1 Tim 2:5; Matt 11:27; Eph 2:18; 1 John 2:23
1665. Matt 5:48
1666. 1 Peter 1:15–16
1667. Isa 43:3, 10–13, 44:6–8
1668. Gen 1:1; Isa 42:5–6; Amos 4:13; Eph 3:9; Rev 4:11
1669. Isa 45:6, 65:16; Eze 36:21–27; Psalm 31:5, 57:10, 69:13, 119:142, 151, 132:11, 147:1–20, Luke 1:4; John 1:14, 14:6, 15:26, 16:13; 1 Tim 2:4
1670. Exodus 19:-24, 20:19, 32:30–33
1671. 1 Tim 2:5
1672. John 6:44
1673. Rev 19:20, 20:15, 21:8
1674. Rev 21:1–3
1675. Gen 19:1–29
1676. 2 Peter 2:4–9; 1 Peter 2:25
1677. Gal 5:4–5; John 14:16; Acts 4:12; Psalm 14:3; Romans 3:12
1678. John 14:6
1679. Gal 2:21, 3:24; Romans 10:4, 9–10
1680. Isa 53:6; 1 John 1:8; Psalm 53:3
1681. Lev 26:14–16
1682. Deut 6:18, 24–25, 30:5–14
1683. Gal 5:19–26; 1 Thess 4:3–8; Col 3:5–12; Philippains 2:3–6, 14–15; Eph 4:17–32, 5:1–5; 1 Cor 7:1–5, 8:12, 13:4–8, 15:33; 2 Cor 5:7–10, 14- 5, 6:3–10; Romans 1:18–32, 2:1–11, 12:9–21
1684. Luke 22:19–20; Heb 10:9–19; Gal 2:16
1685. 1 Thess 2:12; Philippians 1:27
1686. Col 3:14–17; Heb 12:28
1687. Rom 5:5–8
1688. Acts 4:10–12
1689. Matt 10:32–33; Luke 12:8–9
1690. Matt 8:12, 25:30; Heb 11:6; Rev 21:8
1691. Rev 20:11–12
1692. Rev 20:13
1693. Rev 20:15; Heb 10:39
1694. Luke 15:7
1695. Heb 10:36, 13:21; Matt 16:27; Romans 11:29; Phili 1:6; 2 Tim 2:21
1696. Eph 2:10
1697. Matt 5:12
1698. Luke 6:23
1699. 2 Cor 4:6
1700. 2 Cor 4:14
1701. Matt 11:11
1702. Rev 22:12
1703. Isa 29:16, 45:9; Jer 18:6; Romans 9:21

THINGS TO COME

1704. Isa 55:9
1705. Isa 55:8
1706. Luke 6:37
1707. Matt 7:2
1708. Matt 18:22
1709. Matt 6:15
1710. Gen 6:5
1711. 1 John 3:15
1712. Matt 7:21
1713. Eph 5:6; Col 2:8; 1 Tim 6:20; 2 Tim 2:16; Titus 1:10
1714. Gen 9:6
1715. 1 John 4:1
1716. Matt 7:15, 24:4–5, 11; Mark 13:22
1717. Proverbs 3:5
1718. 2 Cor 5:14
1719. 2 Cor 5:15
1720. Eph 2:16; Col 1:20–22; Hebrews 2:17–18, 9:26, 12:2
1721. 2 Cor 5:21; 1 John 3:5; Heb 9:14
1722. Gal 1:4; Eph 2:13; 1 Peter 1:19, 2:24; 1 John 1:9, 2:2; Rev 1:5
1723. John 17:2–5, 20:17; Matt 28:1–7; Mark 16:6; Luke 24:1–8
1724. Rom 8:1
1725. Romans 2:16; 2 Tim 4:1; Rev 19:11
1726. Luke 6:37–38
1727. Romans 16:17–18; 1 Tim 4:7
1728. Matt 6:14–15
1729. Luke 6:37; Matt 7:1–5
1730. James 1:2–7; 1 Peter 1:6
1731. Proverbs 3:11–12; Rev 3:19
1732. Col 3:1–15; Eph 4:17–32
1733. 2 Cor 5:17
1734. John 3:3–7; 1 Peter 1:3, 23
1735. Romans 3:10–12, 23; Phil 2:21
1736. John 3:16, 36, 6:40, 11:25; Romans 5:8, 8:32; Eph 2:4–7; 2 Thess 2:16; 1 John 4:9–10; Rev 1:5
1737. 2 Cor 5:17–19; Romans 4:8; 1 Cor 13:4–6
1738. Hebrews 10:12
1739. Hebrews 7:24–25
1740. Gal 5:4
1741. Phil 3:14–16, The Interlinear Bible, Hendrickson, Jay Green Volume IV
1742. 1 Cor 9:24–27; Heb 12:1–3; 1 Peter 2:9
1743. John 14:16–17, 26, 15:26, 16:7–15; Gal 4:6
1744. Phil 1:6
1745. Deut 5–11 moral duties, 12–16:17 God's statutes, 16:18–26:19 the ordinances of God: civil, social, and duties
1746. Deut 21:18–20
1747. Deut 16:19–20
1748. Deut 19:14
1749. Deut 22:5
1750. 1 John 2: 13–14, 4:4, 5:1–5; Titus 3:5
1751. John 16:13
1752. Col 1:13; John 8:12, 12:46; Acts 26:18; Eph 5:8
1753. John 11:50–51; Matt 16:17; Gal 1:16, Philippians 3:15; Luke 12:12; John 14:26, 16:13; Acts 2:17, 21:11; 1 Cor 12:3; 1 Tim 4:1; Heb 3:7–11; 2 Peter 1:21; Rev 2:7, 11, 17
1754. 1 John 4:10, 19; John 3:16; Romans 5:8
1755. John 15:13
1756. John 20:28
1757. John 20:27
1758. John 20:28–29
1759. Mark 12:31; 1 Cor 13:4–8; Phili 2:3–5
1760. 1 John 5:7; John 1:1–5; Gen 1:26; Matt 3:17–18; 1 Cor 12:3–6, 15:28; 2 Cor 13:14; 2 Thess 2:13; 1 Peter 1:2

417

1761. John 17:21
1762. 1 John 4:19
1763. 1 John 5:1–4
1764. Matt 22:37
1765. Lev 18:21; Eze 16:20–21, 23:37, 39
1766. John 6:39–40, 12:45
1767. 2 Peter 1:10; Eph 1:3–11; Romans 9:11, 11:28; 2 Tim 2:10; Titus 1:1; 1 Peter 1:1
1768. Romans 1:19
1769. John 6:44
1770. John 6:63–65
1771. John 10:4–6
1772. Gen 19:1; Heb 1:14, 13:2; Psalm 34:7, 78:49–50, 91:11, 103:20; Matt 13:41, 49, 18:10; Luke 4:10–11
1773. 1 John 5:19
1774. Psalm 23:5
1775. John 10:16
1776. Gen 3:22
1777. John 13:34
1778. John 7:16
1779. John 8:14
1780. John 8:24
1781. John 8:26
1782. John 8:29
1783. John 8:31–32
1784. John 5:24
1785. John 8:51
1786. John 10:38
1787. John 10:30
1788. Matt 18:14; John 6:40, 47
1789. 2 Peter 3:9; John 10:9; Acts 2:21; Romans 10:9; 1 Tim 2:4
1790. John 6:44, 65
1791. Eph 2:3; Col 3:5–6
1792. Eph 5:11
1793. John 14:6
1794. Matt 12:32
1795. Romans 11:29
1796. 1 John 2:15
1797. 2 Pet 3:9
1798. John 3:15–21, 11:25, 14:6; Acts 2:22–24; Heb 9:28; 2 Cor 5:21; Luke 19:10; 1 Thess 5:9; Romans 10:9
1799. Hebrews 5:8–9
1800. Deut 8:17, 8:11–14, 17
1801. 2 Cor 5:20
1802. John 6:39; 2 Tim 2:10; Matt 24:31; Mark 13:27; Romans 8:28–30; Eph 1:3–13
1803. John 4:34, 5:30, 6:38, 7:16, 9:4, 12:49, 14:31
1804. John 8:29
1805. Phili 2:1–4
1806. Rev 20:14
1807. Romans 3:10–12
1808. Rev 1:8
1809. John 1:1–5
1810. Rev 21:1
1811. John 14:6
1812. Rev 19:20
1813. 2 Tim 2:10
1814. Rev 1:8, 17, 2:8, 21:6, 22:13
1815. 1 Cor 15:40, 44, 46–54; Rev 21:1–5
1816. Rev 20:15; Phili 4:3; Rev 3:5
1817. Exodus 32:32; Deut 29:20; Psalm 69:28; Rev 13:8
1818. Rev 21:1
1819. Rev 21:4
1820. Dan 7:13–14; Rev 21:3; Isa 9:6–6
1821. Matt 25:46; John 5:24, 6:40; 1 John 1:2, 5:11, 20; Rev 22:1–7
1822. 1 John 4:14–15
1823. Rev 21:5
1824. Rev 21:6
1825. Rev 21:2

THINGS TO COME

1826. Rev 21:3
1827. Rev 21:23
1828. Titus 1:2
1829. 1 John 3:20; Isa 44:7
1830. Psalm 139:7–12
1831. Jer 32:17, 27; Job 36:22; Psalm 35:10; Nah 1:6
1832. Titus 1:2; Deut 32:4; Isa 25:1; Heb 6:13–14
1833. Psalm 5:4; Job 34:10
1834. Luke 24:46; Matt 24:30, 25:31, 26:32, 64, 28:6; Mark 16:6
1835. John 20:19–31; 1 Cor 15:4–8; 1 Tim 3:16
1836. John 10:30
1837. 1 Tim 1:16; 1 Peter 2:21; Heb 12:2; Matt 5:45, 11:29, 16:24; Romans 8:15; 2 Cor 6:18; Gal 4:6; Heb 12:7
1838. Phili 2:12–13
1839. Phili 2:15
1840. Phili 1:27
1841. Gen 15:13
1842. Gen 15:16
1843. Gen 21:2
1844. Psalm 102:13
1845. Daniel 8:19
1846. Daniel 11:27
1847. Daniel 11:35
1848. Jeremiah 33:14–15
1849. Jeremiah 33:20
1850. Matt 8:29
1851. Matt 26:18
1852. John 7:6,8
1853. John 7:8 *The Interlinear Bible, Greek / English Translation,* Hendrickson
1854. Romans 5:6
1855. Galatians 4:4
1856. Mark 13:33
1857. Acts 17:31
1858. Phili 2:12–15
1859. John 14:21
1860. Rom 5:19, 2:13
1861. John 15:10
1862. 2 John 1:6
1863. John 1:17
1864. Luke 11:9–10; 1 John 5:14–15; Matt 7:7–8, 21:22; Mark 11:24; John 15:7–11
1865. 1 John 3:24
1866. John 14:21
1867. 1 John 4:4; Romans 8:26–27
1868. John 16:7–15; Romans 8:14
1869. 1 John 2:3–4
1870. 1 John 2:5
1871. 1 John 2:14
1872. 1 Pet 1:15
1873. Rom 3:25; Heb 2:17
1874. 1 John 2:6
1875. Matt 4:8
1876. Matt 16:16–17
1877. Matt 16:22–23
1878. Matt 4:4, 6, 7, 10
1879. Eph 6:16; James 4:7; 1 Pet 5:7–9
1880. Philippians 2:8
1881. John 1:12, 3:16–18, 10:9, 14:6; Matt 1:21; Acts 4:10–12, 5:29, 32, 10:43; Romans 2:8, 5:10, 6:16, 10:9; Col 1:22; Heb 5:7–10; Acts 4:12; 1 Thess 5:9; 2 Thess 1:18; 1 Tim 1:16, 2:4–6; 2 Tim 2:10; Titus 2:11; 1 Peter 1:2, 9, 4:17; Rev 12:10
1882. Psalm 66:18; Isa 59:2; John 9:31
1883. 1 Thess 1:5
1884. 2 Thess 1:5; 1 Peter 5:7–10
1885. James 4:7
1886. Phili 2:6–7
1887. John 14:10–12

TOM NEWMAN

1888. 1 Pet 1:22
1889. 2 Thess 1:8
1890. Gen 4:9
1891. James 2:17, 26
1892. Job 28:28; Proverbs 1:7, 9:10, 15:33; Psalm 111:10; Ecc 12:13
1893. Luke 6:23; Romans 8:18; Matt 5:12; 1 Cor 2:9; 2 Cor 4:17
1894. Matt 6:21
1895. Matt 18:3
1896. Heb 11:1; Romans 8:24; 2 Cor 4:18
1897. Acts 1:8, 5:32; Romans 8:13; Eph 3:16–20; Gal 5:16; 1 John 5:8; 1 Thess 5:19; 1 Cor 15:16–17, 49–54
1898. Proverbs 22:6; Eph 6:4
1899. Jer 29:11
1900. Matt 22:37–38
1901. Phili 1:6, 10
1902. Phili 1:27, 29
1903. Phili 2:3–4
1904. Phili 2:5–11
1905. Phili 2:12
1906. 1 Peter 4:18
1907. 1 Peter 2:21, 4:1, 13; Matt 16:24; Acts 14:22; 1 Timothy 1:16; 1 Cor 11:1
1908. 1 Cor 10:13
1909. 1 John 5:4–5
1910. 1 John 4:4
1911. John 15:10
1912. 2 Timothy 2:19
1913. 2 Timothy 1:9–10
1914. 2 Timothy 1: 13–14
1915. Matt 7:21
1916. John 12:44–45
1917. Col 3:1–2
1918. Col 3:4–6
1919. John 14:11–13
1920. James 4:3
1921. 1 John 3:1
1922. John 6:63
1923. 2 John 1:9
1924. Eph 4:22–24
1925. Eph 4:30–32
1926. James 4:5–8
1927. 1 Peter 1:14–15, 22
1928. Philippians 14–15
1929. Col 2:8, 3:23–24 4:2
1930. Romans 12:2–3, 15:7
1931. 1 John 5:4–5
1932. Luke 6:37–38
1933. Micah 6:8
1934. 2 Cor 5:14–15
1935. John 5:29
1936. Col 2:8; Matt 23:1–36; Mark 7:8, 13
1937. John 14:6
1938. Romans 6:3–14
1939. Rev 12:10; Job 1:12
1940. Romans 3:26
1941. Eph 2:7
1942. 2 Thess 1:7–9
1943. Isa 1:18; Psalm 51:7; Psalm 103:10–12
1944. Rom 10:9–10; 1 John 1:9
1945. Gal 3:24–29, 16:15
1946. Rom 8:6
1947. Eph. 3:16; 1 John 4:4
1948. Eph 1:4–5, 11; Psalm 139:1–16
1949. Eph 3:3–11; 1 John 2:2
1950. Matt 26:41
1951. Eph 2:8
1952. Eph 1:11; Romans 11:25
1953. Romans 9:27, 11:11, 29, 33–36
1954. John 14:6
1955. Romans 8:29–30
1956. 1 Tim 2:4

THINGS TO COME

1957. Eph 5:3–14; John 3:19–20
1958. Matt 7:13
1959. Deut 30:15, 19
1960. 2 Thess 2:13
1961. Phili 1:6; James 1:2–5, 12
1962. Romans 11:29
1963. Proverbs 3:5–6, 16:3, 33, 20:24, 21:31, Phili 4:6–7, 1 Peter 5:7
1964. 1 Cor 10:13
1965. Luke 6:23; 1 Cor 2:9; 2 Cor 4:17; Malachi 4:1–6
1966. 1 Pet 1:6–7; 2 Cor 3:5–6, 4:3–18; Col 1:9–12
1967. Matt 6:33, 7:7–8; Luke 11:9–10; 1 Cor 13:12; Phili 2:8–21
1968. Acts 17:28
1969. Romans 10:9–10; Eph 1:4–10
1970. 1 John 2:1–6, 12–29, 3:1–10, 4:4, 5:4–5
1971. John 16:23, 13:7; Matt 13:14, 19, 24:39; Mark 4:11–12, 12:24; 1 Cor 13:12; Deut 8:3; Job 42:3; Jer 23:20; Micah 4:12
1972. 1 Tim 6:12; 2 Tim 4:7–8
1973. Matt 25:21
1974. Eph 2:10
1975. Philippians 1:6
1976. 1 Corinthians 13:11–12, 15:42, 44, 46–54; Dan 7:9–10, 13–14; Gen 6:1–4; Jude 1:5–7; Rev 4:1–11, 5:1–14
1977. Psalm 46:10, 100:3; Romans 15:13; 1 Peter 5:7; Matt 6:8, 32; Job 12:10, 33:29, 34:10–12, 37:5; Psalm 24:1, 37:23, 50:15, 55:22, 103:3–4, 17, 116:1,12, 121:8, 139:1–6, 145:18–20; Proverbs 3:5–7, 5:21, 8:17, 16:9; 1 Cor 15:10,
1978. Romans 8:28
1979. 1 John 2:15–17
1980. Matt 6:24–34, 13:22
1981. Col 1:12–14
1982. 1 Pet 2:9
1983. John 11:32–35
1984. Jude 23

ADDENDUM

Ample warning and council was given to our Republic by President Abraham Lincoln.

- We the people are the rightful masters of both Congress and the courts not to overthrow the Constitution, but to overthrow the men who pervert the Constitution.

- This country, with its institutions, belongs to the people who inhabit it. Whenever they shall grow weary of the existing government, they can exercise their constitutional right of amending it, or exercise their revolutionary right to overthrow it.

- I am a firm believer in the people. If given the truth, they can be depended upon to meet any national crisis. The great point is to bring them the real facts.

- America will never be destroyed from the outside. If we falter and lose our freedoms, it will be because we destroyed ourselves.

- Any people anywhere, being inclined and having the power, have the right to rise up, and shake off the existing government, and form a new one that suits them better. This is a most valuable—a most sacred right—a right, which we hope and believe, is to liberate the world.

In 1879, the U.S. Supreme Court illegally altered the writing of the Constitution and changed it. How? First, the court declared in U.S. v Reynolds that the Constitution did not define the term "religion." On that basis, that court then went on to make its own definition of that term. And the court chose a broad rendering; it adopted a plural meaning for the term "religion." Hence, they changed the writing of the First Amendment Religion Clause to, in fact, read as follows: "Congress shall make no law respecting an establishment of religions or prohibiting the free exercise thereof."

The Brief—in summary

- Introduction to how the U.S. Supreme Court illegally altered the writing of the Constitution and changed it: p2

- The Analytical Framework and Governing Case Law that aids in understanding the Constitution: p3

- The literal meaning of "religion" in the First Amendment speaks of one, and only one, particular religion, even though no religion is specified therein: p4

- Deriving the lawfully practical application of the Religion Clause using the literal definition of one exclusive religion for the term 'religion': p5

- The U.S. Constitution identifies the unstated religion of the First Amendment to be the teachings of Jesus Christ: p7

- The applicable laws at the time of drafting and ratifying the Constitution and the words and terms used then all clearly corroborate the obvious Christian meaning of the words "our Lord" used in Article 7 of the Constitution: p8

- The intent of Religion Clause is to expunge the sectarianism that plagues the Christian religion: p13

- Critiquing the Reynolds's Decision: p15

> "Of all the dispositions and habits which lead to political prosperity, Religion and morality are indispensable supports. In vain would that man claim the tribute of Patriotism who should labour to subvert these great Pillars of human happiness, these firmest props of the duties of Men and Citizens. The mere Politician, equally with the pious man, ought to respect and to cherish them…Let it simply be asked, where is the security for property, for reputation, for life, if the sense

of moral and religious obligation desert the oaths which are the instruments of investigation in courts of justice?

George Washington, Farewell Address

AMERICA'S HERITAGE: A CHRISTIAN NATION, LIGHT FOR THE WHOLE WORLD

The highest glory of the American Revolution was this: It connected in one indissoluble bond the principles of civil government with the principles of Christianity.

—President John Adams

FOREWORD

A Christian nation, simply, is: a nation whose laws and actions are in concord with the teachings of Jesus Christ, a nation where laws promote and foster Jesus-like behavior in society. As the first Virginia State Constitution states," it is the mutual duty of all to practice Christian forbearance, love and charity towards each other." A Christian nation requires no religious duties of its members other than good civil behavior—no stealing, no killing, no sexual immorality, etc. The religious duties of loving, serving, worshipping and promoting God, on the other hand, is a personal choice and that duty is a matter between the individual and God.

Jeremiah 1.10 says (New American Standard Bible), "See I have appointed you this day over the nations and over the kingdoms, to pluck up and to break down, to destroy and to overthrow, to build and to plant." In this writing you will find a pulling down of the status quo and a building of the founding father's paradigm.

Therefore, the current powers-at-be will find this writing frightening because it destroys their bogus right to lead the people in the direction and fashion as they have.

"Do not separate text from historical background. If you do, you will have perverted and subverted the Constitution, which can only end in a distorted, bastardized form of illegitimate government."—President James Madison, Author of the Constitution

The bottom line to this writing is: Jesus Christ taught that the greatest among you SHALL BE a servant of all. America, with out doubt, is mandated to exercise the commands of Christ by their founding law as you will see. Therefore, America has a moral duty to be a Servant to the whole world. Likewise, Jesus commands one to lay down one's life for the betterment of their brother. Therefore, America must also lay down its life for the life of the World. That is its national duty.

It is my sincere hope America will fulfill its divine destiny as a self-sacrificing servant to the world at large. No man is deserving of the freedom we have here, unless he is willing to fight for and secure another man's freedom. "The kingdom of heaven suffers violence and the violent take it by force." Matthew 11.12

SECTIONS:

- Introduction to how the U.S. Supreme Court illegally altered the writing of the Constitution and changed it: p2

- The Analytical Framework and Governing Case Law that aids in understanding the Constitution: p3

- The literal meaning of "religion" in the First Amendment speaks of one, and only one, particular religion, even though no religion is specified therein: p4

- Deriving the lawfully practical application of the Religion Clause using the literal definition of one exclusive religion for the term 'religion': p5

- The U.S. Constitution identifies the unstated religion of the First Amendment to be the teachings of Jesus Christ: p7

- The applicable laws at the time of drafting and ratifying the Constitution and the words and terms used then all clearly corroborate the obvious Christian meaning of the words "our Lord" used in Article 7 of the Constitution: p8

- The intent of Religion Clause is to expunge the sectarianism that plagues the Christian religion: p13

- Critiquing the Reynolds's Decision: p15

- Opposing Views: p19

- Truth has nothing to fear except if it is foreclosed from shedding its light on error: p28

- What must we do? p29

- Addendum: I have found true reasonable Christianity is the "Law of God" as amended and expounded by Jesus Christ, God's only begotten son: p32

INTRODUCTION

In 1879 the U.S. Supreme Court illegally altered the writing of the Constitution and changed it. How? First, the court declared in *U.S. v Reynolds*[1] that the Constitution did not define the term "religion." On that basis, that court then went on to make its own definition of that term. And the court chose a broad rendering; it adopted a plural meaning for the term "religion." Hence, they CHANGED the writing of the First Amendment Religion Clause to, in fact, read as follows: "Congress shall make no law

---

[1] Reynolds v. U.S., 98 U.S. 145, 162 (1879)

TOM NEWMAN

respecting an establishment of religions or prohibiting the free exercise thereof."

America is a Constitutional Republic, and the Law is king.

Consequently, where the 'Law" goes; so goes this Nation.

True law is eternal, consistent, and unchanging - like the law of gravity. The American Constitutional Republic is supposed to seek and install true social law that is eternal, consistent and unchanging for all generations. And its laws are not supposed to be a reflection of the ever-changing desires of the majority or some power group. President Calvin Coolidge stated that "Men do not make laws. They do but discover them. Laws must be justified by something more than the will of the majority. They must rest on the eternal foundation of righteousness. That State is most fortunate in its form of government which has the aptest instruments for the discovery of law."

Our Nation is currently mired in corruption and division that is unprecedented in its history. So if America is to be a better nation, the Law, and the interpretation of law, must become better. And adopting the true interpretation of the First Amendment Religion Clause will make America a better Nation.

In 1993 in case no. 92-8104, I brought a matter before the Supreme Court that simply said that the 1879 declaration that the Constitution did not define "religion" was absolutely and undeniably wrong: And if the text of the religion clause is parsed according to the rules of grammar, logical reasoning implies a clear and certain definition for the term "religion." The court in 1993 chose to remain with the 1879 declaration in spite of clear and convincing proof that any honest and honorable person would agree with, and they ruled against the truth presented to them without any explanation as to why they decided to remain with the Reynolds precedence.

The court's behavior in 1993 is despicable and criminal. They have acted with total disregard to truth and have consciously misinterpreted the Constitution with a complete understanding of it. The court here is suppressing truth and this is an impeachable

offense under Article 3 and 6 of the Constitution. Justice Antonin Scalia warned the American public in dissenting opinions in 1996, that the court "day by day, case by case, is busy designing a constitution for a country he does not recognize and that a lawyer-trained elite is determined to foist its smug assurances and counter majoritarian preferences onto a helpless and unwitting nation."

After you read through the following clear and convincing truth, I hope you become stirred to rise up and answer 'Justice Scalia's call for help, because now is the time for all the good, the just, the courageous MEN in America to stand up in defense of our Constitution. Together, we must pledge our lives, our fortunes, and our sacred honor in defense of our legal rights, which were purchased with blood, for our children's sake. We must stand and defend our Constitution, the bulwark of our Nation, from those who are destroying it. We must spread the truth of our Constitution. We must put an end to the social corruption, chaos and filth that plague our land and restore a love for truth, honor and respect for one another. We must do our DUTY as required of by THE DECLARATION OF INDEPENDCE, that being: when government becomes abusive (and corrupt) it is the right and the DUTY of the people to throw off such Government and to provide new guards for their future security.

THE ANALYTICAL FRAMEWORK AND GOVERNING CASE LAW THAT AIDS IN UNDERSTANDING THE CONSTITUTION

The Constitution is what 'IT' says it is and its mandates and instruction therein are self-evident and obvious to a reasonable mind. Moreover, no court has the right to use tortured logic to alter the obvious meanings and directives therein.

The true meaning of the religion clause becomes evident through the reasonable application of the following: The first is a reasonable rendering of the terms in the text of the religion clause.

The second is a logical application the rules of grammar governing the text of the religion clause. The third is accurate application of the rules for interpretation of law generated through specific case law. These three criteria will make the absolute truth regarding the First Amendment Religion Clause apparent.

Case Law has developed a number of parameters to aid in coming to an understanding of what the Constitution means and they are:

a) The intention of the instrument is to prevail; this intention must be collected from its words; its words are to be understood in that sense in which they are generally used by those for whom the instrument was intended; its provisions are neither to be restricted into insignificance, nor extended to objects not comprehended in them, nor contemplated by its framers. Ogden v. Saunders (1827) 12 Wheat 332.

b) "The spirit of an instrument, especially of a constitution, is to be respected not less than its letter, yet the spirit is to be collected chiefly from its words." We have no need in this case to go beyond the plain, obvious meaning of the words in those provisions of the Constitution which, it is contended, must control our decision. Jacobson v. Massachusetts (1904) 197 U.S. 22.

c) Chief Justice Marshall said: "As men, whose intentions require no concealment, generally employ the words which most directly and aptly express the ideas they intend to convey, the enlightened patriots who framed our constitution, and the people who adopted it, must be understood to have employed words in their natural sense, and to have intended what they have said." Gibbons v. Ogden (1824) 9 Wheat 188.

d) No word or clause can be rejected as superfluous or meaningless, but each word must be given it due force and appropriate meaning. Knowlton v. Moore (1899) 178 U.S. 87.

e) Where any particular word is obscure, or of doubtful meaning, taken by itself, its obscurity or doubt may be removed by reference to associated words, and meaning of a term may be enlarged or restrained by reference to object of whole clause in which it is used. Virginia v. Tennessee (1893) 148 U.S. 503, 37 L. Ed. 537, 13 S. Ct. 728.

f) Supreme Court is bound to interpret Constitution in light of the law as it existed at time it was adopted, not as reaching out for new guaranties of rights of citizen. Mattox v. United States (1895) 156 U.S. 237, 39 L. Ed. 409, 15 S. Ct. 337.

g) Framers of Constitution employed words in their natural sense, and where they are plain and clear, resort to collateral aids to interpretations is unnecessary and cannot be indulged in to narrow or enlarge the text. McPherson v. Blacker (1892) 146 U.S. 1, 36 L. Ed. 869, 13 S. Ct. 3.

h) The Constitution must receive a practical construction. Railroad Co. v. Peniston ( ) 18 Wall 31.

i) Words in a constitution are always to be given the meaning they have in common use unless there are strong reasons to the contrary. Tennessee v. Whitworth (1885) 117 U.S. 147.

j) That which is implied is as much part of the constitution as what is expressed. Ex Parte Yarbourgh (1884) 110 U.S. 651, 28 L. Ed. 274, 4 5. Ct. 152.

k) An amended constitution must be read as a whole and as if every part of it had been adopted at the same time and as one law. Badger v. Hoidale, C.C.A. 88 F 2d 208 (1937), 109 A.L.R. 798.

TOM NEWMAN

THE LITERAL MEANING OF "RELIGION" IN THE FIRST AMENDMENT SPEAKS OF ONE, AND ONLY ONE, PARTICULAR RELIGION, EVEN THOUGH NO RELIGION IS SPECIFIED THEREIN

In 1879 the U.S. Supreme Court illegally altered the writing of the Constitution and changed it. The court declared in U.S. v Reynolds that the Constitution did not, in fact, define the term "religion" at all—either expressly or implicitly. And on that basis, the court then went on to make up its own definition for that term. The court chose to adopt a broad and plural meaning for the term "religion." And they CHANGED the normal singular meaning of the First Amendment Religion Clause to, in fact, read as follows: "Congress shall make no law respecting an establishment of religions or prohibit the free exercise thereof."

With case law specifying that: the intention of the instrument is to prevail, and this intention is to be collected chiefly from its words understood in their ordinary sense, and although the spirit of an instrument is to be respected not less than its letter, yet the spirit is to be collected chiefly from its words, let us examine the letter of the First Amendment.

The First Amendment of U.S. Constitution states:

"Congress shall make no law respecting an establishment of religion or prohibiting the free exercise thereof."

Note, here that the word 'religion' is in the single case form rather than the plural form (religions); therefore, it literally means a single religious belief by grammatical rule. When we consider the plural rendering of the single case form, which is atypical, there needs to exist some word modifying religion, such as: 'a' or 'any' to change its ordinary meaning. And here, none exists. Therefore, it can be unequivocally stated from this analysis: that the literal meaning of 'religion' in the First Amendment means one particular albeit-unidentified religion.

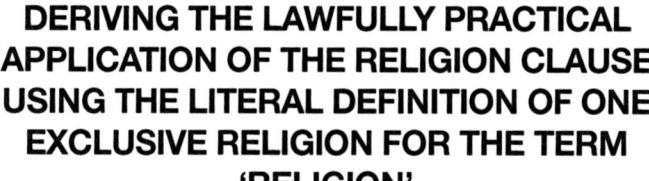

DERIVING THE LAWFULLY PRACTICAL APPLICATION OF THE RELIGION CLAUSE USING THE LITERAL DEFINITION OF ONE EXCLUSIVE RELIGION FOR THE TERM 'RELIGION'

When judges look at new law and they seek to apply it to a case, there is a presumption that the drafters of the law made a reasonable law. And this new law can be applied in a practical, common sense way. And this practical way is in accord to the common meaning of the words used in the law. Furthermore, each word used therein is to be given its full force in defining that law.

The First Amendment Religion Clause reads as follows: CONGRESS SHALL MAKE NO LAW respecting an establishment of religion OR prohibiting the free exercise thereof.

This clause contains two provisions. The first part of the clause is called the establishment provision. The second part of the clause is called the free exercise provision. These two provisions are joined by the conjunction 'or." And according to the rules of grammar, the use of the conjunction 'or" means that the two provisions are equal in importance and can exchange places without changing any meaning. It could have been written - Congress shall make no law prohibiting the free exercise of religion or respecting an establishment thereof- and mean exactly the same thing as it reads above.

In general, the Religion Clause is a total prohibition leveled at the U.S. Congress. Congress can make no law." This is a direct command. It is final and absolute in nature. But what exactly is Congress eternally prohibited from doing?

Looking at the Free Exercise Provision alone, it reads as follows - Congress shall make no law prohibiting the free exercise of religion. What does this mean? Literally, this provision applies to every living soul in the American society - man, woman, child, business, governmental body. And it gives everyone and every group the right to practice religion freely without any restraint. It creates a total freedom of expression for religion for every one.

This provisional absolute, however, is only practical in an environment where there is only one religious belief being acted out in the general society. The Free Exercise Provision does not work in an environment where there is more than one religious belief being acted out in society. The reason is in a society with multiple religions practicing, differing religions will eventually clash with other religions over their religiously mandated behaviors. And when that happens, a judge will curtail the religious exercise of one of the clashing religions in order to bring civil peace. But the Free Exercise Provision specifically forbids any kind of interference with religious exercise, period. Governmental power is absolutely banned from such action.

The following example shows this multiple religion problem clearly: Consider a controversy between devout Hindus and devout Jews. Hindus worship cattle and do them no harm. Jews, however, sacrifice and eat them. It is easily seen that a fight will break out between these opposing beliefs. And to settle this dispute, the courts will restrict some party in their religious freedom so as to bring peace. But the courts cannot do that as the Free Exercise Provision is written. (Currently, the courts are restricting religious practices without any Constitutional authority to do so. This is absolutely illegal and the court has no RIGHT under law to do so.)

In an environment of only one religious belief in society, a religious exercise is either right or wrong when it is measured against doctrine. Therefore if an exercise is correct, the religious exercise cannot be curtailed; however, if it is incorrect it can be restricted lawfully. In this scenario of the Free Exercise Provision, religious controversies are easily resolved. For example, sacrificing a fish is either right or wrong according to Jewish doctrine.

Now, looking at the Establishment Provision alone, it reads as follows - Congress shall make no law respecting an establishment of religion. On the face in the broadest of meaning, this provision compels government to restrict all expression of religion in society.

It, therefore, creates a society devoid of any religion. However, this type of definition is absolutely contrary to the definition of the Free Exercise Provision where every person and institution is granted total freedom to practice religion. There is now an inescapable, inherent contradiction here between the broad definitions of the Free Exercise and Establishment Provisions. The Supreme Court says this is the true situation with the provisions in the case of Walz v. Tax Commission (1969) 397 U.S. 668, 669 which states, "The court has struggled to find a neutral course between the two religion clauses, both of which are cast in absolute terms and either of which, if expanded to a logical extreme, would tend to clash with the other. In other words, the two provisions are at natural odds. However, logically, that cannot be the case. First, no one in their right mind would construct an absurd law that has no logical application ever. That is totally unthinkable, especially if you consider the brilliance of the fore fathers who designed our society. <u>Secondly, and more importantly, such a notion goes against the fundamental legal presumption that the drafters of a law created a practical law in the first place</u>. Therefore, in the name of practicality, there must be a more limited meaning to the term establish. And this limited meaning is in harmony with the concept of total religious freedom.

Since the First Amendment is addressing the powers of Congress only, the establishment of religion restriction applies only to the religious freedoms of the Congress and does not extended out to reach the religious freedoms of the other members of society. The working model of this is: the American society has everyone and every group practicing religion and establishing religion throughout the whole of society except for Congress. Congress is prohibited by law from the one particular religious exercise of establishing a national religious institution like in England where the church and state were wedded.

However, Congress can perform every other form of religious practice that is available to them like giving thanks to God (i.e.—Thanksgiving Day National Holiday), opening the a session of

Congress with a prayer, portraying religious saying on government property, etc. (All of these examples occur now in government circles). Another way to look at it and see the practical application of the Religion Clause is to see a wholly religious society with many communities therein. And then see the government as a subset community in the larger society, practicing religion with all of the other members it organizes. And further see government having no part in managing religious affairs therein.

Therefore, according to the above analysis, the First Amendment is only, I repeat, only practical is a society that acts out the mandates of one and exclusively one religion; the clause is ridiculous otherwise.

THE U.S. CONSTITUTION IDENTIFIES THE UNSTATED RELIGION OF THE FIRST AMENDMENT TO BE THE TEACHINGS OF JESUS CHRIST

The Preamble to the Bill of Rights begins with "The Conventions of a number of the States having at the time of their adopting the Constitution, expressed a desire, <u>in order to prevent misconstruction or abuse of its powers</u>, that further declaratory and restrictive clauses should be added:" With the use of the words 'further declaratory and restrictive clauses (to prevent misconstruction), this charge superimposes the Bill of Rights on the initial constitution and makes the Bill of Rights the heart, and preeminent part, of the Constitution, clarifying the Constitution in a greater and more definite way; and implies a finished work that is wholly reasonable and congruent with the Constitution.

Now that the literal text of the First Amendment is certain in meaning of one and only one unique religion and the amendment does not identify that one religion, one must concluded and assume that the main text to which the amendment has been attached contains that necessary identification.

THINGS TO COME

History shows that the U.S. Constitution was completed on September 17, 1787. And on March 4, 1789 the federal government was inaugurated in New York under the new constitution. And on September 25, 1789 the first Congress, under the new constitution, adopted the first ten amendments, Bill of Rights, to the constitution, which came to force two years later on December 15, 1791.

The fore mentioned case law states that: where any particular word or sentence is obscure or of doubtful meaning, taken by itself (which is what there is here), its obscurity may be removed by comparing it with the words and sentences with which it stand connected. But there are none. Therefore case law deems further that: an amended constitution must be read as a whole and as if every part of it had been adopted at the same time and as one law. All of which leads to the main text of the Constitution.

In examination of the Constitution, there are only two other provisions that have any religious intonation in them: Article 7 and Article 6, both of which precede the First Amendment in time.

For this analysis case law stipulates that: no word or clause can be rejected as superfluous or meaningless, but each word must be given it due force and appropriate meaning, reference is to be had to the literal meaning of the words to be expounded, their connection with other words, and the general objects to be accomplished. But, more importantly, logical assumption has disposed us to seek any meaningful word to identify the unstated religion of the first amendment.

Article 6 of the U.S. Constitution states:

"No religious test shall ever be required as a qualification to any office or public trust under the United States."

Here, there exists no meaningful word which identifies religion. However, Article 7 of the U.S. Constitution states:

(This new constitution is)"Done in convention by the unanimous consent of the states present the seventeenth day of September in the year of our Lord one thousand seven hundred and eighty seven and of the independence of the United States of America the twelfth." (This marks the date the Constitutional Convention completed and signed the new constitution.)

And here it can be clearly seen from the words "Done in convention by the unanimous consent of the States present" that the signers totally assented to the whole contents of the document, the Constitution, as written. And this obviously includes the words "in the year of our Lord" which is a clear inference to Jesus Christ of Nazareth, the founder of the Christian religion. So in writing "our Lord" verses "the Lord," a mere demarcation of time, the framers literally declared their corporate religious belief to be the teachings of Christ in using the plural possessive "our." Thus religion is identified and it is the teaching of Jesus Christ. Therefore, the American society is a Christian Nation that is legally mandated to act out the teaching of Jesus Christ in all aspects.

Even if the signers had used the term "the Lord," the historical record would have confirmed the religious identification to be the teachings of Jesus Christ beyond any doubt. The historical record shows that the country was first a Christian society, which over time grew into a Christian nation. This fact is undeniably true. In 1891 the Supreme Court in its examination of the historical record a century after the country was founded stated unequivocally that the United States is a "Christian Nation" in the case of Holy Trinity v. U.S.

THE APPLICABLE LAWS AT THE TIME OF DRAFTING AND RATIFYING THE CONSTITUTION AND THE WORDS AND TERMS USED THEN ALL CLEARLY CORROBORATE THE OBVIOUS CHRISTIAN MEANING OF THE WORDS "OUR LORD" USED IN ARTICLE 7 OF THE CONSTITUTION

Case law states that words and terms are to be taken in the sense in which they were used and understood at common law and at the time the constitution and amendments were adopted.

THINGS TO COME

In examining the following state constitutions which were applicable at the time of drafting and ratifying of the new federal Constitution and the Bill of Rights, it is found that all sanctioned, advocated, protected, and fostered the exercise of the Christian religion to the affairs of state and man, and granted religious freedom and rights only within the context of such:

Article 22 of the 1776 Delaware Constitution, which was controlling of the five signing state representatives sent to the 1787 U.S. Constitutional Convention, states that: Every person who shall be chosen a member of either house, or appointed to any office or place of trust, before taking his seat, or entering upon the execution of his office, shall take the following oath… "A.B., do profess faith in God the Father, and in Jesus Christ his only son, and in the Holy Ghost, one God, blessed for evermore; and I do acknowledge the Holy Scriptures of the Old and New Testament to be given by divine inspiration.

Article 6 of the 1777 Georgia Constitution, which was controlling of the two signing state representatives sent to the 1787 U.S. Constitutional Convention, states that: The representatives shall be…of the Protestant religion

Article 35 of the 1776 Maryland Constitution, which was controlling of the three signing state representatives sent to the 1787 U.S. Constitutional Convention, states that: No other test or qualification ought to be required, on admission to any office of trust or profit, than such oath of support and fidelity to this state, …and a declaration of a belief in the Christian religion

Chapter 6, Article 1 of the 1780 Massachusetts Constitution, which was controlling of the two signing state representatives sent to the 1787 U.S. Constitutional Convention, states that:

Any person chosen governor, lieutenant-governor,…, or representative, and

accepting the trust, shall…make and subscribe the following declaration, "I, A.B., do declare that I believe the Christian religion and have a firm persuasion of its truth."

Article 3 of the 1778 South Carolina Constitution, which was controlling of the four signing state representatives sent to the 1787 U.S. Constitutional Convention, states that: No person shall be eligible to sit the House of Representatives unless he be of the Protestant religion

Article 32 of the 1776 North Carolina Constitution, which was controlling of the three signing state representatives sent to the 1787 U.S. Constitutional Convention, states that: No person, who shall deny the being of God or the truths of the Protestant religion, or the divine authority either of the Old or New Testaments ... shall be capable of holding any office or place of trust.

Article 19 of the 1776 New Jersey Constitution, which was controlling of the four signing state representatives sent to the 1787 U.S. Constitutional Convention, states that: There shall be no establishment of any one religious sect in this province, in preference to another; and that no Protestant inhabitant of this colony shall be denied the enjoyment of any civil right, merely on account of his religious principles; but that all persons, professing a belief in the faith of any Protestant sect who shall demean themselves peaceably under the government shall be capable of being elected into any office of profit or trust.

Section 10 of the Pennsylvania Constitution, which was controlling of the seven signing state representatives sent to the 1787 U.S. Constitutional Convention, states that: Each member, before he takes his seat, shall make and subscribe the following declaration: I do believe in one God, the Creator and Governor of the Universe, the Rewarder of the good and the Punisher of the wicked. And I do acknowledge the scriptures of the Old and New Testament to be given by divine inspiration.

Article 6 of the Bill of Rights of the 1784 New Hampshire Constitution, which was controlling of the two signing state representatives sent to the U.S. Constitutional Convention, states that: As morality and piety, rightly grounded on evangelical principles, will give the best and greatest security to government, and will lay in the hearts of men the strongest obligations to due subjection, ...Therefore, to promote those important purposes, the people of this state have a right to impower, and do hereby fully impower the legislature...to make adequate provision...for the support and maintenance of public Protestant teachers of piety, religion, and morality...and every denomination of Christians demeaning themselves quietly, and as good subjects of the state, shall be equally under the protection of the law and no subordination of any one sect or denomination to another, shall ever be established by law.

Section 16 of the Bill of Rights of the 1776 Virginia Constitution, which was controlling of the three signing state representatives sent to the 1787 U.S. Constitutional Convention, states that: religion, or duty which we owe to our creator, and the manner of discharging it, can be directed only by reason and conviction, not by force of violence; and therefore all men are equally entitled to the free exercise of religion, according to the dictates of conscience; and that it is the mutual duty of all to practice Christian forbearance, love, and charity towards each other."

Article 38 of the 1777 New York Constitution, which was controlling of the signing state representative sent to the 1787 U.S. Constitutional Convention, states that:

Whereas we are required, by the benevolent principles of rational liberty, not only to expel civil tyranny, but also to guard against that spiritual oppression and intolerance wherewith the bigotry and ambition of weak and wicked priests and princes have scourged mankind, this convention doth further ordain, determine, declare, that the free exercise and enjoyment of religious profession and worship, without discrimination or preference, shall forever hereafter be allowed to all mankind.

Article 39 states that: And whereas the ministers of the Gospel are, by their profession, dedicated to the service of God and the care of souls, and ought not be diverted from their great duties of their function; therefore, no minister of the Gospel, or priest of any denomination whatsoever shall, at anytime hereafter, under any pretense or description whatever, be eligible to, or capable of holding, any civil or military office or place.

The preamble of the 1776 Connecticut Constitution, which adopts the organic English Charter as its constitutional base and was controlling of the two signing state representative sent to the 1787 U.S. Constitutional Convention, states that: The people of this state, being by the providence of God, free and independent, have the sole and exclusive right of governing themselves as a free, sovereign, and independent state and forasmuch as the free fruition of such liberties and privileges as humanity, civility and Christianity call for as is due to every man in his place and proportion.

No state representative was sent to the 1787 U.S. Constitutional Convention from Rhode Island. However, they would have been subject to Rhode Island's constitutional authority, namely: the 1663 English Charter, which states that: Charles the Second, by the grace of God, Defender of the Faith…that all and every person and persons may…bee in the better capacity to defend themselves, in thiere just rights and libertyes against all the enemies of the Christian faith.

All of the signing delegates, by their state constitutions, had a fiduciary duty to uphold the truths and duties of the Christian religion. And 29 of the 36 signing delegates to the constitution were required by their state constitution to affirmatively testify to such in some fashion. Furthermore, 24 of the delegates were trained ministers of the Christian Religion.

Additionally, the representatives of the state legislatures that ratified the new federal Constitution and First Amendment had a fiduciary duty to uphold the Christian religion by their state constitutions, which were controlling at the time under the Federal Articles of Confederation and new Constitution, respectively And therefore when the legislatures ratified those propositions, one must conclude that the representatives perceived those propositions to be congruent with their fiduciary duty to uphold Christian principles, mandated by their state constitution. Otherwise, the representatives would have struck down the ratification of those propositions because of a moral and official imperative. And this sober duty of the state representatives is particularly underscored by their religious text in Matthew 7:21-23 (New American Standard Bible), which warns that:

Not everyone who says to me (Jesus), "Lord, Lord, will enter the kingdom of heaven; but he who does the will of My Father who is in heaven. Many will say to Me on that day, 'Lord', 'Lord', did we not prophesy in Your name, and in Your name cast out demons, and in Your name perform many miracles? And then I will declare to them, I never knew you; depart from Me, you who practice lawlessness.

And this would have a tremendous sobering affect upon a faithful practicioner.

Moreover, the Northwest Ordinance of 1787, which was drafted by Congress on July 13, 1787 at the same time the Constitutional Convention was meeting and drafting our current U.S. Constitution, further enhances the sense of the words and terms as they were used and understood at common law at that time and establishes more applicable law that aids interpretation:

Para. 1: "Be it ordained by the United States, in congress assembled, that the said territory, for the purpose of temporary government "

Para. 13: "And for extending the fundamental principles of civil and religious liberty, which form the basis whereon these republics, their laws and constitutions, are erected to fix and establish those principles as the basis of all laws, constitutions, and governments, which forever hereafter shall be formed in the said territory...."

Art. 3: "morality, and knowledge being necessary to good government and the happiness of mankind, schools and means of education shall forever be encouraged.

Closing salutation: "Done by the United States, in Congress assembled, the 13th day of July, in the year of our Lord one thousand seven hundred and eighty seven and of their sovereignty and independence the 12th."

Therefore in this analysis, the applicable laws at the time of drafting and ratifying the Constitution and the words and terms used then all clearly corroborate the obvious Christian meaning of the words "our Lord" used in the Constitution.

Much more can be said, collaterally speaking, further underscoring the above, but case law stipulates that where <u>the meaning is plain and clear, resort to collateral aids to interpretations is unnecessary and can not be indulged in to narrow or enlarge the text</u>. Consequently, none will follow. Clearly, then, the unstated religion of the First Amendment is the teachings of Jesus Christ.

Before moving on, the following declarations of the U.S. Supreme Court and its members and President John Adams, further, certifies the above conclusion:

In 1833 Rev. Jasper Adams, college president, wrote a pamphlet on the relations of Christianity to civil government in the U.S. that contested the view "Christianity had no connection with our civil constitutions" and contended the "concept of a national religion with it being the foundation for their civil government."

Chief Justice John Marshall wrote Rev. Adams a letter in regards to his pamphlet and stated, speaking for the U.S. Supreme Court,:

"The American Population is entirely Christian, and with us Christianity and religion are identified."

Justice Joesph Story, a member of the Marshall Supreme Court, wrote also a letter to Rev. Adams regarding his pamphlet and stated:

"I have read it with uncommon satisfaction. I think its tone and spirit excellent. My own private judgment has long been (and every day's experience more and more confirms me in it) that government can not long exist without an alliance with religion; and that Christianity is indispensable to true interests and solid foundations of free government,

And the U.S. Supreme Court in 1891 in Holy Trinity v. U.S (143 U.S. 457) states:

"If we examine the constitutions of the various states, we find in them a constant recognition of religious obligations. Every constitution of everyone of the 48 states contains language which either directly or by clear implications recognizes a profound reverence for religion and an assumption that its influence in all human affairs is essential to the well being of the community. p468 There is no dissonance in these declarations. There is a universal language pervading them all, having one meaning; they affirm and reaffirm that there is a religious nation. These are not individual sayings, they are organic utterances. p470 These, and many other matters which might be noticed, add a volume of unofficial declarations to the mass of organic utterances that this is a Christian nation." p471

President John Adams stated that "The highest glory of the American Revolution was this: it connected in one indissoluble bond the Principles of Civil Government with the Principles of Christianity.

THE INTENT OF RELIGION CLAUSE IS TO EXPUNGE THE SECTARIANISM THAT PLAGUES THE CHRISTIAN RELIGION

Preceding the Constitutional Convention that met and created our Constitution, the principle architect of our federal constitution and chairman of the committee that drafted the First Amendment, James Madison published a paper against a bill establishing provision for teachers of Christianity in the State of Virginia. It was called "Memorial and Remonstrance."

Para. 1 states: "It is the duty of every man to render to the creator such homage and such only as he believes to be acceptable to him. This duty is precedent, both in order of time and in degree of obligation, to the claims of society. Before any man can

TOM NEWMAN

be considered as a member of civil society, he must be considered as a subject of the governour of the universe."

Para. 2 therein states: "Because if religion be exempt from authority of the society at large, still less can it be subject to that of the legislative body. The latter are but creatures and vicegerents of the former. Their jurisdiction is both derivative and limited."

Para. 6 states: "Because the establishment proposed by the bill is not requisite for the support of the Christian religion. To say that it is, is a contradiction to the Christian religion itself, for every page of it disavows a dependence on the powers of this world: It is a contradiction to fact; for it is known that this religion both existed and flourished, not only without the support of human laws, but in spite of every opposition from them, and not only during the period of miraculous aid, but long after it had been left to its own evidence and ordinary care of providence. Nay, it is a contradiction in terms; for a religion not invented by human policy, must have pre—existed and been supported, before it was established by human policy. It is moreover to weaken in those who profess this religion a pious confidence in its innate excellence and the patronage of its author."

Para. 7 states: "Because experience witnesseth that ecclesiastical establishments, instead of maintaining the purity and efficacy of religion, have had a contrary operation. During almost fifteen centuries has the legal establishment of Christianity been on trial. What have been its fruits?…Pride and indolence in the clergy, ignorance and servility in the laity, in both supersition, bigotry and persecution."

Para. 8 states: "A just government will be best supported by protecting every citizen in the enjoyment of his religion with the same equal hand which protects his person and his property; by neither invading the equal rights of any sect, nor suffering any sect to invade those of another."

Para. 3 states: "Who does not see that the same authority which can establish Christianity, in exclusion of all other religions,

THINGS TO COME

may establish with the same ease any particular sect of Christians, in exclusion of all other sects?";

From the above paragraph one gleans that Madison saw true society as a manifestation of the teachings of Jesus Christ (something initially the original 13 colony-states constitutionally established); however, he was concerned about the failings and pitfalls of history's prior attempts at establishing religion in society by legal decree. And this perspective gives us the key to understanding the wording of the First Amendment Religion Clause and what it intends to accomplish.

Madison was undoubtedly a brilliant man and one can assume that he knew that the sectarianism that existed then was contrary to the teachings of Jesus Christ, according to John 17.22-23. (Jesus said his followers are to be "one" like he and his Father in Heaven are "one.") One is assured this fact when one considers the letter to Ezra Styles by Thomas Jefferson, Madison's co-leader in the religious liberty movement of that time and author of the misinterpreted and misapplied statement" Wall of separation of Church and State." Jefferson writes "we should all be one sect, doers of good and eschewers of evil. No doctrines of his lead to schism. It is the speculations of crazy theologians which have made a babel of a religion the most moral and sublime ever preached to man, and calculated to heal, and not create differences."

Under our initial federal constitutional instrument, the Articles of Confederations, there was no provision for reconciling the religious sectarianism that existed in the 13 states and this insured a measure of permanent domestic turmoil. This repugnant fact, among other things, drove our forefathers to form a new federal constitution. And this desire to form a more perfect union and insure domestic tranquility is clearly expressed in the Preamble to the current Constitution.

Madison, obviously, figured that logic and reason is the sufficient counter measure to the speculations of theologians and their resulting schisms. And he carefully drafted the Free Exercise provision in the double-negative sense. (The first negative-make NO law; the second negative- PROHIBITING free exercise of religion) This way of the Religion Clause is the logical equivalent of an affirmative drafting [- (-1) = + 1] and means same as if Madison wrote into law every one of the numerous teachings of Jesus Christ that was to govern society. However in using the double negative, he escapes the pitfall of a decree in the affirmative, which also could be used to declare a particular sect above all the other sects.

One also sees that the double-negative construction of the Free Exercise Provision superimposes religious law upon society at large because no religious expression of Jesus' teaching can be prohibited. This then makes society a derivative of religion as Madison stated "society must be" in his "Memorial and Remonstrance."

The brilliance and purpose of the double negative structure is found in the principle that government has a fundamental right to make and pass law and to control behavior. With the double negative structure of the First Amendment, no specific religious doctrine is listed, only the general description of "Teaching of Jesus Christ" is implied to in our legal foundation. This subtle fact has enormous repercussions, however, because it requires every Christian sect to factually and logically establish their religious practice. It requires them to trace their practices back through all of times religious texts and prove their practice is indeed a command of Jesus Christ. If the sects cannot do this, their practice is not protected by the Constitution and it can be restricted by the government. (To paraphrase Luke 21.15, Jesus said that he would give his true followers wisdom that could not be refuted or resisted when they came against enemies of truth.)

Now the brilliance of the Religion Clause double-negative construction is seen because, over time, all ill-founded doctrinal positions causing sectarianism that Jefferson cried against will be exposed. And when remedied, unity and more domestic tranquility will arise, which will create a more perfect union. And then the intent of the Preamble will be achieved.

THINGS TO COME

CRITIQUING THE REYNOLDS'S DECISION

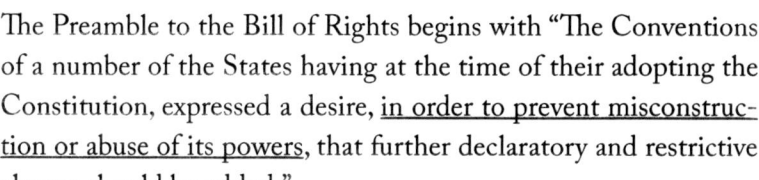

The Preamble to the Bill of Rights begins with "The Conventions of a number of the States having at the time of their adopting the Constitution, expressed a desire, <u>in order to prevent misconstruction or abuse of its powers</u>, that further declaratory and restrictive clauses should be added:"

Before examining the Reynolds decision, let us identify the absolute, inviolate rights and the governmental restrictions contained within First Amendment. Defining such first, will aid in the judging Reynolds more quickly and will show the obvious error in their justifying argument.

The First Amendment in its entirety reads:

"Congress shall make no law respecting (1) an establishment of religion, or (2) prohibiting the free exercise thereof; or (3) abridging the freedom of speech, or (4) of the press; or (5) the right of the people peaceably to assemble, and (6) to petition the government for a redress of grievances."

The First Amendment contains one governmental restriction, namely #1, and five rights, namely #2- #6. Right #3, the freedom of Speech, is the right to think - and believe what you think – and, then, the right to act out, by speaking out on what you think, no matter the topic; therefore this right is the right that protects one's religious ideas and opinions. Right#2, the freedom to exercise your religious belief, is the right to physically act on and act out a religiously held belief. In other words, one can commit overt acts that are religiously based, differing from speaking out, and the government cannot restrict any of those actions at all.

The pertinent portion of the Reynolds decision follows; criticism will shown by bold, center-formatted sentences:

"Congress cannot pass a law for the government of the Territories which shall prohibit the free exercise of religion. The first amendment to the Constitution expressly forbids such legislation. Religious freedom is guaranteed everywhere throughout the United States, so far as congressional interference is concerned.

The question to be determined is, whether the law now under consideration comes within this prohibition.

The court correctly interpreted the freedom to exercise one's religion here.

The word 'religion' is not defined in the Constitution.

This statement is false because it implies to a religion.

We must go elsewhere, therefore, to ascertain its meaning, and nowhere more appropriately, we think, than to the history of the times in the midst of which the provision was adopted. The precise point of the inquiry is, '<u>what is the religious freedom which has been guaranteed?</u>'

The legal question is identified.

Before the adoption of the Constitution, attempts were made in some of the colonies and States to legislate not only in respect to the establishment of religion, but in respect to its doctrines and precepts as well. The people were taxed, against their will, for the support of religion, and sometimes for the support of particular sects to whose tenets they could not and did not subscribe. Punishments were prescribed for a failure to attend upon public worship, and sometimes for entertaining [US. 145. 163] heretical opinions. The controversy upon this general subject was animated in many of the States, but seemed at last to culminate in Virginia. In 1784, the House of Delegates of that State having under consideration 'a bill establishing provision for teachers of the Christian religion,' postponed it until the next session, and directed that the bill should be published and distributed, and that the people be requested 'to signify their opinion respecting the adoption of such a bill at the next session of assembly.'

This brought out a determined opposition. Amongst others, Mr. Madison prepared a 'Memorial and Remonstrance,' (shown earlier herein) which was widely circulated and signed, and in which he demonstrated 'that religion, or the duty we owe the Creator,' was not within the cognizance of civil government. Semple's Virginia Baptists, Appendix. At the next session the proposed bill was not only defeated, but another, 'for establishing religious freedom,' drafted by Mr. Jefferson, was passed. 1 Jeff Works, 45; 2 Howison, Hist. of Va. 298.

In the next segment the court sets their definition of "religious freedom."

In the preamble of this act (12 Hening's Stat. 84) religious freedom is defined; and after a recital <u>'that to suffer the civil magistrate to intrude his powers into the field of opinion, and to restrain the profession or propagation of principles on supposition of their ill tendency, is a dangerous fallacy which at once destroys all religious liberty,</u>' it is declared <u>'that it is time enough for the rightful purposes of civil government for its officers to interfere when principles break out into overt acts against peace and good order.</u>'

This is the correct working of the amendment as shown earlier herein.

In these two sentences is found the true distinction between what properly belongs to the church and what to the State.

This conclusion, Premise 1, is ridiculous and false.

In a little more than a year after the passage of this statute the convention met which prepared the Constitution of the United States.' Of this convention Mr. Jefferson was not a member, he being then absent as minister to France. As soon as he saw the draft of the Constitution proposed for adoption, he, in a letter to a friend, expressed his disappointment at the absence of an express declaration insuring the freedom of religion (2 Jeff Works, 355), but was willing to accept it as it was, trusting that the good sense and honest intentions of the people would bring about the necessary alterations. [98 U.S. 145, 164] 1 Jeff Works 79. Five of the States, while adopting the Constitution, proposed amendments. Three - New Hampshire, New York, and Virginia - included, in one form or another, a declaration of religious freedom in the changes they desired to have made, as did also North Carolina, where the convention at first declined to ratify the Constitution

TOM NEWMAN

until the proposed amendments were acted upon. Accordingly, at the first session of the first Congress the amendment now under consideration was proposed with others by Mr. Madison. It met the views of the advocates of religious freedom, and was adopted.

Jefferson's Wall of Separation Metaphor is next

Mr. Jefferson afterwards, in reply to an address to him by a committee of the Danbury Baptist Association (8 id. 113), took occasion to say: 'Believing with you that religion is a matter which lies solely between man and his God; that he owes account to none other for his faith or his worship; that the legislative powers of the government reach actions only, and not opinions,-I contemplate with sovereign reverence that act of the whole American people which declared that their legislature should 'make no law respecting an establishment of religion or prohibiting the free exercise thereof,' thus building a wall of separation between church and State. Adhering to this expression of the supreme will of the nation in behalf of the rights of conscience, I shall see with sincere satisfaction the progress of those sentiments which tend to restore man to all his natural rights, convinced he has no natural right in opposition to his social duties.' Coming as this does from an acknowledged leader of the advocates of the measure, it may be accepted almost as an authoritative declaration of the scope and effect of the amendment thus secured.

Congress was deprived of all legislative power over mere opinion,

This is a correct interpretation of the Amendment.

but was left free to reach actions which were in violation <u>of social duties or subversive of good order</u>.

This statement that court is inferring in its absolute sense is false because all overt-RELIGIOUSLY INSPIRED-action is protected under the free exercise of religion right, #2. Congress's reach only goes to non-religious actions, and those only; the only exception to this is restriction is a hostile controversy between parties asserting religious reasons, in which case, the court will

decide the reasonableness of their so called religious actions. The rest of the opinion from hereon is corrupted because of the false foundation. For the court to rule on this controversy, it must prove that polygamy in not a true religious expression as defined by the teaching of Jesus Christ, The Lord.

Polygamy has always been odious among the northern and western nations of Europe, and, until the establishment of the Mormon Church, was almost exclusively a feature of the life of Asiatic and of African people. At common law, the second marriage was always void (2 Kent, Com. 79), and from the earliest history of England polygamy has been treated as an offence against society. After the establishment of the ecclesiastical [U.S. 145, 165] courts, and until the time of James I., it was punished through the instrumentality of those tribunals, not merely because ecclesiastical rights had been violated, but because upon the separation of the ecclesiastical courts from the civil the ecclesiastical were supposed to be the most appropriate for the trial of matrimonial causes and offences against the rights of marriage, just as they were for testamentary causes and the settlement of the estates of deceased persons.

By the statute of 1 James I. (c. 11), the offence, if committed in England or Wales, was made punishable in the civil courts, and the penalty was death. As this statute was limited in its operation to England and Wales, it was at a very early period re-enacted, generally with some modifications, in all the colonies. In connection with the case we are now considering, it is a significant fact that on the 8th of December, 1788, after the passage of the act establishing religious freedom, and after the convention of Virginia had recommended as an amendment to the Constitution of the United States the declaration in a bill of rights that 'all men have an equal, natural, and unalienable right to the free exercise of religion, according to the dictates of conscience,' the legislature of that State substantially enacted the statute of James I., death penalty included, because, as recited in the preamble, 'it hath been doubted whether bigamy or poligamy be punishable by the laws of this Commonwealth.' 12 Hening's Stat. 691. From that day to this we think it may safely be said there never has been a time in any State of the Union when polygamy has not been an offence against society, cognizable by the civil courts and punishable with more or less severity. In the face of all this evidence, it is impossible to believe that the constitutional guaranty of religious freedom was intended to prohibit legislation in respect to this most important feature of social life. Marriage, while from its very nature a sacred obligation, is nevertheless, in most civilized nations, a civil contract, and usually regulated by law. Upon it society may be said to be built, and out of its fruits spring social relations and social obligations and duties, with which government is necessarily required to deal. In fact, according as monogamous or polygamous marriages are allowed, do we find the principles on which the government of U.S. 145, 166] the people, to a greater or less extent, rests. Professor, Lieber says, polygamy leads to the patriarchal principle, and which, when applied to large communities, fetters the people in stationary despotism, while that principle cannot long exist in connection with monogamy. Chancellor Kent observes that this remark is equally striking and profound. 2 Kent, Com. 81, note (e). An exceptional colony of polygamists under an exceptional leadership may sometimes exist for a time without appearing to disturb the social condition of the people who surround it; but there cannot be a doubt that, unless restricted by some form of constitution, it is within the legitimate scope of the power of every civil government to determine whether polygamy or monogamy shall be the law of social life under its dominion.

In our opinion, the statute immediately under consideration is within the legislative power of Congress. It is constitutional and valid as prescribing a rule of action for all those residing in the Territories, and in places over which the United States have exclusive control. This being so, the only question which remains is, whether those who make polygamy a part of their religion are excepted from the operation of the statute. If they are, then those who do not make polygamy a part of their religious belief may be found guilty and punished, while those who do, must be acquitted and go free. This would be introducing a new element into criminal law. Laws are made for the government of actions, and while they cannot interfere with mere religious belief and opinions, they may with practices. Suppose one believed that human sacrifices were a necessary part of religious worship, would it be seriously contended that the civil government under which he lived could not interfere to prevent a sacrifice? Or if a wife religiously believed it was her duty to burn herself upon the funeral pile of her dead husband, would it be beyond the power of the civil government to prevent her carrying her belief into practice?

So here, as a law of the organization of society under the exclusive dominion of the United States, it is provided that plural marriages shall not be allowed.

Can a man excuse his practices to the contrary because of his religious belief? [U.S. 145, 167] To permit this would be to make the professed doctrines of religious belief superior to the law of the land, and in effect to permit every citizen to become a law unto himself. Government could exist only in name under such circumstances." (end of opinion)

In regards to the closing paragraph, the court is wrong in thinking that government cannot truly exist being subservient to religious beliefs. James Madison, the author of our Constitution and Chairman of the committee that <u>drafted the First Amendment</u>, specifically states in Para. 2 of his "Memorial and Remonstrance," p13 herein, that "society and government" are nothing but <u>creatures</u> and vicegerents [deputy administrators] of religion and <u>their jurisdictions are both derived from religion and limited by religion</u>. Furthermore, in Para. 1, Madison states that a person's religious duty is <u>precedent</u>, both in order of time and in degree of obligation, to the claims of society. He says that "before any man can be considered as a member of civil society, he must be considered as a subject of the governour of the universe." True religious beliefs are not subjective or caprice in nature, but are in fact universally applicable to all parties; they are verifiable and wholly reasonable in nature and are based on eternal religious precepts and principles.

CPSIA information can be obtained at www.ICGtesting.com
Printed in the USA
LVOW10s1439300716

498290LV00004B/8/P

9 781681 423494